COGNITIVE
INTERVIEWING

COGNITIVE INTERVIEWING

A Tool for Improving Questionnaire Design

Gordon B. Willis

SAGE Publications
Thousand Oaks ▪ London ▪ New Delhi

For information:

Sage Publications, Inc.
2455 Teller Road
Thousand Oaks, California 91320
E-mail: order@sagepub.com

Sage Publications Ltd.
1 Oliver's Yard
55 City Road
London EC1Y 1SP
United Kingdom

Sage Publications India Pvt. Ltd.
B-42, Panchsheel Enclave
Post Box 4109
New Delhi 110 017 India

Printed in the United States of America

Library of Congress Cataloging-in-Publication Data

Willis, Gordon B. (Gordon Bruce)
Cognitive interviewing : a tool for improving questionnaire design / by Gordon B. Willis.
    p. cm.
Includes bibliographical references and index.
ISBN 0-7619-2803-0 (cloth) — ISBN 0-7619-2804-9 (pbk.)
    1. Interviewing. 2. Cognition. 3. Questionnaires—Methodology. 4. Social surveys—Methodology. 5. Social sciences—Research—Methodology. 6. Psychology—Research—Methodology. I. Title: Improving questionnaire design. II. Title.
H61.28.W55 2005
001.4'33—dc22

                         2004013649
This book is printed on acid-free paper.

04 05 06 07 08 10 9 8 7 6 5 4 3 2 1

Acquisitions Editor:	Lisa Cuevas Shaw
Editorial Assistant:	Margo Beth Crouppen
Production Editor:	Julia Parnell
Copy Editor:	Diana Breti
Typesetter:	C&M Digitals (P) Ltd.
Indexer:	Jeanne Busemeyer
Cover Designer:	Glenn Vogel

Contents

Preface   ix

PART I: ORIENTATION AND BACKGROUND   1

1.   Introduction to Cognitive Interviewing   3

    What Is (and Isn't) Cognitive Interviewing?   3
    A Broader Perspective: The Cognitive Testing Process   5

2.   Setting the Stage for Cognitive Interviewing:
    First Principles of Questionnaire Design   12

    Sources of Error in Self-Report Surveys   13
    Why Do Survey Questions Produce Response Error?
      A Sociolinguistic Perspective   17
    How Can We Avoid Problems in Survey Questions?   21
    If We Are Proficient Designers, Why Do We Need
      to Test Questions?   27
    Chapter Summary   30
    Exercise: Question Evaluation   30

3.   Background and Theoretical Origins:
    The CASM Approach   34

    Origins of CASM as an Orienting Framework   34
    Applications of Basic CASM Research   37
    Cognitive Interviewing as Applied CASM Research   39
    Chapter Summary   41

4.   Cognitive Interviewing in Practice: Think-Aloud,
    Verbal Probing, and Other Techniques   42

    Think-Aloud Interviewing   42
    Verbal Probing Techniques   47

Concurrent Versus Retrospective Verbal Probing   51
Choosing Between Think-Aloud and Verbal
    Probing Techniques   52
Vignettes, Card Sorts, and Field-Based Probes   58
Chapter Summary   62

PART II: THE INTRICACIES
OF VERBAL PROBING   65

5. Developing Standard Cognitive Probes   67

    Examples of Cognitive Probing   68
    Logical and Structural Problems   77
    A Systematic Approach to Probe Development:
        The Question Pitfalls Model   79
    Chapter Summary   83
    Exercise: Using the QAS to Develop Probe Questions 84

6. Beyond the Standard Model of Verbal Probing   87

    A Classification of Probe Types   87
    Proactive Versus Reactive Probing   91
    Standardized Versus Free-Form Probes   94
    Chapter Summary   97
    Exercise: Emergent Probing   98

7. A Further Perspective: Cognitive
    Testing as Expansive Interviewing   102

    A Broad View of Cognitive Interviewing   102
    The Ethnographic Interview
        as an Alternative Perspective   109
    Merging Cognitive and Expansive Interviewing   113
    Chapter Summary   114

8. Avoiding Probing Pitfalls   115

    Are We in Danger of Finding Problems
        That Don't Exist?   115
    Practices That Avoid Artificial Problems   116
    Chapter Summary   126

PART III: THE COGNITIVE TESTING PROCESS   127

9. Selection and Training of Cognitive Interviewers   129

    Interviewer Personality: Who Makes a Good
        Cognitive Interviewer?   129
    Technical Background of the Cognitive Interviewer   131
    How Should Cognitive Interviewers Be Trained?   131
    Continuing Education in Cognitive Interviewing   134
    Chapter Summary   135

10. Planning and Conducting Cognitive Interviews   136

    Fitting Cognitive Testing Into the Overall
        Design Sequence   136
    Preparing for the Interview: Subject Recruitment   137
    The Interviewing Process   142
    Twelve Logistical Issues and Considerations   143
    Chapter Summary   150

11. Analyzing and Documenting Cognitive
Interview Results   151

    Characterizing Cognitive Interview Outcomes   152
    The Analysis of Think-Aloud Interview Results   156
    Analysis of the Probed Interview   159
    Persistent Analysis Issues   168
    Chapter Summary   172
    Exercise: Analyzing Cognitive Interviews   172

PART IV: OTHER ISSUES AND TOPICS   175

12. Special Applications of Cognitive Interviewing   177

    Adjusting to Survey Administration Mode   177
    Cognitive Testing of Sensitive Questions   189
    Cognitive Interviewing and Establishment Surveys   196
    Testing Questions on Attitudes and Opinions   199
    Interviewing Across the Age Range   202
    Testing Non-Questionnaire Materials   204
    Chapter Summary   205

13. Evaluation of Cognitive Interviewing Techniques   207

    Theoretical Perspectives   208
    Empirical Evaluation of Cognitive Interviewing   213
    Are We Evaluating the Right Outcome?   224
    Limitations of Cognitive Interviewing   225
    Chapter Summary   228

14. Beyond Cognitive Testing:
    Affiliated Pretesting Methods   230

    (Formal) Expert Review   231
    Focus Groups   233
    Behavior Coding   236
    Reinterview Surveys   241
    How Do Pretesting Methods Compare?   243
    Chapter Summary   253

15. Recommendations and Future Directions   255

    Twelve Recommendations for Cognitive
       Interviewing Practice   255
    Future Directions for Cognitive Interviewing   261
    A Final Case Study   268
    In Conclusion   271

Appendix 1: Example of Cognitive Testing Protocol   273

Appendix 2: Examples of Findings From
Cognitive Testing Reports   287

References   299

Index   321

About the Author   335

Preface

This book centers on a technique—the cognitive interview—that has become increasingly important in the development and testing of survey questionnaires. During the 1990s I wrote several versions of a brief training manual describing how to do cognitive interviewing, due to the absence of literature describing the process in detail. However, it became clear that more was needed; in particular, readers wanted considerably more detail concerning the intricacies of verbal probing techniques. Just as significantly, it was important to be able to place the conduct of cognitive interviewing in the larger context of questionnaire design as it is typically carried out.

Concerning the conduct of cognitive interviewing, I realized from the beginning of this endeavor that the activity is practiced in a number of ways, and that there is no single set of "best practices." This is partly due to the flexible nature of the enterprise, which gives rise to a range of approaches and applications. However, I believe that much of the variation between the practices currently labeled as cognitive interviewing exists simply because there has been little in the way of detailed description incorporating a common vocabulary and set of working principles. This book is an attempt to address this shortcoming. However, I make no attempt to impose a strict set of commandments on anyone who conducts cognitive interviews. Although I present personal (and perhaps idiosyncratic) viewpoints on how best to conduct cognitive interviewing, I do endeavor to distinguish between my own opinions and conclusions that are based on empirical findings. Unfortunately, it remains a fact that there is very little hard evidence concerning the best ways to conduct the interview, so much of my attention is given to documenting the range of approaches, with an emphasis on the approaches that I have personally found to be of most use. Readers should therefore recognize that although my opinions are presumably informed ones, as they are based on fifteen years of experience and hundreds of interviews, they are not the only ones that exist, and reasonable people may disagree. Overall, I have attempted to strike a middle ground between a radically individualistic view and that representing the safe, mutually agreed-upon status quo.

A word on scope: although this volume is explicitly about cognitive interviewing and the assorted details involved in carrying out this activity, I have also addressed several broader issues in order to provide effective context. I had no wish to duplicate other excellent volumes on either questionnaire design (e.g., Fowler, 1995) or the cognitive aspects of survey methods (e.g., Tourangeau, Rips, & Rasinski, 2000; Schwarz & Sudman, 1996). However, readers of my training manuals consistently asked for more information, in particular, (a) How do I get started writing survey questions before testing them? (b) What are the features of a good question in the first place? (c) At what point should I test questions? (d) How do I devise cognitive probes to test questions? and (e) How does cognitive testing compare with other pretesting methods?

Because these are all good questions, I have attempted to provide answers. Without attempting to write a full volume on either questionnaire design or pretesting methods, I consider issues like principles of questionnaire design and how they must be kept in mind when conducting cognitive interviewing. Further, I describe other commonly used methods, including focus groups and behavior coding, in enough detail that the reader can appreciate how they are both similar to and different from cognitive interviewing. I stop well short of proposing a "unified field theory" of pretesting. However, a major theme is that cognitive interviewing does not stand in isolation from the entire context of questionnaire (and survey) development and must be presented as part of a larger picture.

Because the scope of cognitive interviewing has widened, I have also attempted to specify the ways in which it can be used in areas such as testing computerized questionnaires (CATI, CAPI and Web), and for studies that have a cross-cultural emphasis. I hope I have hit the right balance between a focused, microscopic view and a broad, telescopic one. A further balancing act that I found challenging was to resolve the tension between writing a "how to" instructional manual and a more scholarly review of the literature on this topic. I have attempted to do a significant amount of both.

Regarding terminology, ironically, for a field that dwells excessively on wording issues, the survey methods arena has produced a bewildering array of terms that are ill-defined, used variably, or otherwise lead to confusion and miscommunication. In an attempt to address this problem, in Chapter 1 I define explicitly what we are including—and excluding—when we refer to the "cognitive interview." More specifically, it occurred to me that as the focus of the book is methodology, the terminology should be consistent with respect to *method, technique,* and *procedure.* It is not especially helpful to use these terms interchangeably, even though a dictionary search reveals that the definition of each tends to involve the others. Rather, I define them as follows:

I consider *method* to be the most general level; in the context of questionnaire pretesting, this involves a classification of pretest method in the form of cognitive interviewing, behavior coding, or some other gross level of distinction. *Technique* then concerns a more specific level of classification: within the cognitive interviewing method, we may engage in the think-aloud technique, the verbal probing technique, and so on. Finally, I use the term *procedure* to describe process, as opposed to classification; for example, the procedural steps, such as recruitment, selection of interviewers, and so on, that are taken by the investigator through the course of cognitive interviewing. It is my hope that this usage will seem coherent.

I will also note that the order of presentation of topics was a difficult choice, as everything seemed like it should go before everything else. But I settled on a four-part plan. In Part I, the first chapter introduces the overall activity and describes it in enough detail that the reader will have an overview of the entire cognitive testing process. Chapter 2 then delves heavily into questionnaire design as a vital precursor to cognitive interviewing. Chapters 3 and 4 cover theoretical background, and the developments of current techniques—in particular, think-aloud and probing.

Chapters 5 through 8 constitute Part II of the book, which I consider in some respects the core, as it describes the intricate details of probing. Probing is, in my view, the heart of cognitive interviewing, and I made the decision to focus the book on this activity, as opposed to first describing more operational aspects of testing. Then, in Part III, I do cover a wide range of operational and procedural issues involved in the overall cognitive testing process, including training, planning and conducting the interview, and writing up results. Part IV includes a range of specialized applications to which cognitive testing is put, along with evaluation of the method, and a description of some other pretesting methods. I end with recommendations and thoughts about future directions in this very fascinating field.

Throughout almost every chapter, I make heavy use of examples. Some I have borrowed from colleagues, but many of these are from my own archives of cognitive testing results. I do realize that examples do not prove general points, and I am not a proponent of "argument by anecdote." On the other hand, I believe that Mark Twain may have noted that "few things are harder to put up with than the annoyance of a good example," by which I believe he meant that they can be very compelling. As such, I intend them as means to bring otherwise abstract (and potentially boring) discussion to life and to provide clarity. I do hope that they make the book more interesting.

Concerning the support I have received, I would like to acknowledge Trish Royston and Deborah Trunzo, both formerly of the National Center for Health Statistics in Hyattsville, Maryland. Trish and Debbie were responsible for much of what I know in the area of cognitive interviewing, and were instrumental in developing many facets of the approaches that I describe. I thank Jack Fowler for encouraging me to take on the challenge of writing this book. Further, I thank my friends and colleagues in the Federal Interagency Response Error Group (IREG) who have consistently served as a source of useful ideas and as a sounding board for mine. I have been greatly influenced by a number of personal contacts with researchers in the cognitive interviewing field, too many to mention, but I would especially like to thank (in no particular order) Jennifer Rothgeb, Jim Esposito, Paul Beatty, Kristen Miller, Roger Tourangeau, Carol Cosenza, Eleanor Gerber, Barbara Forsyth, Rachel Caspar, Monroe Sirken, Elizabeth Martin, Judy Lessler, Fred Conrad, Johnny Blair, Terry DeMaio, Terry Richardson, Jared Jobe, Barbara Wilson, and Karen Whitaker.

I owe a large debt of gratitude to Lisa Cuevas Shaw, Margo Crouppen, Julia Parnell, Diana Breti, and to Sage Publications in general, for their support and encouragement. I also want to thank my family, who I hope will some day forgive my many hours of solitary pursuit of the goal of finishing this book. If the product of these efforts serves the intended objective of helping either new or experienced practitioners in the art and science of cognitive interviewing, it will have been well worth the effort.

PART I

Orientation and Background

1

Introduction to Cognitive Interviewing

What Is (and Isn't) Cognitive Interviewing?

Across a wide range of disciplines—including health research, market research, political science, and the social sciences in general—we endeavor to develop materials that effectively convey information, such as brochures, cover letters, statistical reports, oral presentations, and computer-based user applications. Very often, we also request information in return by administering data collection instruments, such as survey questionnaires, tax forms, medical forms, and so on. Cognitive interviewing is a general method that developers of such materials can use to critically evaluate this transfer of information. In particular, we use cognitive interviewing techniques to study the manner in which targeted audiences understand, mentally process, and respond to the materials we present—with a special emphasis on potential breakdowns in this process. This book focuses on the cognitive interview as it has most often been used, that is, to evaluate survey questionnaires. More generally, however, researchers can adapt cognitive interviewing to test virtually any type of material, whether delivered orally or in writing, to identify difficulties that may otherwise go unrecognized.

To demonstrate the generality of the cognitive interview, I first refer to an example having little to do directly with survey questionnaires (taken from Willis, Reeve, & Barofsky, in press). Consider an academic subject that is the bane of students everywhere: the math word problem, viewed by many as a particularly insidious form of verbal material. As part of an elementary school educational research project (Fuson & Willis, 1988), I evaluated a set of word problems that included the following:

> The poodle has 9 puppies
> The collie has 5 puppies
> How many more puppies does the poodle have?

To study young children's problem-solving behavior, I read this aloud to a number of first and second graders in a series of one-on-one interviews. To my initial surprise, several gave the same incorrect answer: "none" or "zero." Because I was interested in delving further into the children's thought processes, within each interview I asked additional questions that intensively probed the basis for their answers. This mainly consisted of asking them "How did you get that?"—a practice that is, by definition, cognitive interviewing, although I did not at the time know it by that name. Use of this follow-up probe did provide insights into the reason that this variety of word problem presents particular difficulties for some children. A representative child's explanation was "You told me that she had nine puppies. But then she didn't have any more, so it's none!"

It seemed evident that, from the child's point of view, although it was perhaps nice to hear about the collie, this was not especially relevant to solving the word problem, as it seemed to require only a consideration of the reproductive history of the poodle. Based on this observation, the investigators postulated that some children interpreted the term "more" strictly as an increase in quantity, rather than as a comparison (i.e., "more than something else"). Given the objective of making the comparison clearer, the indicated solution was to rewrite the problem to instead ask "How many more puppies does the poodle have *than the collie?*" Based on further interviews, it appeared that this modification did facilitate understanding and helped the children to learn to successfully solve this variety of problem even when stated in its original, more ambiguous form.

The "puppy word problem" example is, in a nutshell, cognitive interviewing. In application to survey questionnaire evaluation, we test a range of *target questions* that may pose difficulties that generally originate in the cognitive processing of those questions. The questionnaire designer may intend one interpretation yet find that individuals presented with the question adopt an alternate understanding that, in retrospect, appears quite reasonable. If cognitive interviewing leads us to appropriate findings or insights, we may then modify our materials to enhance clarity. This eases the cognitive processing demands for respondents and ultimately increases the likelihood that they will respond in a thoughtful manner and give accurate answers. When we bring about this result, we have achieved our goal of improving the question through cognitive techniques.

AN IMPORTANT EXCLUSION:
A DIFFERENT TYPE OF COGNITIVE INTERVIEWING

I have claimed that a range of developmental and evaluative activities (such as the word problem study described above) implicitly involve cognitive interviewing, even when these activities are not termed as such. A potential source of confusion is that the converse is also true: The label "cognitive interviewing" is sometimes applied to an activity that is outside the realm covered in this book and that involves a somewhat different category of investigation. This type of cognitive interview, introduced by Fisher and Geiselman (1992), does not focus on the testing and development of verbal materials, but is mainly used in law enforcement to enhance the accuracy and reliability of information retrieval by eyewitnesses to crimes. This method has been applied widely, and a literature review of the "cognitive interview" will produce many results related to the Fisher and Geiselman application. However, their interrogation-oriented application has developed separately, involves somewhat different techniques, and serves a fundamental purpose that departs from the goal of evaluating materials such as survey questions. Further, to my knowledge, there is virtually no overlap—and very little communication—between practitioners of these alternate practices. As such, I will not review or otherwise consider the eyewitness-related application. Admittedly, survey-oriented cognitive researchers may "interrogate" people, but not generally for the purpose of solving a crime (notwithstanding the fact that we may consider deficient survey questions to represent a criminal violation of acceptable design practice!).

A Broader Perspective: The Cognitive Testing Process

My opening description of the puppy word problem is somewhat simplistic. In the world of survey questionnaire pretesting, the cognitive interview is usually conducted within a broader testing environment, as part of a sequence of activities that, in aggregate, are referred to as *cognitive testing*. Such testing generally incorporates the properties listed in Text Box 1.1.

Each of the general features in Text Box 1.1 has exceptions, if only because cognitive testing is very flexible and can be tailored to particular situations. However, considering the approach described to be fairly typical, I next turn to an example (Figure 1.1) that involves a hypothetical (but also typical) survey questionnaire, in order to illustrate how cognitive testing might be conducted to evaluate a set of questions or "items" in a real-world context.

Text Box 1.1   General Features of the Cognitive Testing
Process

Cognitive Focus

We study the cognitive processes that respondents use to answer survey questions; in particular, their *comprehension, recall, decisions and judgment,* and *response processes*. However, our goal is to detect a wide range of problems in survey questionnaires.

Timing

Cognitive interviews are typically done between initial drafting and administration in the field, to pretest a survey questionnaire.

Interviewers

Specially trained cognitive interviewers conduct interviews of volunteer *subjects*.

Specialized Recruitment

Researchers often select subjects who have particular characteristics of interest (e.g., the elderly, those who have used illicit drugs in the past 12 months, teenagers who have used chewing tobacco).

Use of Verbal Report Procedures

To identify problems and limitations, cognitive interviewing involves both *think-aloud and verbal probing* procedures.

Reliance on a Range of Probing Techniques

Most interviewers rely heavily on verbal probe questions when interviewing subjects (see Appendix 1 for examples).

Emphasis on Both Overt and Covert Problems

Our objective is not only to obtain evidence of clear, overt problems but to identify hidden or covert ones that are not evident simply by analyzing the normal question-answer sequence.

Laboratory Environment

Interviews are often conducted in a dedicated *cognitive laboratory*, and cognitive interviewing is commonly referred to as "laboratory testing." However, having a physical laboratory is not a critical requirement of cognitive interviewing.

Modest Sample Sizes

Small numbers of individuals are tested—generally between 5 and 15 in an interviewing *round*—before the findings are reviewed and interpreted.

Iterative Testing

Following a round of testing, review, and modification, the revised questionnaire is often tested in a further round; this is a major strength of cognitive testing.

Flexible Application

Although the focus of cognitive testing is limited to the questionnaire, rather than the entire survey process, it is flexible enough to apply to different survey environments (e.g., telephone, face-to-face, paper, or Internet administration). It can be used for factual or attitudinal surveys, and for surveys of individuals (population surveys) as well as those of businesses (establishment surveys).

Information Rather Than Validation

Cognitive interviewing is a useful means for testing survey questions but does not validate questions in a formal sense—we strive to produce better questions, but generally have no proof, statistical or otherwise.

Advisory Nature

The practice of cognitive interviewing does not *in itself* result in improved questionnaires. Cognitive testing serves as "question inspection" and identifies potential problems, but solving these problems requires a skilled questionnaire designer (see Appendix 2 for some sample testing results).

Cognitive testing of a questionnaire containing items in Figure 1.1 could be accomplished through the following steps:

1. Develop a testing plan. Do we need to recruit individuals with particular characteristics? How many interviews should we plan, and how many interviewers do we need? Where and when will the interviews be done?

Part A: Dental Visits

Q1. How many times did you go to the dentist in the past year?

Q2. The last time you visited the dentist, did you have your teeth cleaned?

Q3. The last time you visited the dentist, did you receive any other treatment?

Q4. The last time you visited the dentist, did you have any X-rays or other diagnostic tests?

Figure 1.1   Sample of Dental Questions Submitted to Cognitive Testing

2. Develop a *cognitive testing protocol* consisting of the tested (target) questions along with a variety of *probe questions* to supplement the targeted questions, such as "What time period are you thinking of here?" or "What did you go to the dentist for?" (see Appendix 1).

3. Recruit subjects and invite them into our cognitive lab at appointed times for their interviews.

4. Administer the questionnaire in private, one-on-one interviews, and apply cognitive interviewing techniques, in particular (a) have subjects think aloud as they answer questions, and (b) administer the cognitive probes.

5. With each subject's consent, audiotape or videotape the interview, write notes during the interview, and review the notes and recordings after each interview.

6. If a team is involved, write a testing report (see Appendix 2) and meet with project staff to review the results.

7. Make modifications to the questions based on our findings.

8. If indicated and time permits, conduct a further testing round and then reevaluate the questionnaire.

After carrying out this sequence, the investigators might determine that the targeted questions pose no serious difficulties. This is itself a finding, and provides some assurance that one can go ahead and collect survey data with some confidence. More likely, however, the researchers will make the types of observations in Figure 1.2, which I have assembled from archival reports summarizing cognitive interviews of these target questions. (See Chapter 11 for specific ways to record and process cognitive interview results.)

(a) Three of nine subjects interpreted "the dentist" to mean their main dentist but weren't sure whether to include oral surgeons, dental hygienists, etc.

(b) The term "past year" was interpreted variably. One person thought this meant the prior calendar year, as opposed to the past 12 months. Yet another subject reported visits since January 1 of this year.

(c) Overall, subjects were not that sure of the correctness of their answers; five reported that they couldn't be confident how many dental visits they had made, and three stated that they had assumed it was two times because that is their usual pattern. Overall, the answers given appeared to be "ballpark estimates."

Figure 1.2   Sample Aggregate Findings Based on the Compilation of Interviewer Notes

Based on such results, the designers might consider a few changes to the questions:

1. Through question rewording, make clearer whether we mean "their main dentist," "any dentist," or "a dentist, oral surgeon, dental hygienist."

2. Select "the past 12 months" as the timeframe, as opposed to "the past year."

3. Review our measurement objectives. What level of precision is really needed? If the goal is to broadly classify people into levels of use of dental care (e.g., those who haven't gone at all, those who went one to three times, and those going more than three times), an estimate may be sufficient. If we only want to know if respondents have gone to the dentist at all, maybe that should be asked, rather than visit frequency. On the other hand, if we do require a precise population prevalence estimate of number of dental visits, it might be better to shorten the relevant interval (the *reference period*) in order to obtain more accurate reporting.

4. Ask about X-rays or other tests before the more general question about "any other treatment."

5. Instead of "diagnostic tests," try something simpler like "any other tests done to look for problems."

6. In the treatment question (Q3), try giving a few examples of common treatments to jog their memories.

The researchers might believe that the above modifications constitute reasonable interventions, but to make sure, after making appropriate changes they could test another round of subjects, just to see how the questions now work. Later, the questionnaire could be evaluated further in a field pretest that presents conditions more like those to be used in the main ("field") survey (see Chapter 14 on Affiliated Pretesting Methods). With luck—or, perhaps, as the result of expertise and careful testing—the questions will pose fewer problems, and produce less overall error, than if they had not been tested in this manner.

The example above constitutes a somewhat larger nutshell than the puppy math problem, and describes cognitive interviewing as one part of a larger cognitive testing process. In order to formalize this practice, permanent cognitive labs have been established at several United States federal statistical agencies (e.g., the National Center for Health Statistics, the U.S. Census Bureau, the U.S. Bureau of Labor Statistics). Further, cognitive interviewing is routinely practiced in a range of organizations that conduct surveys, including the U.S. General Accounting Office, several contract research organizations (e.g., Abt Associates, the National Opinion Research Center, Research Triangle Institute International, and Westat), at Statistics Canada, Statistics New Zealand, the National Centre for Social Research in the United Kingdom, in European agencies such as ZUMA in Germany, Statistics Netherlands, Statistics Finland, Statistics Sweden, and Statistics Norway, and at many Universities (e.g., the Universities of Maryland, Massachusetts, Michigan, and Wisconsin). Although initially it was not at all clear whether cognitive interviewing, and especially cognitive laboratories, would simply represent a fad, it does appear that this activity has endured, and is here to stay in one form or another.

Despite wide implementation, cognitive interviewing has also become somewhat unwieldy. The U.S. Census Bureau (2003) has produced a volume describing many of the rudiments of the approach, and I have created several versions of a "how to" manual (Willis, 1994, 1999). However, little has been written concerning the exact details of its practice, and procedures and techniques have evolved along multiple paths, to the point where it is not clear what someone who claims to do "cognitive interviews" actually does (Forsyth, 1990; Willis, 1999). Further, those wishing to learn and apply the method are largely left to their own devices, using the limited existing sources that describe the procedure from something of a distance.

The overall goal of this book is, therefore, to close this gap by describing cognitive interviewing practice as it exists in the early 21st century.

In Chapter 2, I present in more depth the justification for cognitive testing, as this key issue is generally not discussed. Then I address the history and theory behind this method and present the "nuts and bolts" of cognitive interviewing and, in particular, verbal probing techniques in considerable detail. Following this, I describe a number of variations on the general theme that affect the conduct of the cognitive interview, and research results relevant to the validity of cognitive testing results. I end by anticipating future directions in this field.

2

Setting the Stage for Cognitive Interviewing

First Principles of Questionnaire Design

The uncreative mind can spot wrong answers, but it takes a very creative mind to spot wrong questions.

Anthony Jay

Chapter Overview

The reader who is already convinced of the value of cognitive interviewing and wishes to read about *how* to do this may skip to later chapters. However, effective interviewing is not a stand-alone skill. Rather, to be proficient in a range of activities—including identifying potential problems with targeted survey questions, conducting the interview process efficiently, recognizing problems when they occur, and implementing practical and effective solutions—it is vital to understand the principles of questionnaire design. Although this chapter cannot serve as a complete design text, it addresses four critical questionnaire design issues that underlie cognitive interviewing:

1. In the scheme of things, is questionnaire-related error really a serious problem?

2. If so, why do problems abound in survey questions?

3. Can we rely on good design principles to minimize error?

4. If we are good designers, why do we need to test questions?

Sources of Error in Self-Report Surveys

To begin a discussion of error as it relates to survey questions, I first consider the place of the survey within scientific and social research. The self-report questionnaire—in which the respondent speaks for him- or herself—became predominant during the mid-20th century, and has been used in virtually every social science, in the health and economics fields, and even in fields represented by "pure" science (Converse & Presser, 1986). A basic concern throughout the history of surveys has been the accuracy of the information we obtain simply by asking a sample of people (survey respondents) to serve as an integral part of our measurement system and then using the information they provide to produce estimates that extend to the population at large (Stone, Turkkan, & Bachrach, 1999). Put simply, can we get useful information simply by asking for it? This is not self-evident, and at some points in history would have been regarded as scientific heresy; our reliance on the self-report survey reflects what Converse (1987) labeled the "historical ascendance of the subjective realm" over an earlier more purely objective and behaviorist approach.

GENERAL CATEGORIES OF SURVEY-RELATED ERROR

Problems that lurk within the questions we ask survey respondents are the central focus of this book, but these constitute just one potential source of measurement error. From a broad perspective, Text Box 2.1 divides the error associated with the survey process into seven major constituents, based on a synthesis of the views of a statistician (Groves, 1991) and that of a questionnaire designer (Oppenheim, 1966). Questionnaire designers do not usually focus on *sampling* and *coverage error,* as those topics are left to the statisticians. Further, although we may (and should!) consider why people do not want to participate in our surveys (unit nonresponse) or fail to answer particular questions (item nonresponse), we do not typically emphasize *nonresponse error.* Similarly, we do not look ahead to exactly what is done with data after they are collected, with the important exception that we make projections concerning how errors of interpretation or usage might come about. Rather, questionnaire evaluation primarily involves the study of *response error* (and secondarily, *interviewer error*).

A simple view of response error is that it represents the discrepancy between a theoretical "true score" and that which is reported by the respondent (e.g., I have gone to the dentist five times in the past 12 months but report only three times). Across respondents, such errors can have

---

Text Box 2.1   Major Sources of Error in Survey Data

I. Errors of non-observation: Are we surveying the right people?

(a) Coverage error. Certain people or units may not be included in our sample. For example, telephone surveys don't provide coverage of people who don't have telephones.

(b) Sampling error. Because we're selecting a sample, as opposed to asking everyone in the population, we may happen to select individuals who are not representative of that population.

(c) Nonresponse error. If some people who are in the sample aren't surveyed (because they can't be located, refuse to participate, etc.), or if some items are left unanswered, this may introduce bias.

II. Errors of observation: Are we getting the right answer?

(a) Interviewer error. Interviewers may read questions incorrectly, make errors in recording data, and so on.

(b) Response error. Characteristics of questions, and of respondent processing of those questions, may lead to incorrect answers.

III. Post-observation error: Are we doing the right things with the data?

(a) Processing error. Data may be coded or analyzed incorrectly.

(b) Interpretation error. Are we drawing the correct inferences based on our obtained results?[a]

SOURCE: Groves (1991) and Oppenheim (1966).

NOTE:

a. Errors in interpreting our results may be a function of the cumulative errors of other types; for example, the false conclusion that there is no linear relationship between two variables due only to restriction in range in the measured variables. Or, they could simply result from investigator bias (that is, seeing only what we wish to see).

two outcomes. If respondents tend to misreport in the same direction (e.g., they underreport dental visits), this produces a *bias* in the overall statistic (also called *net error*). Or, the question might produce incorrect answers at the individual level that cancel one another, and result in no overall bias. So if another respondent balances my underreport exactly, such that she has gone to the dentist three times but reports five, the obtained measure of number of visits (eight total, or on average, four) is correct.

However, each of us is still wrong, and this can be quantified in terms of *gross error,* which is related to the sum of the absolute values of our individual errors. In this case, even though a point estimate of dental visits would be correct, if an analyst were to relate frequency of visits to another measure, such as dental insurance status, the existence of gross error could water down any true associations between those variables. Readers interested in delving into the multitude of error types that may influence survey-based estimates are encouraged to consult Groves (1989, 1991) or the U.S. Office of Management and Budget (2001). For current purposes, I simply point out that questionnaire evaluation is enhanced to the extent that we keep these basic error categories in mind.

HOW MUCH RESPONSE ERROR REALLY EXISTS IN SELF-REPORT QUESTIONNAIRES?

Concern about response error will be familiar to anyone who has ever reacted to a public opinion poll question by thinking, "That's a biased question!" and then wondered what effect bias may have had on the results. Response error is sometimes overlooked, in part because it is not easily quantifiable (see Groves, 1991). For instance, the results of polls cited in the media often make statements such as "the overall level of error is plus or minus three percent." However, this "overall error" is in truth only the level of sampling error (and parenthetically, also may rely on the oft-violated assumption of simple random sampling). The levels of other sources of error, and in particular nonresponse bias and response error, are generally unknown, and could easily have magnitudes that swamp error due only to imperfect respondent selection. The central premise of this book holds that it is vital to address response error. More specifically, I propose the following as an overall thesis:

> *Response error is a major impediment to survey data quality, and the design of questionnaires that are sufficiently free of such error is a complex process that requires the use of systematic principles of both question design and empirical evaluation.*

This statement may not seem particularly radical, but it is far short of a universally held belief. Questionnaire designers are well known to lament that their skills are unappreciated; as Oppenheim (1966) observed, "the world is full of well-meaning people who believe that anyone who can write plain English and has a modicum of common sense can produce a good questionnaire" (p. vii). In particular, it might seem that question writing requires little of the technical knowledge required to carry out other survey-relevant tasks such as statistical sampling and variance estimation. As such, it is reasonable to demand some convincing evidence that poor question design can really derail our results.

EVIDENCE THAT RESPONSE ERROR EXISTS

There is abundant empirical evidence that the preponderance of response error in survey questionnaires is fact, as opposed to existing only in the imaginations of professional questionnaire designers. There are at least three types of studies that demonstrate such effects:

(a) *Record Check Studies.* Investigators who have made use of objective records—those comparing survey reports with "gold standard" information such as voting records, medical records, and so on—have often reported disturbing levels of response error (Blair & Burton, 1986; Cannell, Marquis, & Laurent, 1977; Harlow & Linet, 1989; Lansing, Ginsburg, & Braaten, 1961; Means, Nigam, Zarrow, Loftus, & Donaldson, 1989). An extreme example involves parents' reports of the details of their children's immunizations. For measures such as the number of each vaccination the child has received, parents' reports may bear little relationship to medical records (Lee et al., 1999). Virtually any record check study of survey responses will reveal at least some degree of non-ignorable error, which often varies across respondent type, and between survey questions, in unanticipated ways.

(b) *Reinterview Surveys.* In studies that simply analyze the consistency of respondents' answers to the same question when asked twice, it is often found that that the responses are seriously unstable, and therefore of suspect validity (Albright, Reichart, Flores, Moore, Hess, & Pascale, 2000; Forsman & Schreiner, 1991; Von Thurn & Moore, 1994). If people can't even agree with themselves, we're led to wonder how good their responses are.

(c) *Studies of Wording Effects.* For many years, researchers have pointed out that even slight wording changes can have major effects on aggregate data distributions (Bradburn & Sudman, 1991; Schuman & Presser, 1981; Sudman & Bradburn, 1982). It is not usually clear which answers are "correct." However, it is evident that because question wording has a major influence, various forms must necessarily induce different levels of response error (as they can't all be right).

In summary, based on available evidence, the important issue before us is not whether response error is a serious problem for questionnaire designers, but rather, why is this so?

Why Do Survey Questions Produce Response Error? A Sociolinguistic Perspective

As I will discuss in detail, there are a variety of reasons why survey questions produce response error. People may not have the information we seek, or they may not remember it, or it may be something they would rather not talk about. Each is an important factor, and it may not be fair to single out any one as the most villainous. I propose, however, that one particular characteristic of survey questions consistently acts to subvert our best intentions and has emerged repeatedly in the literature: the failure to achieve the fundamental goal of *clear communication between the parties* (Schaeffer, 1991). This problem can have a number of sources. For one, we may simply ask questions that are too difficult to understand. In fact, there is some evidence that we routinely overestimate the ability of information recipients to comprehend what we are attempting to convey. Belson (1981) describes research that assessed audience comprehension of radio addresses intended for the general public and reported "a considerable failure to grasp either major or minor points in these talks, the average score for the 26 talks being 27 per cent" (p. 18). The lesson, simply, is that simplicity is a virtue.

QUESTION VAGUENESS: DEFICIENCIES OF GROUNDING

Survey questions fail in a second major way that is subtle but particularly vexing: they exhibit unacceptable vagueness in expressing the designer's intentions, or what is referred to as the *pragmatic* (rather than literal) meaning of the question (Clark & Schaeffer, 1987, 1989; Grice,

1975). If there is room for varied interpretation, exactly what information are we asking our respondents for? It may be surprising that communicating our intentions should be so difficult. Given that most people have a lifetime of experience in asking questions of others, we presumably should be adept at employing this accumulated expertise when crafting survey questions.

However, sociolinguistic analysis suggests that the mechanisms of successful questioning behavior in everyday life are actually very complex and not easily transferable to the survey environment. Researchers who analyze real-life conversations have pointed out that conversers follow implicit rules of interaction (Grice, 1975), such as the assumption that the questioner will not ask for the same information more than once. A particularly relevant observation is that people normally communicate through the critical process of establishing common *grounding* (Clark & Brennan, 1991; Clark & Schaeffer, 1987, 1989; Schober, 1999; Schober & Conrad, 2002). In essence, the argument holds that the solitary, unelaborated query (that is, asking a question and expecting a straightforward answer) is often inadequate, because the strings of words that constitute natural language are inherently ambiguous. Rather, conversations entail additional activities that result in a state of shared interpretation, especially with respect to the speaker's information needs.

A key postulate is that conversation is negotiated and terminated only when the participants have determined that the desired state of common meaning has been achieved, even if this ending state is achieved via a circuitous route. If the inquisitor asks, "How far is it from Huddersfield to Coventry?" and the respondent replies, "About a hundred miles," the former can then add, "No, I mean how long does it take to get there," if his or her objective is to obtain information in terms of time as opposed to distance (Clark & Schaeffer, 1987, 1989; Schober & Conrad, 2002). Speakers rely widely on such *repair mechanisms* to put the conversation back on track when there are indications that an initial interpretation was inadequate.

Perhaps closer to home for some, consider the following hypothetical, but hopefully realistic, morning exchange between wife and husband:

SHE: What are you doing today?

HE: Um—working. It's Monday . . .

SHE: I mean, are you working at home or going in? I have a late meeting so I thought if you were here . . . you could pick up Susie from school.

HE: Yeah, I'm going in, but I can leave early. I'll get her.

As in the previous example, this interchange can be characterized as a "closing in" on a state of shared meaning and purpose, especially as the initial inquiry gives rise to multiple potential interpretations. Additionally, the opening query in this example is vague, and even worse, is only peripherally related to the key item of information required. Rather, it sets the basis for further progression of the conversation towards common ground, and ultimately to the desired outcome: to obtain an answer to the question "Will you pick up Susie from school today?" Of course, there is no guarantee that such adaptive speech mechanisms always work. As may be obvious to married couples, nontrivial misunderstandings between conversers are rife and have caused all forms of calamity throughout history including, presumably, failure to pick up children from school.

In contrast to conversational speech, survey questions usually do not allow for the flexible interactions that establish grounding (Schaeffer, 1991; Schober, 1999; Schober & Conrad, 2002). This is true by definition for self-administered questionnaires, for which the questions are pre-assembled and administered in the absence of any questioner. But this situation also applies to interviewer-administered surveys. By scripting a series of survey questions as a type of artificial conversation, we plan the entire interchange before the fact and attempt to anticipate every move the respondent can make. Such scripting can be a simple series of mostly unrelated questions, but it is often exceedingly complex, such as when the answers to questions have implications concerning the question that should be asked next (that is, they affect *skip patterns,* or sequencing instructions).

As an example of the prototype questionnaire, consider two questions from a U.S. Census Bureau Survey of Income and Program Participation:

(a) Do you have a physical, mental, or other health condition which limits the kind or amount of work you can do? (YES/NO)

(b) Medicare is a health insurance program for disabled persons and persons 65 or over. People covered by Medicare have a card that looks like this (SHOW FLASHCARD). During this four-month period, were you covered by Medicare? (YES/NO)

These formulations do not resemble a natural exchange, such as between spouses. Note in particular that a significant burden is imposed by inflexibility in wording and especially by the assumption that the question will be answered without further cycles of interchange that progress toward a common ground. Consequently, questionnaire designers attempt to design questions that by their nature achieve grounding, rather than leave the interviewer and the respondent to establish shared meaning via flexible forms of adaptive speech. In fact, common survey procedure requires that if a respondent asks "What does [term] mean?" the appropriate response is "Whatever it means to you" (Fowler, 1992); this could be viewed as a somewhat perverse attempt to *avoid* common grounding.

Because of such departures from normal conversation, several authors have advocated the *nonstandardized interview,* which allows the interviewer to deviate from a set script and to effectively interpret and communicate the investigator's objectives (see Beatty, 1995; Schaeffer, 1991; Schober, 1999; Schober & Conrad, 1997; Suchman & Jordan, 1990). This notion is not novel. The "nondirective interview" was introduced during the 1930s (Krueger, 1994), and it is common practice in some fields, including medical research and social work, to rely on nonstandardized *semi-structured* interviews, which typically involve an interview guide as opposed to a fully scripted questionnaire (York, 1998). However, the nonstandard interview has not, at this point, taken hold within the conduct of most large-scale surveys.

WHY DO SURVEYS USE STANDARDIZED QUESTIONS?

There may be good reasons to adopt nonstandard approaches for surveys. Schober and Conrad (1997) experimentally contrasted standard and flexible approaches and concluded that for some items, flexible interviews increased accuracy by almost 60%. In their defense, however, survey administrators have reasons for standardizing question wording (Fowler & Mangione, 1990; Schaeffer, 1991). According to the "black box model," as labeled by van der Zouwen (2002), in order to impose order on the process and to minimize error due to uncontrolled variation among interviewers, we must present the same material to each respondent. In particular, field interviewers may be relatively uneducated in the objectives of the survey after the usual day or two of training in administering the questionnaire. If they are set free to provide whatever information they feel is appropriate based on their interpretations of question objectives, and every interviewer-respondent pair therefore establishes its own grounding, then the designers have ceded control of the information collection system.

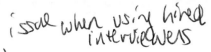
issue when using hired interviewers

Additionally, the survey interview departs from conversation in that the interviewer is not really the inquisitor but rather the conduit of information between researcher and respondent (Houtkoop-Steenstra, 2000). As such, standardization allows us to minimize the need to achieve grounding with respect to two conversations—first between the investigator and interviewer, and then between interviewer and respondent. Finally, as a major practical concern, the standardized interview generally takes much less time to administer than does a more flexible one; Schober and Conrad (1997) reported a mean administration time of 3.4 minutes for their standard questionnaire, but 11.5 minutes for its nonstandardized equivalent.

3 times longer
3~4

IMPLICATIONS OF STANDARDIZATION FOR QUESTION DESIGN

In practice, surveys do not normally feature either strict standardization or nonstandardization (Oppenheim, 1966). Based on a survey of survey research organizations, Viterna and Maynard (2002) found that although such organizations tend to develop standard questions, they also consistently provide significant latitude to interviewers in explaining and interpreting questions. I will not attempt to suggest the appropriate balance in this regard. Rather, I point out that:

(a) Survey questions are typically developed as though they will be administered in standardized fashion, and so wordings are "tied down."

(b) Production of such standardized products requires particular development skills and practices that have no analog in everyday conversation, and that put a premium on the establishment of grounding in the absence of adaptive speech.

(c) To a large degree, it is these requirements that give rise to the formal disciplines of questionnaire design and pretesting, such as cognitive interviewing.

How Can We Avoid Problems in Survey Questions?

Fortunately, several resources exist for minimizing miscommunications and other sources of response error: texts on *psychometrics*, questionnaire design *textbooks*, and *checklist systems*.

PSYCHOMETRICS

Substitution

One perspective on question design deals less with the details of how to write survey questions, or "items," than with how to evaluate them and, in particular, how to assess measurement characteristics that make good questions. For example, the field of psychometrics (literally, "mental measurement") is concerned with several basic question features (see Nunnally, 1978). First, they must be analytically useful. For example, a "Yes/No" question should not elicit a response of "Yes" from every respondent but produce variance in responses. Second, the items should demonstrate reliability and validity. A full review of reliability and validity is well beyond the scope of this book (see Heath & Martin, 1997; Kirk & Miller, 1986). Briefly, reliability can be viewed in terms of either scale consistency (measured through Cronbach's alpha) or test-retest reliability, as in the earlier discussion of reinterview studies in which an item provides consistent information when repeated under similar conditions.

The concept of validity refers to whether measures produce results consistent with our conceptual intent (Turner & Martin, 1984)—not whether the measure is repeatable, but whether it measures what we want it to. There are many subtypes of validity (e.g., criterion, construct, external, discriminant, etc.). In addition to classical psychometrics, modern measurement theory, in the form of Item Response Theory (IRT), relies on mathematical means for evaluating survey questions (Embretson & Reise, 2000; Reeve & Masse, in press). Heath and Martin (1997) have pointed out that psychometrics is infrequently used in social and political research involving survey questionnaires, but that researchers should more often consider the trade-offs involved in applying this method.

I describe psychometrics mainly because this field gives rise to vital concepts in questionnaire design, such as reliability and validity, and because it emphasizes the psychological elements inherent in the questionnaire response process. However, from the perspective of the questionnaire designer, psychometrics has one severe drawback: it is largely dependent on quantitative data that are collected *after* questions are devised and administered, and in some cases (as for IRT models) can require copious amounts of data. For this reason, psychometric approaches are useful for ongoing quality control and evaluation, but not as a means for pretesting at early stages in the question development process.

THE QUESTIONNAIRE DESIGN TEXTBOOK

Independent of the sociolinguistic perspective discussed earlier, questionnaire design specialists have acknowledged for at least 50 years that survey questions must be more carefully formulated than is everyday speech. A number of questionnaire design texts have been written to assist designers in this endeavor, and these often provide specific directives—"do's and don'ts"—largely based on the expertise and experiences of the authors. The classic work is by Payne (1951), who developed a rule book for question design that is still very applicable (e.g., keep questions short; avoid "double-barreled questions" or those that ask two questions in one). A list of sources is contained in Text Box 2.2.

CHECKLIST APPROACHES TO QUESTIONNAIRE DESIGN

Because textbook approaches to questionnaire design are comprehensive and may require a serious commitment to master, they can be

---

Text Box 2.2   Texts on Questionnaire Design

Aday, L. A. (1996). *Designing and Conducting Health Surveys*. San Francisco: Jossey-Bass.

Converse, J. M., & Presser, S. (1986). *Survey Questions: Handcrafting the Standardized Survey Questionnaire*. Newbury Park, CA: Sage.

Fowler, F. J. (1995). *Improving Survey Questions: Design and Evaluation*. Thousand Oaks, CA: Sage.

Labaw, P. J. (1980). *Advanced Questionnaire Design*. Cambridge, MA: Abt Books.

Oppenheim, A. N. (1966). *Questionnaire Design and Attitude Measurement*. New York: Basic Books.

Oppenheim, A. N. (1992). *Questionnaire Design, Interviewing and Attitude Measurement*. London: Pinter Publishers.

Payne, S. L. (1951). *The Art of Asking Questions*. Princeton, NJ: Princeton University Press.

Sudman, S., & Bradburn, N. (1982). *Asking Questions: A Practical Guide to Questionnaire Design*. San Francisco: Jossey-Bass.

somewhat overwhelming. An alternative that attempts to simplify the design process is a systematic checklist approach, which homes in on specific pitfalls to avoid. Instead of providing background and instruction in how to write questions, they focus more on how *not* to write questions by identifying where questions "go bad." Such systems tend to focus mainly at the level of the individual question, as opposed to the questionnaire as a whole. Typically a checklist is applied to each question during a questionnaire review phase, prior to any cognitive or other pretesting, somewhat like a pilot uses a checklist to preflight an aircraft before taking to the sky. My own effort in this regard is the Question Appraisal System (QAS), co-authored with Judy Lesser at Research Triangle Institute International (Willis & Lessler, 1999). The QAS was originally developed for the Centers for Disease Control and Prevention's Behavioral Risk Factor Surveillance Survey (BRFSS), a telephone-administered population health survey. Similarly, Belson (1981); Forsyth, Lessler, and Hubbard (1992); Lessler and Forsyth (1996); and Fowler and Cosenza (2002) have developed checklist-based review systems for population surveys, and Forsyth, Weiss, and Anderson (2002) describe a version that applies to organizational surveys.

A slightly modified version of the original QAS checklist is reproduced in Table 2.1. Using this system, the reviewer critiques a survey question by following a number of steps, each devoted to a major potential source of error. At each step, the reviewer determines whether more specific problem types exist, and if so, checks the "yes" box associated with that type. The system covers a variety of common errors that should be avoided when writing survey questions, and focuses mainly on interviewer-administered (and especially telephone) surveys, although many of the same problems apply in self-administered questionnaires (paper or computerized). Some of these error types, and particularly those related to question clarity (Table 2.1, Step 3), directly involve the concept of grounding. Others deal with basic difficulty due to technical wording, lengthy questions, and so on.

The QAS system includes a manual that discusses each problem type in detail, but many of these simply reflect common sense. For example, if a question is so long it is incomprehensible, it is unlikely the respondent will provide an accurate answer. Similarly, if the question gives rise to multiple interpretations, it stands to reason that at least some respondents may select an interpretation not intended by the designers. Although such problems may seem obvious, following a checklist forces the reviewer to specifically consider potential sources of response error (as an analogy, a flat tire on an aircraft may be obvious, but only once the preflight checklist forces us to look).

Table 2.1   The Question Appraisal System (QAS): Sources of Error in Telephone-Administered Survey Questions

STEP 1 - READING: Determine whether it is difficult for the interviewers to read the question in the same way to all respondents.	
1a. **WHAT TO READ:** Interviewer may have difficulty determining what *parts* of the question should be read.	YES NO
1b. **MISSING INFORMATION:** Information the interviewer needs to administer the question is *not* contained in the question.	YES NO
1c. **HOW TO READ:** Question is *not* fully scripted and therefore difficult to read.	YES NO
STEP 2 - INSTRUCTIONS: Look for problems with any introductions, instructions, or explanations from the *respondent's* point of view.	
2a. **CONFLICTING OR INACCURATE INSTRUCTIONS,** introductions, or explanations.	YES NO
2b. **COMPLICATED INSTRUCTIONS,** introductions, or explanations.	YES NO
STEP 3 - CLARITY: Identify problems related to communicating the *intent or meaning* of the question to the respondent.	
3a. **WORDING:** Question is lengthy, awkward, ungrammatical, or contains complicated syntax.	YES NO
3b. **TECHNICAL TERMS** are undefined, unclear, or complex.	YES NO
3c. **VAGUE:** There are multiple ways to interpret the question or to decide what is to be included or excluded.	YES NO
3d. **REFERENCE PERIODS** are missing, not well specified, or in conflict.	YES NO
STEP 4 - ASSUMPTIONS: Determine whether there are problems with assumptions made or the underlying logic.	
4a. **INAPPROPRIATE ASSUMPTIONS** are made about the respondent or about his/her living situation.	YES NO
4b. **ASSUMES CONSTANT BEHAVIOR** or experience for situations that vary.	YES NO
4c. **DOUBLE-BARRELED:** Contains more than one implicit question.	YES NO

(Continued)

Table 2.1 (Continued)

STEP 5 - KNOWLEDGE/MEMORY: Check whether respondents are likely to *not know* or have trouble *remembering* information.	
5a. **KNOWLEDGE** may not exist: Respondent is unlikely to *know* the answer to a factual question.	YES NO
5b. **ATTITUDE** may not exist: Respondent is unlikely to have formed the attitude being asked about.	YES NO
5c. **RECALL** failure: Respondent may not *remember* the information asked for.	YES NO
5d. **COMPUTATION** problem: The question requires a difficult mental calculation.	YES NO
STEP 6 - SENSITIVITY/BIAS: Assess questions for sensitive nature or wording, and for bias.	
6a. **SENSITIVE CONTENT** (general): The question asks about a topic that is embarrassing, very private, or that involves illegal behavior.	YES NO
6b. **SENSITIVE WORDING** (specific): Given that the general topic is sensitive, the wording should be improved to minimize sensitivity.	YES NO
6c. **SOCIALLY ACCEPTABLE** response is implied by the question.	YES NO
STEP 7 - RESPONSE CATEGORIES: Assess the adequacy of the range of responses to be recorded.	
7a. **OPEN-ENDED QUESTION** that is inappropriate or difficult.	YES NO
7b. **MISMATCH** between question and response categories.	YES NO
7c. **TECHNICAL TERMS** are undefined, unclear, or complex.	YES NO
7d. **VAGUE** response categories are subject to multiple interpretations.	YES NO
7e. **OVERLAPPING** response categories.	YES NO
7f. **MISSING** eligible responses in response categories.	YES NO
7g. **ILLOGICAL ORDER** of response categories.	YES NO
STEP 8 - OTHER PROBLEMS not identified in Steps 1 - 7	
8a. Ordering or context problems *across* questions	YES NO
8b. Other problems not previously identified.	YES NO

SOURCE: Based on Willis & Lessler (1999).

Checklist systems do have limitations. Most importantly, because they focus somewhat microscopically on each question in isolation, rather than on the questionnaire as a whole, they fail to provide an overall assessment (see Converse & Presser, 1986, for a discussion of the distinction between *question* and *questionnaire* evaluation). However, for readers who are interested in this approach, the full QAS manual is available on the Internet.

If We Are Proficient Designers, Why Do We Need to Test Questions?

This book is mainly about pretesting questions, not just writing them, and is based entirely on the assumption that this is, in fact, necessary. Interestingly, this vital assertion is often left unjustified by proponents of pretesting: Assuming that we respect the unique requirements of the standardized questionnaire and become proficient in questionnaire design using appropriate resources and guides, why should we go through the trouble to test them? This question is not at all rhetorical. I have heard prominent questionnaire designers suggest that if we are sufficiently careful when we design questions, there is little added value in conducting cognitive interviews.

I propose several reasons why it is vital to "put the vehicle on the road" and test it on real people, no matter how closely we adhere to practices advocated in texts or checklists.

(a) *Question design rules are by themselves not specific enough.* To illustrate, consider the reasonable "rule" that questions should not be overly long. That is no doubt true, but applying it makes clear that the devil really is in the details. How long is long, exactly? Thirty words or fifty? Might this vary with respondent population? Surveys of physicians may differ from surveys of the general public in this regard, simply due to differences in educational level that may influence responses. Further, does any rule of thumb apply to all types of questions? A well-known study by Bradburn, Sudman, and Associates (1979) suggested that increasing the length of sensitive questions (those asking about personal, private, or embarrassing issues) may *increase* response quality. But it certainly is not generally accepted that all sensitive questions should be long. Further, a general rule we follow is that dates of events tend not to be as well remembered as other metrics, such as age or number of years ago. However, Wellens (1994) found that immigrants' answers to a question asking when they came to the United States were strongly represented by reports of the exact year.

Design rules must be viewed as general guides that have many exceptions, or that would give different types of direction as the problem to be tackled is further specified. The world in which questionnaire designers live is often complex and multivariate, and following rule-based generalizations in a lockstep manner is hazardous. The alternative is to design the product as best we can, but to then do product testing—for example, by conducting cognitive interviews.

(b) *Design rules are blind to the larger picture.* Similarly, a list of rules or commandments is necessarily naive with respect to the vital issue of trade-offs that need to be made as we design questionnaires (see Beatty, in press). There is often no perfect way to ask a question in a particular case, and the varieties of different approaches must be considered with respect to all of the other design decisions we have to make. Worse, rules may produce conflicting advice. Based on general design principles, we may believe that one reference period—say, 30 days—will be better than a longer one, such as 12 months. But in the context of 10 preceding questions that all involve a 12-month period, we may decide to adhere to a different rule—"Don't confuse the respondent by constantly switching the reference period"—and stay with 12 months. Keep in mind that questions don't stand alone but must work as a type of integrated chorus. Design rules and checklists do not handle this truth very well (a limitation that the authors of the QAS system readily admit).

(c) *Rules help us to fashion the question, but is it the right question?* Finally, a subtle and sometimes unrecognized truth is that we must always keep in mind the measurement objectives our questions are intended to fulfill in order to serve as valid measures (Schwarz, 1997). Hammering home an earlier point, we do not ask a question of thousands of survey respondents because we are interested in carrying on a multitude of conversations but because we endeavor to produce some type of aggregate statistic. This may be in the form of a population parameter estimate, such as an unemployment index produced by the U.S. Bureau of Labor Statistics. Or, we may seek to measure association, such as whether educational level is related to Internet-based seeking of knowledge about cancer risk. In every case, it is very possible that our use of good design principles produces questions that function well, but that fail utterly to address our information needs.

Foreseeing these problems is easier said than done; one can study a question from the proverbial armchair for quite awhile without noting problems of interpretation or usage that later become stunningly clear through testing. As an example, consider questions about "why" the respondent has chosen to do something, such as "Why did you go to the dentist for your last visit?" The questionnaire designer may believe that the intent is self-evident, whereas testing such a question often leads to the discovery of additional levels of complexity. Interview subjects may provide a range of responses, such as "I got the reminder card," "It was time to go," "I had some pain," "I got a regular check-up," or "I had X-rays and then a tooth filled." This range of responses reveals our failure to indicate whether we want to know what *prompted* the action (why they went) or about expected or actual *outcomes* (what was done); that is, the question exhibits what Lazarsfeld (1986, cited in Krueger, 1994) labeled *specification error*. In this case, we would be forced to reconsider exactly which of these meanings we intend (or whether we intend both), and rephrase as appropriate.

To state the general point, before we ask others a question we should determine exactly what we want to know; that is, we must achieve "grounding" with ourselves (Fowler, 1992). As I hope to make clear, flaws stemming from vague objectives are often clarified only through the cognitive testing process and not necessarily as a function of following established written practices, rules, or guidelines.

Overall, best practices for questionnaire development depend on a combination of design rules and testing. I have included this chapter because knowledge of questionnaire design rules is vital, especially as this serves as a foundation for testing questions. Yet, "questionnaire design cannot be taught from books; every investigation presents new and different problems" (Oppenheim, 1966, p. vii). We are best served by applying "the rules of the game" and in turn relying on testing results to further hone those rules. As was well-stated by Belson (1981):

> The question designer who uses the question-testing method will discover his failures and be in a position to do something about them. With each new testing operation undertaken he adds to his knowledge about question design and increasingly becomes the competent craftsman. (p. 396)

Chapter Summary

- Errors in self-report surveys are serious. Survey questions produce a range of error types, but questionnaire designers usually focus on *response error*.
- Response errors exist for a range of reasons, but from a sociolinguistic perspective, they occur largely because questions fail to communicate the designer's intent. In particular, they fail to achieve appropriate *grounding*.
- There are a number of ways that we can design questions in order to avoid rampant error, in particular by using (a) textbook-based questionnaire design guides, and (b) checklist-based systems that focus on pitfalls to avoid when designing questions.
- Although these systems are useful, they are incomplete; design rules get us on the path toward our destination, but it is still vital to conduct testing, such as cognitive interviewing.

Exercise: Question Evaluation

EXERCISE 1: SOURCES OF QUESTION MISUNDERSTANDING

To emphasize the point that surveys are unlike conversation, consider how the simple question *"Do you own a car?"* can be expected to function in the structured interview, and

(a) list potential sources of misunderstanding that might work against the development of common grounding,

(b) try to script a survey question to achieve this state of grounding.

SUGGESTED SOLUTION

(a) Answering the question "Do you own a car?" requires consideration of several ambiguous factors related to the questioner's conceptual intent. I may have a vehicle that I drive every day of the week, but am led astray in my interpretation because

    1. It is unclear what is meant by "car." I may say "no" because I have only a pickup truck and a sports utility vehicle.

    2. In response to "you," I could respond "no" because the car is in my spouse's name.

3. Concerning the word "own," I may again say "no" because the vehicle is leased rather than "owned."

Overall, assuming the researcher is interested in whether I am in possession of a vehicle that I have some form of ownership in, that person may not get the desired answer. As described above, in everyday interchange we may have ways of fixing this (I respond but embellish "No, I drive a pickup" and the interviewer says "Yes, I meant that too").

(b) To address these problems in the standardized survey questionnaire, the item might look more like the following:
Do you or (names of household members 18 or older) now own, rent, or lease any type of motor vehicle, including a car, truck, or motorcycle?

EXERCISE 2: DRAFTING QUESTIONS ACCORDING TO DESIGN RULES

The following questions have features that may be problematic. Review them in order to identify problems and issues to investigate during the cognitive interview. Further, (a) Assume telephone-based administration; (b) Evaluate each question for potential problems (either informally, or using the codes from the QAS system; the solutions below assume the latter); (c) Note that questions are not intended to be in a meaningful sequence.

1. How many glasses (8 oz) of milk (whole, 2%, or skim milk) did you drink yesterday?

   Answer: QAS Code 1c: It is clear *what* to read, but unclear *how* to read it. The parts in parentheses can easily be read silently, and would be fine for a self-administered questionnaire. However, if read by an interviewer, the question needs to be rephrased as "How many eight-ounce glasses of whole, two-percent, or skim milk did you drink yesterday?"

2. Do you consider yourself to be overweight, underweight, or about average?

   Answer: QAS Code 7f: Missing category. Some people may not fit any of the given categories. A National Football League lineman (or a horse race jockey) might consider himself to be none of these; he is at a desirable weight, but it is not anywhere near average. Instead, use "overweight, underweight, or about the right weight?"

3. Since you've lived in your current residence, have any special locks been installed on the doors of your home?

   __ Yes   __ No   __ No opinion

   Answer: QAS Code 7b: Mismatch between question and answer categories. The response categories implied do not match those that are given to the interviewer to use. This is not an opinion question. It is either true or it is not, or the respondent does not know. So this question should use "Don't know" instead of "No opinion."

4. Which of the following best describes whether you have a smoke alarm in your home? You own a smoke alarm, and it is installed and working; you own a smoke alarm, but it is broken or not installed; you own a smoke alarm, but the battery is missing; you don't own a smoke alarm because it is too expensive; you don't own a smoke alarm because you don't think it is necessary; or you don't own a smoke alarm for some other reason?

   Answer: QAS Code 3a: Question is too long. A good way to identify long questions is to read them out loud, especially to another person.

5. What kind of doctor treats your diabetes: a general or family practitioner, an internal medicine doctor, a diabetologist, or someone else?

   Answer: QAS Code 3b: Technical term. "Diabetologist" is better conveyed as "a specialist who deals with diabetes" and "practitioner" may be better communicated as "doctor."

6. Thinking about your most recent mammogram, how much did it cost, regardless of who paid for it? Include just the cost of the X-ray itself and not any fee charged by the doctor at the X-ray facility, or the cost for an office visit where the test was ordered.

   Answer: QAS Code 5a: Knowledge. Respondents in a health maintenance organization (HMO) who simply make a co-payment may have no idea how much the mammogram cost. Also, even those who pay out of pocket, or according to a fee-for-service model, may have no way of disentangling the cost of the test from the cost of the office visit.

7. Do you think that ministers, politicians, and other community leaders should speak out against cigarettes and tobacco?

   Answer: QAS Code 4c: Double-barreled. This one is actually triple-barreled, as one could think that politicians and other community leaders should speak out but that ministers should not.

8. Have you had your blood tested for the AIDS virus?

   Answer: QAS Code 3c: Vague question. It is unclear whether this means "Did I take the initiative in deciding to have my blood tested?" or "Was it tested as part of any type of blood test?" Sometimes respondents will say "I needed it tested for my job—but I didn't go out of my way to have it done." If the issue of interest is the act of testing, simply ask "As far as you know, has your blood ever been tested for the AIDS virus?"

9. How often does your arthritis prevent you from doing your usual work or taking part in social activities? Would you say every day, almost every day, once a week, occasionally, or never?

   Answer: QAS Code 4b: Assumes constant behavior. There may be multiple problems with this, but note especially that flare-ups are a common characteristic of many chronic medical conditions. Respondents tend to say that there are weeks when they cannot do these things at all, and then it gets better again. Although this problem has not been solved by questionnaire designers, it might help to first ask a question about the regularity of the experience.

10. Would you support an increase in cigarette taxes if the additional revenue was spent on community cancer prevention and control programs?

    Answer: QAS Code 3c: Vague question. Respondents who smoke, and who are making a serious attempt to answer the question, may object that it does not contain sufficient information. If the increase was a nickel a pack, that may be different than if it was a dollar a pack. The amount needs to be specified. Often a question with this type of problem naturally elicits the response "It depends."

3

Background and Theoretical Origins

The CASM Approach

Chapter Overview

The previous chapter made the case that a blueprint approach (i.e., following question design rules) should be supplemented by product testing. Cognitive interviewing serves this function, but not in a simple or mechanistic sense. Rather, it is—at least in intent—a scientific enterprise supported by historical and theoretical developments. This chapter therefore reviews the roots of the cognitive interview by discussing the Cognitive Aspects of Survey Methodology (CASM) as the broader field from which cognitive interviewing is derived. I first describe the four-stage model of the survey response process on which much CASM research is based, and then distinguish between basic CASM research and applied CASM research, presenting cognitive interviewing as essentially the latter of these.

Origins of CASM as an Orienting Framework

In the early 1980s, the study of survey response error was affected by developments in an emergent field created through the interdisciplinary combination of survey methodology and cognitive psychology and termed the Cognitive Aspects of Survey Methodology, or CASM (Jabine, Straf, Tanur, & Tourangeau, 1984). The CASM approach has come to dominate the field of questionnaire design development, research, and evaluation. The basic tenet of the CASM is that responses to survey questions require a series of complex cognitive processes, or information-processing steps, as opposed to a simple stimulus-response sequence in which the question is asked and the respondent produces an answer (see Lashley, 1923, for a classic behaviorist viewpoint).

CASM was proposed as a framework that would supplement—or even supplant—the more traditional view of questionnaire design as the expression of design rules by emphasizing the vital importance of cognition in the survey response process. That is, researchers across several fields recognized that, for the reasons I pointed out in the previous chapter, design rules are often insufficient. In particular, the fact that questionnaire design lacked a strong underlying theory appeared to be a major limitation that called out for attention. The "cognitive revolution" of the 1970s, in which cognition was applied to a wide range of domains, gave rise to a useful body of relevant theory. Hence the marriage of cognition to questionnaire design appeared to have both theoretical and practical implications, and might even lead to a true science of questionnaire construction (Herrmann, 1999; Jobe & Mingay, 1991; Sirken & Schechter, 1999; Tanur, 1999).

To be fair, the observation that answering survey questions requires thought certainly did not originate with CASM. As I have detailed elsewhere (Willis, in press), the cognitive viewpoint, as extended to surveys, has origins that reach back to the mid-20th century, well before the advent of cognitive psychology as a dominant influence in the social sciences. For example, theories of the survey response process that were cognitive in nature, if not in name, were introduced independently by researchers at the University of Illinois (Lansing, Ginsburg, & Braaten, 1961) in England by Oppenheim (1966), at the University of Michigan by Cannell and colleagues (Cannell et al., 1977; Cannell, Miller, & Oksenberg, 1981), and at the U.S. Census Bureau by Martin (1983).

Although CASM may have had earlier origins, it did assume a relatively subdued profile until the movement began to flourish in earnest following two seminal events: the 1983 Advanced Research Seminar on Cognitive Aspects of Survey Methodology in the United States, now referred to as CASM I (Jabine et al., 1984), and the 1984 Conference on Social Information Processing and Survey Methodology in Germany (Hippler, Schwarz, & Sudman, 1987). One influential outcome of the CASM I conference was the introduction of the four-stage cognitive model proposed by Tourangeau (1984). Table 3.1 depicts the key cognitive steps posited by this model, with indications of issues that may be relevant to each of them. Proponents of this model assert that each processing step must be successful if the output is to be free of error (e.g., if

Table 3.1   The Four-Stage Model of the Survey Response Process

1. Comprehension of the Question

   (a) Question intent: What does the respondent believe the question to be asking?

   (b) Meaning of terms: What do specific words and phrases in the question mean?

2. Retrieval from Memory of Relevant Information

   (a) Recallability of information: What types of information does the respondent need to recall in order to answer the question?

   (b) Recall strategy: What type of strategies are used to retrieve information? For example, does the respondent tend to count events by recalling each one individually, or does he or she use an estimation strategy?

3. Judgment/Estimation Processes

   (a) Motivation: Does the respondent devote sufficient mental effort to answering the question accurately and thoughtfully?

   (b) Sensitivity/social desirability: Does the respondent want to tell the truth? Does he or she say something to make him or her look "better"?

4. Response Processes

   (a) Mapping the response: Can the respondent match his or her internally generated answer to the response categories given by the survey question?

SOURCE: Tourangeau (1984).

the respondent can't retrieve information about how many times she has used sunscreen in the past 2 weeks, she likely cannot report this accurately).

Some of these cognitive processes are automatic, so that the respondent is unaware of their operation, whereas others may reflect a conscious strategy. The processes used to answer survey questions may also vary depending on the type of question asked. Autobiographical questions can place a heavy burden on retrieval processes (e.g., "For how many years have you smoked cigarettes every day?") (Eisenhower, Mathiowetz, & Morganstein, 1991). Sensitive questions may place more demands on the respondent's judgment and decision processes (e.g., deciding to check the "yes" box in response to "Have you ever smoked marijuana?").

Several alternative cognitive models have been introduced (see Jobe & Hermann, 1996, for a review). These are similar, except for two significant features:

(a) Subsequent to comprehension (or encoding) and retrieval (or recall) processes, the next step is variously referred to as a judgment, estimation, or decision stage; the fundamental notion is that the respondent makes conscious decisions concerning features such as the adequacy or plausibility of retrieved information.

(b) Beyond terminological differences, a few models (e.g., the system introduced by Willis, Royston, & Bercini, 1991, now known as the Flexible Processing Model) explicitly reject the notion of a strict sequence of cognitive processes. In particular, rather than enacting an algorithmic series of operations, respondents may instead initiate a decision stage relatively early, before attempting information retrieval. For example, when asked the number of times I have been given a speeding ticket, I may decide to cut short the processing chain and provide a response such as "None of your business!" even prior to attempting to retrieve all occurrences from memory. This view is consistent with observations by several authors that the survey response process is subject to many social and contextual variables, and cannot be fully accounted for by a simple, serial processing model (Ahola, 2004; Collins & Becher, 2001; Snijkers 2002).

Applications of Basic CASM Research

Basic CASM research, as it was termed by Sirken and Schechter (1999), is remarkably broad in scope. It includes a host of empirical studies of cognitive factors that influence survey responses and the ways in which survey questions might be designed to take into account these factors.[1] Some, but certainly not all, of this research is based on a four-stage cognitive model. Entire volumes have been written on these research results; in particular, see Sudman, Bradburn, and Schwarz (1996) and Tourangeau, Rips, et al. (2000). For example, studies related to information retrieval processes force designers to consider the following potential problems:

(a) *Lack of information in memory.* To elaborate on an example from the previous chapter, Lee et al. (1999) studied parental recall of children's immunization records, and determined that in the absence of shot records, reporting of details such as exact type and number of shots was exceedingly poor. The major cause was found to be failure of encoding, rather than information retrieval limitations; that is, parents couldn't report accurately because they had never known the answers, and not because they were unable to remember them. The authors warned against requests for information that has not been stored in memory in the first place.

(b) *Loss of information over time.* Tourangeau, Rips, et al. (2000, p. 84) review the ways that the passage of time influences the correct recall of teacher names, street names, and so on. Not surprisingly, these memories degrade over the years, as presumably do those of survey respondents.

(c) *Blurring of information over time.* In a record-check study of the recall of medical visits, Means et al. (1989) found that, consistent with the general literature on human memory, recurrent events tend to blend into a generic memory, which renders individual episodes and events difficult, if not impossible, to remember. As such, even for information that is retained in memory, the level of detail available to respondents may diminish as the events recede. In the survey environment this may lead to the phenomenon of *telescoping,* in which respondents asked to place an event in time remember it as occurring either sooner or later than it actually did (Neter & Waksberg, 1964).

(d) *Use of varied retrieval strategies.* Blair and Burton (1987) and Burton and Blair (1991) studied the retrieval strategies used by survey respondents to recall the answers to behavioral frequency questions, such as the number of times they had visited a restaurant over a given time period. They found that as the frequency increases, people tend to rely on an estimation strategy, as opposed to enumerating (counting) every episode. It is unwise to assume that questions concerning frequency actually induce our respondents to count episodes, especially for those that are frequent or mundane.

A general theme that has emerged from such studies is that information retrieval is not necessarily direct, but rather is reconstructive in nature (Bartlett, 1932; Hasher & Griffin, 1978; Tourangeau, Rips, et al., 2000).

Findings of the type listed above are perhaps not surprising, as they are consistent with our subjective notions of how people behave. However, there are also interesting findings in the CASM experimental literature that may have been unanticipated. For example, Schwarz and colleagues (e.g., Schwarz, Hippler, Deutsch, & Strack, 1985; Schwarz & Bienias, 1990) have extensively researched the area of open versus closed response categories for behavior frequency questions such as television watching. Their results suggest that respondents use a variety of sources of information to answer such questions—including ones we don't necessarily want them to use. Schwarz et al. (1985) asked two groups of subjects the number of hours per day that they watched television, but one group was given response category ranges from "Up to ½ hour" through "More than 2½ hours" (low ranges), and the other ranges from "Up to 2½ hours" through "More than 4½ hours" (high ranges). They found that subjects who were presented the low ranges tended to select responses that were relatively lower than did subjects presented the higher ranges, and that the overall distributions of responses were markedly different. One interpretation is that people in both cases assumed the middle category represented "usual" behavior, as defined by the survey designer, and that they relied on this as a means for anchoring their own responses. A potential implication for survey practice is that for at least some behavioral frequency questions, it is best to use an open-ended format that simply asks the question without suggesting any particular answers.

Cognitive Interviewing as Applied CASM Research

It is tempting to seize upon results from the CASM research literature as a basis for question design, and the insights gained from such studies are certainly useful. To our advantage, CASM research relies on controlled studies of factors that influence the understanding and answering of survey questions. Such research findings are therefore objective, likely replicable, and provide a rich understanding of the psychological aspects of survey responses. Further, they do seem to reflect science rather than art, as they depend somewhat less on author opinion of effective practice than do the questionnaire design texts and checklists described in the previous chapter. Consequently, the CASM research agenda has achieved the key goal of incorporating theory in a way that enriches our understanding of the survey response process.

That said, CASM research results, just like the pronouncements of question design texts, are generally insufficient in themselves to guide our everyday questionnaire design practices. Again, all such results are subject to case-by-case exception when we face decisions concerning question wording, choice of reference periods, and so on. For instance, even the very reasonable suggestion to use open-ended response categories for behavioral frequency questions, as opposed to ranges, can sometimes be unworkable in practice. Open-ended administration of the question "How many X-rays have you had in your life?" may reduce the chance of bias relative to closed-ended category ranges. However, many respondents would no doubt be at a loss to answer this in totally open-ended form. Instead, it might in this case be better to use ranges (such as "more than 20") that communicate the level of detail required and ease the overall mental processing task, especially as this question may be unlikely to be subject to the biases (or *demand characteristics*) that afflict those reporting on television watching. This solution does not directly challenge the Schwarz et al. results; rather, it represents an adjustment to the specifics of our particular situation.

Sorting through the various trade-offs associated with alternative question formulations is a complex process, and one that cannot normally be solved only through reference to background CASM research, even though this provides a good general knowledge base. As a further development, we have instead come to rely on cognitive interviewing as *applied CASM research* (Sirken & Schechter, 1999). The cognitive interview is certainly one of the more concrete and successful manifestations of the CASM movement in terms of how widely it has taken root and been applied across diverse topic areas, fields, and researchers (Blair & Presser, 1993; Sirken & Schechter, 1999). Cognitive interviewing has generated a body of research that represents applied CASM, some of which is mainly descriptive and some of which attempts to be critically evaluative (see Bercini, 1992; Campanelli, 1997; Campanelli, Martin, & Rothgeb, 1991; DeMaio & Rothgeb, 1996; Dippo, 1989; Esposito & Hess, 1992; Jobe, Tourangeau, & Smith, 1993; Lessler & Sirken, 1985; Royston, Bercini, Sirken, & Mingay, 1986; Sirken, Herrmann, Schechter, Schwarz, Tanur, & Tourangeau, 1999; Willis, DeMaio, & Harris-Kojetin, 1999; Willis & Schechter, 1997, for further reading).

The overall goal of the enterprise is, of course, to evaluate survey questions. Beyond that, a further objective is to feed back into the CASM realm more generally by producing empirical results that yield general principles with a cognitive focus. That is, just as Belson (1981) suggested that testing can make us better questionnaire designers, it should also make us better CASM theorists. Cognitive interviewing is therefore intended to both represent CASM and to reflect back upon it (Schwarz, 1999). In the next chapter I consider more fully the way that specific developments following the CASM I conference resulted in cognitive interviewing as it is now practiced.

Chapter Summary

- At this point, I have discussed two relatives of cognitive interviewing: Chapter 2 covered the use of question design rules, a close cousin; Chapter 3 focused more on parentage, and the manner in which cognitive interviewing is generally viewed as an offspring of the Cognitive Aspects of Survey Methodology (CASM) movement of the 1980s.
- Basic CASM research elucidates cognitive factors that influence responses to survey questions and guides questionnaire design in a general sense.
- However, specific design decisions are often dependent on the outcome of cognitive interviewing as applied CASM research.

Note

1. The objectives of CASM stretch even beyond the survey methods field. One purpose is to study the operation of memory, and other cognitive processes, outside the psychological laboratory in an environment (the survey interview) that may exhibit ecological validity in the sense discussed by Neisser and Winograd (1988).

4

Cognitive Interviewing in Practice

Think-Aloud, Verbal Probing, and Other Techniques

Chapter Overview

Two developments after CASM I produced cognitive interviewing as now practiced: the adoption, and further adaptation, of the *think-aloud interview,* and the wide application of *verbal probing techniques.* Rather than simply describing the details of each technique, I review them from a historical vantage point, which clarifies the context in which they have been used and facilitates the understanding of an accumulated literature that tends to be inconsistent and even confusing. I will then compare and contrast think-aloud and verbal probing in terms of both ease of use and effectiveness. I end with a discussion of vignettes, card sorts, and field-based probing, which can also be viewed as cognitive techniques.

Think-Aloud Interviewing

In a CASM I conference proceedings paper, Loftus (1984) considered how respondents answer questions about past autobiographical events, such as doctor visits. Do they use a present-to-past recall ordering, or do they begin in the far past and work forward? She proposed that such cognitive issues could be studied through verbal report methods—in particular, through think-aloud interviewing, as described by Ericsson and Simon (1980, 1984) and by von Someren, Barnard, and Sandberg (1994). The application to the survey response process is straightforward, at least procedurally: When asking a question about retrieval of doctor visits, we ask the subject to not only answer but to vocalize all of his or her thoughts, and we mainly listen. By doing so, we determine the order in which visits are recalled, and whether obvious problems in responding are evident. Loftus (1984) set the stage for the use of thinking aloud as a means to test survey questions by concluding that "at least in response to these questions, subjects tend to retrieve autobiographical memories in a predominantly past-to-present, or forward, direction" (p. 64).

As thinking aloud has been used for question pretesting, the cognitive interviewer reads each question aloud and then literally records (usually via audiotape or videotape) the subject's verbal think-aloud stream, or otherwise notes the processes the subject uses in arriving at an answer. For example, an idealized think-aloud interview might include the following exchange:

INTERVIEWER: (reading survey question to be tested)	How many times have you talked to a doctor in the last 12 months?
SUBJECT:	I guess that depends on what you mean when you say "talked." I talk to my neighbor, who is a doctor, but you probably don't mean that. I go to my doctor about once a year for a general checkup, so I would count that. I've also probably been to some type of specialist a couple more times in the past year—once to get a bad knee diagnosed, and I also saw an ENT about a chronic coughing thing, which I'm pretty sure was in the past year, although I wouldn't swear to it. I've also talked to doctors several times when I brought my kids in to the pediatrician—I assume you don't want that included, although I really can't be sure. Also, I saw a chiropractor, but I don't know if that's a doctor in the sense you mean. So, what I'm saying, overall, is that I guess I'm not sure what number to give you—not sure what you want.

From this think-aloud *protocol,* or verbal record, the interviewer may observe that although the individual attempts to recall each medical visit individually rather than by estimating or guessing outright, he still has trouble determining whether a particular visit was really in the last

12 months. If, after interviewing a number of subjects, it becomes clear that none could think through with confidence the number of times they had been to a doctor, the investigators might decide that the reference period is simply too long to provide adequate answers. More significantly, the larger problem seems to be vagueness in question intent, as the subject is unsure of what to include and exclude with respect to (a) doctor contacts that pertain only to his health, and (b) the type of physician or other health care provider to be counted. Presumably these flaws can be addressed through appropriate question modification.

CONDUCT OF THE THINK-ALOUD INTERVIEW

Specific written guidance concerning the behavior of the interviewer during the think-aloud session has been sparse. Most importantly, the interviewer must induce the subject to think aloud, and this training generally involves some practice at the start of an interview. One training approach that was suggested to me by a former colleague, David Mingay, was the following:

> Try to visualize the place where you live, and think about how many windows there are in that place. As you count up the windows, tell me what you are seeing and thinking about.

Further training may be necessary, prior to or during the core part of the interview, to keep the subject thinking aloud. However, Ericsson and Simon (1984), as original proponents of this method, cautioned against excessive training in thinking aloud, arguing that the ultimate objective is not to focus attention on that task, or to produce subjects who are proficient at thinking aloud, but rather to use this as a tool to understand their mental processes. Usually the most critical and complex issue related to think-aloud interviewing is not its relatively simple conduct, but rather the variable, and often complex, analysis of the think-aloud protocol. (Chapter 11 is devoted specifically to the issue of analysis of the results of cognitive interviews.)

MAKING THE CASE FOR THINK-ALOUD INTERVIEWING: ERICSSON AND SIMON'S THEORY OF VERBAL REPORTS

In using information derived from think-aloud interviewing to evaluate survey questions, we implicitly make the claim that these verbal reports are veridical; that is, they provide information reflecting actual cognitive processes, and these processes are relevant when determining whether the questions function as we hope. Our reliance on think-aloud varieties of cognitive interviewing therefore depends on the truth of such assumptions, and this matter has received significant attention in the cognitive psychology literature. Ericsson and Simon (1980, 1984) were the major proponents of the use of verbal report procedures in psychological research. They proposed a means for the study of cognitive processing based on a model of memory introduced by Newell and Simon (1972), which mainly (but not exclusively, as is sometimes believed) emphasized the use of the think-aloud interview (see Willis, in press). Thinking aloud produces a verbal stream which is submitted to *protocol analysis*—detailed coding and subsequent review of the verbal output—in which particular behaviors or patterns are discerned. Ericsson and Simon reviewed a range of studies using such verbal reports applied to problem solving and concept formation. Usually these tasks were rather complex and involved multiple steps, such as playing chess; solving a "Tower of Hanoi" puzzle, in which a series of three rings must be moved according to a defined set of rules; or descrambling an anagram such as ECOAN to produce the word OCEAN (or, CANOE).

Ericsson and Simon based the use of think-aloud interviewing on two important premises: (1) Self-reports are veridical to the extent that they involve output from short-term memory, rather than long-term memory. (2) Under this circumstance, subjects can provide self-reports through think-aloud interviews that are *non-reactive;* that is, the act of thinking aloud does not in itself contaminate the subject's verbal processes. They went to great lengths in reviewing the available evidence before concluding that

(a) thinking aloud tends to slow cognitive processing relative to a silent control condition, but it does not fundamentally alter the subject's level of task performance; and

(b) even when thinking aloud does appear to alter task performance, the effects are relatively minimal compared to other features of the experimental setup that influence responses.

Following Loftus's (1984) advocacy of the application of think-aloud techniques to the survey domain, survey researchers adopted the think-aloud interview as a means for pretesting survey questions, and christened this approach the cognitive interview. In an applied context, the U.S. National Center for Health Statistics sponsored a demonstration project that incorporated cognitive interviewing into the development of the National Health Interview Survey (see Lessler & Sirken, 1985; Lessler, Tourangeau, & Salter, 1989; Royston et al., 1986). The U.S. Census Bureau was also early to adopt this technique as applied to a wide range of census surveys (DeMaio et al., 1983), and since that time, investigators have applied and further developed the think-aloud interview (Bolton & Bronkhorst, 1996). To this day, some researchers refer to cognitive interviewing as "think-aloud" (e.g., Smith, 2003), even when it is not especially clear how much classic thinking aloud is occurring in the interview.

DOES THINK-ALOUD INTERVIEWING MAKE SENSE WHEN APPLIED TO SURVEY QUESTIONS?

Despite Loftus's seemingly reasonable application of think-aloud interviewing to the study of retrieval, and the enthusiasm with which it was originally co-opted, practitioners have never established, on theoretical grounds, that the think-aloud interview applies to the general testing of survey questions. In particular, researchers have seldom considered whether the necessary underlying assumptions hold, and background theory is very seldom invoked or considered in a serious manner. Most significantly, the application of think-aloud interviewing to the study of question comprehension processes is common, as we listen to determine whether the subject is interpreting the questions, phrases, or terms correctly. However, comprehension processes were not strongly represented in the original Ericsson and Simon reviews. The psychological tasks they reviewed were typically first described to the subject, and the think-aloud task was targeted toward problem solving, as opposed to the understanding of the task (Whitney & Budd, 1996). Extending think-aloud interviewing to the comprehension of survey questions therefore represents a fundamental extension of the Ericsson and Simon approach, and in fact the use of think-aloud interviews to study comprehension (such as in text reading) is very controversial (see Magliano & Graesser, 1991; Trabasso & Suh, 1993; Whitney & Budd, 1996).

Further, think-aloud interviewing in classic form was somewhat less social in nature than is the interviewer-administered survey questionnaire, as it mainly involved direct interaction with the psychological laboratory task, rather than with another human being. As such, Ericsson and Simon (1984) emphasized the importance of minimizing social contact between the interviewer and subject. They counseled the interviewer to avoid the word "me," in order to refrain from interjecting him- or herself into the social interaction (e.g., "Keep talking" as opposed to "Tell me what you're thinking"), and to go so far as to sit facing away from the subject.

With respect to think-aloud interviewing as applied to surveys, Bolton and Bronkhorst (1996) emphasized the complete opposite by advocating *back channeling*—"nodding, making encouraging sounds, or offering feedback, such as saying 'okay'" (p. 45)—to encourage respondents to think aloud effectively. It does seem that the Bolton and Bronkhorst approach, involving a greater level of social interaction, is much more widely accepted as appropriate practice by cognitive interviewers. This reiterates the point made by sociolinguists that the survey represents a social and often conversational interchange, as opposed to simply the completion of a psychological task, and this has a significant effect on the nature of the think-aloud interview. (On the other hand, self-administered instruments may represent a significant departure in this regard, as will be clarified in Chapter 12.)

Readers who are interested in a more complete discussion of these background issues are encouraged to consult a theoretically oriented review paper (Willis, in press). For present purposes, I hope it suffices to state that although think-aloud procedures have frequently been applied to survey question evaluation, this has been mainly because the method is practical and seemingly useful. In fact, it is somewhat unfortunate that Ericsson and Simon's theory has been largely ignored by survey researchers, as more explicit attention might provide the basis for informing and tailoring cognitive interviewing practice.

Verbal Probing Techniques

As an alternative to the think-aloud interview, intensive verbal probing is a core verbal reporting technique that has increasingly come into favor with cognitive researchers (Willis et al., 1999). Assuming a face-to-face interview, the interviewer asks the target question and the subject answers it, but the interviewer then follows up (either immediately or at the end of the interview) by probing for other specific information relevant to the question or to the specific answer given. Table 4.1 contains basic categories of now "classic" probes, and an example of each (adapted from Willis, 1999). Note, however, that this is a skeletal and incomplete listing. Probing is a varied and complex endeavor, and I will devote several chapters to this activity.

Table 4.1   Common Cognitive Probes

Cognitive Probe	Example
Comprehension/Interpretation Probe	What does the term "outpatient" mean to you?
Paraphrasing	Can you repeat the question I just asked in your own words?
Confidence Judgment	How sure are you that your health insurance covers drug and alcohol treatment?
Recall Probe	How do you remember that you went to the doctor five times in the past 12 months?
Specific Probe	Why do you think that cancer is the most serious health problem?
General Probes	How did you arrive at that answer? Was that easy or hard to answer? I noticed that you hesitated. Tell me what you were thinking.

THE HISTORICAL BASIS OF THE VERBAL PROBING TECHNIQUE

Reminiscent of the observation that CASM itself had roots earlier than 1983, the use of what today would be called cognitive probing was described by Cantril (1944) and Cantril and Fried (1944), who advocated the *intensive* interview, well before it became fashionable to refer specifically to cognition (see also Selltiz, Jahoda, Deutsch, & Cook, 1959). Somewhat later, Belson (1981) introduced an extremely intensive form of comprehension oriented probing, and this again can be seen as an expression of a long-held belief that (a) respondents need to think in order to answer survey questions, and (b) we can ask them pointed questions about their thinking (Blair & Presser, 1993).

As a particularly illuminating illustration, Schuman (1982) discussed the very famous example of a survey question that failed because it produced data indicating that innkeepers would refuse service to Asians, when their behavior showed they did no such thing. Schuman wondered how the hypothetical situation described by the survey question had been interpreted by respondents, and just what it was that the surveyed innkeepers were actually envisioning as they answered the questions. He suggested that in order to assess this,

> One good way, not perfect by any means but among the best available, is to ask and then to listen as well as we can for each proprietor's personal definition of the situation. If we attempt to do this with a concern not merely clinical, but with the goal of representing a meaningful population of proprietors; of proceeding systematically so as to avoid bias in our inquiry; and of gathering information in a form that can be analyzed internally and connected to such social categories as age and sex, then we have reinvented the attitude survey in its richest form. (pp. 26–27)

Schuman's recommendation clearly foreshadows what today we routinely refer to as the cognitive interview.

Despite these earlier strands, the resurgence of probing techniques in the late 1980s was greatly kindled by developments subsequent to the CASM I conference. For one, survey methodologists at the newly formed NCHS Questionnaire Design Research Laboratory began to utilize probe questions as an adjunct to the think-aloud interview (Lessler et al., 1989). Further, several reports began to appear suggesting that the sole use of think-aloud interviewing was perhaps of limited usefulness, and in its place, probing was advocated. To quote from Royston and Bercini (1987), "because many respondents found it difficult to think aloud as they answered, responses were probed extensively to get at the cognitive aspects of the response process" (p. 829).

Beyond simply accepting that generic forms of probing were useful, researchers at several locations realized that the processes within the four-stage cognitive model could naturally be mapped to cognitive probe questions that address each process. For example, comprehension issues could be addressed through the use of explicit comprehension probes (e.g., "What does the term 'abdomen' mean to you?"); retrieval could be assessed by asking "How easy or difficult is it to remember how many times you went to the doctor in the past 12 months?"; decision and judgment processes could generally be tapped through "How did you come up with that answer?"; and response processes through formulations such as "Was it easy or difficult to choose an answer from that list?" From this point, cognitive probes were increasingly applied, especially as they seemed to represent a very focused and productive approach when compared to pure forms of think-aloud interviewing. In fact, reliance on the four-stage model as a basis for verbal probing has, as much as any factor, contributed to the ongoing attractiveness of this cognitive model.

THE THEORETICAL BASIS FOR VERBAL PROBING TECHNIQUES

Probing makes intuitive sense, and because of this, practitioners seem very willing to apply probes. However, from a theoretical point of view, applying these in the pursuit of question evaluation activities requires that we make several key assumptions:

(a) Definable features of survey questions (e.g., question length, terminology, and so on) impact the information processing chain at various points—specifically, where comprehension, information retrieval, judgment and decision processes, and response processes are enacted.

(b) We can apply verbal probing techniques to literally "probe" the processing system; we ask the subject probe questions that are meant to tap the various subprocesses, such as comprehension, retrieval, etc.

(c) The information we receive from the subject's verbal report, in the form of a response to the probe question, can be used to make judgments about the operation of that subprocess, and in particular, whether the question has been processed as we intend.

The simple example in Figure 4.1 represents this processing chain as applied to a sample question.

Beyond asserting that responses to probes have at least something to do with the processing of the question, we also make the strong assumption that probing does not bias further question processing; that is, it does not produce reactivity. In truth, we cannot prove that either of these conditions holds, but throughout the book, I will emphasize the importance of probe construction practices and cognitive interviewer behavior that increase the likelihood that they are satisfied, and will eventually revisit the theoretical arguments surrounding our reliance on probing techniques (see Chapter 13).

(1) Question is submitted to cognitive system for processing: "In the past year, have you worked at more than one job for pay?"

(2) Question undergoes *comprehension* processing: "past year"; "work"; "job"; "for pay."

(3) Question undergoes *retrieval* processing: Access to memories concerning past year, job history.

(4) Question undergoes *decision/judgment* processing: Does answer pass internal plausibility test? Does the subject want to report the value retrieved in unaltered form?

(5) Question undergoes *response matching*: Answer is to be in the form of "yes" IF job > 1; "no" IF job = 0 or 1.

(6) Response is produced: "Yeah."

Figure 4.1   Information Processing Chain

Concurrent Versus Retrospective Verbal Probing

For cognitive interviewers who rely on probes, as opposed to pure think-aloud interviews, a key decision concerns the choice of *when* to probe—during the interview, as it is integrated within the asking and answering of target questions, or afterward, as a completely separate activity. Most of the examples that I will present presume that probing is done in an interactive, conversational manner in which the cognitive interviewer and subject take turns asking and answering both target questions and cognitive probes. For such exchanges, the interchange is normally characterized by the following sequence:

1. the interviewer asks the target (survey) question,

2. the subject answers the question,

3. the interviewer asks a probe question,

4. the subject answers the probe question,

5. possible further cycles of (3–4)

6. the interviewer asks the next target question

Somewhat confusingly, this common sequence has been referred to both as *concurrent probing* and *immediate retrospective probing* (Willis et al., 1991). On the one hand, such probes are concurrent with the interview, as they are embedded within it. On the other, they are arguably retrospective, because they follow the subject's response to the target question (and can therefore be distinguished from thinking aloud, which is more literally concurrent). An important alternative to this procedure is to avoid disrupting the interview with probe questions, and to hold off until the end before conducting any probing (or even until the next day, as by Belson, 1981). This variant has been referred to as *delayed retrospective probing*, as *retrospective probing*, and as *subject debriefing*. For purposes of simplicity, I will use the terms *concurrent* and *retrospective* probing to distinguish probing done during questionnaire administration from that done after.

Currently, concurrent probing is more frequently used. In an empirical study of three cognitive labs, DeMaio and Landreth (in press) determined that approximately 95% of probes were administered concurrently rather than retrospectively. It might seem more effective to wait and debrief the subject by probing after the questions have been administered, in order to avoid reactivity effects due to the cumulative effects of probing. However, most cognitive interviewers appear to agree with Ericsson and Simon (1980, 1984) that information should be fresh in subjects' minds at the time that we probe it. Absent this, we face a significant danger that subjects no longer remember what they were thinking as they answered a question, and instead fabricate an explanation (Snijkers, 2002).

Retrospective probing, rather than the concurrent form, is chosen under certain circumstances: (a) when testing self-administered questionnaires, especially when the purpose of testing is mainly to determine the subject's ability to manage a self-completion instrument unaided (this issue is discussed at length in Chapter 12); and (b) in later stages of questionnaire development, when the designers want to simulate field procedure, absent interjected probe questions.

Choosing Between Think-Aloud and Verbal Probing Techniques

Having discussed the history and theoretical underpinning of each major verbal report method, the next natural question would be "Which is better?" I address this conflict through a consideration of pros and cons, ending with a plea for something of a truce. I first draw the reader's attention to the points of similarity and contrast between probing and think-aloud as major alternative approaches. In truth, verbal probing and think-aloud are not completely independent; note that the general probe "Tell me what you were thinking" is virtually identical to the key instruction often used in think-aloud interviewing to elicit response. From this perspective, the think-aloud interview can be conceptualized as the most general form of verbal probing. That said, think-aloud and probing do represent different levels of specificity, and I present the following list of relative trade-offs.

GENERAL ADVANTAGES OF THE THINK-ALOUD TECHNIQUE

(a) *Freedom from interviewer-imposed bias.* Because the interviewer contributes little other than the reading of the survey question, except to occasionally ask what the subject is thinking, he or she interjects little that may serve to influence responses. Therefore there is relatively little danger that the interviewer will "throw a wrench in the works" by making a comment or asking something that is biasing in nature.

(b) *Minimal interviewer training requirements.* Given that the interviewer mainly just needs to read survey questions and then listen to the respondent talk, little training or special expertise may be necessary.

(c) *Open-ended format.* Again, because the subject's verbalization is guided only minimally, he or she may provide information that is unanticipated by the interviewer. Therefore think-aloud interviewing is especially valuable when the subject is outgoing, articulate, and has had significant experience with the topics covered by the survey questions.

POTENTIAL DISADVANTAGES OF THE THINK-ALOUD TECHNIQUE

(a) *Need for subject training.* Because thinking aloud is a somewhat unusual activity for most people, the technique may require a non-trivial amount of preliminary training of subjects in order to elicit a sufficient amount of think-aloud behavior. Such training may eat into the amount of productive time that can be devoted to the interview itself.

(b) *Limited subject think-aloud proficiency.* Several researchers have commented on this drawback—even given training in the activity, many individuals are simply not good at thinking aloud when answering survey questions (Royston, 1989; Von Thurn & Moore, 1994). In particular, they tend to automatically answer the questions when asked, without further elaboration. More seriously, both Bickart and Felcher (1996) and Wellens (1994) found a positive relationship between ability to produce a think-aloud protocol and educational level, and Wellens reported that especially for individuals with low English language skills, think-aloud was much less effective than verbal probing.

(c) *Burden on subject.* Related to the point above, the think-aloud activity places the main burden on the subject. The alternative of verbal probing places more of the relative burden on the cognitive interviewer.

(d) *Tendency for the subject to stray from the task.* Under think-aloud, the subject controls the nature of much of the elaborative discussion. Therefore it is very easy for a freely associating individual to wander completely off track, and to spend a significant amount of time on one question, often delving into irrelevant areas, so that the interviewer must struggle to bring the subject back to the task. In general, the think-aloud technique results in relatively few survey questions being tested within a particular amount of time, compared to verbal probing (Snijkers, 2002).

(e) *It is difficult to tell whether the respondent can answer the question.* One of our objectives is normally to determine whether the subject can give an answer that can be coded into one of the given response categories (e.g., the question "In the past 12 months, in how many months did you have a job or business?" requires a numeric response between 0 and 12). Normally, survey respondents know that they are to give an answer, but in think-aloud mode, they are encouraged to simply talk. Because there is little emphasis on asking for an answer, or determining if they can really be tied down, it is possible that they never quite get around to answering the question. Bolton (1993) found that in a pure think-aloud task, 40% of subjects gave uncodeable responses for the first three questions tested; however, it is possible that this was in part a function of the think-aloud task, rather than intrinsic difficulties with the questions.

(f) *For many tested questions, even capable subjects fail to supply useful think-alouds.* In their detailed study of think-alouds, Bickart and Felcher (1996) found that over a third of their behavior frequency questions were answered using direct retrieval strategies; that is, subjects simply answered them rather than supplying elaborated think-aloud streams. As such, even when our subjects are generally able to think aloud effectively, some questions are answered directly from memory, without complex strategizing. In these cases, think-aloud is not particularly revealing.

(g) *Potential bias in subjects' information processing tendencies.* By its nature, thinking aloud forces subjects to think. As such, subjects may invest a considerable amount of mental effort in processing the survey questions, relative to what they do when simply answering the questions. Thinking aloud typically entails more intensive effort, and more justification of each answer, than when one simply provides an answer such as "yes," "no," or "I agree." Therefore it is possible that the activities associated with think-aloud speech may serve to violate the Ericsson and Simon assumption of non-reactivity, and to burden or contaminate the cognitive processes used in answering the question. This issue is clearly still open to debate.

ADVANTAGES OF VERBAL PROBING TECHNIQUES

(a) *Maintaining control of the interview.* The use of targeted probing to guide the subject tailors the interchange in a way that is controlled mainly by the interviewer. This practice avoids a good deal of discussion that may be irrelevant and non-productive. This is a very important operational consideration that I believe was instrumental in spurring the widespread adoption of probing.

(b) *Investigative focus.* The interviewer can focus on particular areas that appear to be relevant as potential sources of response error by actively searching for problems. Put another way, this allows us to examine what may be thought but left unstated, even under think-aloud.

(c) *Ease of training of the subject.* It is fairly easy to induce subjects to answer probe questions as these probes often do not differ fundamentally from the survey question they are otherwise answering. In fact, in reviewing the accumulated cognitive interviewing literature, it is striking to see the number of practitioners who have independently commented that they found verbal probing to be a much more natural activity for respondents than think-aloud (Holland & Willis, 1991; Royston, 1989; Von Thurn & Moore, 1994; Wellens, 1994; Willis, 1999).

DISADVANTAGES OF PROBING TECHNIQUES

(a) *Potential for reactivity.* The validity of verbal probing techniques, and especially the concurrent variety, is suspect to the extent that the interjection of probes by interviewers produces a situation that is not a meaningful analog to the usual survey interview, in which the interviewer simply administers questions and the respondent answers them. In particular, if probing influences the subject relative to what he or she would do when unprobed, this produces reactivity. On the other hand, verbal probing is certainly no more unrealistic than the alternative of thinking aloud. Further, probes often resemble survey questions themselves, and it may be somewhat difficult for the subject to even tell the difference (e.g., the probe "When did you first go to an herbalist?" could be either a survey question or a follow-up probe). Hence although adding probes may have some effect, it is not clear that it introduces any more bias than does the usual practice of asking a series of survey questions on the same topic. This is a very important issue that I will revisit in a later chapter.

(b) *Potential for bias.* The misuse of probes may lead the subject to particular types of responses, the same way that biased survey questions do. To counter this, practitioners carefully select non-leading probing techniques that minimize bias. This will be further clarified later, but briefly, rather than suggesting one possibility ("Did you think the question was asking just about physicians?"), it is preferable to list all reasonable possibilities ("Did you think the question was asking only about physicians, or about any type of health professional?"). Probes should be characterized by unbiased phrasing, in the same manner that any good survey question is.

(c) *Need for careful training.* Following directly from the point above, probing is a complex activity in which sources of biases may emerge. As such, this activity demands proficiency, and significant attention to training requirements (see Chapter 9).

IS CHOICE OF VERBAL REPORT
TECHNIQUE AN EITHER-OR DECISION?

To some extent, I have presented think-aloud and verbal probes as somewhat antagonistic, and have chronicled an evolution toward probing rather than think-aloud in the sense envisioned by Ericsson and Simon (1980). Further, in an earlier work (Willis, 1994), I attempted to further move the pendulum in this direction by advocating probing at the expense of the think-aloud interview. This may have been a somewhat extreme reaction, as more recent studies suggest that cognitive interviewing is best characterized as a combination of think-aloud and probing procedures (DeMaio, Rothgeb, & Hess, 1998). In particular, systematic observation by Beatty, Schechter, and Whitaker (1997) and by DeMaio and Landreth (in press) reveal that that even within interviews that rely on verbal probing, subjects tend to spontaneously engage in a considerable amount of thinking aloud. DeMaio and Landreth state that

> Perhaps the act of probing suggests . . . that their thoughts are important, and this elicits spontaneous verbalization of thoughts without explicit instruction. Thus we can only conclude that think-aloud instructions are not necessary to conduct think-aloud interviews.

Conversely, discussions with several authors have convinced me that even for interviews that are described as "think-aloud" in a pure sense, the interviewers usually engage in a fair degree of verbal probing; it is rare to find researchers who engage strictly in unprobed think-aloud, telling subjects only "Tell me what you are thinking," bereft of any probing. Most interviews, therefore, consist of a mixture of techniques. It is likely that our lack of specificity in uses of terminology has created an appearance of differences in approach that may not truly exist.

Ironically, then, we seem to have found that (a) inducing "pure" think-aloud is difficult and unwieldy; (b) the view that we instead rely only on verbal probing is also inaccurate, given that probing tends to induce think-aloud behavior; and (c) the resultant hybrid may even obviate the need to provide special think-aloud instruction. In practice, think-aloud and verbal probing actually fit together very naturally. I find it helpful to ask subjects to think aloud as much as possible (we do want to get them to be talkative), but do not hesitate to jump in with probe questions whenever I feel this to be appropriate. Some people are naturally gifted at thinking aloud, and in this case the best the interviewer can do is listen, while also trying to keep the interview moving along. In other cases (the example that comes to mind is male teenage smokers), the notion of thinking aloud is alien to the subject, and we are lucky to motivate any behavior other than monosyllabic verbal responses and occasional facial or body gestures. Rather than being dogmatic, a flexible approach to probing that can be adjusted to the particular subject is optimal.

Vignettes, Card Sorts, and Field-Based Probes

Besides think-aloud and basic verbal probes, there are a few other "orphan" techniques that exist in the cognitive interviewing toolbox. These were described in basic form by Forsyth and Lessler (1991), and are described in somewhat more detail by DeMaio, Mathiowetz, Rothgeb, Beach, and Durant (1993). I will therefore not attempt an exhaustive review, but will provide enough detail to compare and contrast these with the more common forms of cognitive interviewing. In particular, I cover the use of (1) vignettes, (2) card sorts, and (3) field-based probes.

VIGNETTES

Vignettes are short stories or descriptions of a hypothetical respondent that are used to investigate a subject's cognitive processing with respect to survey-relevant decisions (Bates & DeMaio, 1989; Gerber, 1994; Gerber, Wellens, & Keeley, 1996; Lee, 1993; Martin, 2004; Morrison, Stettler, & Anderson, 2002; Pascale & Mayer, 2002). Gerber et al. (1996) studied comprehension of rules for assignment of individuals to households within a census form, using vignettes such as the following:

> Maria is a live-in housekeeper for the Smiths during the week, but spends weekends with her husband and children at their apartment. Where should Maria be listed on a census form?

According to the survey instructions, the correct answer is that Maria should be included with the Smiths, but respondents were correct only 36% of time, indicating potentially serious problems with these instructions.

An inventive use of the vignette approach was that by Smith, Mingay, Jobe, and Weed (1992), who examined the problem of incorrect reports by physicians on death certificates. In order to understand physician comprehension of key terms related to causes of death—especially the assignment of "immediate" versus "underlying" cause—they devised vignettes describing recently deceased patients (e.g., an 85-year-old male having arteriosclerotic heart disease who died in the hospital of acute myocardial infarction after experiencing chest pains). In the cognitive interview, the physician subject was to state immediate cause of death, underlying cause, contributing causes, and mode of death (e.g., respiratory arrest, heart failure); the investigators also had subjects define these terms.

Smith et al. found that key terms were clearly misunderstood (quoting one subject, "I'm not sure what they mean by that—mode of dying—I have no idea"). Further, they found that only 3 of 16 physicians demonstrated understanding of the distinction between "underlying cause" and "other significant conditions." The authors noted that physicians often receive no formal training in filling out death certifications, and this showed in their lack of knowledge concerning key terms. In this case, the vignette approach was useful as a specific, controlled procedure for investigating matters of comprehension of a limited number of concepts. As a limitation, the approach may have been less useful for a long questionnaire with a multitude of terms and phrases to be investigated; that is, vignettes are most practical and efficient when a small number of key comprehension issues can be defined at the outset and intensively targeted.

Vignettes have been used in similar ways in a field survey environment. Martin and Polivka (1995) conducted an extensive study using vignettes to examine respondent interpretation of the term "work" as part of the redesign of the U.S. Current Population Survey (CPS). In a debriefing session following a field experiment, respondents were asked a series of vignettes, such as the following:

> Earlier I asked you a questions about working . . . Now I want you to tell me how you would answer that question for each of the persons in the following imaginary work situation . . . Sam spent 2 hours last week painting a friend's house and was given 20 dollars.
>
> CONTROL VERSION: Would you report him as working last week, not counting work around the house?
> TEST VERSION: Would you report him as working for pay last week?

The experiment revealed that the concepts of "work" that were introduced by the different question wordings were measurably different. The

TEST version produced a narrower conception of "working" that was more consistent with the intent of the researchers; it could be used in scripting CPS questions that would likely lead to more consistent and valid reporting.

CARD SORTS

Card sorting is another systematic means to determine the ways in which subjects think about a key topic. More specifically, it is used to determine how individuals organize concepts, and in particular, what they believe a concept includes or excludes. Brewer and Lui (1996) reviewed the use of this technique and the statistical analysis of results. To illustrate, Brewer, Dull, and Jobe (1989) used a card sort task to investigate subjects' perceptions of medical conditions by instructing subjects to sort cards containing names of chronic diseases into piles that "go together," and then applying statistical clustering techniques to ascertain the nature of the resultant patterning. They found that subjects' conceptualization of disease tended to rely on the dimensions of body part affected and symptoms, as opposed to the underlying commonality of disease mechanisms that characterizes a health professional's view. On this basis, the authors suggested organizing the conditions in a survey checklist to be consistent with the schema likely to be held by respondents.

This type of task could also be used to investigate how individuals define complex concepts, such as what "having any kind of sex" means. Cards would be made up containing a number of explicit descriptions, and the person instructed to read them and place them into two piles—the first labeled "a kind of sex" and the second "not a kind of sex." The cards could contain as many detailed descriptions as the investigators cared to have sorted in this way, including some that may clearly be sex in the usual sense, as well as those that may not (e.g., "touching genitals with the hands"). The sorting patterns could then be used to determine how a complex concept such as "any kind of sex" is likely to be interpreted.

Card sort tasks are much more rarely used than the varieties of cognitive interviewing I have described previously, especially in cognitive interview studies that emphasize question pretesting. The reasons may be obvious—it takes considerable time and effort to put together, and then to administer, a card sort task that examines just one topic or concept. Further, knowing how a number of individuals conceive of a term is very useful, but card sorting is not the only way to do this. In application, it usually makes little sense to use it for a concept (such as "any kind of sex") that would very likely be found to be vague, and not universally agreed-upon, simply based on a limited degree of probing.

FIELD-BASED PROBES

A hybrid procedure that has existed for some time consists of qualitative probing within the field interview. This approach can be thought of as cognitive interviewing in the field rather than the lab (DeMaio & Rothgeb, 1996), with the exception that the probes may be administered by a field interviewer who is generally untrained in cognitive techniques. Like lab-based probes, field-based probes can be administered either concurrently or retrospectively. Converse and Presser (1986) describe the use of concurrent *embedded probing* to evaluate questions such as "Government is trying to do too many things that should be left to individuals and private businesses." They followed up with standardized probes, such as "What things do you feel should be left to individuals or private businesses?" (p. 43).

The investigators found that a quarter of the subjects who had agreed with the first question could not answer the probe, and that others gave irrelevant answers like "taxes are too high." Their conclusion was that respondents were simply expressing a general attitude that "government is too big," and this was seen as casting light on the quality of the initial question. (I might conclude that the question as posed is somewhat over-specific with respect to the nature of the responses one might get when asking it.) Converse and Presser also describe a field-based activity that is a variation of the embedded probe technique. The *random probe* technique, as described by Schuman (1966), involves a generalized follow-up: "Can you tell me a little more about what you mean?" Here, questions to be probed are literally selected at random.

As an alternative, DeMaio and Rothgeb (1996) and Hess (1995) describe retrospective (rather than concurrent) field probing, or *respondent debriefing*. Again, the primary objective of such probing is to assess respondent interpretation of key terms and concepts, and to determine if they match those of the investigator. Within a relatively small field pretest, such debriefings can be conducted with every respondent, whereas for large investigations, respondents can be sampled, or probes targeted toward subgroups of particular interest (DeMaio & Rothgeb, 1996). Debriefing probes may be closed-ended, as are survey questions (e.g., "I asked several questions about vacation homes. Does this make you think of places that you own, that you rent, or both?"). Or, they can be open-ended, and might even make use of the respondent's prior responses. For example, Fowler and Roman (1992) followed up respondents who had reported reading works of fiction by asking them to describe these, and found that over 20% of the open-ended responses were erroneous, as they were instead works of non-fiction such as self-help books.

Field-based probing does provide large sample sizes relative to usual cognitive interviews. Because the pretests in which they appear occur relatively late in the development process, these probes can sometimes be developed through earlier rounds of developmental cognitive interviewing, and are therefore used in addition to, rather than in place of, the more standard cognitive approach. For this reason, the combination of lab- and field-based cognitive interviews provides a very powerful approach to the qualitative analysis of survey questions.

Chapter Summary

- The two techniques now associated with cognitive interviewing—think-aloud and verbal probing–were adopted within the CASM field as means for applied research, in the form of questionnaire testing.
- Loftus's 1984 paper introduced the think-aloud interview as key to the study of retrieval processes. Since that time, the technique has been applied more widely, despite limited theoretical support for this extension.
- Verbal probing, although introduced decades previously, re-emerged as a second major technique after Tourangeau's (1984) introduction of the four-stage cognitive model.
- As a fundamental decision, probing can be conducted concurrently or retrospectively. Concurrent probing can be viewed as the default procedure, as a probe administered at the time the question is answered puts minimal demands on the subject's memory. However, retrospective debriefing probes are commonly used in testing self-completion instruments, or where researchers have a desire to emulate field procedures.
- Think-aloud and verbal probing techniques present different advantages and disadvantages. The major strength of the think-aloud is that it allows us to monitor ongoing cognitive processes. Verbal probing is useful because we are able to take control of the interview and to target particular cognitive subprocesses.

- From the interviewer's point of view, think-aloud is relatively easy to learn, whereas verbal probing requires significant training due to its more directive nature.
- Although cognitive interviewing was originally viewed in terms of pure think-aloud, intensive verbal probing is now more often viewed as the technique that defines cognitive testing.
- In practice, cognitive interviews typically involve a combination of think-aloud and verbal probing approaches.
- Beyond think-aloud and verbal probing, researchers can also use vignettes, card sorts, and probes embedded in field interviews.

PART II

The Intricacies of Verbal Probing

5

Developing Standard Cognitive Probes

Chapter Overview

Chapters 1 through 4 presented context, background, and theory related to cognitive interviewing. However, new cognitive interviewers tend to be most interested in learning about technique, as in "How exactly do I conduct cognitive interviews to evaluate survey questions?" There are two levels at which this can be answered: (1) the tactical, involving the details of cognitive *interviewing* "in the trenches"; and (2) the strategic, concerning the overall process of cognitive *testing* of the survey questionnaire. Both levels are important, but over the next several chapters I will adopt the former, more narrow interpretation, as an appreciation of the details should make later discussion that is broader in scope more meaningful.

In approaching the cognitive interview, one can have in mind either the think-aloud or the use of verbal probes. Conducting the think-aloud interview is relatively straightforward, as it leaves little room for latitude in interviewer behavior beyond deciding when to ask, "What are you thinking?" and back-channeling, or providing other nondirective feedback. Consequently, I have already provided as much instruction in think-aloud interviewing as should be necessary.

Verbal probing, on the other hand, is a much more varied and complex activity. To date, the biggest missing piece in the cognitive interviewing puzzle appears to be a rational explanation of exactly how one decides *which* questions to probe and *what* probes to develop. Because I consider probing to be the key to cognitive interviewing, I devote several chapters to the intricate details of this activity. This chapter provides guidance in basic probe construction by including

1. a series of concrete examples of survey questions that were tested with verbal probing, along with the cognitive issues investigated, relevant findings, and suggested question modifications, to clarify the types of cognitive probes that are useful in detecting problems;

2. a discussion of *logical and structural* problems that are revealed through probing;

3. the introduction of a systematic general approach to probe development that merges the principles of questionnaire design from Chapter 2 with the CASM orientation of Chapter 3.

Examples of Cognitive Probing

This section contains a series of individual case studies, adopted from one of my earlier training manuals (Willis, 1999), that illustrate the use of cognitive probing. The tested questions were intended for use in the NCHS National Health Interview Survey (NHIS), a household interview health survey of the general U.S. population. Each example consists of the following elements:

1. The question in its original (tested) form.

2. A list of potential cognitive issues that were identified for investigation though probing; that is, comprehension, retrieval, decision,[1] or response processes (or several of these).

3. Suggestions concerning probes that would be appropriate for examining these issues. These probes would normally be embedded within a cognitive testing protocol,[2] which consists of the tested questionnaire with probe questions placed at strategic locations (see Appendix 1 for an example).

4. A short description of the problems found through cognitive testing of the question, using probes of the types suggested.

5. A suggested resolution to the problem, based on the testing results.

EXAMPLE 1

1. Original version of the tested question:

Has anyone in the household ever received vocational rehabilitation services from:

The State Vocational Rehabilitation program?
Any other vocational rehabilitation program?

2. Issues to investigate:

The question contains a number of technical terms (vocational, reha-bilitation). How well are these understood? Further, given the reference period of "ever," might there be a knowledge or retrieval issue concerning how much people know about other household members in this regard?

3. Appropriate probe questions:

(a) Can you repeat the question in your own words?
(To test how well the subject comprehends the question.)

(b) What, to you, is a "vocational rehabilitation program"?
(To test comprehension of a particular term.)

(c) How sure are you that [person] got (or didn't get) this type of service?
(To determine the subject's ability to recall information confidently.)

4. Results of testing:

Comprehension problems. Subjects found it difficult to understand the question because of its length and technical nature. Further, the mean-ing of "vocational rehabilitation" was not at all clear; some subjects thought this just meant any type of physical therapy.

5. Suggested revision:

Has anyone in the household ever received job rehabilitation services; that is, services to help a person with a disability to work?

If YES, ask WHO, and:

Was [person's] job rehabilitation from the state or from another job rehabilitation program?

In brief, the question was "decomposed," or divided up, and a defin-ition was provided to make it easier to understand. The term "voca-tional" was also changed to the more understandable form "job." Note that question decomposition is a frequent result of cognitive testing, as many problems occur simply because designers pack too many concepts into one question.

EXAMPLE 2

1. Original version of the tested question:

How long has [person] used the [cane, wheelchair, walker, etc.]?

2. Issues to investigate:

This may involve a long time period. How well does the respondent remember this?

3. Appropriate probe questions:

(a) How did you get the answer of x years?
(To determine the overall cognitive strategy used.)

(b) When did [person] first use the [device]?
(To test comprehension and interpretation of the question.)

(c) How well do you remember this?
(To test recall of the relevant information.)

4. Results of testing:

Although we had targeted recall, a more serious comprehension issue arose. For individuals whose use was intermittent over a long period of time, the question was interpreted in two distinctly different ways:

(a) How long has it been since [person] first used the [device]? For example, the subject may say, "Since 1960, so about 30 years."

(b) For how long, overall, has [person] actually used the device since first having it? The subject counts up periods of use within a longer time, for example, "For two five-year periods since 1960, so 10 years."

The identified problem can be considered to be a comprehension problem, but it doesn't involve a failure of comprehension of a key term, as did the last example. Rather, it suffers from vagueness, as subjects simply have alternate, but reasonable, interpretations of the question intent. Addressing the problem identified required consultation with the client, in order to clarify question objectives.

5. Suggested revision:

How long ago did [person] first use a [device]?

The revised question represented a further specification of measurement objectives, based on the discovery that a pertinent issue was more conceptually complex than had been initially appreciated.

EXAMPLE 3

1. Original version of the tested question:

About how many miles from here is the home [child] lived in before he/she moved to this home?

(The response categories are printed on the questionnaire, but not read.)

[ ] less than 1 mile
[ ] 1–50 miles
[ ] 50+ miles

2. Issues to investigate:

Knowledge. Do subjects know the answer?

3. Appropriate probe questions:

  (a) How sure are you of your answer?
       (To determine overall level of confidence.)

  (b) How hard was this to answer?
       (To determine level of difficulty, and likelihood of estimation or guessing.)

4. Results of testing:

No subject appeared to have difficulty understanding the question as posed. However, a few needed to think for a fairly long time before giving an answer. Further, subjects tended to struggle needlessly with the level of specificity they thought was required (for example, deciding whether the distance was closer to 20 or to 25 miles, when this information was ultimately irrelevant, as the interviewer would mark "1–50 miles" in either case).

The problem can be described as one involving a difficult *recall task,* or perhaps as one involving *response* (mapping) processes, as opposed to a comprehension problem. A rephrasing of the question to incorporate response alternatives was necessary to make clear the desired degree of precision in their answers.

5. Suggested revision:

About how far from here is the home [child] lived in before he/she moved to this home: less than a mile, 1 to 50 miles, or more than 50 miles?

Although one might argue that providing closed-ended response categories could induce bias, it seemed unlikely that the question was especially prone to social desirability effects due to our suggestions of possible responses, and the possibility of bias was far outweighed by the need to ease information retrieval.

EXAMPLE 4

1. Original version of the tested question:

We are interested in your lifetime exercise patterns.

First, when you were 14 to 19 years old:

How many hours a week of brisk walking did you do?

How many hours a week of vigorous exercise such as running, cycling, swimming, or aerobics did you do?

How many hours a week of activities that required you to be on your feet (excluding running or walking) such as dancing, hiking, did you do?

2. Issues to investigate:

A lifetime reference period is long. How well do subjects remember this? Further, how do subjects comprehend key terms?

3. Appropriate probe questions:

   (a) Was this hard or easy to answer?
       (To determine comprehension and overall ability to recall.)

   (b) How do you remember this?
       (To study recall strategy.)

   (c) How sure are you of your answer?
       (Confidence probe.)

   (d) What, to you, is "vigorous exercise"?
       (Comprehension and interpretation of a specific term.)

4. Results of testing:

Several subjects found it extremely difficult to remember back to the time period specified at the required level of detail. In fact, it seemed that some subjects could not even answer this question series with respect to their *current* behavior, let alone their behavior many years ago. *Recall* of information (assuming it was ever "learned" in the first place) seemed to be the dominant problem.

The cognitive interviewing staff conferred with the client to clarify question objectives, and were able to determine that use of a broad scale of level of activity, comparing past and present behavior, would satisfy the data objectives.

5. Suggested revision:

We are interested in your lifetime exercise patterns. When you were 14 to 19 years old, were you more active than you are now, less active than now, or about as active as now?

In subsequent testing, some subjects did consider this to be a "dumb question" (of course they were more active when they were young). As such, this may not best be described as a "good" question. We did, however, feel that field respondents would be able to answer it confidently, and that it addressed the stated measurement objectives as defined by the analysts.

EXAMPLE 5

1. Original version of the tested question:

During a typical work day at your job as an [occupation] for [employer], how much time do you spend doing strenuous physical activities such as lifting, pushing, or pulling? (Categories are contained on a card shown to respondent.)
___ None
___ Less than 1 hour
___ 1–4 hours
___ 4+ hours

2. Issues to investigate:

Can people confidently provide an answer in terms of number of hours? If so, does this report appear to match their occupational activities?

3. Appropriate probe questions:

(a) What type of work do you do? Describe a typical work day.

(b) How did you arrive at the answer of x hours?
(Such probes target a range of processes, including those related to decision and judgment.)

4. Results of testing:

Testing that relied on these probes revealed that people who gave reports of 1–4 hours often were office workers who did little or no heavy physical work. This appeared to be due to biasing characteristics of the question; saying "none" makes one appear to be completely inactive, which is socially undesirable. This problem was related to respondent *decision* processes, rather than to comprehension or recall. A revision was needed to make it easier for someone to report little work-related physical activity.

5. Suggested revision:

The next questions are about your job as a (FILL JOB TITLE) for (FILL EMPLOYER).

Does your job require you to do repeated strenuous physical activities such as lifting, pushing, or pulling heavy objects?

(IF YES) During a typical work day, how many minutes or hours altogether do you spend doing strenuous physical activities?

Note that the results of a field-based survey experiment by Willis and Schechter (1997), discussed further in Chapter 13, have supported the contention that the revised question form is very likely a better expression than was the initial version.

EXAMPLE 6

1. Original version of the tested question:

Do you believe that prolonged exposure to high levels of radon gas can cause

	YES	NO	Don't Know
Headaches?	—	—	—
Asthma?	—	—	—
Arthritis?	—	—	—
Lung Cancer?	—	—	—
Other Cancers?	—	—	—

2. Issues to investigate:

In testing attitudinal questions, it is generally useful to determine whether the individual appears to harbor beliefs at the level of detail asked. If so, are there indications that they are trying to please the interviewer, or to just guess what is appropriate to say (i.e., Do we observe the demand effects or social desirability effects often seen in psychological experiments)?

3. Appropriate probe questions:

    (a) What, to you, is "radon gas"?

    (b) Why do you say this?

    (c) How sure are you of this?

    (d) Do you remember where you may have heard or read about this?

    (e) Is it easy or difficult to answer these?

(Probes can be viewed as targeting the entire range of cognitive processes.)

4. Results of testing:

Independent of probing, simple observation of subjects made it clear that this question was difficult to answer. They required a very long time to respond to each item, and tended to be unsure about several of the items, and hedged by providing answers such as "Oh, I guess that makes sense," as opposed to "yes" or "no." Further, our probing revealed that the format encouraged a "guessing" response strategy, rather than actual retrieval of information—for example, several subjects assumed that the correct answer for at least one of these would be "yes." Finally, for people who *did not* believe that exposure to radon is harmful, it became very tedious, and sometimes even offensive, to repeatedly ask about the specific harmful effects of radon. In this case, it mainly appeared that the subject's *decision* and *response processes* were excessively burdened by the question as posed.[3]

5. Suggested revision:

Do you believe that prolonged exposure to radon is unhealthy, or do you believe that it has little or no effect on health?

[IF radon believed unhealthy, SHOW CARD TO RESPONDENT]
Which, if any, of these conditions do you believe can be caused by
radon exposure?

___Headaches   ___Lung Cancer

___Asthma   ___Other Cancers

___Arthritis   ___Don't Know

The revised phrasing provides the respondent with a way to report,
one time, that he or she does not believe that radon is harmful. If so, the
next question simply allows him or her to "pick and choose" the items
that seem appropriate. Using this alternative, the burden on decision
processes appeared to be reduced. As usual, one can argue that the question isn't perfect. In particular, survey respondents may be able to guess
that we wouldn't be asking unless we thought radon was harmful.
However, the revision at least appeared to be less guilty of "leading
them down the garden path" toward affirmative responses to particular
items.

Parenthetically, again note the use of question decomposition, which
is a useful "fix," especially for questions in interviewer-administered
questionnaires.

EXAMPLE 7

1. Original version of the tested question:

What is the primary reason you have not tested your home for radon?

2. Issues to investigate:

Is there a primary reason? How difficult is it for subjects to say why
they haven't done this? Do they appear to get confused between radon
testing and other forms of testing?

3. Appropriate probe questions:

(a) Is it hard to think of the main reason?

(b) Can you think of any other reasons?

(c) How much have you thought about having your home tested?

4. Results of testing:

Although the question is easily enough understood, it was very difficult for subjects to produce a reasonable answer, especially if they had

never given the issue much thought. Instead of simply saying "I never thought about it," or "I haven't gotten around to it," they tried to think of answers that were more specific or defensible. Here one could argue that potential problems affected any or all of recall, decision, and response processes.

5. Suggested revision:

Delete the question. The client agreed that it was not especially useful to ask the reason why someone *had not* carried out this activity. This is reminiscent of the perennial observation that people are best at telling us *what* they do, not quite as good at telling us *why* they do what they do, and worst at revealing why they *don't* do certain things (Fowler, 1995).[4]

Logical and Structural Problems

I have referred to "comprehension probes," "recall probes," and so on. Admittedly, though, for some of the "bad question" examples presented above, it may not be especially clear that one particular cognitive process was primarily at work. For example, we might ask what is nominally a recall probe—"How well can you remember jobs you had in the past 12 months?"—and instead detect a comprehension problem—"Twelve months? I though it was asking about my whole life." Consequently, despite our reliance on the mapping between a cognitive stages model and cognitive probing, I suggest not worrying excessively about exactly how to classify either the probe (e.g., as a "comprehension" probe, etc.) or the identified problem, as long as the nature of the problem is clear.

Further, beyond such mismatches in cognitive labeling, there are also cases in which it is exceedingly difficult to place any cognitive "tag" on the problems we observe. To this point, my description of cognitive interviewing has been dominated by a pure cognitive perspective, focusing on problems that involve general comprehension, recall, and decision and response processes. However, a related beneficial outcome of testing is to detect categories of problems that do not have such a strong cognitive focus, and are termed *structural* or *logical* problems.

Royston (1989) and Willis, Royston, and Bercini (1991) noted that many of the problems emerging from cognitive interviews appeared to represent logical flaws in questionnaires that simply did not fit the basic cognitive model. More recently, several other authors have reached a similar conclusion, and have included the category of logical problems, or its equivalent, in their problem classification scheme (Akkerboom & Dehue, 1997; Conrad, Blair, & Tracy, 2000; Fowler & Cosenza, 2002; Snijkers, 2002; van der Zouwen, 2002; Willis & Lessler, 1999). Skip pattern errors, redundancy, and questions that are double-barreled or simply do not apply to some respondents may produce cognitive problems, but these are not by nature especially "cognitive" in origin.[5] Consider the question "How are your vegetables usually cooked? Are they steamed, broiled, fried, or sautéed?" This may have worked fine in 1950, but the world has changed since then, and it may be evident after even one cognitive interview that the modern category of "microwaving" is missing. In brief, the question fails to apply to the world as it now exists.

As another type of logical problem, subtle forms of redundancy may only become evident in a live interview when a particular person's situation is brought to light. For example, one tested series of questions about child health included questions, strewn throughout the questionnaire, on:

1. The number of physician contacts in the past two weeks

2. Whether the child was taken to a physician in the past two weeks because of a cold

3. The time since the last medical contact about the child

4. Whether the child has seen a doctor in the past 12 months

Although these questions are not literally redundant, they represent the common problem in which questionnaire design is encumbered by "multiple chefs with different recipes," and testing made clear that these items could all ask about the same event (e.g., a single visit to the pediatrician in the past week). My recommendation was to pool similar questions in one section, and to sort them into a logical sequence that made appropriate use of *skip-outs* (that is, instructions that send the interviewer to a following section of the questionnaire).

Finally, to address attitudinal surveys, we often find that a question like "Do you feel you get enough support from your immediate family?" is logically flawed because some respondents have no "immediate family." Again, we often fail to think of problems related to flawed premises until we are faced with the flesh-and-blood subject who renders the flaw inescapable. As I will follow up in detail in the following chapters, elucidating such problems may require skills somewhat different from those we apply in purely cognitive probing.

A Systematic Approach to Probe
Development: The Question Pitfalls Model

The specific examples appearing earlier in this chapter should be useful in guiding readers toward development of probes; new cognitive interviewers have typically learned the craft somewhat inductively by studying such examples. Further, when fashioning probes, interviewers can attempt to adhere to the basic four-stage model of the survey response process. Still, probe development is an acquired skill, and the main complaint of new interviewers seems to be that it is simply not clear how probes should be written. This may be because our trumpeting of the four-stage model as a recipe for probing is insufficient. Although that model is useful for describing the survey response process (as was the original intent), it refers mainly to the human information processor—and not as much to the details of the survey questions that are processed. Optimally, to develop probes we must not only consider cognition, but also *the characteristics of survey questions that interact with respondent cognition to produce problems.*

In practice, to keep probing from getting unwieldy, it is necessary to probe selectively, so that particular classes of probes are assigned to particular varieties of questions. Obviously, it would be a frustrating and boring exercise for both interviewers and respondents to mechanically establish whether each and every question exhibits comprehension, recall, decision, judgment, and response problems by force-feeding each type of probe in an exhaustive manner. Rather, we need to formulate probes more cautiously, but in a manner that still maximizes our chances of detecting underlying problems. A systematic approach to probe development would optimally be based on a theory of cognitive probing (Forsyth & Lessler, 1991) that relates question features to cognitive ones. Unfortunately no such model exists, and for this reason the practice of developing probes remains somewhat interviewer-specific, ill-defined, and mainly based on intuition and common sense as opposed to the expression of a solid theory.

APPRAISAL-BASED PROBING

Although still short of a true theory, I propose that cognitive interviewers extend the four-stage model by systematically analyzing the unique contributing features of target questions. Instead of simply asking, for example, "Does the person comprehend the question?" probe development can be facilitated by asking a subtly different question: "Does the question have particular features that make it likely that the item will not be understood?" If not, and other potential problems (e.g., recall) may be more germane, it pays to focus our probes on those problems. Put more concretely, if I am confronted with the question "How many dental X-rays have you had in your life?" I might be more concerned about retrieval demands than by the comprehension of either "dental X-ray" or "life."

Extending a major theme from Chapter 2, developing probes is therefore dependent on our understanding of where errors tend to crop up in questions in the first place (Blixt & Dykema, 1993). The examples presented earlier in the chapter represent this approach, as the suggested probes are keyed to particular expectations concerning problem defects. What is not so clear, however, is what gave rise to those expectations. To establish this, I suggest the straightforward approach: prior questionnaire review based on a checklist system. Wilson, Whitehead, and Whitaker (2000) have advocated the QAS system, described in Chapter 2, for this purpose. Although the QAS was devised for question appraisal, it can also be extended as a framework for probe development. Wilson et al. (2000) proposed an informal process, in which QAS problem categories can be "kept in mind . . . when conducting interviews or analyzing results" (p. 990).

Formalizing this process somewhat, we can systematically (a) apply the QAS to appraise target questions for potential faults, and then (b) devise probes appropriate to the types of defects that we suspect exist. A version of the QAS that includes suggested probes associated with the different varieties of potential problems is contained in Table 5.1. Some problem categories require no probing; for example, potential difficulties for interviewers are mainly determined by attending to the demands of the question on the individual asking it. However, Wilson et al. (2000) reported that forced attention to these categories did result in discovery of reading problems for the interviewer. As such, this approach might help to address the findings by Rothgeb, Willis, and Forsyth (2001) and by Von Thurn & Moore (1994) that cognitive interviewing often fails to detect interviewer-oriented problems in survey questions. Finally, the existence of a fairly large number of probing categories within the QAS also addresses a finding by Foddy (1998) that probes are more effective when they are specific, as opposed to diffuse and general. Although the QAS may not be comprehensive (as it does not do particularly well in identifying question ordering problems, for example), it is at least useful as a guide to anticipating problems, and then fashioning probes that investigate them.

Table 5.1   Sources of Error in Survey Questions, With Probes Appropriate
to Investigation of Those Problems

STEP 1 - READING: Determine whether it is difficult for the interviewers to read the question in the same way to all respondents.	
1a. **WHAT TO READ:** Interviewer may have difficulty determining what *parts* of the question should be read.	PROBE: None. Interviewer should attend to this potential difficulty and note it.
1b. **MISSING INFORMATION:** Information the interviewer needs to administer the question is *not* contained in the question.	PROBE: None. Interviewer should attend to this potential difficulty and note it.
1c. **HOW TO READ:** Question is *not* fully scripted and therefore difficult to read.	PROBE: None. Interviewer should attend to this potential difficulty and note it.
STEP 2 - INSTRUCTIONS: Look for problems with any introductions, instructions, or explanations from the *respondent's* point of view.	
2a. **CONFLICTING OR INACCURATE INSTRUCTIONS,** introductions, or explanations.	PROBE: [*At the end of a long intro, but before the question itself*] Before I get to the actual question, tell me what this introduction is telling you.
2b. **COMPLICATED INSTRUCTIONS,** introductions, or explanations.	PROBE: Same as above
STEP 3 - CLARITY: Identify problems related to communicating the *intent or meaning* of the question to the respondent.	
3a. **WORDING:** Question is lengthy, awkward, ungrammatical, or contains complicated syntax.	PROBE: Can you tell me in your own words what that question was asking?
3b. **TECHNICAL TERMS** are undefined, unclear, or complex.	PROBE: What does the word [term] mean to you as it's used in this question?
3c. **VAGUE:** There are multiple ways to interpret the question or to decide what is to be included or excluded.	PROBE: Tell me what you were thinking when I asked about [topic].
3d. **REFERENCE PERIODS** are missing, not well specified, or in conflict.	PROBES: (1) Can you remember what time period the question was asking about? (2) You said [answer]. What time period does that cover?

(Continued)

Table 5.1 (Continued)

STEP 4 - ASSUMPTIONS: Determine if there are problems with assumptions made or the underlying logic.	
4a. **INAPPROPRIATE ASSUMPTIONS** are made about the respondent or about his or her living situation.	PROBES: (1) How well does that question apply to you? (2) Can you tell me more about that?
4b. **ASSUMES CONSTANT BEHAVIOR** or experience for situations that vary.	PROBE: Would you say that mostly stays the same, or does it vary or depend?
4c. **DOUBLE-BARRELED:** Contains more than one implicit question.	PROBE: Tell me more about your opinions on that.
STEP 5 - KNOWLEDGE/MEMORY: Check whether respondents are likely to *not know* or have trouble *remembering* information.	
5a. **KNOWLEDGE** may not exist: Respondent is unlikely to *know* the answer to a factual question.	PROBE: How much would you say you know about [topic]?
5b. **ATTITUDE** may not exist: Respondent is unlikely to have formed the attitude being asked about.	PROBE: How much thought would you say you've given to this?
5c. **RECALL** failure: Respondent may not *remember* the information asked for.	PROBES: (1) How easy or difficult is it to remember [topic]? (2) You said [answer]. How sure are you of that?
5d. **COMPUTATION** problem: The question requires a difficult mental calculation.	PROBE: How did you come up with that answer?
STEP 6 - SENSITIVITY/BIAS: Assess questions for sensitive nature or wording, and for bias.	
6a. **SENSITIVE CONTENT** (general): The question asks about a topic that is embarrassing, very private, or that involves illegal behavior.	PROBE: (1) Is this OK to talk about in a survey, or is it uncomfortable? (2) In general, how do you feel about this question?
6b. **SENSITIVE WORDING** (specific): Given that the general topic is sensitive, the wording should be improved to minimize sensitivity.	PROBE: The question uses the word [term]. Does that sound OK to you, or would you choose something different?

6c. **SOCIALLY ACCEPTABLE** response is implied by the question.	PROBES: (1) How did you come up with that answer? (2) Do all the possible answers here seem OK, or did it seem like there's one that's supposed to be the right answer?
STEP 7 - RESPONSE CATEGORIES: Assess the adequacy of the range of responses to be recorded.	
7a. **OPEN-ENDED QUESTION** that is inappropriate or difficult.	PROBE: Was it easy or difficult to decide what answer to give?
7b. **MISMATCH** between question and response categories.	PROBES: (1) How easy or hard was it to find your answer on that list? (2) You said [answer]. How well does that apply to you?
7c. **TECHNICAL TERMS** are undefined, unclear, or complex.	PROBE: In this list, what does [term] mean to you?
7d. **VAGUE** response categories are subject to multiple interpretations.	PROBE: Tell me what you were thinking when I asked about [topic]
7e. **OVERLAPPING** response categories.	PROBES: (1) How easy or hard was it to choose an answer? (2) Tell me why you chose [answer] instead of some other answer on the list
7f. **MISSING** eligible responses in response categories.	PROBE: How easy or hard was it to choose an answer?
7g. **ILLOGICAL ORDER** of response categories.	PROBE: How was it for you to go through that list? Did that cause any difficulties?
STEP 8 - OTHER PROBLEMS not identified in Steps 1 - 7	
8. Other problems not previously identified.	PROBE: Can you tell me more about that?

Chapter Summary

- Some problems in survey questions are inherently cognitive in nature, and we examine these by devising probe questions targeted toward comprehension, retrieval, decision, judgment, and response processes.

- Other problems are logical or structural and may be easy to observe.
- In fashioning probes, it is helpful to rely on a framework that relates types of problems to particular features of tested questions. I advocate a checklist-based review that brings potential problems to the forefront and that also provides probe questions useful for investigating these problems.

Exercise: Using the QAS to Develop Probe Questions

Review each target question (Q1-Q5) for potential problems, and indicate what types of probes might be appropriate. Suggestions are provided.

Q1. Have you ever had any form of ischemic heart disease?

Problems/Probes: QAS Step 3b: Focus on comprehension of the technical term "ischemic heart disease" by asking "What, to you, is ischemic heart disease?" whether the answer given was "Yes" or "No."

Q2. Since age 25, have you gone a period of three months or longer without working at least ten hours a week for pay?

Problems/Probes: (a) It doesn't seem that there is any particular term that would be expected to cause difficulty. Still, based on QAS 3a, the question appears to be long and perhaps difficult to keep in mind. Consequently, to determine what is actually being heard, ask "Can you remember what that question asked?"

(b) QAS 5c: For someone in his 60s, accurate long-term recall might be challenging. Accordingly, especially right after a simple response to the question was "yes," we can test recall: "Can you tell me more? When was that, and for how long?" If the person then describes a difficult year-long period of no employment, we could conclude that this seems consistent with the question as posed, and that no particular problems are in evidence.

Q3. Overall, how satisfied are you with the cable TV service you now receive?

READ CATEGORIES:
Extremely satisfied
Somewhat satisfied

A little satisfied
Not at all satisfied
Neither satisfied nor dissatisfied
No opinion
Don't know

Problems/Probes: (a) QAS 3c: First, the term "cable TV service" might be interpreted in a variety of ways. This could refer to reception, cost, or even the quality of the shows the cable system carries. It would be interesting to probe to find out "What kind of cable TV service are you thinking about?" or "What do you like or not like about your cable TV service?"

(b) QAS 7e, 7f: The response categories beg attention. It seems that there could be a category missing between "Extremely" and "Somewhat," such as "Mostly satisfied"; also, it's not clear where "Neither satisfied nor dissatisfied" fits in the list, and how "No opinion" is intended to differ from "Don't know." This could be probed by asking them "Was it easy or difficult to choose one of the categories I read?" or "In your own words, how satisfied would you say you are?"

Q4. How often do you plan your route to avoid certain dangerous places?

Problems/Probes: (a) QAS 4a: Always be on the lookout for questions in the form "you do X in order to do Y," because they normally make the assumption that condition Y is true, which may not be the case. Here, the question assumes that the person had dangerous places to avoid. But if the survey includes both those who do and don't face such dangers, "never" responses would be uninformative, as this could mean that (a) I face dangerous places but never avoid them, or (b) I never face them in the first place so I never plan with them in mind. This would be a classic inappropriate assumption, and could be probed with "How often do you normally face dangerous places?" or "Tell me why you said 'never.'"

(b) QAS 3c: The question asks about planning my route, but it doesn't ask whether I follow the plan, and presents potential vagueness. Depending on the subject's answer to the question, follow-up probing could be accomplished by asking "What does it mean to you when it asks about planning your route?" and "When you plan that kind of route, how often do you stick to it?"

(c) Finally, we might want to make sure that the types of dangerous places the subject has in mind match our intent (again, to avoid potential vagueness of expression). A simple probe like "What does 'dangerous place' mean to you?" or "What kinds of places do you avoid?" would be useful to distinguish, for example, locations with high crime rates from those that are dangerous because they present geographic obstacles (e.g., I avoid a path that poses the risk of falling down a mountainside).

Q5. Do you have close friends in the neighborhood?

Problems/Probes: QAS 3c: The question is short and simple, yet very possibly is quite vague. One could probe with "What, to you, is a 'close friend'?"; "What do you think of as your neighborhood?"; and "Tell me who you are counting, and why." Testing of this question has revealed that people's concept of "close" can vary greatly. They may assume it refers to travel distance rather than degree of friendship.

Notes

1. I use the term "decision" to refer in aggregate to processes that have been called "judgment," "estimation," and "decision" by the various cognitive models.

2. The term "protocol" has a somewhat different meaning here than in the think-aloud protocol, as the former consists of the materials to be used by the interviewer to conduct the interview, whereas the latter refers to the subject's verbal stream, and constitutes the key data to be analyzed.

3. The reader may wonder why a potentially vital issue—comprehension of the term "radon"—is not mentioned. In this case, a preceding question asked whether the person had heard of radon, so this problem had been explicitly addressed by the questionnaire.

4. If this "rule" was found to be consistent, it would be a good example of a generally useful finding that emanates from cognitive interviewing of particular questions, and that would then feed back at a general level to the arena of questionnaire design (again, an ultimate objective of this endeavor).

5. I have heard it argued that these problems remain "cognitive" in nature because they can cause cognitive problems. This, however, is not the key issue. For example, if a bridge washes out due to a structural defect, this may cause cognitive problems for drivers who need to figure out other ways to get across the river. It would be a stretch, however, to label the bridge failure a "cognitive problem."

6

Beyond the Standard Model of Verbal Probing

Chapter Overview

The "standard model" of probing within the cognitive interview, as I have presented it, consists of:

1. questionnaire review to identify anticipated problems;

2. probe development prior to the interview as a means to investigate these problems;

3. the administration of probes as planned, within the cognitive interview (whether concurrent or retrospective).

This sequence does characterize many cognitive interviews, and has been described before (Willis, 1994, 1999). But this is only part of the story: probing behavior is, in practice, considerably more complex and flexible. In this chapter, I delve more deeply into the details of several important variations of probing with respect to the manner in which probes are developed and administered.

A Classification of Probe Types

For all cognitive interviews that rely heavily on probing, two primary factors dictate the development and use of probes. One involves the nature of probe *construction:* Are probes universally standardized, as presumed by the discussion in the previous chapters, or can they be fashioned on-the-spot, during the course of the interview? The second

Table 6.1   Model of Verbal Probing in the Cognitive Interview

	Proactive Administration (initiated by the interviewer/researcher)	Reactive Administration (triggered by subject behavior)
Standardized Construction (constructed *prior* to the interview)	(1) Anticipated Probes	(3) Conditional Probes
Nonstandardized Construction (constructed *during* the interview)	(2) Spontaneous Probes	(4) Emergent Probes

factor concerns the conditions for probe *administration:* Is the probe administered *proactively,* based on interviewer initiative, or is it done *reactively,* depending on the behavior of the subject? These two factors combine to produce the four probe varieties illustrated in Table 6.1. Because major controversies and variations in probing practice center on the practitioner's selection from among these varieties, I will discuss the relative merits of each, starting with the proactive-reactive dimension.

PROACTIVE PROBES

Under the standard model of cognitive interviewing, verbal probing is proactive in nature; that is, the interviewer adopts an investigative stance in which probes are used to actively search for problems. I label the two proactive varieties *Anticipated* and *Spontaneous* probes. Anticipated probes are represented by all of the examples in Chapter 5, and address what Cosenza (2002) calls "pre-identified, concrete concerns." These are, by definition, (a) developed prior to the interview (whether by an individual or team), and (b) normally intended for use by interviewers in a standardized manner.[1] If it is expected that a particular term or phrase may not be universally understood, cognitive interviewers can be instructed to apply a particular Anticipated probe (e.g., "What does 'non-married partner of a biological parent' mean to you?"). Such probes are normally added to the questionnaire draft to create a test protocol containing explicit programmed probes. The probes may be identified by a different color, typeface, or by the label "PROBE" (See Appendix 1). Anticipated probes have also been referred to as "planned" or "structured" or, most frequently, as "scripted" probes. I have chosen yet another term for such probes because the defining element involves anticipation of their use, and not the fact that they are literally scripted. In fact, anticipated probes often use unscripted wording, as in "Probe to determine comprehension of 'living at home.'" Further, as described below, some probes that *are* scripted fall into a fundamentally different category.

As the second variant of proactive probing, *Spontaneous* probes are developed during the interview by the individual interviewer. Spontaneous probes are therefore nonstandardized, although the cognitive interviewer should strive to formulate them using the same (non-biasing and clear) language that applies to Anticipated probes. Spontaneous probes are often used when the interviewer decides that it is important to ask a probe not contained in the interviewing protocol. In some cases, experienced interviewers may rely completely on Spontaneous probes. For example, I have conducted cognitive interviews with draft questionnaires that were literally warm from being just finalized and photocopied, with no time to develop any Anticipated probes. I do not suggest that this practice is an ideal one, as it does stretch the boundaries of the cognitive interview as a flexible activity!

REACTIVE PROBES

Reactive probes represent a probing philosophy that is fundamentally opposed to the proactive approach. It addresses Oppenheim's (1966) observation that, despite our best efforts, "fatal ambiguities may lurk in the most unexpected quarters" (p. 26); that is, we cannot fully anticipate problems. Reactive probes therefore respond to the unexpected; they are triggered by something that the subject has said or done that may signal a problem, rather than a search for problems by the interviewer. In a metaphorical sense, where the proactive interviewer is a fire inspector, the reactive interviewer is the fire engine driver. As an example of reactive probing, consider the following selection from an interview I conducted on the issue of lead paint exposure:

INTERVIEWER: (Target question)	Inside your home, are there any walls that have peeling paint?
SUBJECT:	Peeling? Uh . . . no . . . not on the walls, anyway.

INTERVIEWER: Is there any paint that's peeling, inside?
(Probe)

SUBJECT: Yeah, the window frames . . . paint is peeling
                right off. The original paint, I suppose.

In this case, the reactive probe ("Is there any paint that's peeling?")
was unanticipated, and was prompted by the subject's comment indicating
that even though the walls weren't peeling, something was. The interviewer
chose to pursue that response by probing reactively to obtain further information. Admittedly, a set of proactive probes could have been (and probably was) fashioned as an attempt to focus on potential problems, perhaps
by asking how much peeling had occurred, whether it is inside or outside
the dwelling, and so on. However, it might not have been anticipated during the probe development process that the question had neglected to consider other painted surfaces that could be peeling and potentially pose a
lead paint hazard to occupants. In this case, the need for reactive probing
became evident only during the course of the interview.

Just as proactive probes can be constructed either prior to or during
the interview, two variants of reactive probes also differ in the timing of
their construction: (a) *Conditional* probes, which once elicited by subject
behavior are selected from a set of prepared and standardized formulations; and (b) *Emergent* probes, which are extemporaneous and developed flexibly at the time of the interview on the basis of some behavior of
the subject.[2]

Conditional probing was introduced by Conrad and Blair (2001),
whose rules governing its use are set out in Table 6.2. Emergent probing,
on the other hand, gives rise to no particular set of rules but appears more
like an extended conversation. The lead paint example presented above
constitutes a segment of an interview that includes Emergent probing.
Emergent probes are the most discrepant from the standard probing model,
both because (a) they are not based on the anticipation of problems, and
(b) they make little use of any formal principles of probe construction.

I have expounded at length upon the typology in Table 6.1 because
all of these probes are commonly in use. However, it is not clear which
is preferable, and deciding among them is a complex and a somewhat
contentious issue that divides cognitive interviewers into different camps.
I next discuss the pros and cons of the two major dimensions: (1) proactive versus reactive probing, and (2) standardization versus free-form
construction during the interview.

Table 6.2   Rules for Use of Conditional Probing

Condition	Conditional Probe
1. Subject cannot answer or does not know the answer.	"What was going through your mind as you tried to answer the question?"
2. Subject answers after a period of silence.	"You took a little while to answer that question. What were you thinking about?"
3. Subject answers with uncertainty, using explicit cues such as "um," "ah," changing an answer, etc.	"You seem to be somewhat uncertain. If so, can you tell me why?" "What caused you to change your answer?"
4. Answer is contingent on certain conditions being met, e.g., "I'd say about 25 times if you don't need a super precise answer."	"You seem a little unsure. If so, can you tell me why?"
5. Erroneous answer; verbal report implies misconception or inappropriate response process.	Clarify respondent's understanding of the particular term or the process used. For example, if the respondent appeared to misunderstand the word "manage," probe the term ("So you don't manage any staff?")
6. Subject requests information instead of providing an answer.	"If I weren't available or able to answer, what would you decide it means?" "Are there different things you think it might mean? What sorts of things?"

SOURCE: Conrad & Blair (2001). Slightly modified for purposes of clarity.

Proactive Versus Reactive Probing

This dimension truly addresses the heart of cognitive interviewing practice: Should probing be done in order to actively search for problems, or should it be done to follow up problems that have appeared during the course of the interview? Each practice can be both supported and criticized on logical grounds. On the one hand, proactive probing appears more systematic in nature because it is based on hypotheses concerning flaws in the questionnaire to be evaluated, which I have advocated as good practice. Further, the exclusive use of standardized forms—that is, Anticipated probes—generally limits variance between interviewers, as they are all "on the same page" in this regard. Consequently, studies that include novice interviewers sometimes rely to a large extent on fully proactive protocols involving Anticipated probing (e.g., Willis, Al-Tayyib, & Rogers, 2001).

In contrast, Conrad and Blair (1996, 2001) in particular have made an opposing argument, warning against the potential overuse of proactive approaches. They suggest that the extensive fishing for problems that is induced by such probes may create the appearance of difficulties with survey questions that do not truly exist. Instead of looking for problems, Conrad and Blair propose that we should probe only when the individual gives some indication that a problem exists—that is, reactively.

These opposing arguments present a paradox for the cognitive interviewer. On the one hand, we want to probe proactively to delve into problems that we suspect may exist. On the other, we don't want to create the appearance of problems simply by probing questions to death in order to identify any imaginable flaw. At this point, there is little empirical evidence that will resolve this debate. Conrad and his colleagues have experimented with reactive techniques, and have shown that the use of Conditional probes may result in good agreement among researchers in identifying questions that are problematic, relative to proactive approaches to probing.

Such findings are not conclusive, however. In particular, we might expect that problems that are identified through reactive probing (e.g., those that are witnessed) produce good agreement, as they are generally obvious, and represent the low-hanging fruit on our tree of problems. That is, if a subject expresses clear confusion, this should lead to good inter-observer agreement. In contrast, hidden problems that are elucidated only through proactive probes (that is, through searching) may be more subtle, complex, and variable, and therefore lead to lower agreement. These problems, however, may be real.

I will concede that by conducting only reactive forms of probing we limit opportunities for creating illusory problems, simply because we are "raising the bar." However, there is also a very real possibility that such a restriction hamstrings the interview, and effectively throws a very important baby out with the bathwater. If we accept that a key objective of cognitive interviewing is to identify *covert* problems, as opposed to only those that are *overt*, or in evidence, then neglecting to actively search beneath the surface risks the failure to detect what DeMaio and Rothgeb (1996) have referred to as *Silent Misinterpretation*.

To illustrate this key phenomenon, a consistent finding from cognitive interviewing appears to be that subjects fully believe they understand a term as intended, but they are utterly wrong (Schober & Conrad, 2003). As an example, a health survey question tested in the NCHS cognitive lab on several occasions is "Do you or any members of your family have dental sealants?" (see Lessler et al., 1989). Each time, interpretation of the term "dental sealant" has been found to be problematic: subjects tend to interpret this as "getting a cavity filled" (which seems logical, as this does seal a tooth). However, given that a dental sealant is, in fact, a material placed on the teeth to prevent decay, a respondent who confidently answers "yes" may be in error. In this case, there is nothing in the individual's behavior that indicates the question poses a problem, and in the pure application of reactive forms of probing, we would simply move on to the next question. It is only by actively probing using proactive techniques (e.g., "What, to you, is a dental sealant?") that the interviewer is able to determine that a problem exists in the target question.

As a further example, testing the question "During the past 30 days, how many days did symptoms of asthma make it difficult for you to stay asleep?" produced no problems, until probing with "Tell me how asthma affected your sleep?" revealed that what subjects heard was not "stay asleep" but "fall asleep"—a critical difference (Willis, Bornstein, Sand, & Alakoye, 2000). Similarly, Beatty (in press) tested the question "In the past 12 months, how many times have you seen or talked on the telephone about your physical, emotional, or mental health with a family doctor or general practitioner?" Upon probing subjects who had answered quickly and clearly, it was determined that several had misreported because they had not processed the term "on the telephone."

I contend that the detection of such silent misinterpretations is a keystone of the cognitive interviewing approach and cannot depend solely on observation. As theoretical support, I resurrect the psycholinguistic concept of the grounded conversation, as discussed in Chapter 2. In order to justify sole reliance on reactive probing, we must assume that cognitive interviewers can rely strictly on overt cues that signal failures of grounding. That is, we must believe that all such failures will be evident, because the subject having difficulties with a target question will employ conversational mechanisms to ensure that the conversation does not proceed until the current exchange is successfully grounded. Put simply, when communication has failed, the subject will make the interviewer aware of this.

I find it doubtful that these conditions generally apply within the cognitive interview (or even within many natural conversations outside of the survey environment). Reiterating previous observations, standardized survey questions often fail to incorporate mechanisms that effectively identify and repair misunderstandings. As a result, reliance on reactive probing to detect misunderstandings will fail whenever the exchange itself fails to produce overt signs that grounding has not been achieved. Van der Zouwen (2002) states this eloquently, in discussing the pitfalls of relying on what linguists refer to as the *paradigmatic sequence,* or an interaction between interviewer and respondent that proceeds without obvious error:

> A sequence proceeding in a paradigmatic way is neither a guarantee that participants do not have problems nor that the quality of the data collected via this sequence is optimal. For example, a respondent's misunderstanding of the question is only recognizable if the respondent does something other than select one of the response alternatives offered. (p. 62)

My conclusion is that in order to detect cases of silent misinterpretation, the cognitive interviewer must probe—proactively—even when there is no overt sign of trouble.

Standardized Versus Free-Form Probes

A further major dimension, reflected in Table 6.1, concerns a critical issue for cognitive interviewers: Whether proactive or reactive, should probes be specifically constructed prior to the interview, or is it acceptable to make them up during its course? Again, under the proactive category, the critical contrast is between the relatively standardized Anticipated probes, and the Spontaneous types that may simply occur to the interviewer to ask. Under the reactive category, the distinction is between the standardized Conditional probes favored by Conrad and Blair (2001) and the nonstandard, on-the-spot Emergent ones.

Not surprisingly, some researchers (i.e., Conrad & Blair, 2001) look askance at probes that are made up during the interview. An overarching issue that is implicitly wrapped up in this debate concerns interviewer style in general—whether it is better to take a "professional" or a "personal" approach (Dijkstra & van der Zouwen, 1988; Schaeffer, 1991). The use of Spontaneous and Emergent probes clearly represents the latter, and departs markedly from our usual field interviewing procedures. As it may already be a stretch to add in our structured Anticipated probe questions, the more extreme practice of fashioning probe wording on the fly might appear unscientific, haphazard, idiosyncratic, and—most seriously—potentially biasing (reactive in the sense described by Ericsson and Simon, 1980).

While there may be some truth to these charges, depending on who is conducting the interview, there are particular advantages to maintaining a flexible approach to probe construction. In practice, I have found that the most interesting and productive forms of probing often develop through the course of the interview, as the product of the particular relationship between the interviewer, subject, and survey questionnaire. In these cases, no previously scripted probe is readily available. Over time, interviewers tend to become very proficient in developing these Spontaneous and Emergent probes.

Spontaneous probing is useful when the interviewer develops an insight about a potential source of question failure, especially in the context of the "real world" situation presented by the test subject. To illustrate this, I again rely on an example from personal archives, involving a cognitive interview of an elderly man:

INTERVIEWER: (Target question)	Over the past 12 months, when you used margarine how often did you use a reduced-fat margarine?
SUBJECT:	Never.
INTERVIEWER: (Spontaneous probe)	How aware would you say you are of the type of margarine that's in the food you eat?
SUBJECT:	Sure—if you mean . . . what I put on my food at the table. But my wife does the cooking—who knows what she does at the stove? I guess there's margarine in there . . .

In preparing probes for the cognitive interview protocol, we had envisioned people who had control over cooking ingredients, and planned to address potential flaws by developing a number of Anticipated probes concerning recall over a 12-month period, of what the subject considered "low-fat" margarine to be, and so on. This elderly male subject presented an unanticipated situation, however. I had already discovered during the course of the interview that he did no cooking for himself but relied fully on his spouse. Given that context, asking the margarine question brought out the possibility of a further problem involving a potential deficit in knowledge required to provide a meaningful answer. This realization led to the production of a Spontaneous probe, which turned out to be well worth asking (and note that the subject had given no overt indication of the problem to this point, again validating the interviewer's proactive approach).

Pursuing this line of reasoning further, even very free-form Emergent forms of probing can be profitable, despite their uncontrolled nature. I have found that it is useful to retain the ability to script these on the spot, rather than to rely on a ready arsenal of standardized Conditional probes. The subject may give some indication of a problem such as hesitation, qualifying a response, or providing inconsistent responses, and the nature of logically appropriate follow-up probing may be so specific to the question that we must fashion these in an imaginatively Emergent manner. Though it is admittedly only one illustration, consider the following paraphrased interchange based on cognitive testing of an HIV risk factors questionnaire at an urban sexually transmitted disease clinic:[3]

INTERVIEWER: (Target question)	How many sex partners did you have in the past 12 months?
SUBJECT:	Well . . . two. Two steadies . . . the others weren't exactly what you'd call my partner or whatever.
INTERVIEWER: (Emergent probe)	The others? Tell me more about them.
SUBJECT:	You know, a couple of ladies I met at clubs, that type of thing. Just for a night of partying and carryin' on, nothing serious. You forget their name.
INTERVIEWER: (Emergent probe)	So are you saying that you do or you don't consider them to be sex partners?
SUBJECT:	Well, yes to the sex part, but no, they're not my partner.
INTERVIEWER: (Emergent probe)	How about if I asked you the question like this: In the past 12 months, how many people did you have sex with?
SUBJECT:	Oh, now that would be about four. You know, two steadies, two lucky ladies . . . (laughs)

The exchange made evident that the use of the term "sex partner" was inappropriate, as the subject considered a "partner" to be someone with whom one has an ongoing relationship. Other noteworthy features of this segment are that

1. the interviewer applied reactive probing based on the subject's qualification of his initial answer to the question;

2. the probing was Emergent—not scripted or otherwise "canned" but more like a conversation about the question;

3. probing was complex, multipart, and resembled a type of follow-on conversation (that is, it pursued grounding as an objective), as opposed to an isolated set of cognitive probes in the classic sense;

4. one purpose of probing was to try out a different form of the target question, based on an on-the-spot diagnosis of a problem with the original. This served to both verify the nature of the suspected problem and to test a potential alternative.

The type of exchange above is very common in the cognitive interview and represents an approach that is markedly different from the administration of purely scripted and anticipated probes according to a predetermined sequence.

Chapter Summary

- Proactive probing has a vital function. Probing should *not* be restricted only to cases in which clear difficulties are observed, or we will miss problems that exist below the surface, that is, those that are covert and reflect silent misunderstandings. To be fully effective, probing should be proactive, searching, and investigative, and apply the types of probes presented throughout Chapter 5.
- Reactive forms of probing are also fundamental to cognitive interviewing. If we were to completely reject the use of reactive probes and rely only on programmed proactive approaches, we would miss many unanticipated problems, as proactive approaches alone only provide verification, and not discovery, of suspected problems.
- As a general rule, Anticipated probing is especially practical and useful when (1) there is sufficient *time* to prepare for interviews and to plan a cognitive testing protocol; (2) cognitive interviewers

are relatively *inexperienced* and would benefit from the guidance provided by a structured approach (inexperienced interviewers often appreciate the presence of fully scripted probes, given that determining how to probe spontaneously is an acquired skill); and (3) the questionnaire has a complex or otherwise hard-to-follow format, and simply administering it requires considerable attention (in this case, the production of Anticipated probes frees the interviewer from the burden of also inventing probe questions on the fly).

• Whether proactive or reactive, probes cannot be selected as though they were articles of clothing that can be expected to fit a particular situation. Often, the appropriate probe cannot be constructed before the fact, and should be either Spontaneous or Emergent in form.

Exercise: Emergent Probing

The following exchanges all involve Emergent approaches to probing; the probes are not anticipated or scripted, but are based on something the subject has said. This type of probing is the most difficult because it involves on-the-spot recognition of problems that may be very subtle. In order to get an idea of what is involved, read up to the point at which the subject first responds to the target question, and think about how you might probe at that point. Then look at the suggested probes, which are based on interview transcripts. As there are many effective ways to probe, there are no "right" answers; these probes serve as illustration.

EXAMPLE 1

Subject is female, aged 56.

INTERVIEWER:	What is the most you have ever weighed?
SUBJECT:	Oh, the most? 130, but luckily that was done and over with pretty quick.

Suggested Probes:

INTERVIEWER:	Oh? When was that?
SUBJECT:	When I was pregnant with my first child.

INTERVIEWER: What about during times when you weren't pregnant? What's the most you ever weighed then?

SUBJECT: I was always a skinny thing, no more than 110.

The interviewer is able to determine that the question fails to make clear whether we want women to include or exclude pregnancy, and either way, this needs to be specified in the question. Clearly no one had thought of this when writing the question or fashioning probes, but it came out during the cognitive interview simply as a result of further (Emergent) discussion.

EXAMPLE 2

INTERVIEWER: During the past 30 days, how many days did symptoms of asthma make it difficult for you to stay asleep?

SUBJECT: No, asthma doesn't make it difficult to fall asleep.

Suggested Probe:

INTERVIEWER: What about staying asleep, once you are asleep? Does asthma make that difficult?

The interviewer noted that the question didn't ask about "falling asleep," but whether it was difficult to "stay asleep," and that the subject seemed to have misinterpreted it. But unless the interviewer is also fully awake and attending to the relationship between the question and the subject's responses, it is easy to miss such problems.

EXAMPLE 3

INTERVIEWER: Do you believe that police should have the right to stop drivers who they suspect of illegal activities?

SUBJECT: Sure. (Pause. Puzzled look.) Sure—uh, wait, definitely no to that one.

Suggested Probe:

INTERVIEWER: I noticed that you first said "sure," and then changed to "no." Can you tell me why?

> SUBJECT: First I thought you were asking about them stopping someone they see committing a crime, but then it occurred to me that you said "suspect." That's a different story.

First, the interviewer was in no hurry to move on to the next question (as the field interviewer frequently is), and waited as the subject paused and then changed his mind. Then, probing this change revealed that the person had initially been unsure of the meaning of the question.

EXAMPLE 4

> INTERVIEWER: Which of the following do you think causes the most deaths each year: cancer, heart disease, stroke, or motor vehicle accidents, or AIDS?
>
> SUBJECT: Oh . . . uh, heart disease . . . that's more than cancer, and the other stuff.

Suggested Probe:

> INTERVIEWER: Can you remember what that other stuff was?
>
> SUBJECT: (Laughs) Well, no, actually. I got the cancer and heart disease, but there were a few more I missed.

The "other stuff" induced the interviewer to determine whether the subject had actually heard, and could consider, the different listed items (in this case, no).

EXAMPLE 5

Finally, consider an example that involves multiple cycles of Emergent probing:

> INTERVIEWER: In what year did you first work full-time for pay?
>
> SUBJECT: Let's see. . . my first real job . . . 1972.

Suggested probes:

> INTERVIEWER: Real job? Tell me more about what you were doing then.

SUBJECT: That was after I got out of college, right when I got my first serious job, in a bank. Before that I had just had summer jobs.

INTERVIEWER: What about those summer jobs? Were they full time, or part time, or something else?

SUBJECT: Well, I did summer work that was 40 hours a week, but this wasn't permanent, just a couple of months.

INTERVIEWER: So when I asked about when you first worked full time for pay, were you thinking about the summer jobs or not?

SUBJECT: No. I didn't think you meant summer. Just, you know, when I had my first real, regular, full-time job. If you mean summer jobs, then it would go back to high school—different story.

The initial response included the subject's mention of a "real job," which wasn't contained in the question itself. This caused the interviewer to simply ask for some further explanation. Through further discussion of the question the interviewer pins down a mismatch between the subject's interpretation of first working full time and what the question may be seeking.

Notes

1. As a complication, such probes can also be devised by each interviewer individually and are therefore not truly standardized, except perhaps within the interviewer. Here I simply submit that any conceivable classification scheme will fail to cleanly encompass every possibility.

2. The notion of Emergent probing, though perhaps not defined exactly as above, has been informally discussed by Kristen Miller and Paul Beatty at NCHS, and is described by Beatty (2003).

3. Previously unpublished example selected from the author's archive of cognitive testing results.

7

A Further Perspective

Cognitive Testing as Expansive Interviewing

Chapter Overview

Although I initially introduced cognitive interviewing by reviewing its history, development, and practice through a cognitive lens, it may appear that the last few chapters have begun to seriously drift from the cognitive orientation. First, I introduced the notion that some problems, and some probes, may not really be cognitive in nature, but are better classed as logical or structural. Then, in the previous chapter, I described a number of probing approaches—especially the Emergent kinds—that seem to represent open-ended conversation, rather than a practice that can meaningfully be viewed as the infusion of cognitive psychology into the question evaluation process. In this chapter, I will continue this conceptual thread by proposing a fundamentally different viewpoint concerning the basic nature of cognitive interviewing: that interviewing is often *expansive*.

A Broad View of Cognitive Interviewing

Since the establishment of cognitive interviewing there have been occasional objections from its practitioners that, despite the proliferation of the CASM movement, the cognitive model is insufficient. They do not claim that the cognitive orientation is wrong, but rather that it is the tip of the proverbial iceberg. Some years ago, Trish Royston of NCHS remarked to me that she preferred the term "intensive interview" to "cognitive interview," as many of our laboratory findings seemed to have less to do with the study of cognition, per se, than with the intensive study of tested survey questions.

Several other authors have also suggested that much in the world of cognitive interviewing is not especially cognitive (Blair & Presser, 1993). This alternative viewpoint has never been fully developed but has mainly remained implicit, bubbling beneath the surface in a number of guises. Across authors, a number of terms and concepts have been applied to describe this perspective, incorporating terms such as logical problems, Emergent probing, Elaborative probing, the ethnographic interview, the nonstandardized cognitive interview, and the Grand Tour approach. To combine these themes, I propose that, at least in some cases, the cognitive interview is not best characterized as "cognitive" or even as "intensive," but rather, as *expansive,* to adopt a term introduced by Beatty, Schechter, and Whitaker (1996). That is, the interview is done *as a means to extend our understanding of the phenomenon under study, and the way in which the survey questions we are testing address that phenomenon.* Although this description sounds vague, several authors have independently given it significant depth and credence—if at times unintentionally. I therefore discuss the trends in the field that point toward a somewhat unified conclusion.

IMPLICATIONS OF THE LOGICAL/ STRUCTURAL PROBLEM CATEGORY

I have already introduced a non-cognitive perspective by outlining cases of structural deficiency. By nature, these problems are inherent in the questions, and therefore are not dependent on how our subjects mentally process them. Although this definition may be subject to philosophical debate (especially as it is risky to suggest to CASM adherents that a problem may not be cognitive at its core), it is in one sense noncontroversial, as it expresses a long-standing view that the respondent and the survey instrument each contribute some amount of response error (Groves, 1989).[1] During the interview, these problems may be painfully obvious as soon as we become aware of the facts concerning the subject's life. As a very simple example, "How long have you owned your house?" will be found deficient once we observe a single renter among our tested subjects.

In theory, it is unnecessary to conduct interviews of live subjects in order to identify logical problems. That is, full knowledge of the relevant domain (as through an infallible armchair review process) should in itself be sufficient. For example, we determine that some people own their house and some rent or, to borrow an earlier example, that food can be cooked in a microwave as well as by other means. Similarly, we might determine which foods to include in a dietary assessment to be conducted in China by conducting a broad observational study of the range of foods that the Chinese respondent population actually eats.

As an alternative, the cognitive interview provides a convenient substitute for an appropriately rich knowledge base, and a means for locating logical holes. In order to probe for these errors, our usual cognitive probes are often inappropriate, as we need to supplement our knowledge concerning cognitive processing to also determine whether the question matches our respondents' life situations (again, it does no good for our question to be understood if it is the wrong question). We presumably could rely on a formulation that literally asks "How well does this question apply to you?" and this is occasionally done.

However, cognitive interviewers typically adopt a more circumspect approach and simply ask subjects to "Tell me more about that," which induces them to elaborate on the particulars. Further, this type of probe is generic, in the sense that it can be expressed as any of the subcategories I introduced in the previous chapter (it can be Anticipated, Spontaneous, Conditional, or Emergent in nature). In effect, we research an area of interest by regarding our subjects as substantive experts in that area, and probe them for an expanded description. Because no one is more knowledgeable about the minute details of illicit drug use than drug users, obtaining an *expansive* "description of reality" from these individuals simply puts the interviewing team in position to tailor questions on drug use more appropriately.

ELABORATIVE (EXPANSIVE) PROBING

An almost identical theme—that cognitive interviewers often focus outward toward a broader context, as opposed to inward toward the question itself—has been made explicit by Beatty and his colleagues at NCHS. In two studies, they sought to determine what experienced interviewers actually do, as opposed to what the instructions in the cognitive protocol indicate they should do, or what they say they do. In one such observational study, Beatty, Willis, and Schechter (1997) distinguished two observed probe categories, beyond those defined in previous chapters:

1. Reorienting probes. These are focused back toward answering the tested question, "So, can you give me a number for how many days in the last 30 your health was not good?"

2. Elaborative probes. These focus attention toward a more complete verbal report, often to determine details about the subject's life that are relevant to evaluating the survey question– "Tell me more about why you weren't working then."

It is not my wish to introduce a pantheon of probe categories and systems, as the previous chapter was fairly detailed in that respect. However, beyond issues I have discussed concerning probe standardization and triggering, Beatty, Willis, et al.'s classification forces yet another important qualitative division. These probe varieties differ fundamentally with respect to the direction they induce the subject to proceed along the track established by the target question. The Reorienting probe travels toward an answer to that question, whereas the Elaborative probe takes a side-track in which the question topic is expanded. Interestingly, Beatty, Willis, et al. found that the type of probe used had a major influence on subjects' subsequent behaviors. A quarter of the responses that followed Reorienting probes were precise, or consisted of codeable answers to the target question, whereas only about 5% of those following Elaborative probes displayed the same level of precision. Besides indicating that (not surprisingly) the nature of probing does influence subject behavior, this illustrates how our choice of probe might itself be based on our test objectives. That is, we either (a) reorient, to determine whether a subject who has just given a vague or otherwise uncodeable answer can be induced to answer the question when prompted, or (b) elaborate, to examine in wider scope the basis for the individual's response.

Beatty, Willis, et al. (1997) suggested that cognitive interviewers are less often interested in determining whether they can force a response to a target question than they are in obtaining broader information relevant to the evaluation of the question in its entirety. That is, our purpose is not to badger people into giving codeable answers (for better or worse, that is one function of the field interviewer). Rather, we strive to determine whether even precise, codeable answers are meaningful, and if not, why not. The authors suggested that Elaborative probing, even in the very simple form of "Can you tell me more about that?" can be extremely useful in this regard, as it expands the conversation beyond the strict confines of the question itself.

Even more relevant to the concept of Expansive probing, Beatty et al. (1996) found it useful to specifically introduce the Expansive probe by name, as a result of analyzing cognitive interviewer behavior. Based on a review of interviews done in the NCHS cognitive laboratory, they defined the following probe types:

(a) Traditional cognitive probes (as described by Willis, 1994)

(b) Confirmatory probes: "So, for the last 30 days you were only unhealthy for one day?"

(c) Expansive probes designed to obtain additional narrative information: "Tell me more about your arthritis."

(d) Functional remarks that redirect the subject back to the original question, and are the opposite of Expansive probes: "Yes, I'm talking about how you felt in the last 30 days."

(e) Feedback probes: "Thanks, that's just the sort of information I'm looking for."

Interestingly, Beatty et al. (1996) found the classic cognitive probes to be relatively rare, and a number of alternative and previously unrecognized probe types were observed. Some types, such as Feedback, do not even probe for information, but resemble the speech acts normally used by questioners in natural conversation (e.g., acknowledging that the respondent has answered).

Most significant is the Expansive probe category, which appears to be the Elaborative probe by another name, as it simply asks subjects to provide further information. The constant re-emergence of the Expansive (i.e., Elaborative) probe, along with the Beatty et al. (1996) finding that traditional cognitive probes were relatively rare in their study, forces a reinterpretation of what the cognitive interview achieves. In particular, it appears to very often serve a dual checking function, as follows:

(a) We administer probe questions that are Expansive, as they induce the subject to talk about issues relevant to the targeted survey questions. Such probing provides a "grounding check," as the expanded information we receive reveals whether subjects are thinking about the questions as we intend.

(b) As a second type of check, the information elicited by Expansive probes serves as a means to verify the answer the subject gives to the tested question; that is, Expansive probing provides "a description of reality against which to evaluate answers" (Cosenza & Fowler, 2000, p. 996).

As a simple, hypothetical example, we may ask, "How often is household trash collected?" and the person answers, "Twice a week." We then rely on Expansive probing—"Tell me more about your trash pickup"—and are told that "The garbage gets picked up on Monday, and the recycling on Wednesday." If our measurement objective is to measure only the collection of trash and to exclude recyclables, we have detected a problem in question interpretation. Our expanded conversation is in this case useful in establishing that (a) the target question failed to achieve grounding between the subject and ourselves; and that (b) the original answer was wrong, given our intent.

The logic of this question-evaluation sequence was hinted at years ago by Converse and Presser (1986), and a review of the cognitive interviewing literature suggests that the identical philosophy has emerged repeatedly (e.g., Rho & Sangster, 2003). In fact, several researchers have modified this logical approach by obtaining Expansive information prior to, as opposed to after, asking target questions. Cosenza and Fowler (2000) describe their use of the *Prospective* probing procedure, in which the interviewer asks the subject to talk about the general topic of the questionnaire, prior to a more carefully structured cognitive interview. By first eliciting a prospective story (e.g., related to health care utilization in the past year) from which to draw upon during the cognitive interview, the authors found that they could detect and resolve inconsistencies that emerged as the person answered the tested survey questions. Likewise, Wilson and Peterson (1999) have independently implemented the prospective approach, which they imaginatively labeled the "Grand Tour approach" to the subject's life.

A case study by Groenvold, Klee, Sprangers, and Aaronson (1997) reflects the Expansive orientation to instrument development in an implicit but powerful manner. Working in the field of quality-of-life research (which is somewhat outside of survey methodology and therefore unencumbered by the cognitive model of the survey response process), they evaluated a patient questionnaire by having subjects complete the instrument unaided, and then conducted expansive qualitative interviews that probed each question more fully. Again, the qualitative interview elicited an enhanced picture of the person's health, which was then used to validate the responses given previously. Because they found good agreement between these two sources of information, they concluded that the shorter, more efficient approach (the questionnaire) was an adequate representation of a more elaborate interview that presumably best reflected the person's true status.

In pushing the notion of the Expansive interview to perhaps its logical extreme, Friedenreich, Courneya, and Bryant (1997) applied Expansive probing techniques to a physical activity questionnaire. Rather than using the expansive description as a check on the restricted, standardized version of the instrument, however, they decided instead to simply adopt the expanded version as the data collection instrument *itself*. At this point, the researchers were no longer conducting cognitive interviewing as a form of pretesting, but crossed the line into the collection of field data.

THE EXPANSIVE INTERVIEW AS
NONSTANDARDIZED PRETEST INTERVIEW

As I stress above, from a technical perspective, Expansive probes are generic in nature, and can be developed and administered in a variety of ways. That is, they can be Proactive or Reactive, or standardized or non-standardized (e.g., we can, and sometimes do, script a probe of the form "Tell me more about that" prior to cognitive testing; alternatively, we can develop it during the course of the interview in a fully Emergent fashion). That said, based on available descriptions of its use, Expansive probing does seem to be somewhat conversational, and therefore nonstandardized in the sense discussed in Chapter 2. It also tends to be Emergent, as the term was used in Chapter 6. In this form, the approach might be characterized as simply the nonstandardized survey interview, but for purposes of pretesting, rather than for data collection proper. That is, in our quest to probe further to obtain useful validating information for evaluating the standardized target questions, we have in effect become proponents—and implementers—of the nonstandardized approach. Further, it seems that *cognitive interviewers implicitly adopt the spirit of nonstandardization due to a belief that the benefits this confers can in turn be applied to the tested, standardized version.* That is, we not only believe that nonstandardized Expansive interviewing provides an enhanced view that renders that interview a better measure than the tested instrument, but also that we can use this information to in turn improve that instrument.

Put another way, cognitive interviews are often based on the following unstated assumptions: Through Expansive probing, we translate the questionnaire into a (nonstandardized) form which we believe to represent a more sensitive, and overall superior, data collection instrument. We then compare this full, muscular version to the relatively emaciated standard form we intend to field. Based on the nature of the gaps and errors we uncover, we attempt various forms of surgery on our standardized version, in the hope that it will behave as much as possible like the enhanced version. This is exactly the logic represented by the Groenvold et al. (1997) study cited above, but with the exception that we do not stop after making our critical comparison of these implicit "versions," but go on to modify and improve the standardized form when it is found lacking.

If we are successful, we have achieved two desired outcomes: (1) The standard questionnaire mimics the functioning of the nonstandard form, but (2) also retains the benefits of the standardized field interview. Our overall objective is therefore to have it both ways: to produce an instrument that provides grounding and other beneficial features of conversation, but without conceding the structured approach. This is a tall order, and is certainly a lot to ask of the cognitive interview! It is far too early to decide whether, to the extent this viewpoint is an accurate depiction, we are successful in this regard.

The Ethnographic Interview as an Alternative Perspective

As the topic of this chapter is alternative ways to view cognitive interviewing, I also describe another important development in the cognitive interviewing field: the conceptualization of this activity as an anthropological exercise, as opposed to a strictly cognitive one. The ethnographic approach to cognitive interviewing emphasizes cultural variables, such as belief systems and everyday practices, that determine whether or not a particular question even makes sense to respondents across the cultural spectrum (Gerber, 1999; Martin & Tucker, 1999; von Thurn & Moore, 1993).

For instance, surveys of physical activity have traditionally focused on leisure time activities most appropriate to relatively well-educated office workers, but have not been designed with other groups in mind (Ainsworth, 2000). As a result, the questions tend to overlook physical activities that some respondents do engage in, and therefore misrepresent their activity (e.g., Ainsworth mentions low-income Hispanic women, who are typically active in household physical chores rather than in leisure time activities). Here, the fundamental questionnaire-based flaw is not primarily due to limitations in the cognitive processing of questions on physical activity, although these problems certainly may exist (Warnecke et al., 1997). Rather, even if understood perfectly, the questions fail to provide a fit to respondent lives (note the strong similarity to the earlier description of logical problems, but here with an explicit cross-cultural focus).

Such problems of culture are increasingly important as survey researchers endeavor to take into account cultural variation across the populations they survey. In order to address these problems, Gerber (1999) and Von Thurn & Moore (1993) in particular have advocated the *ethnographic interview* as a means to elicit background discussion that enhances the investigator's understanding. In proposing this as an alternative to cognitive interviewing, there are actually two considerations: (1) To what extent is the cognitive interview already ethnographic in nature? and (2) If it is not, do we need to consider the ethnographic interview as an explicit alternative to the cognitive interview, or as an extension?

ARE COGNITIVE INTERVIEWS ALREADY ETHNOGRAPHIC?

As strong as the argument is that attention to cultural factors is vital, practitioners of cognitive interviewing have not been blind to this fact. Gerber (1999) suggests that anthropological methods are already sometimes woven into the cognitive interview:

> Cognitive interviews often take on the function of providing ethnographic information to survey researchers. From this point of view, one of the functions currently served by cognitive interviewing is what was elsewhere called "backup ethnography." (p. 222)

Cognitive interviewing techniques may be very useful for addressing the cultural variables that influence question design and for identifying survey questions that do not account for cultural variation. For example, a careful cognitive interviewer might probe by asking a female Hispanic subject to describe her day and, on that basis, determine that questions limited to physical activities such as aerobics classes, yoga, and jogging are grossly inadequate. In fact, cognitive interviewing reports appear to be replete with comments denouncing survey questions for failing a variety of cultural tests. For example, I once remarked that the question "Are you regularly exposed to loud noises, such as from riding a motorcycle, playing in a rock band, or operating a chain saw?" seemed to lack examples that are universally appropriate, after administering this to an elderly, double-amputee, diabetic African-American female who had responded simply, "No, I don't do none of those things."

Wellens (1994) also successfully applied existing cognitive interviewing techniques to evaluate the quality of census-based citizenship information for the foreign-born population, finding, for example, that the term "born abroad" wasn't well understood but was interpreted as "born on a ship," or "first-generation born in the U.S." Further, the term

"American parent" was deficient because this could refer to anywhere in the Americas.

DO WE NEED AN EXPLICIT ETHNOGRAPHIC INTERVIEW?

Cognitive interviewers may, in the course of their usual activities, already be dabbling in the field of anthropology. The more important question would seem to be whether this is enough, or whether we should further modify any activities to make them more culturally sensitive. There are several implications of the anthropological perspective that have ramifications for interviewing practice. To a great extent these involve subject recruitment, simply because the first challenge is to ensure that we are interviewing a sufficient range of appropriate subjects (see Chapter 10).

Beyond subject recruitment, with respect to specific practices during the interview, Gerber (1999) advocates the ethnographic interview as one in which the researcher actively endeavors to focus on understanding the interviewed individual's cultural background, so that the questions asked are appropriate to that individual's life. Gerber has also suggested that the ethnographic interview be conducted differently from the strict cognitive interview, and envisions divergent approaches to probing: "Ethnographic questioning leads respondents into a description of the wider schema, while the cognitive interview must stay focused on the question context" (p. 232). That is, ethnographic probing leads subjects to elaborate on their conceptualization of relevant concepts and question "fit." Gerber advocates a multi-step process in which interviews that are heavily ethnographic precede those that are devoted to assessing the cognitive properties of the targeted survey questions.

After reading my earlier description of Expansive probing, Gerber's conception of ethnographic probing may seem extremely familiar. In fact, these seem to be virtually synonymous, in that both are defined in terms of elaborating the discussion in order to provide the interviewer with a greater appreciation of background and context. Even if these concepts are not technically identical, they reflect the same stubbornly recurrent theme: Cognitive probing is useful because it provides supplemental information about "reality," including information relevant to culture. Further, if the Expansive interview already incorporates ethnographic probing, then to the extent that interviews are conducted in a sufficiently expansive manner, we may already pay sufficient attention to problems of culture. Hence the distinction between ethnographic interviewing and cognitive interviewing may not be so stark that it is necessary to introduce a new form of interview.

HOW SHOULD WE APPLY ETHNOGRAPHIC/EXPANSIVE PROBING?

Admittedly, however, even if we do possess an existing tool, whether named the expansive or ethnographic interview, this does not address a fundamental point Gerber (1999) makes, which is that we should perhaps make increased use of this tool to appreciate how issues of culture impact the development and testing of survey questions. Following Gerber's suggestion, it is perhaps advisable to conduct a series of early interviews that make use only of Expansive/Ethnographic probes, and later, once we are relatively certain that we at least know *what* questions to ask, to tailor probing more toward the classic cognitive formulations, in order to determine *how* to ask them.

To be specific, especially when studying populations that we are not familiar with, or when we study a range of cultural or ethnic groups, we should endeavor to include a number of ethnographically inspired (Expansive) probes:

1. Tell me about the types of activities you do that take physical effort or that make you feel physically tired.

2. The question has a list of foods in it. Are these the types of foods that your family usually eats?

3. What types of things do you think of as "work"?

4. Are you always paid in cash for the work you do, or are there other ways in which you get paid?

Finally, keep in mind that issues of culture may involve a much wider domain than race, ethnicity, or other variables typically associated with anthropology or ethnography. In addition, cultural differences between investigators and respondents may involve variables such as profession, even within the same nominal culture. For example, a transportation planner and a typical respondent will have different experiences and viewpoints concerning the concept of "commuting" (Tourangeau, Rips, et al., 2000). It is the job of the cognitive investigator to find ways to bridge these cultures, especially by attending to sufficiently investigative forms of probing.

Merging Cognitive and Expansive Interviewing

Reflecting on my experiences in the cognitive lab, I believe that there is considerable merit to the view that cognitive interviewing is, in large part, Expansive. Further, although it is perhaps a special case covered by the Expansive umbrella, the ethnographic approach is becoming increasingly important. The implication is not, however, that we should either jettison our usual reference to our activities as cognitive or reject the cognitive framework. First, it is important to distinguish between cognitive *probes* and cognitive *problems*. That is, our probes may be fully Expansive rather than classically cognitive in nature—yet they might still reveal a host of serious problems that are obviously cognitive. In fact, as I will show in Chapter 11, many of the problems we observe clearly are cognitive by definition, mainly involving comprehension difficulties.

Most importantly, it is perhaps best to infuse multiple perspectives into the work of cognitive interviewing, as is reflected in a report by Loomis (2000) involving questions on welfare benefits. In her cognitive testing protocol, the author combined Expansive and Cognitive probes:

> The types of probes used most often asked respondents to describe the assistance they received, which helps verify "yes" responses, and to paraphrase questions in their own words, which helps to verify their comprehension of the question and elicit potential alternative wording to use in question design. (p. 3)

As in the examples I presented earlier, Loomis (2000) used Expansive probing as a check on the subject's answer, so the investigator could assess its accuracy. In addition, a cognitive probe—paraphrasing—was used to search for sources of misunderstanding that might give rise to an incorrect answer. Consequently, by combining probing types, the interviewer is able to measure both error and its cognitive source (see Pascale, 2003, for a further example). The major lesson to be gleaned in recognizing this coordinated approach is that it is fruitless to argue whether cognitive interviewing is really cognitive, or is something else—as it is no *one* thing. To fully understand how our subjects respond to evaluated concepts (e.g., "pain in the abdomen"), we need to investigate their cognitive processing of the relevant concepts (e.g., "What does 'abdomen' mean?") and also the background context (e.g., "Tell me more about that pain").

Chapter Summary

- Although we normally adopt a heavily cognitive orientation in terms of both theory and the varieties of probes as we describe them, many probes that interviewers commonly use do not appear to be targeted toward cognition.
- Rather, the probes used by a wide range of practitioners often simply request elaboration, as in "Tell me more about that."
- Such Expansive probing provides information that in turn is used as a check on the accuracy of the answers to targeted survey questions.
- Expansive probing is most often nonstandardized, and in that sense reflects a nonstandard questioning approach within the pretesting domain.
- As a radical interpretation, Expansive probing can be viewed as a means for molding a standardized instrument into a form that provides the benefits of the nonstandard approach, in terms of minimizing error, but without its training and administration costs.
- Ethnographic interviewing represents a further alternative view of cognitive interviewing; this form of probing is also fundamentally Expansive.
- These alternative concepts do not eclipse the cognitive perspective but enhance it; best practice in cognitive interviewing involves recognizing and implementing multiple approaches.

Note

1. CASM could be viewed, in a formal statistical sense, as the study of the interaction between the instrument and the respondent. This leads to a very interesting discussion of the statistical modeling of error that is beyond the scope of this book (see Groves, 1989).

8

Avoiding Probing Pitfalls

The difference between the right word and the almost-right word is the difference between lightning and the lightning bug.

Mark Twain

Chapter Overview

Probing is the key to finding problems in questions, but misuse can create more problems than we solve. In particular, we must avoid (a) inducing subjects to invent problems, and (b) inventing them ourselves. There are several practices that can help us to avoid biased probes, to repair ineffective ones, and to check our tendency to overprobe or overinterpret.

Are We in Danger of Finding Problems That Don't Exist?

Thus far, most of the discussion of probing has emphasized the development of probes that are effective—they can be used to find problems that really exist. But returning to an important point made by Conrad and Blair (1996, 2001), we do need to be careful, in our zest to uncover problems, to avoid inappropriate probing techniques that create the appearance of problems that do *not* exist within our target survey questions. Presumably, such errors could have two origins: (1) *local reactivity effects,* in which the act of probing a target question produces evidence of spurious problems in that question, and (2) *extended reactivity effects,* where the cumulative effect of probing is to induce, within questions that follow, problems that do not exist in the absence of probing.

Concerning the first of these possibilities, Beatty (in press) has chronicled his attempts to evaluate questions that ask, "In the past 30 days, on how many days was your (physical or mental) health not good?" Although NCHS-based cognitive laboratory interviews revealed that subjects had considerable difficulty answering in terms of number of days, the survey sponsor pointed out that field interviews tended to produce few overt problems, and suggested that perhaps the activity of probing itself was creating the illusion of problems. This possibility led Beatty, Willis, et al. (1997) to systematically test this hypothesis by training interviewers to apply Reorienting probes (as defined in the previous chapter), thereby inducing subjects to provide answers to the question. As the sponsor had anticipated, subjects were able to provide answers. However, a series of retrospective debriefings of subjects pointed to a very different conclusion. At that point, subjects indicated that they had significant difficulty providing answers they considered accurate. They had failed to articulate this, however, because the interviewer had not pressed them to report problems but instead had pushed them to provide codeable responses.

As a result, the investigators concluded that problems found through our usual cognitive probes are more likely to be actual issues that are normally suppressed than artificial problems that do not otherwise exist. This interpretation is buoyed by Viterna and Maynard's (2002) observation that in the field survey environment, interviewer probes tend to be radically reorienting, as they are focused exclusively toward inducing a codeable answer (in effect, instructing the respondent to "Give me a number!").

Practices That Avoid Artificial Problems

Still, avoiding problem creation, as opposed to problem discovery, presents a severe challenge to cognitive interviewers, and especially to adherents of probing approaches that are strongly proactive and therefore "go looking for problems." To minimize these effects, we have several means at our disposal:

1. *Avoid bias and other classic questionnaire design problems.* Because probe questions are similar to survey questions (as I've mentioned, subjects often don't seem to even know which is which), *the interviewer needs to realize that our cognitive probes are subject to all of the same question design flaws as our tested questions.* Schaeffer (1991) has pointed out that normal speech is often formulated in order to promote agreement between speakers, and subjects may simply acquiesce to whatever

our probes ask (see Martin, 1964 for a description of acquiescence bias). Reiterating a point from Chapter 4, one approach to this problem is to be especially careful to ask probe questions that are balanced and do not suggest certain outcomes:

- Instead of asking simply, "Do you consider volunteer work to count as work?" balance the probe by adding "or is it something else?"

- Rather than asking, "Was that a hard question to answer?" ask "Was that question easy or difficult to answer?"

- Rather than implicitly blaming the subject ("Do you understand those directions?"), put any possibility of blame on the materials ("Are these instructions clear, or are they confusing?").

2. *Be especially careful when using paraphrasing.* Paraphrasing, in which we ask the subject to repeat the question back to us in his or her own words, is normally thought of as a useful member of the family of classic cognitive probes, and has been used quite often (e.g., Hess, 1999; Jenkins & Von Thurn, 1996; Pascale & Mayer, 2002; Rothgeb, 2001; Schechter & Beatty, 1994). However, a debate has emerged concerning its use. Specifically, several authors have noted that paraphrasing is sometimes difficult for cognitive laboratory subjects, especially those who are not particularly articulate or well educated. Therefore a failure to read back a question may not necessarily indicate that the individual has failed to understand the question (especially given that there is much that we can understand yet not repeat back fully, including perhaps the evening news). Use of paraphrase probes may therefore lead us to overestimate difficulties of question comprehension (Prufer & Rexroth, 2004; Rho & Sangster, 2003). Further, de Leeuw, Borgers, and Strijbos-Smits (in press) counsel against the use of paraphrasing for interviews of younger children, which again hints at the particular difficulties of this technique.

I suspect that an important determinant is how paraphrasing is used and the criteria we set. If we indeed request that subjects repeat the question verbatim, this could be a very difficult and unfair task. On the other hand, it is advisable to view the paraphrase mainly in terms of concepts to be recounted, rather than words. That is, if a question contains four key components, the subject's paraphrase should presumably include those, in order for us to conclude that he or she has appropriately understood the question. Even short of requiring that much, we often hear paraphrases like "Oh, it was some longwinded thing about health insurance and Medicaid, or maybe Medicare." Such cases do not confer confidence that the individual knows what we are asking him or her, and it would be quite a stretch to conclude that he or she probably understood, and is just unable to articulate all of the words.

Hess (1999) describes an approach that is perhaps a self-validating mechanism for paraphrase probes. For the target question "Was there ever a period of three months or more when [child] did not live with his or her biological father?" several subjects gave incorrect, and in some cases completely reversed, paraphrases such as "They want to know if he ever did live with his biological father." These subjects had also already answered the question "No" prior to the paraphrase. Through further Expansive probing, however, Hess was able to determine that the true answer to the tested question was "Yes" for these individuals. Hence the initial, incorrect answer was consistent with the initial, incorrect encoding reflected by the paraphrase. In this case, the investigator used the logic of Expanded interviewing to determine that (a) upon further review, the initial response was incorrect, and (b) based on the use of the paraphrase, the reason appeared to relate to comprehension difficulty. By combining probing approaches (e.g., the cognitively oriented paraphrase probe with the Expansive probe), we obtain a rich description that provides logical support for the use of each. Overall, paraphrasing can be dangerous or revealing, depending on how it is linked to other relevant sources of information.

3. *Retrench when our probes "don't work."* It is somewhat paradoxical that probes—no matter what their origin or category—are themselves subject to misinterpretation (Belson, 1981). So, in the extreme, it might seem necessary to cognitively test our probes to see if they can be understood, which leads to an endless loop. To avoid writing unclear probes, the cognitive interviewer should obviously not introduce new forms of complex vocabulary, and should severely limit the length of the probes in order to minimize demands on the subject's short-term memory. However, the best means for resolving such problems is to expect them—and to flexibly adjust through nonstandardized means. The following segment from a cognitive interviewing exchange, reported by Wellens (1994), is telling:

INTERVIEWER: (target question)	Are you a citizen of the United States?
SUBJECT:	No.
INTERVIEWER (probe):	In your own words, what does the term "citizen" mean to you?

SUBJECT:	I don't . . . I don't understand.
INTERVIEWER: (probe)	I just want to know what you think the definition of the word "citizen" is.
SUBJECT:	A citizen is a person who belongs to this country. That person has the right to vote or join the government.
INTERVIEWER: (probe)	Can you tell me more about why you are not a citizen of this country?
SUBJECT:	A person must live here for five years, take a test, obtain history course, then the person can become citizen. (p. 1206)

In this case, the originally targeted question was clear enough, and ultimately was found to pose no particular problems, as the subject appears to have an impressive notion of citizenship. Far less clear, ironically, was the probe used to test the target question. However, once this became evident, the cognitive interviewer simply rephrased it. The revised probes seemed to have worked, and provided the basis for making the intended determination. Hence probes—like survey questions themselves—are imperfect, but this fact does not mire us in an inescapable logical morass as long as we are ready to adjust as necessary (somewhat interestingly, in a flexible manner that leads to conversational grounding with respect to the probes themselves).

4. *Limit speculative probing.* We can also strive to avoid inventing problems by keeping in mind the degree to which our probes may induce subjects to speculate or to otherwise focus on issues that are not especially germane to the mental processing of the survey question. For example, Miller (2002a) suggests that we avoid probe questions such as "If you had cancer, would you have answered 'yes' to this question?" As an illustration of a somewhat more subtle case, in testing a question such as "In the past year, how many times have you seen a doctor, nurse, or other health professional?" it is common to probe the interpretation of vague terms such as "other health professional" simply by asking subjects to indicate what this means to them. I have found it very easy to elicit reports that include all sorts of fringe providers—acupuncturist, herbalist, and so on—which may not be what the question had really intended. But does this indicate a problem with the question?

For one such investigation (Willis, Bornstein, et al., 2000), I concluded not, because the elaborated descriptions I had induced did not seem strongly related to what the subjects had been thinking about as they answered the target question. For most subjects, asking about doctors and nurses covered the majority of visits, and the "other provider" segment of the question was irrelevant. In that case, asking about conceptualization of the term "other health professional" was perhaps of academic interest but had expanded the scope of the inquiry beyond that which was relevant to the task.

Returning to a theme from the previous chapter, it is precisely this potential for probing overuse and misinterpretation that led Conrad and Blair (1996, 2001) to challenge the Proactive approach in particular—and the point is well taken. The lesson may be that it is acceptable to probe, but we also need to avoid a judgment that interesting responses to the probe invalidate the target question. There are even ways to firm up our judgment through further probing. If the subject mentions an herbalist when I ask about interpretation of "other health professionals," I can probe elaboratively and ask whether she has seen one in the past 12 months. If the answer is "no," and the person has simply been spouting multiple exemplars of that category, there is no evidence from this interview that a problem has been detected—even though I may still believe that "other health professionals" is a vague term.

5. *Be conservative in the number of probes asked.* This is a tricky and somewhat subjective issue. Cognitive interviewers vary greatly in the sheer number of probe questions they administer (DeMaio & Landreth, in press). It is difficult to know whether the simple activity of asking numerous probes can in itself induce problems—especially when these are proactive and are therefore not in reaction to observed difficulties. Based on concerns that have been expressed by Conrad and his colleagues (Conrad & Blair, 1996, 2001; Conrad, Blair, & Tracy, 2000) my personal view has evolved. Whereas I once felt as though my probing was insufficient if I could not think of a probe to ask for every question (either in an Anticipated or Spontaneous sense), I am now inclined to be somewhat more selective—and purposely avoid probing some questions when there is no evidence of any problem and I can think of no clear issue to investigate further. If we leave some questions unprobed, we may avoid conditioning subjects to expect probes for every single targeted item, which might unduly influence their cognitive processing. It does seem that in at least some cases, lack of evidence of a problem *does* mean that there is no problem, and we can therefore choose our battles and apply probes somewhat judiciously, as opposed to probing indiscriminately on the off chance we'll find something substantial. As a

caveat, there may be other experienced interviewers who would dispute this particular point.

6. *Don't view the subject as a questionnaire design critic.* If our explicit focus is on finding problems in survey questions, and we have invited subjects to assist us in this endeavor, does this risk a wild inflation of problems because we have induced subjects to helpfully and imaginatively create them? If so, the cognitive interview is a very heavy hammer, and the poor survey questionnaire a very enticing nail, and all sorts of deficiencies could be ascribed to a questionnaire that may not be all that poor (see Beatty, in press, for a more detailed discussion of this issue). Of particular concern is the possibility of extended reactivity effects, in which probing in general serves to reinforce subject behaviors that focus on any conceivable type of shortcoming.

There are several reasons to be reassured on this count. First, Converse and Presser (1986) presented evidence that interviewed individuals are simply not prone to engage in questionnaire critique, and may be totally unaware of question failings even when their responses clearly reflect gross forms of response error. For example, Hunt, Sparkman, and Wilcox (1982) found that even when severe errors were purposely built into questions, respondents failed to notice much wrong. This observation is very consistent with my experiences with cognitive interviewing—it simply is not characterized by academic discussion between interviewer and subject concerning the failings of survey questions. In fact, explicit attempts to lead subjects to give opinions on questions has sometimes been shown to be ineffective. For instance, Sangster and Fox (2000) reported that subjects' preference for alternate versions of questions on housing rental costs were poorly related to their accuracy in answering the questions.

One might think that our typical introductory instructions to our cognitive subjects—especially the outright statement that our job is to find problems—would induce them to engage in extensive opinionating. I have not observed this, either in my own interviews or in recordings of other interviewers. On the contrary, it is more often necessary to give subjects explicit permission to point out problems by indicating that I did not write the questions, and they shouldn't worry about being nice to avoid hurting my feelings (Chapter 10 expounds on these operational issues more fully). Despite these exhortations, subjects more often provide verbal reports that signal clear problems with question interpretation or other question features, yet they seem to be oblivious to these. Rather than commenting on issues I believe to be obvious, they simply await my next query.

The following cognitive interview segment is very typical in this regard:

(1) INTERVIEWER: (Target question)	The next question is about all the fruits and vegetables you ate at your evening meal yesterday. First, what vegetables did you have?
(2) SUBJECT:	Oh, gosh, let's see . . . I had rice, some green beans, and—oh, and an orange.
(3) INTERVIEWER: (Probe)	Do you consider rice to be a fruit, a vegetable, or something else?
(4) SUBJECT:	Rice? Yeah, uh, that's about the only veggie I eat.
(5) INTERVIEWER: (Probe)	And what about an orange—vegetable, fruit, or something else?
(6) SUBJECT:	[Pauses] Uh, an orange? You mean . . . [uses hand to outline circular shape approximately the size of an orange, and pauses] Fruit, right? Like, an orange you eat?
(7) INTERVIEWER:	OK, I'm just checking on your thoughts on this stuff.

It is illustrative to decode this exchange. The subject's response in (2) indicated to the interviewer that (a) he may consider rice a vegetable, whereas researchers consider this to be a grain and therefore out of scope; and (b) unless the subject truly believes an orange to be a vegetable, he probably believed that both fruits and vegetables were to be reported, given that the instruction had mentioned both and that he had failed to fully process the limitation (to vegetables alone) in the question following the instruction. In order to investigate this, the interviewer then asks, in (3) and (5), for the subject's categorization of each food.

The subject's puzzled pause and tentative response in (6) indicates that he believes it strange to be asked about whether an orange is a fruit. However, it was fortuitous that the interviewer chose to ask this "dumb" question, as the rejoinder seems to clarify the source of the erroneous inclusion of orange: the subject does classify it as fruit, but reported it anyway after mishearing the question. On the other hand, he apparently mentioned rice because he does consider it to be a vegetable (as do many people who are not nutritionists or health researchers).

I presented this analysis in detail to make several points:

The subject wasn't much of a critic. He didn't notice any problems, either with the original question or after the interviewer's probes provided some clues that a problem may have existed. This is critical when considering whether probes are biasing; that is, does the interjection of probing cause the subject to alter his or her behavior and to more carefully process subsequent questions, based on the experience of being "challenged" by earlier probes? Although this can of course happen, in my experience the type of exchange above is very typical. Even after probing very obvious misunderstandings, the subject does not fully appreciate *why we are probing,* or the implications of this for questionnaire design. I might administer the next question and literally find the same problems, with the subject demonstrating no awareness that anything may be amiss, consistent with the Hunt et al. (1982) results. This exhibits, perhaps, a form of ignorance—but this benefits us, as it markedly reduces extended reactivity effects.

A fundamental reason for subjects' lack of awareness of questionnaire problems seems to be that they are not explicitly focused on possible sources of response error and have no inkling of our measurement objectives. Instead, they treat the exercise as a conversation—and tend to answer the questions we ask. Although subjects try to be as helpful as possible, they are not trained in the identification of problem pitfalls any more than a member of the public glimpsing an old bridge would distinguish between surface rust and deep structural decay.

Second, note that the interviewer chose not to explain the relevant issues to the subject. Based on the exchange above, the interviewer may have come to the following conclusions: (a) The question should be rewritten in a way to avoid misreports of rice as a vegetable; (b) more seriously, the question in its original form is confusing, and the initial mention of "fruits and vegetables" elicits reports of both, even though the question itself asks only for vegetables. It might therefore be better to mention only vegetables initially, and fruits in a later question series.

However, the interviewer chose to discuss none of these issues with the subject. He probed to the extent necessary to come to appropriate conclusions, but without attempting a detailed discussion about what he was investigating. Such a reticence to engage in a full critique is appropriate interviewer behavior. For one, we prefer not to spend time discussing issues of questionnaire design that the subject is likely not that interested in. Further, there is no reason to introduce the risk of bias by training the person in questionnaire design. Finally, it is very counterproductive to point out every time the person appears to have misunderstood a question because we want to avoid making him or her feel besieged or put on guard against failure (i.e., we have no desire to go out of our way to *induce* reactivity).

There is, of course, no reason to take an extremist position; we can ask for subjects' opinions on some aspects (e.g., "How about if I used the term 'stomach' or 'torso' rather than 'abdomen'? Do any of those work better for you, or not really?"). If someone mentions a questionnaire problem on his or her own—"What? That question is like listening to the whole Gettysburg Address!"—we of course listen to the subject and note this reaction. The critical point is that, as interviewers, we should not get heavily involved in questionnaire design-related discussions with subjects. This is sometimes difficult to resist, and presents a challenge to new interviewers—as above, when the subject's response implies that the interviewer is a simpleton for asking whether an orange is a fruit. However, explaining oneself would be complicated and is unnecessary. It is much better to simply respond in a neutral manner, indicating once again that we're just asking about the subject's thinking on a number of topics.

7. Finally, we can avoid inventing problems by accepting that our expectations may be wrong. Garas, Blair, and Conrad (in press) have suggested that researchers who overprobe may find problems simply because they are intent on finding them, and that proactive forms of probing might lead to a self-fulfilling prophecy. I have no proof that this does not occur, but will suggest a simple solution: Cognitive interviewers should regard probes as just that—means by which we probe for potential problems that may or may not exist. If we probe and fail to find problems, we should be prepared to accept this outcome.

Although it has not been possible to conduct a systematic review of cognitive interviewing reports, it is enlightening to review write-ups from different cognitive laboratories, in order to get some indication of the stance represented by the researchers. If this seemed to indicate a desire to be severely critical and to tear the questionnaire to pieces, then we might be especially concerned that cognitive interviewing simply provides a handy weapon. Somewhat reassuringly, a number of interviewing outcome reports from the U.S. Census Bureau, the Bureau of Labor Statistics, and NCHS suggest that cognitive laboratory personnel are measured in their comments. Loomis (2000) details cognitive testing results from the Income Supplement to the Current Population Survey, and explicitly notes that due to the difficulties of changing the instrument, "a conservative approach

> How many of your four closest friends smoke cigarettes?
>
> a. None   b. One   c. Two   d. Three   e. Four   f. Not sure
>
> FINDING: We had expected to observe problems, given that someone may not have four close friends, or may have difficulty determining which four were the closest, etc. On the contrary, this was generally well understood. Respondents appeared to react well to this, to be somewhat thoughtful in their responses, and to be able to answer our probes concerning their friends.

Figure 8.1   Targeted Question, With Results, Based on Cognitive Testing of Teen Smokers

was taken for making recommendations for revisions to the question" (p. 3). Based on fairly typical probing practices, the author investigated seven subsets of questions, and for six of these recommended no changes, making comments such as "For the most part, these questions worked well" (p. 4). Several other reports identify relatively more problems (Hess, 1999; Hughes & DeMaio, 2003; Goldenberg & Phillips, 2000; Miller 2002b; Pascale, 2003; Rothgeb, 2001), but are still balanced in finding that some questions create problems and others do not (e.g., Hughes & DeMaio suggested changes for roughly 60% of the questions they tested). Overall, the results in these reports are nuanced; questions do not have fatal flaws, but may not work in particular (indicated) cases, and should either be slightly reworded or further studied.

Finally, following my practice of providing explicit examples, Figure 8.1 is another example from my accumulated files that represents a typical outcome of the probed interview. The interviewing team was not committed to proving the item was problematic, but instead considered the failure to identify anticipated problems to be a positive result. (At the least, this is one fewer question we need to worry about modifying!) If investigators establish a reasonably high threshold, and are more interested in finding actual problems than in proving the ones we anticipated do exist, it should not be especially difficult to resist the temptations of problem fabrication. Admittedly, neither this example nor the other reports cited above constitute proof that the problems we do find are "real" (see Chapter 13 on method evaluation). However, it is possible to conduct probing that does not result in a litany of severe problems for any question we could imagine testing.

Chapter Summary

How can we avoid biased probing? By being aware that

- our probes may well be biasing, and we do need to be sensitive to evidence that this is the case;
- we are able to implement balanced forms of probes, in order to avoid biases, mainly by applying good questionnaire design principles to probe design;
- subjects may still not understand our probes, and we must be able to fix them on the spot;
- we may anticipate a problem, probe, and still find nothing wrong;
- even if we do probe and obtain an interesting result, we must still decide whether this actually constitutes a problem for the tested survey.

PART III

The Cognitive Testing Process

9

Selection and Training
of Cognitive Interviewers

Chapter Overview

The past few chapters placed a strong emphasis on the flexible use of probing procedures. Effective implementation of these requires a particular combination of background, training, and practice. To focus more specifically on the person who is conducting the interviews, this chapter addresses the following:

Issue 1: What types of individuals make effective cognitive interviewers?
Issue 2: What type of education or previous experience is necessary?
Issue 3: What type of training produces proficient interviewers?
Issue 4: How can interviewers undergo continuous training in order to provide a common approach and to avoid bad habits?

The first two issues are related to interviewer selection and are mainly relevant if one is engaged in development of a cognitive interviewing lab capacity (as readers who are interested in doing interviewing themselves have already made their choice of interviewer). The latter issues, pertaining to training, presumably apply in all cases.

Interviewer Personality: Who Makes a Good Cognitive Interviewer?

The question could also be modified to ask, "How much of my own personality should I express when I do interviews?" It might seem that we can bypass problems rooted in variations in interviewer personality simply by constraining interviewer behavior to only what is directly relevant to the task of cognitive interviewing. By conducting interviews in a laboratory or other controlled environment and standardizing all of the interchanges, including initial contact with the subject, probing, and follow-up activities, we might try to establish a system that exhibits tight control, leaving little room for extraneous interviewer behavior. This practice is reminiscent of the standardized field interview, as well as the prototype psychological lab-based think-aloud interview described by Ericsson and Simon (1980).

However, as discussed in Chapter 2, the notion that the survey interview is a purely programmed exchange of this type is unrealistic. Further, if the field survey interview is in actuality largely a social encounter, this is even more true of the cognitive interview. As such, there are two facets to cognitive interviewer behavior that must be balanced and coordinated for maximum effect: (a) technical ability and (b) interpersonal skills. Previous chapters concerning the investigative nature of probing techniques have largely addressed the former, but the latter is also vital, especially at the beginning of the interview. It is important to be able to put a wide variety of subjects at ease, and to seamlessly move between social interaction (e.g., greeting the subject) and the conduct of practices that technically constitute cognitive interviewing.

I feel that individuals who are successful interviewers have not only technical skills but also *the ability to be flexible, spontaneous, and cool under duress.* There is no script that we can turn to when a subject shows up late for the interview in a distracted and possibly foul mood because she has just driven around lost for an hour. Or, the individual might show up at the correct time but on the wrong day, and the interviewer must make a choice between turning a subject away and dropping what she is doing and quickly preparing for an off-the-cuff interview. Off-site interviewing presents the most challenging circumstances in this regard. Interviewers may need to visit an unfamiliar and possibly dangerous part of town to visit appropriate subjects (for example, homeless shelters or drug rehabilitation clinics), and they must be prepared for a range of unanticipated interactions. For instance, an interviewer on one of my projects reported conducting an interview while a young child continually scribbled on her testing protocol, without any attempt at intervention by the parental subject. I was myself once induced, at the end of an inner-city health clinic interview, to "please hold my baby for a second" by a mother who then disappeared for over an hour. (Perhaps she considered babysitting service as compensation for my having badgered her with probe questions.)

Sometimes the interview itself can unleash strong emotional reactions. In these cases, I would rather rely on an interviewer fresh out of college and otherwise unaccomplished—yet appropriately sensitive and unflappable—than on a Ph.D. with a long list of impressive research publications who is rigid, impersonal, and unable to adapt to the unanticipated. In sum, interviewers must exhibit clinical as well as technical skill.

Technical Background of the Cognitive Interviewer

Certain types of technical or training background are helpful. Good cognitive interviewers tend to be those who

(a) have some type of social science background, and have been exposed to measurement phenomena such as bias, context effects, acquiescence effects, and so on;

(b) have basic knowledge and experience in questionnaire design;

(c) have had exposure to the type of subject matter inherently involved when testing questionnaires; for example, employment and labor force issues for U.S. Bureau of Labor Statistics surveys, the health and medical arena for health surveys, or issues of demography for U.S. Census Bureau surveys;

(d) have experience; the best interviewers seem to be those who have simply done this a lot, as there is no set of background readings or magical scripts that one can follow to become instantly proficient.

How Should Cognitive Interviewers Be Trained?

Training, and perhaps even certification, of new cognitive interviewers is one of the most important though least documented aspects of cognitive interviewing. I have seen many cases in which investigators have reported on the use of cognitive interviewing—but without reporting *who* did the interviewing, *how* they did it, or how they were trained (and by whom). Given the wide variety of activities that cognitive interviewing may entail, this may lead to a number of questions about the degree of similarity in techniques across practitioners (Willis et al., 1999). As mentioned above, cognitive interviewing is a multifaceted skill. Good interviewers serve as technicians who can administer a protocol, as detectives who can locate problems in survey questions, and as engineers who work toward developing workable solutions to identified problems. Attainment of mastery for the latter, in particular, is gradual. Interviewers can be taught in an incremental, stepwise fashion, consisting of as many of the following steps as possible:

(a) *Gaining familiarity with questionnaire problems.* Trainees should conduct appraisals of several questionnaires to determine potential problems (perhaps using a checklist system, as described in Chapter 2). In institutional settings, they also attend early questionnaire design meetings, as well as meetings where cognitive interviewers discuss the results of testing.

(b) *Knowledge of the CASM approach.* Trainees can familiarize themselves with material on the general philosophy and objectives related to the Cognitive Aspects of Survey Methodology (Sudman et al., 1996; Tourangeau, Rips, et al., 2000).

(c) *Training in probing techniques.* Assuming verbal probing rather than pure think-aloud is to be applied, interviewers are taught specific probing procedures by means of written materials or lecture-based training (such as a short course at a survey methods conference). This training should emphasize specific examples of the way that probing is used to detect problems in survey questions (see Chapter 5), as opposed to abstract or theoretical discussion. Probing techniques are especially brought to life through the use of audio and videotaped recordings of cognitive interviews, if these are available.

(d) *Exposure to cognitive interviews.* Trainees observe experienced interviewers conducting interviews. Unless a topic is very sensitive, subjects generally have little objection to being observed in the same room by an individual who is described as "in training." (Permanent laboratories normally make use of remote viewing capabilities.)

(e) *Exposure to field interviews.* It is particularly valuable to expose new cognitive interviewers to field interviews. Seeing or hearing how interviews go awry in the field (through monitoring telephone interviews or accompanying a household interviewer), and learning to appreciate the conditions that field interviewers must work under (e.g., television blaring, loud argument in adjacent room), is a very illuminating experience.

(f) *Practice.* Trainees perform one or more interviews while being observed by a practiced interviewer, or they compile tape recordings of their interviews for review by other staff. The trainee can then be given appropriate feedback. An especially useful practice is the mock interview, in which the new interviewer conducts a cognitive interview of another who is more experienced, and who can assume the role of subject in a number of challenging guises.

(g) *Fixing the problems.* Trainees attend questionnaire review meetings subsequent to the interviews and can suggest specific recommendations to solve the observed problems.

(h) Finally, this book will hopefully be useful in facilitating at least several of the described activities.

CAN FIELD INTERVIEWERS BE TRAINED TO BE COGNITIVE INTERVIEWERS?

A common question is whether field interviewers—especially very experienced ones—can be taught to perform laboratory cognitive interviews of interviewer-administered instruments. Results obtained by DeMaio and Landreth (in press) have suggested that they can; a team consisting of field interviewers (but with two years of experience in cognitive interviews) were found to be as effective as two other teams consisting of professional survey researchers. Concerning the more basic issue of whether field interviewers can be quickly "reprogrammed" to conduct cognitive interviews, I have had success by addressing accumulated habits that are valuable in field interviews but that may be counterproductive for cognitive interviewing. In particular, individuals with extensive field experience must be prompted to

(a) *Find problems, rather than work around them.* Field interviewers have typically learned "to make a question work," for example, by rewording it so that a confused respondent will ultimately provide a codeable response. It must be emphasized that our task in the lab is different: to *find,* rather than to adjust for, flaws in the questions.

(b) *Slow down.* Interviewers tend to work as fast as possible in the field, usually in order to complete the interview before the respondent becomes uncooperative. Interviewers must be reminded to work at an unhurried pace in the cognitive lab.

(c) *Be flexible and forgiving of formatting problems.* Field interviewers often focus on formatting and structural features such as question layout and skip pattern errors. Unless assessing these is a key objective of cognitive testing (e.g., when testing a self-administered format), interviewers must be instructed to instead focus on questionnaire *content*, as the format might be extremely rough. Similarly, field interviewers are taught not to deviate from the instructions contained in the instrument. In contrast, cognitive interviewers must be comfortable with adapting to situations in which draft questionnaires contain sequencing instructions that are incorrect or completely absent (which often involves the rule "Find the next question that makes sense to ask").

As an important caveat, even if field interviewers can conduct the cognitive interview effectively, they may not be particularly adept in other key phases of this activity. Cosenza (2001) found that professional survey interviewing staff who were given minimal specific training in cognitive techniques could administer standardized probe questions and identify problems, but were not especially effective in determining why these problems occurred, or in suggesting modifications to address question defects.

Continuing Education in Cognitive Interviewing

There is a tendency for organizations using cognitive interviewing to train a group of individuals (or themselves) in this endeavor and to then set them loose without much further monitoring or retraining. The eventual effects of this approach are unknown. It is very possible that, over time, interviewers begin to diverge, practice idiosyncratic techniques, and develop bad habits. In fact, the failure to control discrepant approaches even within the same lab is partly responsible for objections by Conrad and Blair (1996, 2001) and Tucker (1997) that cognitive interviewing practices sometimes lack appropriate scientific rigor.

Just as scientists must come to some agreement on how procedures should be carried out in the biology lab, cognitive interviewers should strive for common standards by reviewing each other's work (e.g., by reviewing videotapes), meeting periodically to revisit overall approaches, addressing harmful tendencies that may have developed (in particular, leading forms of probing), and considering developments in the field that may point to the need to alter practices. For example, with respect to the latter, I have recently been informed by several practitioners that they have begun to experiment with a procedure in which two staff members jointly administer the cognitive interview. One asks the target questions as written, and the other asks probe questions. This practice may be effective in helping the subject to keep straight the distinction between these fundamental types of queries; conversely, this division of labor may be unnecessary or confusing.

The inherent flexibility of cognitive interviewing is a strength but also a potential danger if we cannot be self-critical, open to change, and sensitive to the fact that rugged individualism in approach may not always be a virtue. A useful example of such revisitation was provided by the aforementioned Beatty, Schechter, et al. (1997) study, which systematically evaluated several categories of probing behavior by each NCHS cognitive laboratory interviewer. Although that study was not done to evaluate individual interviewers, the general approach would be useful for monitoring performance and providing an important quality-control function.

Chapter Summary

- Effective cognitive interviewing is not a function of academic qualifications but of interpersonal skills; the best interviewers are able to flexibly adapt to the unexpected and to generally make subjects comfortable in order to induce them to speak freely.
- Interviewers should also be familiar with surveys in general, demonstrate technical skill in questionnaire design, have knowledge of the CASM approach, and be familiar with the topic of the survey.
- Training can be accomplished through a multi-step approach that focuses on observation of both field and cognitive interviews, a systematic introduction to each step in the cognitive testing process, and active participation in the conduct of both mock and real cognitive interviews.
- Even for very experienced cognitive interviewers, training should be an ongoing process in order to ensure that bad habits are not developed and that an agreed-upon approach is applied across the interviewing staff.

10

Planning and Conducting Cognitive Interviews

Chapter Overview

If not already transparent, my bias has been to focus on the application of verbal probing in the conduct of the cognitive interview and to focus considerably on the details of that activity. Probing does not occur in a vacuum, however, but exists as part of a wider cognitive testing process involving planning, subject recruitment, and attention to myriad logistical issues. This chapter therefore adopts a more operational stance, viewing cognitive interviewing as an activity that is conducted in a real-world context where we must attend to deadlines, coordinate activities, and make efficient use of limited resources.

Fitting Cognitive Testing Into the Overall Design Sequence

Cognitive interviewing fits into a more general developmental sequence. Again, before jumping into the lab to test questions, it pays to carefully develop working drafts that pass appropriate "first-stage" tests (see Aday, 1996, and Chapter 2 of this book). Table 10.1 places cognitive interviewing in the context of these activities as well as those that may occur subsequent to testing.

Cognitive interviewing is just one of the 10 steps identified, and the timing of this step is vital. In particular, we don't want to make the mistake of testing too early or too late in the process. If accomplished too early, other influences (e.g., thinking about objectives, finding precedent surveys) can interfere with a smooth testing process; if too late, there may not be enough time to make changes based on interview results.

Table 10.1   Sequence of the Questionnaire Development Process

(1) Determine *analytic objectives* of the investigation

(2) Interview experts or "informants," respecify objectives and approach as necessary, develop listing of general concepts to be covered.

(3) Conduct *focus groups** as necessary to further develop key concepts.

(4) Translate concepts into draft survey questions.

(5) Check the fit between questions and objectives (Do the former address the latter?).

(6) Conduct expert appraisal of questions for common pitfalls.

(7) Evaluate questions empirically through cognitive interviewing.

(8) Produce field test version of questionnaire.

(9) If possible, conduct field-based pretesting procedures such as *behavior coding.**

(10) Finalize questionnaire and administer in field environment.

---

*See Chapter 14.

COGNITIVE TESTING IN CONTEXT: A CLOSER LOOK

Figure 10.1 further magnifies Step 7 above, outlining in detail the activities normally associated with the cognitive testing process. This flowchart embodies several features and operations that are, in practice, somewhat variable. I will discuss several of these, starting from the top.

Preparing for the Interview: Subject Recruitment

Prior to the interview we must develop the questionnaire to be evaluated and then the cognitive testing protocol containing our probe questions. I have described in some depth the activities involved in developing cognitive probe questions and placing these in the questionnaire (Appendix 1 contains a sample protocol, with instructions for both interviewers and subjects, and probes embedded in the tested questionnaire). Most importantly, however, we must locate suitable subjects on which to test our

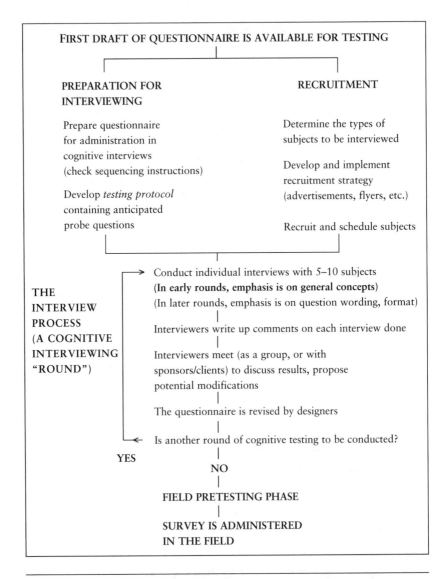

Figure 10.1   Cognitive Testing in the Context of Questionnaire Development

materials. *From a practical point of view, recruitment is the "500 pound gorilla" that determines the feasibility of cognitive interviewing.* We may have a questionnaire to test, highly trained and motivated interviewers, and a ready protocol, but we must then locate subjects who are appropriate, willing, and available when we want to conduct interviews. Several considerations present themselves:

WHO IS APPROPRIATE? DEFINING
AND RECRUITING THE "RIGHT" PEOPLE

Some survey questionnaires are targeted toward the general population (e.g., a federal census; a survey of attitudes toward a political candidate); others focus on defined subpopulations (e.g., children, users of illicit drugs, dry cleaning equipment operators). Subjects recruited for cognitive testing optimally should exhibit demographic and other characteristics that parallel those of the intended survey population. General survey populations typically call for general recruitment (e.g., any person 18 or older), whereas surveys of special populations call for a more focused recruitment effort (e.g., parents of children under 18; proprietors of dry cleaning establishments).

As a complication, however, surveys often serve a filtering function; they start out with a general population but rely on what are variably labeled *screener, filter,* or *gateway* questions to identify a specific subpopulation of individuals of interest. A survey on drug use may present a screener checklist to all surveyed adults asking about use of a variety of drugs in the past 12 months (marijuana, cocaine, misuse of prescription medications); a podiatry survey will screen for people with foot problems. We consider those who respond positively to critical gateway items to be positive occurrences and normally follow them up with more detailed questions.[1] In such cases, designers must be concerned with how well the gatekeeping questions function. If they are too liberal, they allow too many respondents to be counted ("enumerated") and to branch to the follow-up set; if too conservative, we erroneously exclude those who are in truth eligible.

In order to evaluate gateway questions, *it is important to conduct pretesting on both people who do and those who do not exhibit the key characteristic(s) of interest* (e.g., drug use, foot problems). This practice helps us to determine whether gatekeepers serve the vital function of appropriately routing respondents for follow-up. For example, subject recruitment for cognitive testing of the 1990 National Health Interview Survey Podiatry Supplement was broad in scope and not limited to advertising for "people with foot problems." Interviews of such people might determine that the tested questions successfully identified true positive occurrences. What would remain unknown, however, is the extent to which the critical screening questions in effect set the bar too low and falsely identified people who did *not* have the types of problems intended. Similarly, Loomis (2000) tested a Current Population Survey on welfare reform through active recruitment of both subjects who received assistance from welfare programs and those who did not. Although cognitive interviewing will normally not tell us whether our gatekeeper questions are set at exactly the right level, it often informs us when they are grossly inadequate and likely to lead to biased survey results (e.g., a gateway question asking generally about "any type of foot problems" was found to produce many false positives and was rejected in favor of a more specific checklist that screened for a number of defined conditions).

LOOKING IN THE RIGHT PLACES TO GET SUBJECTS

Subjects are typically recruited through newspapers, flyers, service agencies, and support groups. If payment will be involved, flyers and newspaper ads should emphasize this fact (and monetary incentives do tend to be very effective). Figure 10.2 is a mock newspaper advertisement (the information required for such ads is often determined by an organization's Institutional Review Board, or IRB).

Statistical sampling methods are not normally used to obtain laboratory subjects, although there are exceptions: Caspar and Biemer (1999) used a geographical block method to select subjects; and Willis, Bornstein, et al. (2000) tested a telephone survey by recruiting subjects via random digit dialing by a telephone call center, scheduling interviews (with promise of payment), and then calling back at the appointed time to conduct the cognitive interview over the telephone. Willis et al. reported that the individuals they interviewed in this manner were at a somewhat lower educational level than those typically recruited for cognitive studies, although in other regards—in particular, how they responded to the task—they appeared to be very similar.

Most frequently, recruitment depends on quota sampling, in which the recruiter strives to obtain a range of ages, genders, and socioeconomic levels, or to select from each major group of interest (e.g., for a survey of child custody, Schaeffer and Dykema [in press] selected divorced mothers, divorced fathers, mothers involved in paternity cases, and fathers involved in such cases). Overall, our focus should be on subject *variation* across a range of characteristics, as opposed to statistical representativeness. That is, we cannot produce a statistical sample; rather, we desire representation in the sense that we are able to *interview the greatest cross-section of the population as is possible, in order to identify a wide range of problems.*

RECRUITING THE RIGHT PEOPLE:
A CROSS-CULTURAL PERSPECTIVE

Chapter 7 introduced the notion of the ethnographic interview as a means for conducting the interview in a way that is sensitive to issues of

---

PAID VOLUNTEERS NEEDED

TO TEST SURVEY QUESTIONS

Cognitive Interview Associates in Rockville MD needs volunteers to spend one hour answering survey questions on a variety of health topics.

We need WOMEN aged 18-44 who have AT LEAST ONE CHILD, and we especially need women who have children under age 3.

All information is confidential, and you will receive $40.

For more information, please call
(301) 555-1234

Figure 10.2   Sample Newspaper Advertisement for Subject Recruitment

cultural variation. To successfully conduct such testing, we must address cultural variation during the recruitment phase. That is, beyond recruiting the groups that specifically address the topic of the questionnaire (e.g., the working and the unemployed), we strive to include the natural range of demographic and cultural variation in the population, on the assumption that the survey may not operate uniformly across subgroups (see Johnson, 1998, and Kagawa-Singer & Blackhall, 2001, for a discussion of the issue of cross-cultural equivalence of survey questions).

As an eye-opening example of the importance of *who* we interview, Miller (2002c) conducted cognitive interviews in a very poor rural area of Mississippi, to study the way that variations in background health care systems and cultural beliefs affect the adequacy of health-related survey questions, such as those on cancer screening tests (e.g., mammography and pap smear). Miller found that the problems she observed were qualitatively similar to those obtained from previous testing in the Washington, DC, area, but were much intensified. She points out that limiting subject recruitment to constrained geographic areas, or among homogeneous groups, may distort the picture obtained from cognitive interviews. Remedying this problem is admittedly challenging, especially because vital populations of interest may be difficult to recruit. It does help to conduct interviews at locations that are comfortable for otherwise reticent groups, such as medical clinics, offices of service agencies, churches, libraries, or even in subjects' homes, as long as privacy can be maintained. In determining the interview location, the main focus should be "What do we have to do to interview the people we need?"

The Interviewing Process

Once our recruited subject arrives at our laboratory or other interview location, we must take pains to communicate our purposes and procedures. Normally the person will be asked to read and sign an IRB-approved confidentiality form that explains the entire testing process. Further, at the start of the interview, it is important to orally convey several points. Here is a somewhat generic script that incorporates some of these elements, assuming that the interview involves concurrent probing[2] (see Appendix 1 for a slightly different approach):

> Thanks for coming here today to help us test out our survey questions. At this point, we are *not* collecting information about you. Instead, we're first trying out our questions on a few people such as yourself, so that we can improve them. I will read you the questions, and I'd like you to answer them. However, I'd also like to hear about what you're thinking. Please try to think aloud—just tell me everything that comes to mind, whether it seems important or not. I'll also be asking you about how you come up with your answers and how you're interpreting the questions, and I'll take lots of notes. If any question seems unclear, is hard to answer, or doesn't make sense, please tell me that—don't be shy. We'll just take our time and get as far as we can in an hour. Do you have any questions before we start?
>
> Ok, here we go: [READ FIRST QUESTION]

A few issues for emphasis throughout the interview:

(a) *Focus on questions, not answers.* The interviewer stresses that he or she is not primarily collecting survey data on subjects, but is testing the questions.

(b) *Emphasize our goal of finding problems.* Make clear that although we are asking the subject to answer the survey questions as carefully as possible, we are primarily interested in the ways that they arrived at those answers and the problems they encountered. Therefore any detailed help they can give us is of interest, even if it seems irrelevant or trivial. Again, as described in Chapter 8, it is very important to orient all defects toward the questions, rather than the subject: rather than asking "Do you understand this?" phrase this inquiry as "Is the question clear?"

(c) *Introduce think-aloud.* If thinking aloud is to be emphasized, tell subjects, at the least, to "think out loud to the extent possible, so we can tell what you are thinking about when you answer the questions." In many cases this introduction may not produce a great amount of continuous think-aloud, in the classic sense. However, as DeMaio and Landreth (in press) have pointed out, some subjects helpfully think aloud no matter what we tell them.

(d) *Help the subject to feel uninhibited in expressing difficulties.* To reiterate a previous point, subjects normally tend not to be critical of tested questions, in part because they simply don't notice problems. However, another contributing factor may be that norms of politeness in everyday conversation prevent them from saying "That's a totally ridiculous question!" As we do want to hear this from subjects, it can be helpful to detach the interviewer from the questions by adding, "I didn't write these questions, so don't worry about hurting my feelings. My job is to find out what's wrong with them." This helps to "bring out" subjects who may otherwise strive to avoid insulting the interviewer.

Twelve Logistical Issues and Considerations

Issue 1: How long should an interview be? Although cognitive interviews can take from 15 minutes to 2 hours (Hunter & Hughes, 2003), a common view is that a 1-hour cognitive interview is reasonable (see Hess, Rothgeb, & Nichols, 1998, for an example). Most subjects can attend for an hour, but longer periods make excessive demands on attention and motivation (for the interviewer, as well!). In general, the interview process should be flexible, and questionnaires that are too long to test in one session can sometimes be broken up into separate pieces, especially early in development.

Issue 2: How long a questionnaire can be tested in a 1-hour cognitive interview? This tends to be difficult to determine, as the concept of questionnaire length is a vague notion that is variably expressed in terms of number of questions, number of pages, and administration time. Given our 1-hour limit, time is normally the relevant concern, and the pertinent question becomes: How long a questionnaire, in "field-minutes," can be tested in a 1-hour cognitive interview? As a general rule of thumb, I suggest aiming for a 2:1 ratio between "cognitive interview time" and "field time," so that *60 minutes of cognitive interviewing time will be used to test a questionnaire that requires 30 minutes to complete in the field.* At least somewhat close to this, in an empirical study of cognitive interviewing, DeMaio and Landreth (in press) report an approximate 3:1 ratio between cognitive interview and field durations (which implies that the instrument to be tested should be no longer than 20 minutes to fit comfortably within the cognitive interview).

Keep in mind that these estimates can vary widely depending on the amount of probing the interviewer does and subject characteristics that control the amount of the questionnaire that is covered during testing. For example, cognitive testing of a tobacco questionnaire will normally involve a high proportion of subjects who smoke, and this increases administration time relative to the fielded survey, as the latter will mainly contain nonsmokers who skip most questions. Predicting the amount that one will get through in the cognitive interview is also difficult because questionnaires often have skip patterns that result in widely varying questionnaire lengths for different individuals, and because subjects vary in overall speed and in the degree to which they respond in detailed ways to the targeted survey questions or to probe questions.

Issue 3: How many interviews should an interviewer do in one day? Cognitive interviewing can be a taxing activity, especially if the interviewer is actively listening to the respondent and formulating Emergent forms of probing (as opposed to just following a fully standardized Proactive protocol). I recommend that any individual do *no more than three interviews in a single day.* As always, exceptions apply. I have, on occasion, been engaged in very concentrated activities, for example, traveling to a drug treatment clinic where interviewers each carried out up to six interviews in a day. This was certainly productive and efficient. I would not, however, have chosen to do this every day for a week.

Issue 4: What is an appropriate subject payment (remuneration)? As of 2004, the industry standard appears to be *$25–$50 for a one-hour interview,* depending mainly on how difficult it is to induce individuals to participate. For subjects who truly represent a "needle in a haystack," even more may be necessary. The proper amount to pay depends in part on variables such as the subjects' travel time. Payment should be enough that it is not simply a token remuneration; this way, we are less likely to recruit individuals who are practiced volunteers and who may participate mainly out of academic interest (and who may therefore be very different from the usual household survey respondent). Keep in mind that money is not always the proper inducement—professionals with high levels of personal income may be more responsive to a request from a respected colleague than to a money-waving recruiter.[3]

Issue 5: How many interviews should be conducted? This question pertains to both (a) the number to be conducted within a testing round, and (b) the number of rounds to be conducted. Concerning the former, this determination depends on several factors:

(a) *Problem seriousness.* If it becomes obvious after several interviews that there are major problems to be rectified, then there is little benefit in conducting more interviews before modifications are made to the questionnaire. Especially in the very early stages of development, as few as two interviews may be sufficient to cause us to stop and retrench (Hess, 1999). This may seem grossly insufficient, but often simply addresses what is best termed "a goof"— a clear flaw that we should have noticed earlier, but didn't.

(b) *Limitations to "beating a dead horse."* Even if it appears that more interviews should be done, it is seldom necessary to conduct more than 12–15 interviews before meeting or delivering comments concerning that round of interview results. If subtle problems exist, this may require many interviews, but we do reach a point of diminishing return, where additional interviews obtain only a little more useful information. Decisions about when to stop and revise also depend greatly on whether additional testing rounds are to be conducted. If so, note that questions that have not yet been altered will receive further testing in those later rounds, such that the effective sample size for those questions is increased.

(c) *Operational limitation.* Federally supported research that involves data collection from the public is limited by the Office of Management and Budget to nine individuals for whom data will be analyzed as a set, unless a special type of generic clearance for cognitive testing is obtained (this is normally done only by the large U.S. federal labs at Census, BLS, and NCHS). This then becomes the ceiling for a round of cognitive interviews. Once questions are revised, a new round can then be conducted with another group of nine subjects.

Concerning the second issue, the number of rounds to be conducted, one of the greatest strengths of the cognitive interviewing technique is the ability to test our modifications subsequent to a first testing round. Therefore *it is always helpful to be able to conduct at least two such rounds.* In fact, I argue that if the objective is to improve the questionnaire, as opposed to simply evaluating a static instrument, it is more useful to conduct three rounds of 9 subjects than one round of 27. After the questionnaire has been revised based on the comments from meetings and on any discussions with clients or sponsors, a new round of interviewing can be conducted to test the changes made and to provide additional testing of questionnaire segments that were not yet changed. The nature of the interviewing rounds tends to change over the course of development of a questionnaire. Early in the process, findings relate not only to particular question wordings but to more global issues, such as the appropriateness of the survey measurement of major concepts that the questionnaire is attempting to cover. Later rounds focus mainly on polishing specific question wordings.

But, one could ask, how do we know when to finish testing? A questionnaire presumably could be tested forever and still have problems (as the perfect survey question may not exist). Optimally, we test until all the major problems have been detected and satisfactorily addressed. Usually, however, this ends up being a moot issue. Surveys are subject to strict developmental timeframes, and limited time is available for pretesting. As a result, our usual approach is to conduct as many iterative rounds as practical (usually up to three), prior to a field pretest or field administration. Although limited lab testing may not produce a perfect questionnaire, the final product should be markedly better than if not subjected to any evaluation of this type. To cite a perhaps overused expression, the perfect is very much the enemy of the good.

Issue 6: How much time is required for the various activities? Several critical periods are generally involved. The amount of time required to conduct the cognitive interviews is important, but practitioners must also allow time to develop a testing protocol, to write up testing results, to confer with other interviewers, and to modify the questionnaire both between rounds and subsequent to the final round. Generally it requires at least a week, and more often several, to recruit subjects, especially if newspaper ads will be developed and run. Conducting a round of nine interviews then requires 1 to 2 weeks; writing up and aggregating results takes anywhere from a day to several weeks; and we typically require another week or more to consider revisions and to draft a new version.

Rounds that are separated by a month are comfortable; reducing this time is possible but puts a premium on close attention to planning and staying on track.

An activity that eats up more time than one might imagine is the interview itself. Even though each interview may take only an hour, the entire interviewing process requires considerably more time. Preparation, interviewing, and writing up results usually take at least 3 hours and sometimes considerably longer. This appears to be an area in which cognitive interviewers vary considerably; organizations that require interviewers to review video or audio recordings of every interview need to allow more time.

Issue 7: What kind of staffing is needed to run a cognitive testing operation? Ambitious practitioners may be interested in not just conducting interviewing, but also in establishing a cognitive laboratory. Based on experience working in both staff-oriented (Federal government) and project-based (contract research organization) environments, I have found that there is no single organizational structure that is necessary to support an effective cognitive interviewing capacity. It is very helpful to develop a cadre of staff members who have a history of cognitive interviewing experience to avoid turnover and constant retraining. It also helps greatly to have a laboratory manager who is responsible for subject recruitment—placing advertisements, developing flyers, making phone calls, scheduling, and generally monitoring interviewing operations. At least one staff member should have experience in communicating with clients or sponsors of questionnaires. Finally, to revisit a consistent theme, staff must have the questionnaire design experience necessary to translate laboratory findings into realistic and practical solutions.

Issue 8: Is it necessary to have multiple interviewers? Yet another operational variable concerns the number of cognitive interviewers who should be engaged for a particular project or testing round. Apparently successful projects have involved a single cognitive interviewer (e.g., Hess, 1999), and I have done this as well. However, I feel that even if the size of the interviewing sample is small (9 or fewer), it is useful to involve several interviewers and have a variety of interviewer contributions. That is, it seems at least as beneficial to have two interviewers conduct four interviews apiece as it is to have one interviewer conduct eight. This statement is likely controversial, as it violates scientific principles that direct us to reduce sources of error by limiting variance such as that due to the interviewer. However, I do not necessarily view the individual contributions of interviewers as error, but rather as a source of information necessary for evaluating and improving survey questions. Further, I have often been reassured by the level of overall correspondence between independent interviewer findings and appreciative of the additional perspectives gained (or just happy to be able to share the load!). There is little direct evidence on the efficacy of various interviews-per-interviewer ratios, so this is another facet of the cognitive interview that is open to debate. In practice, logistical issues (such as availability of other cognitive interviewers) often drive these decisions.

Issue 9: Is there any value in limited cognitive interviewing efforts? The aforementioned notions of cognitive laboratories, permanent staff, and multiple players might alienate potential practitioners who are "lone agents" and who may object that they do not have the resources to put together a cognitive laboratory. So is there still value in conducting small amounts of ad hoc testing, perhaps with just one interviewer? Although it is of course beneficial to rely on the services of a full-service cognitive laboratory, this is not necessary. Small-scale informal cognitive interviews of friends, colleagues, and family members do appear to be effective in at least identifying problems that the designer has overlooked (that is, in serving as a backup to basic questionnaire design). We must, of course, keep in mind that results based on two or three subjects could be misleading. However, I find it difficult to believe, especially if we remain aware of the possibility of bias, that the conduct of any number of cognitive interviews produces worse results than the alternative of doing none at all.

Issue 10: What are the physical requirements of the cognitive laboratory? Organizations that conduct relatively large numbers of cognitive interviews—such as NCHS; the Bureau of Labor Statistics; the Census Bureau; Westat; RTI International; and Abt Associates—have dedicated laboratory facilities containing multiple interviewing rooms, video and audio equipment, and remote observation capability. Although one-way mirrors are sometimes used, an alternative is to rely on live video that is distributed to one or more observation rooms. Such capabilities are important for permanent cognitive laboratories, but for most applications *cognitive interviewing does not require special physical environments or sophisticated recording equipment.* As mentioned above, many interviews have been conducted outside the cognitive laboratory, such as in service organization offices or homes. Any quiet and private room, such as a conference room or empty office, can serve as a "laboratory." Equipment needs are also minimal; a portable tape recorder is valuable, as it is useful to record interviews, and most subjects do not object as long as privacy and confidentiality requirements are met.

Issue 11: Maintaining privacy and confidentiality. Discussion of the recording of interviews leads directly to a critical point: We must at all times be careful of issues of privacy and confidentiality, especially where private or sensitive information is to be gathered. If subjects are to be videotaped, it is helpful to hide the camera or to make it unobtrusive (although informed consent from the subject is still necessary). A separate consent for videotaping or audiotaping can be used so that subjects can consent to an interview but not to recording. Taped interviews must be carefully handled; they should be stored in a locked location, labeled with subject ID numbers rather than personal identifiers such as names, and destroyed within a reasonable time after they are reviewed.

If tapes are to be shown to collaborators or colleagues, this must be made clear in the consent form. Under no circumstances should these be shown in classes or in scientific conferences unless the subject has given specific consent for such use. Finally, consent should normally be obtained in writing, unless the only contact with subjects will be over the telephone and written consent cannot be obtained in some manner such as through the mail. Again, institutional IRB regulations may govern cognitive interviewing operations. Even if not, we should be conservative in the use of information that we obtain, and regard each interview as a private conversation to be held in strict confidence.

Issue 12: In an organizational environment, how should clients and sponsors be integrated into the process? Sponsors are mainly involved in the communication of results, to be discussed in the next chapter. It is, however, beneficial if our sponsors participate in cognitive testing, especially as observers. Clients or sponsors should be encouraged to observe interviews, or to listen to recordings, as the impact of a question that is confusing or long-winded is very difficult to ignore when such evidence is presented directly. Very often, where abstract discussions concerning the flaws contained in a questionnaire are unconvincing, the evidence from only a few laboratory interviews can have a potent impact. This is a point worth stressing: Beyond its strength in *identifying* problems, a major positive feature of the cognitive laboratory approach is the relative *persuasiveness* of the information it collects (seeing truly is believing).

Chapter Summary

- Cognitive interviewing is best placed at an intermediate point between initial question development and fielding.
- Subject recruitment is the key to cognitive testing as a process— locating the right people and motivating them to participate requires active steps such as advertisement, perhaps working with community contacts, and appropriate payment.
- The outcome of the cognitive interview process is influenced by the manner in which we introduce the task; we should make clear our objectives and the subject's role in helping us to achieve them. In particular, we must ensure that subjects are comfortable relating all of their thoughts to us in an uncensored manner.
- A range of logistical issues present themselves. Decisions must be made on a case-by-case basis, but I have made a number of recommendations. Most importantly: (a) hour-long cognitive interviews are effective; (b) within a testing round, 8–12 interviews are usually sufficient; (c) it is useful to conduct multiple iterative rounds and to stop after three of these; (d) within production environments, staffing should include a laboratory manager who can handle recruitment and operations; but (e) it is not necessary to develop a formal laboratory, and even small-scale efforts by a single practitioner can produce gains in questionnaire quality.

Notes

1. Although it is beyond the scope of this book to fully discuss this approach, note that follow-up questions can be used either to enhance our knowledge of positively identified cases (e.g., drug users), or as a check to determine if the initial gateway items have appropriately diagnosed a true positive case (e.g., those suffering from serious mental disorder).

2. If probing is only to be done retrospectively, it is more appropriate to conduct the interview "straight"—that is, as though it is an actual data collection—and instructions emphasizing the detection of problems are then introduced prior to retrospective probing.

3. On the other hand, in hundreds of interviews, I have only had monetary remuneration refused one or two times. When in doubt, pay!

11

Analyzing and Documenting Cognitive Interview Results

Chapter Overview

By diligently studying and applying the techniques presented to this point, the reader can become proficient in the conduct of cognitive interviews and even become a master prober, if such a designation makes sense. Unlike conducting a symphony orchestra, however, interviewing is not itself the desired outcome, but rather a means for producing a coherent set of results and recommendations that become the basis for further action. To be efficient and effective in this regard requires procedures for:

(1) chronicling what we find from the interviews;

(2) performing data-reduction steps that result in concise statements; and

(3) successfully conveying this information to collaborators and decision makers.

There is no formula that we can apply to any of these requirements, as the journey between the cognitive lab and the final outcome report typically involves a significant degree of judgment and interpretation. Put another way, *the application of cognitive interviewing procedures does not in itself provide precise direction in question design.* To borrow a report title from Conrad et al. (2000), "Verbal Reports are Data" to be used in making decisions—but do not in themselves supply us with the answers we seek. The nature of the steps that cognitive interviewers take between data collection and decision making is largely uncharted territory, so I devote this chapter to issues of analysis, documentation, and communication.

Characterizing Cognitive Interview Outcomes

Earlier chapters were devoted to the questions "What are we looking for?" and "How do I find it?" Here I follow up with "What do we find?" and "What do I do with it?" In considering how to process our results, it is useful to first review the major categories of outcomes that emerge from cognitive testing:

---

(1) *Item-specific recommendations* for changes to wording (cognitive, logical/structural, culturally oriented defects)

(2) Need for further *specification of objectives* or the manner in which the questions satisfy them

(3) Problems related to *ordering* (of items, sections, and so on) and other interactions between survey questions

(4) Problems related to reduction in overall instrument *length or burden*

(5) Limitations on *what can be asked* of survey respondents using the intended procedures

---

1. *Item-specific recommendations.* This category constitutes the result most consistent with our usual dogma: cognitive interviewing results provide information that we use as a basis for recommending (or making) changes to question wording, such as, "Instead of 'oncologist,' questions should use the term 'doctor who treats cancer.'" This is an important outcome—but not the only positive one.

2. *Respecification of objectives.* Cognitive interviews force further consideration and respecification of unclear question objectives and result in comments such as the following:

Target question [ASK IF 12–17]: Do you ever smoke alone or by yourself?

COMMENT (Interviewer #2): The intent is unclear. Are we interested in finding out if (a) they smoke "alone" in the sense that they're not with anyone else at the time (like hiding in a closet at home, driving alone), or (b) they are "alone" in that they may be with others but are the only one smoking? One subject said that he smokes when he is with his nonsmoking friends and in that case is the only smoker. But he is not alone, so he didn't know how to answer it.

This is a classic example of an insight obtained through the testing of flesh-and-blood lab subjects. The subject was able to provide useful information based on his elaboration of life experience. As a result of this one interview, the designer is forced to reevaluate objectives and presumably to better specify the question intent. Cognitive interview write-ups pertaining to such issues are most helpful when they (a) convey precisely how the concept is nuanced or multi-faceted and (b) also suggest how specific question wordings can be linked to each alternative objective. However, we may not be able to suggest precise solutions, as the establishment and satisfaction of measurement objectives often presents a morass of complex issues requiring the input of staff other than the cognitive interviewing team. Consequently, the outcome of testing is often a question rather than a recommendation. As Rothgeb (2001) observes, "obviously, without the objectives it is difficult to know whether a question will obtain the necessary information required for analysis" (p. 2).

An important variation on this theme is a situation that I have already discussed often enough that it warrants its own designation: the *Wrong Question Effect*. The objective is clear enough, but the target question, as a measurement tool, simply missed the boat in addressing it. An example would be attempting to measure sources of financial livelihood through questions on formal, legal, money-based employment when surveyed individuals are, in truth, involved in informal, illicit, or barter-based activities that we have failed to account for. Our comments, therefore, will address the logical/structural failings of the instrument and often suggest how the questions can be refocused to eradicate erroneous assumptions the designer has made.

3. *Issues of ordering and other interactive effects.* Although probing is focused on the individual question, cognitive interview outcomes very often transcend the question level and explicitly address problems related to the interaction between items. Cognitive interview results related to question ordering effects sometimes correspond nicely to findings from the basic (as opposed to applied) CASM literature (see Chapter 3). For instance, consistent with data from Schwarz, Strack, and Mai (1991), cognitive interview results suggest that when we administer items that are conceptually related,

but that convey different levels of specificity, the order in which these appear is a critical factor. For example, through cognitive testing of a questionnaire on complementary and alternative medicine, I observed that when subjects were asked separately about their use of (1) an acupuncturist and (2) a Chinese healer, asking the more general item (Chinese healer) first induced them to include the more specific member of that category (i.e., acupuncturist) that, unbeknownst to them, will appear later in the list. In fashioning recommendations that address this overlap, we might advise reversing the order so that the more specific term appears first. Under this ordering, respondents are more likely to report this item and then to exclude it when next presented with the more general one (in effect, interpreting the latter as "Any other type of Chinese healer").

Another category of adverse cross-item effects uncovered by cognitive interviews is gross redundancy; Wilson et al. (2000) reported that a pregnancy questionnaire they tested contained a total of 16 different reference periods and was, as a result, confusing to subjects. At a more global level, cognitive interviewers may also recommend changing the order of question subsections that jump between topics or ask questions in a way that will induce bias due to the effects of earlier questions on later ones. As a perennial issue, health researchers frequently measure both attitudes and behaviors toward issues such as medical tests for disease—yet in the cognitive laboratory, asking either set is found to sometimes influence the other (i.e., asking about what I *think I should do* influences my reporting of what I *have done,* and vice versa). In such cases, the researcher might determine which set is of primary importance and place that first. Or, we can attempt to determine through our testing process whether carryover effects are asymmetrical, such that one ordering will likely produce less bias than the other, and proceed on that basis.

4. *Issues of burden.* A further category of outcome addresses overall burden of the instrument, or of particular sections or questions (Caspar & Biemer, 1999). It may not appear from an armchair-based review that answering a checklist of 50 varieties of physical activity is excessive, but forcing our subjects through the list may change our minds. It is, however, difficult to assess overall field burden in the cognitive lab—on the one hand, if we are doing substantial probing, this itself may contribute to perceived burden, relative to the (unprobed) field situation, and certainly increases interview duration. On the other hand, cognitive lab subjects tend to be attentive and patient, relative to the field (especially if we are paying them), which alleviates subjective burden.

It is possible to administer a questionnaire straight, without probes (or to probe retrospectively), when our testing objective is to measure section or overall administration time and to analyze those times. This can be risky, however, unless we also factor in the degree to which our lab interviews are representative of field interviews, in terms of interviewer behavior (speed of asking questions), subject behavior (speed with which they answer), and subject characteristics that affect burden (mainly those determining the parts of the questionnaire that are administered). Although the cognitive laboratory has been used for such purposes (Caspar & Biemer, 1999), I do not view timing measurement as the main strength of the cognitive method.

5. *Limitations on what can be studied via survey questionnaire.* Not everything we attempt to measure in the survey environment is necessarily measurable at reasonable cost simply because we choose to script and administer survey questions. Based on the notion that "You can't get blood from a stone," there may be no manner in which we can feasibly modify questions such that they satisfy our measurement objectives. Instead, we may face inherent limitations because (a) the topic is so complex that it would require more questions than we can devote, or (b) respondents cannot give us the information because they failed to encode it (i.e., they don't know) or are unable to retrieve it from memory at the time we request it (i.e., they can't remember).

For example, Hunter and Hughes (2003) discovered that a survey on pension and retirement benefits might be impeded by knowledge limitations, based on the simple observation that many of their test subjects knew very little about their own benefit plans. Akkerboom and Luiten (1996) nicely summarize the relevant issue as "a balance between information supply and demand" (p. 911). An important outcome of cognitive interviewing is therefore the assessment of what is and isn't likely to exist in the minds of most respondents, and of that part that does exist, what part is reportable, given that the survey interview normally presupposes almost instantaneous retrieval (as it does us no good for the answer to spring to the respondent's mind an hour, day, or week after the interview).

In sum, cognitive interviewing results in a wide spectrum of findings, some dealing with questions, some with the questionnaire, and others with the survey in a broad sense. In keeping with the philosophy that examples can be illuminating, Appendix 2 contains a compilation of questions that were tested in several cognitive laboratories. In particular,

I have included the findings obtained in these cognitive interviews and have chronicled the range of outcomes they represent.

The Analysis of Think-Aloud Interview Results

Having described the types of recommendations we strive to produce, I now turn to the issue of how we use cognitive interviewing results to this end. First I describe the analysis of the think-aloud protocol and then turn to interviews that are more dependent on verbal probing approaches. Although the conduct of the think-aloud interview is relatively straight-forward and uncomplicated, *protocol analysis* is not, as it is necessary to analyze a sometimes complicated and meandering stream of verbal information and to determine what part of this is relevant to evaluating and modifying survey questions.

INFORMAL ANALYSIS OF THE THINK-ALOUD PROTOCOL

The simplest means for analysis of the think-aloud protocol would be to write (very quickly!) as the subject is thinking aloud during the interview, in order to record issues that are significant. This is not ideal, as it involves some fairly great cognitive demands on the interviewer, who must listen carefully, pick out what is relevant, and record this while continuing to listen to the think-aloud stream and (under interviewer-administration) at the same time prepare to administer the next target question. Somewhat better, the interview can be live-evaluated by others; Bolton (1993) describes a procedure in which observers witness think-aloud interviews as they are conducted and form impressions of how well the tested questions function. A significant improvement is to videotape (or at least audiotape) the interview, and perhaps to transcribe it, so that it can be reviewed at leisure.

By following these informal means of review, the analyst (whether the cognitive interviewer or another researcher) can focus on all of the types of potential problems—cognitive or otherwise—discussed so far. The following example of a think-aloud stream transcription consists of the raw data produced by one subject in reaction to a question requesting income information:

> Well, the question is asking me about my "family income last month before taxes," but I'm having some difficulty with this. My son works, but . . . really, I don't even know how much he made last

month. Even for me . . . my work . . . I can't give you a monthly amount that's before taxes. I can tell you how much I get in my monthly paycheck after they take out the taxes . . . I can give you my annual total, before taxes . . . and divide by 12, I guess. But that isn't really it either, because there's a bonus in there too . . . so this . . . uh . . . if you really take it seriously it's just not that easy to come up with . . . I'd have to give you a round guess . . . or something.

The analyst reviews such think-aloud protocol segments on a question-by-question basis and records interpretive notes in descriptive and often open-ended form. If problems can be precisely described, and specifically linked to features of the presented questions, this information is useful. That is, clues such as the subject's obvious misunderstanding of a question, or an admission that she is at a loss to provide an answer confidently, lead to hypotheses that there are perhaps better ways to ask the question.

After reviewing the above transcript, the analyst may note that "the subject was unable to provide information about monthly income at the level of detail asked—he expressed difficulty in reporting for other family members, and could not report his own pre-tax monthly income." Once a number of subjects are interviewed, observations of this sort are summarized across interviews, especially where consistent themes can be noted ("None of my subjects could answer this question with any confidence"). The burden of determining what is—and what is not—a problem depends at each step on the ability of the analyst to systematically and objectively make decisions of this type. The analyst also provides written recommendations, such as to reconfigure the question so that it better matches respondent knowledge. For example, one might consider asking for net rather than gross monthly income, or presenting a series of income ranges, as this may avoid respondent agonizing over the specific amount.

USING CODING SCHEMES TO ANALYZE THINK-ALOUDS

The informal analysis of think-aloud protocols may appear subjective, imprecise, and impressionistic. An arguably more rigorous way to analyze think-alouds is to apply a formal coding scheme in which segments of the verbal protocol can be examined and assigned objective coding categories, based on the presence of explicit "triggers." Bickart and Felcher (1996) review such schemes, and propose their own, which contains several dozen coding categories such as:

(1) Respondent changes question to fit her knowledge

(2) Recall episode about self

(3) Positive qualitative frequency assessment about self

(4) Statement about what self normally does

(5) Trait knowledge about self

These codes do not so much reflect problems, per se, as the precise behaviors or strategies represented in the verbal protocol. As such, this type of system is mainly useful in basic CASM research concerning the survey response process (e.g., Bickart and Felcher examine the strategies that subjects use to answer behavioral frequency questions). This approach is of limited utility in the applied world of question pretesting, where our focus is more on problems with survey questions than on cognitive processes, per se.

A variant of the coded think-aloud is the automated computer-based coding described by Bolton and Bronkhorst (1996). This procedure is, in theory, useful for question evaluation, as it is intended to locate specific flaws. In brief, the system consists of the following steps:

(a) Audio-recording and transcription of the think-aloud interview

(b) Transcript preparation. The investigator (or more likely, a research assistant) divides the protocol into segments by marking the beginning and end of each individually identifiable part of the response to each target question.

(c) Code specification. For each tested question, the investigator assigns a list of verbal and nonverbal codes thought to be relevant to cognitive processing of the items, and a list of behaviors to be associated with each code. (For a question on overall quality of telephone service, Bolton and Bronkhorst assigned "Forget" as one code, and then developed a list containing the terms "forget," "don't remember," "can't think," and "I'm trying to think" as behaviors representing the "Forget" code.)

(d) Computer-based coding. Transcriptions of each written segment are submitted to a computer program that examines the segments for the presence of each behavior and assigns the appropriate code.

The outcome of this rather elaborate system is a report that indicates how frequently each type of code (such as Forget) is triggered in the verbal protocol for each evaluated question. If two versions of a questionnaire are tested, the researcher can assess whether one version produces fewer such codes than the other. An advantage the authors cite is that the computer is unbiased and objective. The obvious disadvantages of this approach are its complexity and, for many applications where quick turnaround of results is necessary, its impracticality, as the very intensive coding and processing operations described could simply not be conducted quickly. In their 1996 study, Bolton and Bronkhorst focused on a test of three target survey questions, whereas cognitive interviewers are normally responsible for evaluating dozens of questions at a time. Hence although the formal, systematic approach is better represented in the published literature than is the informal, it is doubtful that this is frequently carried out in practice. Finally, Bolton (1993) herself has noted that a limitation to automatic coding is that it is ineffective in diagnosing problems that require expert judgment, such as faulty question ordering. To some extent, subjective interpretation remains key to analysis.

Overall, despite the fact that think-aloud interviews are relatively easy to conduct, their analysis, especially in terms of precisely what types of utterances constitute "problems with questions," has not been as well-specified. Although most cognitive interviewers presumably rely on very informal means of analysis (and this is often left unspecified in testing reports), little research has been carried out to determine whether some levels of coding of the verbal protocol are more effective than others. Unanswered questions include the following:

(a) How useful is it to transcribe the think-aloud interview, as opposed to relying on live or recorded review?

(b) Is it worthwhile to invest the resources into formal coding, or is informal interpretation sufficient?

(c) Who should analyze the protocol, and what training and experience are necessary?

Analysis of the Probed Interview

DATA COLLECTION: HOW ARE RESPONSES TO PROBES COLLECTED?

An important distinction between think-aloud and probed interviews concerns the fundamental nature of our data. Under think-aloud, data consist of the subject's response—that is, the verbal stream. For the probed interview the situation is more complex and murky, as data to be analyzed can consist of either (a) the subject's responses to the probes, or (b) the interviewer's or analyst's notes and interpretations of subject responses. As a simple example, we can consider as data either the interviewer's comment that "The subject didn't understand the question" or the subject's statement "I don't get that question." Researchers disagree on exactly what our cognitive interview outcome data should consist of. Tourangeau, Rips, et al. (2000) have noted that "the conclusions drawn from cognitive interviewing are only loosely constrained by the actual data they produce" (p. 333). Conrad and colleagues (Conrad & Blair, 1996; Conrad et al., 2000) have suggested that interviewers should tighten this connection by relying more heavily on subject responses than on interviewer comments, given that the former are closer to the level of the observed data and therefore not filtered through the minds of interviewers. Beatty (2003, 2004) has conceptualized this debate as a philosophical divide—the cognitive interviewer as relatively passive data collector versus more active investigator.

In practice, cognitive interviewers tend to rely on a mix of information—some observed directly, some inferred. Typically, the data relevant to questionnaire evaluation do consist of the written comments of cognitive interviewers, who not only record the subject's answers to targeted questions but, more importantly, record free-form written notes as the subject answers probes. It is these data that must somehow be analyzed. This is yet another black box within the practice of cognitive interviewing—practitioners may indicate how they probed and what they believe they have found, but it is not especially clear what process they took to travel this distance (Cosenza, 2001). This is the topic of the next discussion.

INFORMAL ANALYSIS OF INTERVIEW RESULTS

I first will refer solely to informal means of analysis, rather than formal coding schemes. As for think-alouds, there are a variety of procedures for compiling the results from cognitive interviews that rely on heavy use of probes, and no one way is necessarily best. Some organizations will use a separate report for each interview that was conducted, in order to maintain the "case history" integrity of each interview; others will produce one written report which aggregates the results across interviews, in order to provide a more summarized, question-oriented version of the results. For readers desiring a specific recommendation in this regard, a fairly efficient means for processing data, representing a trade-off between completeness and timeliness, is the following:

1. *Review and document the individual interview.* To do this, one might transcribe each interview. This provides the full context for every asking of every question, and represents the most detailed level of analysis. I do not recommend this, however, as it is time consuming, costly, and tends to prevent us from seeing the forest for the trees. Rather, it is useful to rely on handwritten comments that we have made during the interview or during a subsequent review. These comments can later be typed into an electronic copy of the survey questionnaire under each target question, creating a record of each interview. The following is an example of a comment pertaining to a single question from one interview:

Q 8a. Would you say your health in general is excellent, very good, good, fair, or poor?

COMMENT: The subject is 18 years old, has no health problems, and is a competitive runner. I expected to hear "excellent" but he said it was only "fair" right now because he's suffering from shin splints.

Further, the analyst should also look over the entire interview to search for results that are not question specific but that cross the tested questions, and add a more general comment:

COMMENT: We have three sets of questions asking about income, but these appear in three different places. The subject expressed some annoyance that we kept returning to this topic.

2. *Compile results across interviews.* It is then important to further aggregate by producing a version of results that combines interviews across all interviewers, and that elucidates trends that occurred consistently. This can be done by compiling, for each question, all the comments that were made on that item. Comments for each question can be summarized in both a qualitative and quantitative sense. From a qualitative point of view, we look to see what the problems were and whether they were similar across interviews. From a quantitative point of view, one can sometimes get a notion of the severity of the problem from the frequency with which problems emerged.

> A1. How far do you routinely travel to get health care? Would you say less than an hour, one to two hours, or more than two hours?
>
> COMMENTS: Of ten subjects tested by the three interviews, five had significant problems answering this question. Three of them objected that this really varied depending on the type of provider they're visiting. The fourth one stated that the answer to "how far" would be five miles; and the fifth said "it's right next door." Note that the question is internally inconsistent, because the question implies a distance, while the answer categories are all represented by amounts of time. Also it wasn't really clear what the reference period is. One subject had been to the doctor once, in the past year or so, and so didn't know how to handle the "routine" part, or how far back he should go in thinking about an answer. We need to rethink whether we want to know how long it takes people to see the provider they saw the most during the past X months, or how long it takes them when they go for a routine checkup (assuming they do), or something else entirely.

Note that this comment is fairly involved, points out several problems, and instead of simply suggesting a rewording, explicitly brings out the need to better specify question objectives.

3. *Write an organized testing report.* The final annotated questionnaire containing these collapsed question-by-question comments then becomes a major section of a *cognitive interviewing outcome report.* In order to be clear concerning what the project entailed, the report should generally contain several important items of information:

(a) an introductory section describing the evaluated survey (including its mode of administration), and the specific purposes of testing;

(b) the nature of the subject population, and a description of recruitment procedures used;

(c) the number of subjects tested, with a tabular summary, such as the following (modeled on the testing of a health insurance survey by Pascale, 2003):

Subject ID	Gender	Age	Hispanic	Race(s)	Educational Level	Health Insurance
#1	M	22	No	White	12	No
#2	F	48	No	Asian	14	Yes
#3	F	60	Yes	White	10	No

(d) the number of cognitive interviewers, and their level of experience;

(e) the cognitive interviewing techniques used, specifically with respect to think-aloud versus probing, category of probing done (concurrent, retrospective, Proactive versus Reactive, degree of probe standardization, and so on);

(f) a question-by-question review of results, with recommendations for each tested question;

(g) a section listing the potential limitations of the testing and anticipated next steps, and even final decisions about question wording, when possible.

It is also helpful to include the testing protocol, consisting of the tested questionnaire and the Anticipated probes, at the end. Alternatively, the probes can be included along with question-specific comments. Overall, to the extent that cognitive testing reports routinely include the level of detail described, this enables other researchers to replicate and to evaluate cognitive investigations.

The report writer should provide the level of detail that will most effectively communicate results. It is also sometimes useful to provide a written summary of the most significant problems that were found, prior to the detailed question-by-question listing. The problems should be prioritized so that more attention is given to the most serious problems (Rothgeb, Loomis, & Hess, 2000). Finally, keep in mind the audience for the cognitive testing report, and what readers are likely to want. Very often, clients or sponsors are not much interested in process. Rather, they assume that the pretesting staff is credible and proficient, and they simply want to know (a) what was found to be amiss, and (b) what can be done about it. A sample report of this type is provided by DeMaio and Wellens (1997), who only briefly mention the fact that 20 cognitive interviews were conducted and then immediately get into the results. There is, of course, a natural tension in the cognitive interviewing field between the desire for complete documentation of procedures and the production of user-friendly reports. A compromise might be to include an appendix containing all the details that only a methodologist could love.

Reiterating earlier discussion of the CASM literature as a base, it is useful for purposes of report writing to be aware of the results of past question testing, of the general questionnaire design literature, and of the results of survey-oriented experiments, such as those covered by Tourangeau, Rips, et al. (2000). Because our testing results are often somewhat subjective, the report writer can legitimately lend an additional air of credibility to specific comments by pointing out they are consistent with results that have been obtained elsewhere. When commenting that questions about why the person has done something, or in particular, has failed to do something, simply do not produce useful information, I have cited Fowler (1995), who concludes that questions concerned with *what* typically work better than those asking *why,* and that we ask *why not* at our peril (for an example, refer to Chapter 5). Further, a recurrent theme of cognitive testing results is that complex questions need to be broken down into component parts, or decomposed. This conclusion again has strong support in the CASM literature (Tourangeau, Rips, et al., 2000).

FORMAL ANALYSIS OF PROBED INTERVIEWS: CODING SCHEMES

As for think-alouds, informal rather than formal means of analysis are normally used in cognitive interviewing. However, formal coding systems can be applied by assigning summary codes to either interviewer comments or subject behaviors. Researchers who have applied coding systems to interviewing results have mainly done so for purposes of method evaluation, rather than as a means to guide the review and modification of questions (Rothgeb et al., 2001). However, I will review these systems at this point, because they are available to practitioners who may favor systematic data processing procedures. Further, the results of these systems are extremely pertinent for clarifying the outcomes of interviews that rely on probe administration.

Formal codes tend to be descriptions of problems embedded in survey questions (and look very similar to the QAS codes listed in Chapter 2). The main variations among these coding schemes are (a) the number of codes and (b) their scope, particularly with respect to the degree to which they focus strictly on cognitive processes. For example, Willis et al. (1991) proposed a very simple coding scheme that classified questions as either

(a) cognitive or (b) structural-logical in nature, mainly in order to make the point that the latter category had been neglected by the four-stage cognitive model. At a more detailed level, Presser and Blair (1994) conducted an influential study that determined whether the results from a number of pretesting techniques, including cognitive interviewing, fell into the following seven categories:[1]

(1) The interviewer has a problem reading the question or recording the answer.

(2) The respondent has difficulty understanding what the question means.

(3) The respondent has difficulty remembering the question.

(4) The respondent has difficulty understanding the meaning of particular words or concepts.

(5) Different respondents have different understandings of the question.

(6) The respondent has difficulty recalling, formulating, or reporting an answer.

(7) The analyst will have a problem using the data.

Presser and Blair found that categories 2 through 5 ("Semantic Problems") dominated their cognitive testing results. What is most interesting about this scheme is that, from the point of view of the four-stage cognitive model, it is seriously distorted: Of the categories that can be viewed as "cognitive" in nature, four of these (2 through 5) involve the comprehension process, and the remaining cognitive processes (retrieval, decision/judgment, and response) are compressed into one category (6). Conrad and Blair (1996) and Willis, Schechter, and Whitaker (1999) independently developed coding systems that more closely reflect our dominant cognitive model. Specifically, the Willis et al. system proposed the following problem types: (1) *Comprehension/Communication,* which reflects the encoding process (e.g., "Subjects tend not to understand what we mean by vigorous exercise"); (2) *Recall/Computational,* which captures the retrieval process (e.g., "Subjects had problems remembering over 12 months); (3) *Bias/Sensitivity,* which reflects the judgment process (e.g. "The question makes it sound like you should report a lot of hours of work each week"); and (4) *Response Category,* which reflects the response process (e.g., "The

Table 11.1   Overall Percentage of Problem Type Codes Assigned for
Cognitive Interviews

	CO (Communication)	RE (Recall)	BI (Bias)	RC (Response Categories)	LO (Logical)	Total
NCHS Cognitive Interviews	70.5% (332)	11.0% (52)	1.9% (9)	12.1% (57)	4.5% (21)	100% (471)
NORC Cognitive Interviews	58.1% (358)	13.3% (82)	1.3% (8)	19.8% (122)	7.5% (56)	100% (616)

SOURCE: Willis, Schechter, et al. (1999).

NOTE: The number of codes assigned in each method is given in parentheses.

given categories don't match the answers that people normally use"). A fifth problem code was used to cover logical issues that cannot easily be conceptualized as due to problems in the cognitive processing chain.

Similarly to Presser and Blair (1994), Willis et al. (1999) applied this coding scheme to a set of cognitive interviews done at two labs (NCHS and the National Opinion Research Center). The results of the coding analyses, in terms of code distribution, are depicted in Table 11.1.

The immediately apparent result is that, for both labs, the lion's share of the codes was concentrated in one category (Comprehension/ Communication). The authors then decomposed this global category into several more subcategories related to encoding and comprehension processes and concluded that, despite the dictates of the four-stage model, Presser and Blair (1994) had in fact paved the correct path by focusing on the subtypes of comprehension problems (though it still may be useful to separate the remaining varieties of cognitive problems). As further confirmation that a variety of comprehension problems tend to dominate cognitive interviewing outcomes, DeMaio and Landreth (in press) reported that across three cognitive laboratories, over 60% of problems were classed as stemming from comprehension difficulties, and response category problems were the next most frequent. In another study involving three cognitive laboratories, Rothgeb et al. (2001) found that 70% of problems belonged to the Comprehension/Communication category (with memory retrieval second most frequent). In departure from this pattern, in a study of self-administered questionnaires to be discussed more fully later, Daugherty, Harris-Kojetin, Squire, and Jaël (2001) obtained a more complex set of findings, in which comprehension problems were in evidence but not universally more frequent than were other problem categories.

Coming full circle, the conclusion that cognitive interviewing largely involves communication—or as Gerber and Wellens (1997) stated, that pretesting largely involves the study of meaning—fits nicely with the key assertion in Chapter 2 that survey questions present problems because they simply fail to effectively communicate our intent. Although one might produce a plethora of codes to define the outcomes of cognitive testing, it appears advisable to focus them on processes variously described as encoding, comprehension, communication of intent, interviewer-respondent interaction, establishment of grounding, and so on.

ARE CODING SCHEMES WORTH THE TROUBLE?

Having used coding schemes, I can attest that applying them to define the particular problems in survey questions requires considerable time and effort, as each question must be categorized in terms of its component problems—and very often multiple problems arise within the same question. Finally, the codes must be summarized in order to review questions for potential modification. In the course of everyday cognitive interviewing to pretest questions, it may be unnecessary to go to this level in order to diagnose problems and make question modifications. Rather, the qualitative written comments are often wholly suitable—and even preferable—for this purpose.

For instance, if an interviewer's comment states that "the term 'EMT' should be specified as Emergency Medical Technician," or "Parents don't seem to have any idea what shots their children have gotten at the doctor," the additional coding of these as "terminology problem" or "failure to encode desired information," although systematic, does not supply additional information. Worse, because coding invariably involves data reduction, the code, in the absence of the original comment, contains *less* information, as it does not indicate exactly what the problem was. Fixing the question would require returning to the detailed descriptive information, rendering the coding fairly useless (see DeMaio & Landreth, in press, for further discussion). It is for this reason that coding schemes are useful mainly for characterizing the overall results of cognitive interviewing as a methodology ("what we find"), rather than on evaluation of individual survey questions ("what we found"). What these systems have taught us, however, is that even when we apply our usual informal approach, we should expect many of the problems we find to be related to issues of meaning, comprehension, and communication.

Persistent Analysis Issues

Several details plague cognitive interviewers as they go about the business of analysis. I address these as a series of issues to contemplate, and provide guidance where possible.

1. *Once-through versus revisitation.* In a once-through procedure, the interviewer probes, records notes, and writes them up—without further review of the interview. At the other extreme, using a revisitation procedure, the interviewer might focus only on administering the questionnaire and probing; any note taking or coding would occur after the fact, as the interviewer or other investigators review recordings. In between these approaches, there are a number of possibilities. For example, interviewers may listen to recordings after the interview to supplement their notes, or another analyst may do so.

The most basic question is whether to revisit the interview at all, assuming it can be video- or audiotaped. Although I feel that very experienced interviewers can get away with a once-through approach without replaying the interview, this may be risky; it puts considerable demands on the cognitive interviewer, who must, within one session, (a) administer the questionnaire, (b) conduct intensive probing, and (c) write comprehensive and intelligible notes. There is some evidence that this may be asking too much. DeMaio and Landreth (in press) compared organizations that reviewed questionnaires with one that did not do so, and although the interpretation is somewhat difficult due to the limited sample of organizations, found that the former were able to identify more problems than did the latter.

Admittedly, the review of tapes is a very time-consuming activity, and the appropriateness of this activity depends on the nature of the testing. In cases where time pressures are severe, or where revisions are made at a fairly quick rate, it is often not possible to devote the resources necessary to record, or to review interview recordings (Rothgeb, 2001). In such cases, it may be necessary to rely on written outcome notes alone.

If we conclude that interviews are to be reviewed expressly for purposes of comprehensive analysis of our findings, should the original interviewer do that review? To reiterate discussion from Chapter 9, it is instructive to listen to one's own interviews, if only for purposes of continuing education and self-monitoring. An alternate approach, of course, is to unburden the interviewer by having another staff member review the interview, and to obtain an independent review of the problems that emerge. This is also an excellent means for training new interviewers, as it allows them to develop a capacity to listen for problems without the simultaneous requirement of conducting the interview (see Chapter 9). Overall, although this puts additional demand on staff, I am convinced that an independent review of the interview is a very worthwhile endeavor.

2. *Should we be concerned with how the subject answers the tested questions?* A subtle but critical issue in the conduct and analysis of cognitive interviewing is whether it is necessary to record the quantitative answers to the target questions we are testing, as we would in a field survey (e.g., marking that the subject reported "good" health), or to instead focus only on recording notes about *problems* with the question—such as "The term 'practitioner' is technical in nature and should be simplified." At times, survey sponsors or clients seem very fixated on exactly "how the subjects answered the questions," whereas my own view may be that they *couldn't* answer them, because they are faulty questions. Cognitive interviewers do seem to differ in the degree to which they treat the cognitive interviews as a data collection exercise focusing on quantitative distribution (e.g., "Three subjects said their health was good, four said it was fair," etc.) (Beatty, 2004). In fact, to resurrect an earlier point, interviewers vary considerably even in the extent to which they attempt to obtain such answers in the first place, such as through Reorienting probing that induces subjects to provide answers (Beatty et al., 1996).

Because of the known dangers of forcing subjects to provide answers that may be meaningless, it is dangerous to rely heavily on the answers to such questions as a primary outcome measure. Again, we are not conducting cognitive interviewing to collect survey data, and our intent is normally not to determine that we can force people to answer the question if we try. Rather, we should record and summarize the responses for target items that are answered without difficulty but consider this a secondary outcome. The literal answers can be very instructive. However, in departure from the field survey, what is most important is a measure of reactions to the questions, and not the answers to the questions themselves.

3. *Do we count up the frequencies of problems with questions?* If we agree to focus less on the *answers* to targeted questions than on the

presence of *problems* they contain, should those problems be quantified? That is, should we report that

(a) "The question was difficult to understand and should be simplified," or

(b) "Five of nine subjects found the question to be difficult to understand."

The second approach may seem obviously superior, as it communicates the extent to which the problem was observed and can be useful in assessing its potential severity. Accordingly, I do try to provide such quantification whenever it appears to convey useful information: if a problem occurred 10 times in 10 interviews, this likely indicates greater severity than if the problem appeared only once. Interestingly, despite the increased specificity of the quantitative approach, the qualitative approach is more often represented in cognitive testing reports, such as those produced by the NCHS and Census Bureau labs (e.g., DeMaio, Landreth, & Hughes, 2003; Hughes & DeMaio, 2003; Miller, 2002b). I do not consider this to be a major failing, though, for an important reason: in many cases, *problem frequency is not a measure of problem existence or seriousness.*

Consider a problem that has occurred only one time in nine cognitive interviews. Even if we are committed to an approach that emphasizes quantification, keep in mind that our quantitative base consists only of the subjects we happened to have interviewed, and not the population to be surveyed. The key issue is, therefore, not how often a problem has been observed in our tiny cognitive interviewing sample, but rather, how often it can be expected to occur in the field environment. In this regard, we must be prepared to make an educated judgment. If the one person having the problem is representative of a large (or important) proportion of respondents, then this may be considerable and noteworthy.

As a pointed example, consider a question I tested to determine risk behavior for HIV and STDs: "The last time you had sex, did you drink alcohol within an hour before?" In a study of high-risk subjects, the question did appear to be understood well enough, and to serve its intended purpose of assessing whether people neglect safe sex practices when under the influence of alcohol. A problem emerged only when I interviewed a married man who reported that yes, this wouldn't be at all unusual, as drinking a glass of wine tended to put him and his wife in a romantic mood. It then occurred to me that for a large segment of the population, the question did not serve its intended purpose of measuring risky behavior. Further, it seemed unnecessary to measure the severity of the problem by testing a dozen more married people. Rather, a fundamental logical requirement—that we establish the relationship between the respondent and his or her last sex partner—seemed obvious, even based on one interview.

Especially because of the small samples involved in cognitive interviews, there is often little in the way of "truth in numbers," and it is dangerous to conclude that if problems are found in 25% of cognitive interviews, they are to be expected in that percentage of field interviews. We instead apply a subjective correction factor to our results, based on an assessment of likely differences between the subjects that were tested and the respondents who will be surveyed. If tested subjects are more highly educated than the population to be surveyed, even relatively modest levels of documented comprehension problems might motivate the designers to simplify the questionnaire. In summary, *the capacity of the interviewing and questionnaire design staff for applying judgment, interpretation, and subjective correction is basic to the analysis of cognitive interview results.*

4. *Should cognitive interviewers opinionate about the presence of problems?* I believe that a legitimate function of cognitive interviewing is to indicate where problems may exist, even when we have not observed these problems. In one respect this is a fairly radical suggestion, as it seems to violate the notion that we should only report the facts, not what we believe. On the other hand, interviewer opinionating is nothing more than questionnaire appraisal—the very technique that presumably was already used to get the questionnaire into shape and to develop probe questions. Although we theoretically obey a strict sequence in which appraisal is superseded by objective empirical testing, the real world is not so clean. Very often a prior review process is incomplete, and an accomplished cognitive interviewer can contribute to this process later, even after cognitive interviewing. DeMaio and Landreth (in press) found that all three cognitive labs they studied made use of such empirically unsupported interviewer comments.

A fair way in which to handle these opinions is to simply make clear which comments are based on objective testing results and which reflect at least some degree of interviewer subjectivity. For example, this quote from a testing report by Hughes and DeMaio (2003) contains strong elements of admitted subjectivity:

Although we did not probe on the introduction, we feel that reference to personal computers and personal use seemed to lead respondents to think the questions are only asking about the use of computers at home. (p. 2)

The use of such comments reflects an implicit recognition that the cognitive testing process is not guaranteed to be comprehensive—we may have recruited a biased sample that fails to include a sufficiently wide range of subject ability, knowledge, or motivation. Or, we may have neglected to probe something that could be significant. Practitioners who are offended by these strongly judgmental influences are free to restrict the types of freewheeling comments they will allow, especially when there are doubts about the questionnaire design proficiencies of the cognitive interviewers. Rather than focusing the argument around the question of what best defines the most rigorous scientific approach, I instead encourage investigators to consider the mix of empiricism and judgment that is most likely to result in the best possible outcome in their own environment, and to make reasonable use of a variety of sources of information.

Chapter Summary

- To determine what problems we have found, we need some means for analyzing cognitive interviewing results.
- Outcomes are varied, and relate to question-specific features as well as to question objective, ordering, overall burden, and determining what we perhaps should not be attempting to measure through survey-based self report.
- Analysis of the think-aloud interview involves protocol analysis—the interpretation of the subject's verbal stream—and can be done informally or through a coding scheme.
- Analysis of heavily probed interviews is normally informal. Alternately, an explicit problem coding scheme can be relied upon; these are objective and systematic, but difficult to apply in production work.
- Compilation of interview results is similarly informal in nature, but is systematic in the sense that interviewers and analysts attempt to make use of all available forms of information that inform the questionnaire design and evaluation process.

Exercise: Analyzing Cognitive Interviews

EXERCISE 1: INTERPRETING A THINK-ALOUD INTERVIEW

In response to the question "How much did you pay last month in total for household utility bills?" we may hear the following:

Let's see. I really can't say how much I spent on my utility bills last month, unless I get the receipts out, which I'm SURE I wouldn't want to do if you called up and did the interview on the phone . . . I'd say that it was probably a hundred . . . no, say a hundred twenty for the electric, because that's for the A/C, which is a lot during the summer months. What else . . . I have the telephone bills—but that gets complicated because now there's the cell phone and that's a different bill from the main phone. I don't know—maybe 40 last month for the cell phone, because that's what it always is . . . but the other phone really varies. Fifty, last month? So say around 90 for phone, and 120 for the electric, plus I don't know what other utilities there may be that I'm forgetting. The water bill only comes every three months, and we didn't get that one last month. Really, one dollar amount . . . is hard . . . if you could just say "Between 100 and 150" or something, I could probably do it, but otherwise . . . no.

Where did the person have difficulty? What would you propose doing about it?

SUGGESTED SOLUTION

Without invoking much theory—and simply by summarizing major themes—one might be inclined to comment that this individual had difficulty in reporting an exact dollar amount and was left to think for herself about what should be included as a "utility." As a suggestion, the cognitive interviewer might add that the investigators should make clearer what they mean to have included in utilities, either by using a checklist or by providing a short list that covers the main areas of interest. Further, the subject herself suggested another modification—using a list of category ranges, as opposed to asking for an exact amount. Most importantly, the complex computational demands may simply preclude an approach that requires the aggregate reporting of all forms of utilities.

EXERCISE 2: USING COGNITIVE
INTERVIEWING RESULTS TO REDESIGN QUESTIONS

Assume that we have decided to review our cognitive interviewing results in a fairly informal manner, and it is our job to identify problems from written summaries and to make recommendations. Using the following three examples—most of which are real-life findings from cognitive interview reports—what changes to these questions might you suggest?

Q1. Tell me whether you strongly agree . . . strongly disagree: There are few homeless people in your community.

INTERVIEWER COMMENT: This came across several times as "There are *a few* homeless people in your community"—which leads to a reversed interpretation of the item!

Suggested Solution: We might try a few other wordings—"There are very few homeless people in your community," or "There is a problem with homeless people in your community"—depending on whether it's the fact or the perception of impact that's more important.

Q2. When you go out, how often do you take something with you that could be used for protection such as a dog, mace, gun, or knife?

INTERVIEWER COMMENT: A woman from a wealthy neighborhood said, "Every night I go out and take my dog—she's big and loyal so she'd definitely protect me." This obviously isn't getting at the point—she doesn't carry the other things on the list!

Suggested Solution: Remove "dog" from the list.

Q3. During the past year, has a doctor or other health professional talked with you about your diet and eating habits?

INTERVIEWER COMMENT: This was pretty vague. Subjects weren't clear about what "talk with you" means—is this just asking if you're eating well/healthy, asking something more specific, or counseling you if all you eat is potato chips. They weren't sure what we want here, and I'm not either.

Suggested Solution: It's difficult to know how to change the question at this point. Instead, discuss the results with the survey development team, sponsor, or client, and get clarification on precise objectives.

Note

1. I have renumbered and rephrased these but retained the original intent of the authors.

PART IV

Other Issues and Topics

12

Special Applications of Cognitive Interviewing

Chapter Overview

To this point I have discussed cognitive testing as it is applied to surveys of the general household population, when an interviewer is asking the questions, and where the questions mainly pertain to factual and autobiographical issues. This is a common situation, and describes several large U.S. surveys, such as the National Health Interview Survey and the Current Population Survey. However, surveys vary tremendously in terms of several key variables that influence the conduct of cognitive interviewing, including:

(1) administration mode (telephone, paper, computer-based);

(2) sensitivity of question content;

(3) target population (the individual versus the establishment);

(4) type of question (autobiographical versus attitudinal);

(5) age of survey respondents.

Additionally, cognitive interviewing is useful for testing materials other than questionnaires (Snijkers, 2002), such as information forms, brochures, Web sites, and so on. This chapter addresses these variations on the basic theme.

Adjusting to Survey Administration Mode

It is no stretch to say that when we design surveys, administration mode is as important as any other consideration. The survey methods field is currently undergoing an evolution in this area as the range of administration methods has increased to include not only face-to-face, telephone, and mail, but also Internet, e-mail, and mixed-mode surveys. Several of these methods may also present the choice of either paper-and-pencil or computer administration (see de Leeuw & Collins, 1997, and Tourangeau, Rips, et al., 2000, for reviews). This proliferation of procedures has led to a variety of new acronyms, for example, CASI (Computer-Assisted Self Interview), ACASI (Audio-Computer-Assisted Self-Interview), CATI (Computer-Assisted Telephone Interview), and CAPI (Computer-Assisted Personal Interview). In part, these developments represent an attempt to enhance data quality, and perhaps also to address declining levels of survey response. Their implementation may also reflect the recognition that interviewers do deviate from strict standardization, or themselves introduce error; van der Zouwen (2002) notes that solutions involving computerized self-administration are designed to remove the human interviewer completely from the interaction.

Tourangeau, Rips, et al. (2000) devote a full chapter to the ways in which administration mode may interact with the respondent's cognitive processes. For example, the use of a self-administered questionnaire (whether paper-and-pencil or computer-based) provides visual information that is unavailable under interviewer-administered (in-person or telephone) modes. Because the way in which we present our materials to individuals has cognitive ramifications, this necessarily also has implications for question design, and by extension, for cognitive interviewing practice. Two decisions predominate in this regard: (a) What mode should be used for the cognitive interview? and (b) What additional procedures in the cognitive interview need to be tailored to fit the mode of the survey?

Table 12.1 illustrates how cognitive interviewing is related to survey mode, at least based on past practices. It may seem logical that these modes should match exactly, but this is not always the case.

INTERVIEWER-ADMINISTERED FACE-TO-FACE SURVEYS

The most straightforward case is the in-person field interview, such as the U.S. Census Decennial long form. For these surveys, cognitive testing is typically also done in person, whether in a laboratory or at an outside location such as an elders' center or subject's home. When possible, the cognitive interview is conducted in a way that reflects the technology of administration; if the interviewer-administered questionnaire is contained on a computer, as for a Computer Assisted Personal Interview

Table 12.1   Mode of the Cognitive Interview as a Function of Mode to be Used in the Fielded Survey

Survey Mode	Cognitive Interviewing Mode
Interviewer-administered (IA) face-to-face	IA face-to-face
Interviewer-administered (IA) telephone	(a) IA face-to-face (b) IA telephone
Self-administered (SA) (paper or computer-based)	(a) IA face-to-face (b) SA/IA hybrid (c) SA followed by IA debriefing/probing

(CAPI), it is best to conduct cognitive testing of a computer-based draft version. However, as I will detail later in the chapter, this practice can present logistical difficulties.

INTERVIEWER-ADMINISTERED TELEPHONE SURVEYS

In violation of an approach that matches cognitive interviewing mode to field mode, surveys intended for the telephone are often tested through face-to-face cognitive interviews (Schechter, Blair, & Vande Hey, 1996). One rationale for this mode mismatch is that in-person cognitive interviews present the advantage of making evident nonverbal cues that cannot be observed in a telephone interview (e.g., the subject's puzzled look). Or, the researchers may be willing to believe that major cognitive problems existing in telephone interviews are also present when questions are administered face-to-face. Still, as anyone who has ever participated in a long telephone survey may have experienced, there are important differences between telephone and face-to-face communication concerning intelligibility of speech, potential fatigue effects, and inability to rely on visually oriented materials (such as "show cards" containing written response category options). Consequently, there are also clear advantages to conducting the cognitive interview over the telephone.

One way to get the best of both worlds is to make use of multiple testing rounds, in which earlier interviews are conducted face-to-face and focus on more global, mode-independent questionnaire flaws. After appropriate revision, further interviews can be conducted using the telephone in order to determine how the questionnaire will function in its intended environment (Schechter & Beatty, 1994). Telephone-based cognitive interviewing does pose some logistical considerations. Because the interview is not conducted in person, it is not strictly necessary to have the subject (or the interviewer) travel to the interview. Hence recruitment can be very different from the usual cognitive lab testing project.

An interesting variation of the telephone-based cognitive interview has been implemented at NCHS, involving

(a) normal recruitment procedures for bringing subjects to the lab;

(b) conduct of the interview over the telephone, with the interviewer in one room and the subject in another;

(c) video monitoring of the subject during the interview;

(d) following the interview, an in-person retrospective debriefing.

This procedure maintains important features of telephone-based interaction, but also allows observation of subjects' nonverbal cues and provides the opportunity for more in-depth probing during the subsequent in-person debriefing.

SELF-ADMINISTERED PAPER QUESTIONNAIRES

To the extent that investigators are interested in sources of response error that are mode independent, interviewer-administered cognitive interviews for self-administered questionnaires can be effective, especially early in the development process (Schechter et al., 1996). Certainly, many problems with terminology, question vagueness, and so on, persist no matter how the questions are presented (e.g., confusion over the term "solid waste recycling practices"). For example, although the Question Appraisal System described in Chapter 2 was developed strictly for interviewer-administered questions, many of the problem codes apply very well to self-administered questionnaires. Again, face-to-face cognitive interviewing can be useful for detecting these problems, and many investigations that involve self-administration have benefited greatly from unabridged forms of the cognitive interview.

That said, there are good reasons to consider the additional challenges that self-administration presents to the cognitive interview. To a great extent, the transition from interviewer- to self-administration presents a very different cognitive world. Most obviously, whereas the former involves auditory information processing based on a series of verbal exchanges between interviewer and respondent, the self-completed questionnaire is visual in nature. Further, it makes no use of a human interviewer to read questions, control question sequencing, and answer questions the respondents may have. Cognitive interviewing must therefore be concerned with two vital issues unique to self-administered instruments: (a) How does the respondent cognitively process information he or she is presented visually? and (b) In cases in which users must make decisions that control instrument flow (e.g., following sequencing instructions or "skip patterns"), how well do they do in navigating the instrument? (Dillman & Redline, in press; Redline, Smiley, Lee, DeMaio, & Dillman, 1998). As an example of the potential impact of visual characteristics, Wolfgang, Lewis, and Vacca (1994) tested a paper-based, self-administered agricultural report form questionnaire and found that a large physical distance between the end of the printed question and the answer box caused 5 of 17 subjects to fill in the wrong box. Further, subjects sometimes mistakenly interpreted oversized answer boxes at the bottom of the form to be places to sum responses they had entered above, rather than places to enter new information.

THINK-ALOUD VERSUS RETROSPECTIVE PROBING FOR SELF-ADMINISTERED QUESTIONNAIRES

One approach to investigating the unique cognitive requirements posed by self-administered questionnaires is to utilize think-aloud in its pure sense (Daugherty et al., 2001; Hak, van der Veer, & Jansen, 2004). Although earlier I suggested that investigators infrequently apply think-aloud in the absence of supplemental interviewer-based verbal probing, there may be theoretically driven reasons for believing that think-aloud in its original guise has a place in the evaluation of self-administered questionnaires. In particular, unlike interviewer-administered questionnaires, the self-administered questionnaire represents the prototypic problem-solving task envisioned by Ericsson and Simon, in which the subject interacts directly with the to-be-completed materials and the interviewer is superfluous to that primary task. Therefore, a subject filling out a self-administered questionnaire might reasonably be left alone to answer questions and navigate the form in the absence of interviewer interjection, but to think aloud while doing so.

On the other hand, Redline et al. (1998) suggest that think-aloud might induce classic reactivity effects in self-administered interviews by slowing subjects down and causing them to process sequencing information (skip patterns) more fully than they otherwise would. Gower and Dibbs (1989) make the opposite argument, supposing that the think-aloud interview leads subjects to read less, causing them to miss skip instructions. Either way, the basic concern of these authors is that thinking aloud may produce biased responding, and for that reason it might not be considered the front-runner among means for conducting cognitive interviews of self-administered instruments.

An almost diametrically opposed approach to self-administered instruments is to rely on probing that is purely retrospective, involving after-the-fact debriefing. This approach adheres most closely to the practice of leaving the subject alone as he or she completes the questionnaire: the interviewer simply observes the subject and conducts a debriefing afterward in which the questions are revisited. The interviewer asks the usual types of cognitive probe questions, either Proactively, when based on a debriefing script, or Reactively, when based on observations made during the self-administered part of the interview ("It seemed like you paused for a while on this question; can you remember what you were thinking?"). In my experience in conducting such interviews (mainly with teenage smokers), such retrospective probing is effective only if it is done immediately after completion of the questionnaire.

Redline et al. (1998) conducted a fairly extensive (55-subject) experimental test that compared think-aloud and retrospective procedures to determine whether thinking aloud leads to enhanced attention to paper-based questionnaire content.[1] These procedural variants produced similar findings concerning navigation of the instrument, with the important exception that subjects with low educational levels tended to miss skip patterns under the think-aloud condition, possibly because they were focused on the verbal content to the detriment of the visual or navigational realm. Overall, the authors concluded that both interviewing approaches were useful.

CONCURRENT AND MIXED
APPROACHES TO SELF-ADMINISTRATION

Think-aloud and retrospective debriefing approaches have opposing strengths and weaknesses; think-aloud is potentially more disruptive, but is less prone to bias resulting from reconstructing thoughts that existed at the time one answered the questions. Perhaps because of this, a third approach attempts to judiciously interject concurrent verbal probes of the type that characterize the testing of interviewer-administered questionnaires (Bates & DeMaio, 1989; Schechter et al., 1996).

(a) The subject is asked to complete the questionnaire, and perhaps to think aloud as much as possible.

(b) During the interview, the interviewer interjects a limited number of targeted probe questions (usually for key target questions).

(c) The interviewer may also conduct a full retrospective probing.

When all three of these elements are included, this "kitchen sink" approach attempts to rely on all of the major approaches to cognitive interviewing in a way that balances the relative advantages and disadvantages of each.

As always, it would be helpful to have access to empirical results to help us choose among techniques, and several studies have compared various approaches to the cognitive testing of self-administered questionnaires. Bates and DeMaio (1989) compared (a) a combination of concurrent and retrospective probing, which they labeled Observation, with (b) pure think-aloud, to evaluate a Census Bureau Decennial Census form. Interestingly, the authors concluded that "in general . . . , the problem areas that were detected in the census form were similar in both the observation and the 'think aloud' sessions" (p. 268). In both cases, the problems found tended to be unique to self-administration, involving key issues of navigation. For example, subjects often did not start at the correct place and so skipped important parts of the instrument.

Schechter et al. (1996) also compared concurrent and retrospective approaches to probing of a self-administered instrument, and despite expectations that interviewer probing would interfere with subjects' processing of sequencing instructions, the concurrent probe group actually made *fewer* skip errors. Overall, the authors concluded that it is best to mix techniques; some subjects should be probed as they complete the questionnaire and others left to complete it unaided and then probed retrospectively. The key conclusion from both the Bates and DeMaio (1989) and Schechter et al. (1996) studies seems to be that cognitive interviewing of self-administered paper-based instruments should certainly investigate issues of navigation, and that both think-aloud and retrospective probing are effective to this end.

As a comparison of three variations of cognitive interviewing, Daugherty et al. (2001) systematically pretested a paper-based self-administered questionnaire on health plans by comparing the results from 21 interviews that involved either (a) think-aloud, (b) concurrent probing, or (c) retrospective probing. Based on a count of the number of problems identified under each approach, they concluded that think-aloud and concurrent probing were both useful, and advocated those techniques for cognitive testing of self-administered instruments. They were less impressed with the retrospective procedure, in part based on the somewhat smaller number of problems identified by that approach. However, the authors admitted that the target questionnaire had already been well-tested and had few serious problems, and was therefore not typical of the more troublesome instruments we normally evaluate.

Finally, the most systematic hybrid approach to the cognitive evaluation of self-administered questionnaires is the Three-Step Test Interview (TSTI) introduced by Hak et al. (2004). In their own words:

> The Three-Step Test Interview (TSTI) is an instrument for pre-testing a self-completion questionnaire by *observing actual* instances of interaction between the instrument and respondents (the response process). Because this process mainly consists of cognitive processing ('thinking') and is therefore hidden from the observer, *(concurrent) think aloud* is used as a technique for making the thought process observable. (p. 2)

> The TSTI consists of the following three steps:
>
> 1. Concurrent thinking aloud aimed at collecting observational data.
>
> 2. Focused interview aimed at remedying gaps in observational data.
>
> 3. Semi-structured interview aimed at eliciting experiences and opinions.

The first step is conducted as what I label "pure" think-aloud and the second two as retrospective debriefings. The difference between the latter steps is that step 2 is limited to following up, reactively, behaviors of interest that the interviewer observed during the initial step (e.g., a long pause at a certain question). Step 3 is a wrap-up in which the interviewer and subject can more freely discuss issues that pertain to the questions in a less structured form, and the interviewer can engage in Proactive forms of probing. Hak et al. (2004) provide a number of case study examples to illustrate the types of findings obtained from the TSTI, such as the example in Figure 12.1.

Target Question:

How often did you drink six or more glasses in one day, during the last six months?

[Response categories range from "(1) every day" through "(8) never" and "(9) don't know," with one answer permitted.]

The expert review did not predict problems with the response categories, but some appeared during the TSTI.

Step 1: Observation

Subject marks two response categories: 3 (3 or 4 times a week) and 9 (don't know).

Step 2: Focused Interview

INTERVIEWER: So it is about three or four times a week you drink six glasses or more?
SUBJECT: [There] may also [be] a week that I don't drink . . .
INTERVIEWER: And you also marked "don't know."
SUBJECT: Well, the one time three, and the other time, nothing.

Step 3: Semi-Structured Interview (Comment)

It appears that this respondent is a shift worker at a brewery. He only drinks alcohol in weeks in which he does not work. In such weeks he often drinks more than 6 glasses.

Conclusion

The respondent wants to express the variability of his drinking.

Figure 12.1   Results of the Three-Step Test Interview

SOURCE: Hak, van der Veer, & Jansen (2004), modified slightly for clarity of presentation.

Overall, there is probably no "correct" way to test a self-administered questionnaire. If we are particularly interested in determining how our subjects are able to follow a self-administered questionnaire that requires nontrivial navigation, I would leave them alone to complete it and then conduct a retrospective debriefing. If, on the other hand, we are concerned primarily with issues of information processing related to the targeted questions, a more concurrent assessment (involving either think-aloud or concurrent probing) may be more appropriate, as this minimizes the retention interval for key types of information. Further, a procedure that divides the task into a series of systematic and qualitatively varied steps, such as the TSTI, is also promising (or at the least, logical in principle).

ADJUSTING TO COMPUTERIZED QUESTIONNAIRES

A consideration that I have touched on, but that deserves more discussion, concerns the ramifications of the evolution of the survey methods field toward computer-based instruments. Sophisticated systems have proliferated in the realm of computer-assisted survey information collection (CASIC) for computer-assisted personal and telephone interviews (CAPI and CATI, respectively), as well as for self-administration (CASI), sometimes where a digitized voice serves as the interviewer (ACASI). These technological innovations pose a number of challenges to survey practice (Couper et al., 1998). Some of the inherent cognitive issues relate to social-cognitive interaction. In particular, for interviewer-administered surveys (especially CAPI), what happens when the computer is introduced as another "actor" in the interchange between the interviewer and the respondent?

Further, from the field interviewer's point of view, the notions of program usability and user-friendliness also become vitally important. On the one hand, the computer controls skip patterns and sequencing instructions, and so automates navigation. On the other hand, the computerized questionnaire presents a type of black box relative to a paper questionnaire; it tends to provide only a myopic snapshot of each presented question section and often fails to provide cues as to the total length of the instrument or where we are in it.

COGNITIVE INTERVIEWING
AND COMPUTER-BASED INSTRUMENTS

The study of the cognitive aspects of computer-based systems has largely been subsumed under the practice of "usability testing" (Couper et al., 1998). Usability and cognitive testing exhibit clear commonalities, and the nature of the relationship between them was best stated by Couper (1999):

> Usability laboratories . . . can be seen as an extension of cognitive laboratories. Much of what we have learned about conducting research in the latter can be applied to the former. Many of the other techniques used in usability research and testing (whether experimental design, think-alouds, expert review or conversation analysis) are part of the survey culture, in part, due to the success of the CASM movement. (p. 293)

Despite Couper's observation, in some ways cognitive interviewing and usability testing have developed as strangers, with limited consideration on either side concerning how these should be integrated. Further, relevant investigations have typically been carried out in usability labs rather than in the cognitive lab, often by very different types of staffs. Although this development may seem perplexing, it may in part be due to a divergence in the professional affiliations of practitioners, given that usability testing (or Human-Computer Interaction, or HCI) is often affiliated with the technology-intensive fields of survey operations or computer science. Many cognitive interviewers, on the other hand, have been trained in paper-based questionnaire design or human cognition.

There have, further, been discrepancies between these fields in emphasis, especially concerning precisely *who* we define the subject of our investigation to be. To a great extent, usability testing has attended to computerized survey administration systems that are operated by the survey interviewer (in particular, CATI and CAPI), and where it is mainly the interviewer's interaction with the machine that is of interest (see Couper et al., 1998). Cognitive interviewing, on the other hand, has largely maintained a focus on the respondent as opposed to the interviewer. Hence, with the advent of CATI and CAPI systems, the questionnaire pretesting field seemed to subdivide into two paths, in which one of these—usability testing—was technologically oriented, and sought to determine whether the interviewer could deal with the mechanism that presents the questionnaire (rather than the questionnaire itself). The other path—cognitive interviewing—continued to investigate the respondent's interaction with the questionnaire, without much enhanced emphasis on either the mechanism or the survey interviewer.

In fact, because CATI and CAPI systems retain the element of verbal delivery of questions by the interviewer, the changeover from paper-based administration was not generally viewed by most cognitive interviewing practitioners as particularly dramatic from the respondent's perspective. Even though we recognized that the incorporation of the machine did have potential effects on respondents, there still was relatively little impetus for cognitive interviewers to modify their procedures, as we have been content to rely on either paper drafts or facsimiles of computerized versions.

The gap between usability and cognitive testing can surely be narrowed. For example, in a rare departure from the norm, Hansen, Couper, and Fuchs (1998) evaluated human-machine interaction in a study of 52 laboratory-based cognitive interviews involving the National Health

Interview Survey, with interviewers as subjects. Their observations therefore focused almost exclusively on the interviewer side of the exchange, an element typically neglected in cognitive interviewing reports. Clearly, the concepts and methods of cognitive interviewing and usability overlap greatly, and in the spirit of the Hansen et al. study should be more closely coordinated in the future. Further, as the survey world further evolves to newer forms of computerized administration, such as Web and e-mail surveys, it will be vital for cognitive interviewers to adapt to these trends. Increasingly, designers need to consider the visual aspects of Web-based surveys, such as whether questions should appear one screen at a time or as a long list that the user can scroll up and down through (Bowker & Dillman, 2000; Couper, 2001; Dillman & Bowker, 2001; Dillman, Tortora, Conradt, & Bowker, 1998). Chapter 15, which anticipates the future course of cognitive pretesting, presents several thoughts on how cognitive interviews could be of assistance in designing Web-based surveys.

OPERATIONAL CHALLENGES OF CAPI/CATI QUESTIONNAIRES

More critical to cognitive interviewers, the migration of interviewer-administered questionnaires from paper to computer format has introduced a somewhat more mundane but very serious problem: Computerized questionnaires are difficult to test (Bethlehem & Hundepool, 2002). In particular, once the questionnaire is computerized, it is not a simple matter to convert it into a cognitive protocol containing probes and to make iterative modifications to the questions. Several practices make the job of testing computerized instruments more efficient:

(a) *It helps to conduct cognitive testing prior to the beginning of programming.* Most questionnaires begin life on paper (typically through word processing), and are later converted to a programmable format. They can be cognitively tested during the paper phase of the questionnaire's life, prior to metamorphosis into electronic form (or into a paper form that contains computer "specifications" in addition to the questions). For example, for the NCI Tobacco Use Supplement to the Current Population Survey, the sponsor produced a paper version of the draft instrument, and Census Bureau staff conducted several rounds of cognitive interviewing prior to the target date for programming. This does tend to extend the development cycle for the instrument, and the limiting factor for testing is the date on which the questionnaire must be "locked down" so that programming can commence.

(b) *A testable version of the computerized questionnaire can be developed.* Sometimes cognitive interviewing is conducted for instruments that have already been programmed. It may be possible to use a printout of the computer program to produce a cognitive testing protocol, but the presence of copious programming code tends to make the instrument very difficult to follow. The questionnaire can be simplified by having computer code deleted, and in some cases, skip patterns need to be simplified if a human is simply unable to follow them.

(c) *Cognitive testing can be done using the computerized version.* It is not always necessary to convert a computerized version to paper in order to conduct cognitive testing, if cognitive interviewers have access to computer equipment (normally a laptop system). However, this does complicate the task of including anticipated probe questions in the protocol, as these must be printed separately and then related to the question that is in electronic form. Interviewers can still write comments on paper, but they must at some point have access to a version of the questionnaire that they can annotate. To date, cognitive testing has not relied extensively on computer-only formats, although the use of purely computerized approaches (e.g., with capability of switching between target questions and probes) would certainly be a welcome development.

Cognitive Testing of Sensitive Questions

> *Because surveys involve people, it can be hard*
> *to get to the truth.*
>
> Conrad (1999, p. 301)

Conrad's statement was intended to be general, but the feeling that "our respondents stand between us and the truth" seems especially germane when we deal with sensitive subject matter. Increasingly we are faced with the prospect of asking questions about issues that are very private, potentially embarrassing, involve illegal behavior, or are otherwise termed "sensitive" in nature (Schaeffer, 1999). Referring to the four-stage cognitive model, such questions present serious issues concerning respondent Decision/Judgment processes. Most importantly, will we get accurate and truthful answers to such questions? Additionally, as we may not even know at the outset the degree to which our questions will be considered sensitive by respondents, we are sometimes also interested in issues of question comprehension, definition, and conceptualization.

Cognitive interviewing can be very useful in studying these issues. However, probing into sensitive behaviors can involve several complexities that induce us to modify our approaches. Probing sensitive content may be the single most challenging variety of cognitive interviewing, and there are several considerations to take into account when preparing to evaluate sensitive questions.

WHAT IS A SENSITIVE QUESTION?

When we anticipate testing sensitive materials, a primary issue to consider is just what is likely to be "sensitive" as the term is normally used (Lee, 1993). In particular, it is important to distinguish between sensitive *questions* and sensitive *answers*. Some questions are sensitive because asking them is offensive (e.g., asking a 60-year-old woman if she has paid for sex), whereas for others, it is the *answer* that is sensitive because the respondent has engaged in the behavior and not because the question itself is especially objectionable (e.g., "Have you used heroin in the past 12 months?"). These concepts have been labeled *intrusive threat* and *threat of sanction,* respectively (Lee, 1993). In the cognitive interview, we can assess the former without necessarily asking the person to divulge information about him- or herself, but for the latter, it is sometimes helpful to know whether the person has engaged in a particular activity. The latter, in particular, can make the cognitive interview itself sensitive, depending on how it is conducted.

IS INTENSIVE COGNITIVE TESTING OF SENSITIVE QUESTIONS POSSIBLE?

Investigators faced with the prospect of administering sensitive questions often find the notion of cognitive testing to be very seductive: If in doubt about how people will react to the questions, why not test them in the lab? Paradoxically, however, if people are likely to be reticent to answer sensitive questions in the first place, the act of probing these behaviors, or asking for elaboration, might only make the situation worse. In fact, we must recognize that the cognitive laboratory is limited in the degree to which it can study the issue of sensitivity in an ecologically valid manner. We often cannot answer the (admittedly important) question, "Will respondents in my survey find these questions sensitive and answer them truthfully?"

Based on earlier work in this area (Willis, 1996; Willis et al., 2001), I believe that we are limited by the fact that sensitivity is not a static attribute of the item to be isolated for laboratory study. Rather, it tends to be a dynamic entity that is dependent on the physical and social environment. In some environments (e.g., a sexually transmitted disease clinic in which our subjects are waiting for examination and treatment), even very personal detailed questions about sex and drug use have proven to be effectively nonsensitive. In such environments it is relatively easy to intensively discuss the tested questions. However, there still exists the important caveat that it is difficult to say, based on such investigations, how these questions will function in a field survey. Asking about number of sex partners within the past 12 months in the privacy of the cognitive laboratory may be very different from asking the same question in a household-based telephone interview, especially if the respondent's spouse might be listening in on the call.

Making use of our background cognitive model, I view cognitive interviewing as particularly effective for investigating comprehension and recall processes associated with sensitive questions. That is, we are normally willing to make the assumption that comprehension of terms such as "condom," or the recall of the number of partners over a defined interval, are not strongly influenced by the interview location. Studying such issues is very useful, and may be as much as cognitive interviewing can reasonably be called upon to accomplish.

PROCEDURES FOR TESTING SENSITIVE QUESTIONS

Even if one accepts that cognitive interviewing is mainly useful for evaluating the questions themselves, and less useful for predicting reactions to the questions, such testing still presents a significant challenge. Again, some questions are inherently embarrassing or private (e.g., they present intrusive threat), and even discussing these—let alone asking for answers—may bring out some aspect of resistance or discomfort. Consider the following question subset (from Willis et al., 2001), asked of male respondents:

When, if ever, was the last occasion you had anal sex with a woman? By anal sex, we mean a man's penis entering a partner's anus or rectum.

Have you EVER had painful sores or blisters on your sex organs?

Have you EVER had dripping or oozing or a discharge from your sex organs that had a strange color or smell?

Have you ever had sex with a man involving genital area/penis contact?

To make testing of such questions work effectively, several strategies can be applied, beyond our usual cognitive testing approaches:

(a) *Prepare and protect the subject.* It is unlikely that most people will react positively to being probed in depth, without warning, about questions such as "Have you ever given money for sex, or received money for sex?" or "Have you ever taken money or equipment from your place of business without permission?" Rather, it is useful to provide relevant information from the start (at the time of recruitment) so that they will know what they are in for. Sometimes the recruitment ad will make the situation evident (e.g., "Needed: people to answer survey questions about drug and alcohol use"). Even so, the issue of informed consent—although always important—takes on special significance, and I would be sure to emphasize in a consent form that "all of your responses will be treated as confidential, and only used by researchers working on the study. Your name or other personal identifiers will not be connected to any answers you give."

(b) *Consider indirect probing.* Sometimes we do not need to literally ask people to answer the sensitive questions. Rather, we can learn a lot simply by asking about term interpretation (e.g., "What does 'any kind of sex' sound like it means?") or recall (e.g., "Does 12 months seem OK, or is it too long to remember how many times you've been drunk?" or "Without telling me your answer, how sure are you that it's accurate?"). For example, for self-administered questionnaires (which are often used for sensitive topics, as they remove the interviewer from the scene) we can (1) ask the subject to read through the questionnaire, answering the questions directly on the form, and then (2) without viewing their answers, review the questions with them in a way that focuses on the questions rather than on their particular answers. Of course, this approach is hampered by the fact that answers to such probes may only be informative to the extent that we also know whether the subject has engaged in the behavior. However, sometimes subjects who would otherwise be reticent to answer will spontaneously volunteer information about their actual behaviors, simply in order to clarify their explanations in a way that is difficult when we only "talk around" the issues.

(c) *Focus on defects of the questions, not of the person.* One of the main reasons we can induce subjects to freely divulge sensitive information is our ability to convey the notion that our overall purpose is to judge the *questions*, rather than to obtain information about *them*. By maintaining an explicit focus on question features that may create problems, the cognitive interviewer can elicit discussions that one would rarely have with relative strangers in the course of everyday life. For example, a subject who has engaged regularly in sex for pay may be prompted to object that a question about exact number of lifetime sex partners is defective due to unrealistic demands on memory, suggesting that the researchers consider the use of response category ranges for very high frequencies of the behavior.

(d) *Maintain a neutral interviewer approach.* The subject normally reacts to social and behavioral cues from the interviewer, and one who is nervous, embarrassed, hesitant, or apologetic in asking sensitive questions will likely elicit similar reactions from the subject. To defuse resistance, it is helpful to (1) ask a series of nonsensitive questions first, as a warm-up; (2) announce matter-of-factly that we will then switch to some questions that some people find personal, reminding subjects that they do not have to answer any question that makes them feel uncomfortable; and then (3) launch ahead, in a direct but personable manner, in the same manner one would use if discussing the weather.

Most importantly, if direct questioning is used, the interviewer must not display overt reactions to the person's *answers*. That is, rather than communicating surprise or shock at a report of 80 sex partners in the past 6 months, or commenting on how that might be somewhat higher than the norm, I would instead be inclined to ask further probes: "Do you remember what time period the question was asking about?" "To you, what is a 'sex partner'?" "How did you arrive at that answer?" "Would you say that these were pretty even over that time period, or were there times when you had more or fewer partners?" As a result, the subject can be induced to be responsive, but without receiving strong cues indicating *how* he or she should respond in order to receive any form of social reinforcement.

(e) *Forgo recording of the interview.* When discussing dental visits, people seldom care if the interview is audiotaped or videotaped, and almost always give consent readily. This may not be the case when illegal behaviors, in particular, are asked about. Interviewing without recording does have implications for data collection and review, as there will exist no think-aloud stream to analyze, and in general this procedure places a burden on the interviewer to take careful notes as the only source of data. On the other hand, Miller (2002b) conducted a cognitive lab study of sexual identity, attraction, and behavior that was recorded, apparently without negative incident.

(f) *Match on demographic variables?* When strong sexual content is involved, it does help to gender-match the interviewer and subject, in order to avoid embarrassment. One might also attempt to carefully match on age, or as is sometimes strongly suggested, race and ethnicity. The justification for the latter is that people may be more open toward others who share their background and culture (Jourard, 1964) and who may be better suited to understand uses of language, such as slang terms. This is a very important issue, as it influences decisions concerning staffing and whether individuals should be disqualified from interviewing based on demographic status.

Requirements of strict racial and ethnic matching have not been demonstrated in any empirical sense in the cognitive interviewing domain, and based on personal experience, I think it can be unnecessary and, in some cases even counterproductive. Consider first that subjects themselves may not care whether we match them demographically or culturally. To illustrate, in a cognitive interviewing study of female reproductive history involving African American subjects at an inner-city health clinic, my team happened to consist of one black and one white interviewer, both female. The former was very careful and methodical, but once word got around to potential subjects that her interviews took much longer, new subjects spontaneously voiced a preference for the white interviewer, simply based on the expectation of less time investment. I suspect that if an even quicker white male interviewer had been available, he would have been favored. Subjects make decisions about participation based on many factors, and we should not impose upon them the restriction that race or ethnicity is necessarily the dominant one.

Of course, the fact that subjects may not care about the demographics of the interviewer fails to address whether they provide good information to individuals who are dissimilar. Although counterintuitive, there is reason to believe that subjects might be more forthcoming with an interviewer who is demographically dissimilar, in particular because this tends to limit the potential for interaction once the interview is over. Brannen (1988) suggests that it is imperative, for discussions of sensitive topics, that the interviewer and participant are extremely unlikely to ever cross paths again (this is reminiscent of the "stranger on a plane" effect described by Krueger, 1994, in which people reveal all manner of intimate personal details to the person sitting next to them). Consistent with this notion, a subject at an inner-city clinic remarked that she would be reticent to reveal sensitive information to another black woman, but that she did not fear running into me in church or on the street, so I posed no threat. In summary, I claim that a wide variety of individuals can make effective cognitive interviewers, across a wide variety of respondent populations, as long as we are sufficiently sensitive ourselves to the universal human concerns that impact the process of answering sensitive questions.

SUMMARY: SENSITIVE QUESTIONS ARE STILL QUESTIONS

Although sensitive questions can be challenging, it is also important not to overemphasize the above points. Despite some differences, interviews of sensitive questions share many features with those of more mundane topics. As an illustrative case study, Miller (2002b) describes a cognitive lab project involving 30 cognitive interviews of subjects of varying sexual orientation, across several ethnic and racial groups. Subjects first completed the questionnaire via computer, and then were intensively probed using a direct-questioning approach. Miller reported no particular issues surrounding sensitivity of the testing process itself, and was able to elicit detailed discussions concerning sensitive sexual questions:

TARGET QUESTION: In your lifetime, with how many men have you had sex?

(MALE) SUBJECT COMMENT: That's kind of difficult. I mean, because . . . you never keep track. You never think to count, and it was just a question to—it's just never been asked of me before. So, I had to really sit and think . . . (p. 17)

Miller also noted that the (ACASI) survey computer administration system was programmed to actively control the time available to answer questions, but provided very little time for such reflective thought, as the designers assumed that responses would be quick. However, the subject quoted above was apparently unable to retrieve such information using a direct retrieval strategy, and indicated that enumeration of this event would be fairly difficult. This implied that the computer system should perhaps be reconfigured to take into account such difficulties of retrieval. The author documented further problems concerning question comprehension, including vagueness regarding the phrase "had sex." Overall, the types of problems discovered were not significantly different from those that emerge in many cognitive interviewing studies.

Cognitive Interviewing and Establishment Surveys

WHAT'S "SPECIAL" ABOUT ESTABLISHMENTS?

Researchers who regularly conduct cognitive interviews of businesses and other establishments—that is, where the unit of analysis is not the individual but the organization—might question the description of this as a "special application." That is, at least some practitioners at U.S. federal agencies (e.g., the Census Bureau, Bureau of Labor Statistics, Department of Agriculture, Energy Information Administration, General Accounting Office, etc.), at Statistics Canada (Laffey, 2002), and in European agencies (e.g., Giesen, 2004) focus their efforts solely on establishment survey development and pretesting. However, based on reports of their cognitive interviewing projects, I consider this to represent a special case due to its increased complexity. In particular, in addition to all of the processes and procedures required for testing individuals, the establishment survey presents an important additional feature: It relies on the reporting of information that may be distributed among a number of individuals or other sources, in particular written or computerized records (Goldenberg, Anderson, Willimack, Freedman, Rutchik, & Moy, 2002; Rutchik & Freedman, 2002). Hence the information retrieval and information processing stage in particular is often multifaceted, and involves the selection and combination of human memory (internal memory) and record-based sources (external memory). Edwards and Cantor (1991) presented a model that extends the Tourangeau-style cognitive model to the realm of establishment surveys, in part by including the retrieval of record-based data.

WHAT NEEDS TO BE DONE
DIFFERENTLY FOR ESTABLISHMENT SURVEYS?

There are several unique features that need to be taken into account when surveying establishments:

1. It may be necessary to conduct interviews that focus on the operation of the organization as an entity or system, in order to devise logical questions (Rutchik & Freedman, 2002); this can be conceptualized as the "Ethnography of Business" (McCurdy, 1997).

2. Issues to be examined tend to emphasize the organization and location of information needed to complete the survey, and identification of the appropriate respondent (Cantor & Phipps, 1999). Tomaskovic-Devey, Leiter, and Thompson (1994) and Goldenberg (1996) describe the potentially varied role of each individual in terms of authority, capacity, and motivation to serve as survey respondent.

3. Subject recruitment can pose a particular challenge: Goldenberg (1996) reported that cognitive testing of the Business Births Pilot Study required 183 telephone calls to 55 establishments to obtain 18 interviews. O'Brien, Fisher, Goldenberg, and Rosen (2001) recommend stratifying recruitment of establishments, so that size of firm and industry type can be at least minimally represented in the cognitive interview sample.

4. For practical reasons, cognitive testing often needs to be done "on the road" (e.g., at one or more business locations, rather than in the cognitive laboratory).

5. Establishment subjects may not be willing to complete a tested form in the presence of the cognitive interviewer, due to the inconvenience involved in retrieving record information (Stettler, Willimack, & Anderson, 2001). In an attempt to compensate for this limitation, Stettler et al. asked hypothetical probes that focus on retrieval processes (e.g., "Where would you go in your records to get this information?"), and that stop short of requiring actual record lookup. The authors also developed vignettes that mimic relevant business situations and asked subjects to complete the form using those data.

Davis, DeMaio, and Zukerberg (1995) reported that as of the mid-1990s, there was little literature available that addressed the cognitive interviewing of establishments, and that such testing was not widespread, presumably due to the types of challenges listed above. Davis et al. made a fledgling attempt to bypass some of these limitations by attempting cognitive interviewing of establishments by mail, a procedure they concluded to not be particularly effective. More recently, however, this situation appears to have changed, as administrators of establishment surveys have increasingly begun to incorporate cognitive methods into pretesting (Willimac, Martin, Whitridge, Japec, & Lyberg, in press).

Despite their differences, cognitive interviews of establishments and of population surveys use similar procedures, and may find similar problems. Wolfgang et al. (1994) conducted 24 in-person cognitive interviews of farm and ranch operators to test a form used for a U.S. agriculture census that is done every 5 years. Their approach and findings are reminiscent of multiple themes that have emerged in previous chapters:

1. *Limited scope of questions to be tested.* Only the sections suspected to be the most problematic or important were tested, in order to keep interviews at reasonable length.

2. *Varied recruitment.* They maximized geographic variability and variance in relevant subject characteristics (e.g., poultry farmers in Maryland, grain farmers in Michigan, cattle feedlot operators in Texas, ranch operators in Colorado, and fruit and nut growers in California).

3. *Use of probing techniques to study comprehension processes.* The investigators focused on question misunderstanding; for instance, the term "this place" as the unit to be reported on was misinterpreted by 12 of 24 subjects (e.g., farmed land that was rented rather than owned was mistakenly omitted). Similar to what is often found in cognitive testing, subjects also tended to display a general rule of excluding unmentioned items when provided a list of examples meant to be general prompts. In general, comprehension-related problems may be a major nemesis of establishment surveys, as for those of populations; after testing a survey on job openings and employee turnover, Goldenberg and Phillips (2000) also noted that the largest source of measurement error they identified consisted of "communication problems that interfered with respondent comprehension" (p. 6).

4. *A focus on the ways in which subjects handle written instructions.* Wolfgang et al. (1994) found that several subjects set an information sheet aside and didn't look at it, even when the questions instructed them to, and that 12 of 24 didn't notice or read particular instructions contained in the form. Interestingly, they also reported a finding that seems to be ubiquitous for self-administered questionnaires: Parenthetical instructions were often ignored, as though the parentheses indicated the material to be of secondary importance and not worth reading.

5. *An evaluation of the match between subject's records and those assumed by the instrument to exist.* As an example of a type of finding that was unique to establishment surveys, more than half the subjects

complained that tax records they used as a basis for responding weren't broken down the way the questionnaire asked for information (e.g., fuel costs weren't itemized in a manner required to complete the form, because for tax purposes they were aggregated).

Rutchik and Freedman (2002) point to several lessons learned concerning cognitive interviewing of establishments: (a) At least some cognitive interviews should be very unstructured, in accordance with an ethnographic approach; (b) especially for technical matters (e.g., energy production and pricing), unless the cognitive interviewer is a content expert, it is helpful to have an expert present at the interview to provide explanations; and (c) when the experts are stakeholders in the survey results, it is especially illuminating for them to observe firsthand the complexities and difficulties associated with the data collection. Again, each of these recommendations has parallels within the broader world of cognitive testing.

Testing Questions on Attitudes and Opinions

As a very gross oversimplification, but one that may nevertheless be useful, survey researchers fall into two camps: (a) those who study facts and events, and (b) those who study attitudes and opinions (and of course, some straddle both worlds). The former include, in particular, staffs of U.S. and European federal agencies who are concerned with "the hard facts" about unemployment rates, industry statistics, frequency of medical visits or other health events, and so on, whereas the latter focus on political views and a range of public policy issues (e.g., attitudes toward government spending). Consistent with this view of a two-headed field, Tourangeau, Rips, et al.'s (2000) textbook on CASM research devotes separate chapters to factual questions and to attitude questions (see Tourangeau, 1987, 1992; Tourangeau & Rasinski, 1988, for general cognitive issues pertaining to attitude questions).

However, although there tends to be a difference between these question types with regard to measurement goals, and even to some extent in professional orientation, it is not clear that this leads to major differences in pretesting—and especially cognitive testing—of these variants. Despite treating these separately, Tourangeau, Rips, et al. (2000) state that "there are more similarities than differences between the response process for the two types of questions" (p. 166). Given that cognitive interviewing techniques (at least theoretically) derive from cognitive response processes, this would seem to imply that cognitive testing of these items should be very similar.

To a great extent this is true: Many surveys undergoing cognitive testing in fact mix factual-behavioral and attitudinal items (such as questions on smoking behavior and attitudes toward smoking restriction in public places), yet cognitive protocols or testing reports tend not to highlight any particular distinctions relating to this dimension. Consider the example of an attitudinal item from a survey of teen smoking: "Tobacco companies use advertising to fool young people—definitely yes, probably yes, probably not, or definitely not." Based on usual forms of probing, my interviewing team detected several problems related to the intent of this item. Interviewed teenagers sometimes professed negative attitudes toward *cigarette manufacturers*—but failed to recognize these as "tobacco companies." The question also turned out to be unclear because it does not specify whether we mean to ask (a) whether the purpose of advertising is to fool young people, or (b) whether this is done successfully. As usual, cognitive testing appeared to be useful for exposing otherwise hidden problems.

As such, it is tempting to conclude that we do not need to limit or modify our cognitive techniques based on whether we are dealing with attitudinal or factual questions. However, the proverbial fly in the ointment in this case is a review paper by Wilson, LaFleur, and Anderson (1996) that very directly addressed the issue of verbal reporting concerning attitude questions. Wilson et al. presented evidence, based on psychological laboratory findings, that survey questions on attitudes and, in particular, questions asking *why* a person harbors a particular attitude, may be unreliable and produce classic reactivity effects (i.e., answering such questions influences answers to later questions). To some extent this is not a surprising conclusion, and it is likely that experienced cognitive interviewers would agree with this assessment.

The potential difficulties this analysis poses for cognitive interviewing are twofold. First, if people really don't have much access to the basis for their attitudes, what good does it do to probe them through cognitive testing? That is, what can probes about attitudes really tell us, when people don't know why they harbor these attitudes? Second, perhaps hitting more closely at the core of cognitive interviewing as a method, if survey questions that ask "why" are unreliable, then are not cognitive probes asking "why" similarly suspect? Put differently, if asking "why" produces problems, it likely does so generally, for probe questions as well as for survey questions, per se.

For cognitive testing of factual questions, we can sidestep both of these arguments. First, we are not asking about attitudes but presumably about issues that respondents have more cognitive access to (e.g., their "life histories"). Further, our probes are not normally phrased in terms of "why." For example, the probe "How did you come up with that answer?" focuses on the processes used to answer a survey question; "What does the term X mean to you?" requests a fairly direct report of semantic knowledge.[2] Such probes therefore avoid the Wilson et al. objections to asking subjects to self-report why they exhibit a particular belief. However, the Wilson et al. analysis cannot be so blithely dismissed with respect to probes normally applicable to attitudinal questions. If they are correct, probe questions like "Why do you believe that smoking shouldn't be allowed in bars?" or "Why do you say that your health in general is excellent?" do run the risk of promoting unreliable answers, or reactive effects.

There are no data refuting the argument that probing of attitudinal questions represents a misguided use of cognitive interviewing. However, to address this logically, consider the criticism that probing leads to unreliable verbal reports. Certainly there are cases in which probing leads us nowhere—and especially when we ask "Why?" we may be requesting information that subjects cannot reasonably provide. However, by concentrating on our testing goals, and on how these lead us to develop probes, we can strive to avoid this problem.

For example, when testing the attitudinal question "Do you believe that smoking should be allowed in public places?" our objective is to test the question—not to literally understand why this particular subject believes what he or she does, but rather to judge whether the question effectively represents that belief. Therefore I might, in this case, refrain from probing with "Why do you believe this?" because it does not help to evaluate the question to hear that it is "Because it's annoying" or "Because secondhand smoke hurts you." Rather, based on a suspicion that the term "public places" is vague, I might instead ask, "What types of public places are you thinking of?" or "What, to you, does 'public place' mean in this question?" I might also probe to determine if they are thinking only of cigarette smoking or also of cigars. In this case, we can test attitudinal questions, avoid the "why" conundrum, and still (ideally) get useful information.

Consider a second question that can be classed as attitudinal in nature: "Would you say your health in general is excellent, very good, good, fair, or poor?" Here, an issue for investigation may be the way the person conceptualizes the response categories (Schechter, 1993, 1994). In this case, use of "why" in the probe "Why do you say 'very good'?" would seem to invite criticism, as we appear to be requesting a self-evaluation of belief. We may, in fact, only elicit a longwinded and possibly irrelevant explanation (an occupational risk for the cognitive interviewer). However, somewhat subtly, the use of "why" is not mainly geared toward eliciting a report of the reasons the subject harbors a particular attitude. Rather, we are asking them why they selected a particular term to represent their belief. In other words, we are not asking them to justify the attitude itself but to revisit the process that led them to select a particular term as their answer, based on our suspicion that matching a broad term ("good") to one's internal concept of health status may sometimes be difficult.

The general point I again propose is that rather than avoiding particular words when we probe (e.g., "why"), we are best served by following a path in which we develop our probes based on an analysis of potential problem pitfalls. Consistent with Wilson et al.'s (1996) results, asking unguided, open-ended questions about why people believe things is probably inadvisable, as this information may not be readily available on reflection. However, in pretesting questions, to the degree that we are targeted in approach and make use of a model of question defects that is general enough to cover both factual and attitudinal items, this should lead to cognitive probes that are effective. Again, the QAS model cited in Chapter 2 represents an attempt to address the features of both types of questions, and gives rise to probes that we can use in cognitive interviewing to investigate potential problems. I conclude by mirroring the Tourangeau, Rips, et al. (2000) assertion that there is more commonality than separation between factual and attitudinal questions, and this pertains not only to subjects' cognitive processes but to cognitive pretesting procedures as well.

Interviewing Across the Age Range

A premise of the cognitive approach to questionnaire evaluation is that rather than making reference only to generalized rules of question design, we can aim our testing toward the particular groups of interest to the survey. Although the concept of special populations can involve a large number of variables—including varied occupation, education, physical disability, and so on—many of the interviewing issues are related to recruitment (that is, getting the right people) rather than modification of the procedures used in the cognitive laboratory. Here, I will focus on one additional concern that sometimes arises: whether we need to modify our interviewing approaches to take into account respondent age.

INTERVIEWING CHILDREN

Based on a review of the limited number of cognitive interviewing studies across the age range, it appears that cognitive testing procedures generally work for children. To test a self-administered questionnaire on school issues, Zukerberg and Hess (1996) interviewed 12- to 17-year-olds using both think-aloud and probing techniques. Their results mirrored those pertaining to adults: Teenagers had trouble following skip patterns and demonstrated departures from researchers in interpretation of key terms (e.g., unsurprising in retrospect, their view of "year" involved the school year, as opposed to the previous 12 months). Subjects were found to be able to think aloud and to answer probe questions and, in summary, Zukerberg and Hess concluded that "conducting cognitive interviews with adolescents may not be that different from similar research conducted using adult respondents" (p. 952).

These results are in at least partial agreement with those of Stussman, Willis, and Allen (1993), and Holland and Willis (1991), who also tested teenagers and were able to apply cognitive interviewing effectively to find problems. Stussman et al. did report the caveat that some teens were not particularly adept at think-aloud, and that interviewers relied on a heavy dose of cognitive probing. Again, however, this same observation has also been made many times in cognitive interviews of adult respondents. Finally, in a review of this literature, de Leeuw et al. (in press) report that 12- to18-year-olds generally react well to a combination of think-aloud and probing, including the use of paraphrasing.

De Leeuw et al. (in press) have pointed out that interviewing younger children (aged 7 to 12) may require special procedures and suggest being careful to put the child at ease, introduce the task by carefully explaining "the rules of the game," give clear examples of what we want them to do, and adjust for attention lapses. They also report that younger children are good at thinking aloud but not particularly adept at question paraphrasing, due to the cognitive demands of that task. Finally, with respect to interviews of children at a very young age, I can cite the experiences I described when opening the book, involving cognitive interviewing of first and second graders, in this case on mathematical word problems. Like other researchers, I found this to be effective and not fundamentally different from interviewing adults, except for perhaps being somewhat more enjoyable. Overall, it again seems that cognitive interviewing of children is entirely feasible, and in terms of procedural modification, mainly requires that we simplify our materials and procedures to be age appropriate. One lesson that has emerged from these studies is that we must always remember that children develop quickly, and that for a survey of teens, a 13-year-old may respond very differently from someone who is 19. Recruitment must therefore encompass this spread.

INTERVIEWING THE ELDERLY

Moving now to the other extreme of age, cognitive interviews of the elderly have been done frequently and effectively (e.g., Jobe, Keller, & Smith, 1996; Jobe & Mingay, 1990). Again, I do not believe that there are fundamental modifications that we must make to do such interviews. It may be necessary to speak loudly and to make sure that written materials use sufficiently large type. As for field interviews, there is a possibility that elderly respondents will meander, and it is necessary to gently bring them back to the topic of the interview. Although elaborate personal histories are not always directly relevant to the testing of our target survey questions, I will profess to finding interviewing the elderly especially fascinating, rewarding, and especially useful in providing unique perspectives. Cognitive probing, by its nature, elicits a lifetime of memories, both good and bad. I have witnessed the recounting of the deaths of spouses, life in World War II concentration camps, and racial oppression, as well as positive outcomes, such as the very elderly man who reported "excellent" health despite multiple chronic medical conditions, and then answered my probe of this response by remarking "I got up this morning, didn't I?"

Testing Non-Questionnaire Materials

One promise of the cognitive approach is that it applies to a variety of materials other than survey questionnaires (and to math word problems, the only other area I have so far described). Rather than providing an in-depth discussion of this range of application, I simply provide a list of examples to make the point that such testing is not limited strictly to questionnaires.

(1) Pickle, Herrmann, Kerwin, Croner, and White (1994) conducted a cognitive laboratory experiment to determine how professionals interpret disease rate maps, in order to develop effective visual mapping techniques.

(2) Caspar and Biemer (1999) used a cognitive lab to estimate issues of production survey costs and respondent burden.

(3) DeMaio and Hughes (2003) interviewed lab subjects to investigate their perceptions of confidentiality of information when it is collected at several points from different household members.

(4) Landreth (2001) used cognitive techniques to evaluate advance letters used for the U.S. Census Bureau's Survey of Income and Program Participation (SIPP).

(5) Kennet, Wilson, Calvillo, Whitaker, Garber, and Pinder (2000) applied cognitive interviewing to development of a brochure intended to counter mistrust-based survey refusals.

(6) Apart from math word problems, there are a range of educational applications (e.g., text comprehension) to which cognitive interviewing techniques have been extended (e.g., Trabasso & Suh, 1993).

Chapter Summary

• Cognitive interviews apply in many "special" situations. As the survey (and other fields) progress, these situations are becoming more commonplace, and cognitive techniques must adjust accordingly. I have described the way in which interviewing can be done across a limited number of nonstandard situations, beyond the interviewer-administered individual interview.

• For *self-administration,* we must adjust to the fact that an interviewer is missing, and the respondent will go through the instrument unaided. If we have doubts about how this will work, we should let subjects complete the instrument undisturbed and probe them afterward.

• *Sensitive topics* are difficult because we must often talk about embarrassing or illegal subject matter. Cognitive interviewing can be accomplished if we modify our methods but at the same time adopt a stance during the interview that communicates to subjects that we are simply asking them normal questions.

• *Computer administration* ultimately should make things easier for interviewers and respondents, but it does make things difficult for cognitive interviewers. If it is not possible to use a draft computer program to conduct interviews, one can decide to use a paper mock-up, although this is not ideal.

- *Establishment surveys* present operational difficulties to the cognitive testing process. Concerning the conduct of the interview itself, we must focus on both business ethnography, in order to create meaningful questions, and on the information retrieval process, which may involve multiple sources, including written records.

- *Attitudinal questions* are amenable to the cognitive interview, just as are factual-autobiographical ones. However, we must be careful not to induce subjects to speculate on the sources of their attitudes, which they may not have direct access to.

- *Interviewing children and the elderly* mainly differs from the norm in that these interviews are likely to be especially enjoyable to the interviewer; otherwise, both groups make excellent subjects.

Notes

1. It is not clear from the Redline et al. report whether the think-aloud condition also included verbal probes; I assume that it did.
2. Some cognitive probes intended for factual questions do literally include the word "why," as in "Why do you say that?" However, this use of "why" can be seen as an equivalent to simply "How did you come up with that?" which again departs from the usage criticized by Wilson et al.

13

Evaluation of Cognitive Interviewing Techniques

What is truth?

Johnny Cash
© Songs of Cash/Bughouse
© 1970, CBS Records

Chapter Overview

Cognitive interviewing is widespread and has gained considerable acceptance. However, popularity does not automatically confer validity, and several authors have encouraged survey researchers to directly face the question "How do we know that the cognitive approach to testing survey questions really works?" (O'Muircheartaigh, 1999; Tucker, 1997; Willis et al., 1999). Cognitive interviewing can be evaluated from a number of perspectives. First, I will revisit the theoretical underpinnings of the method and consider whether they serve to provide a base of support in the manner intended by its proponents. Following this, I turn to the empirical evaluation of the cognitive interview by

- considering the complexities involved in defining method effectiveness;
- proposing a framework that organizes the evaluation studies that have been conducted to date;
- summarizing the findings of those studies; and
- indicating where gaps exist in evaluation efforts.

Theoretical Perspectives

ARE WE REALLY MIND READERS?

One way to view the effectiveness of cognitive interviewing is to assess its supposed role as a means for "opening a window to the mind." A critic might challenge this assertion, objecting that cognitive interviewers who rely on verbal report techniques cannot *really* tell what people are thinking; Groves (1996) has expressed the key issue as a chapter title: "How Do We Know What We Think They Think Is Really What They Think?" The risk we face is that there might be little relationship between verbal reports and underlying mental processes, and that verbalized descriptions of thinking are therefore uninformative or even misleading. Our adaptation of Ericsson and Simon's (1980) theoretical viewpoints, as described in Chapters 3 and 4, might simply be misguided.

In support of this contention, it has sometimes been demonstrated that people's verbal reports of *why* they have behaved in a certain manner are inconsistent with objective measures of their behaviors. The most compelling evidence to date is an oft-cited study by Nisbett and Wilson (1977). Fueling skepticism toward verbal report methods, the authors demonstrated that they could arrange experimental situations in which subjects appeared to have no conscious awareness of subtle factors that influence their behavior. In one representative experiment, Nisbett and Wilson presented word pairs, such as "ocean-moon," that were intended to elicit (or "prime") particular mental associations (e.g., "tide"). Later in the experiment, when asked to name a detergent, subjects who had viewed these word pairs were more likely than controls to mention "Tide." More significantly, when probed as to *why* they had chosen Tide, these subjects tended to mention factors other than the priming word pairs (e.g., "Tide is the best-known detergent"; My mother uses Tide"; "I like the Tide box").

The Nisbett and Wilson study prompted a great deal of critical response, too extensive to cover here; but in summary, proponents and skeptics of verbal report methods agree that, as the authors stated, *in some cases* verbal reports can be misleading. This is entirely consistent with Ericsson and Simon's original contentions. In particular, if we ask subjects to speculate—especially about the reasons for their behaviors—they will tend to do so, even when we cannot reasonably expect them to have useful insights. This observation is in accordance with recommendations for avoiding probing pitfalls that were presented in Chapter 8.

To a great extent, the current debate concerning the veracity of verbal reports in psychological research has narrowed from the global question of *whether* verbal reports are veridical to *when* they are (Austin & Delaney, 1998; Smith & Miller, 1978). Which types of cognitive tasks, verbal report instructions, and research objectives represent best uses of verbal reporting? This is a largely unresolved issue (Crutcher, 1994). For current purposes, three observations are relevant: (1) Circumstances *can* be developed in which subjects have little insight into the motivations for their actions; (2) subjects will nevertheless attempt an explanation when asked to; and (3) misleading self-reports are, in these cases, most likely when people are asked probes requiring them to justify their behaviors.

VERBAL REPORTS AND COGNITIVE INTERVIEWING

The general debate among psychologists over the veracity of verbal report methods has not directly concerned the cognitive interviewing of survey questions (or of other materials). Elsewhere (Willis, in press) I have considered the theoretical basis for this extension, and Beatty, Willis, et al. (1997) have suggested logical arguments supporting the use of verbal reports in questionnaire design. I will briefly recap—and extend—these arguments. First, in support of the notion that there is a meaningful correspondence between the thoughts that produce survey responses and the verbal reports given by our tested subjects, we do have the advantage of relying on a cognitive model that makes defensible assumptions about the relationships between specific cognitive processes (e.g., comprehension) and response quality. For one, we accept that understanding a question increases the probability that one can answer it correctly, and that evidence of misunderstanding is a reasonable indication that the question may be problematic.

Further, we make the assertion that subjects do, at least in some cases, have awareness of cognitive problems, and that when they do express these, the expressions are veridical. That is, when subjects state that they are confused, we believe them, based on our willingness to also believe it unlikely that someone who says "I don't have any idea what that question is asking me" actually does, and is falsely reporting difficulty. Similarly, we accept that subjects who produce verbalizations such as "Sorry, I can't remember all the times I've been to a restaurant in the past 6 months" do so as a result of their conscious awareness of retrieval failure.[1] In sum, we reject a radical behaviorist view claiming that conscious thought is epiphenomenal; that is, it exists, but is not relevant to behavior (Skinner, 1950). This view is reminiscent of the psycholinguistic concept of the grounded conversation; speakers realize when they are unclear or confused, and take active steps on this basis to communicate these facts to their conversational partner and to apply repair mechanisms. Such naturalistic exchanges simply do not seem to support an extreme (and perhaps distorted) interpretation of Nisbett and Wilson's (1977) results, which would propose that speakers literally do not know what they are thinking and are unable to express their thoughts.

MUST SUBJECTS BE AWARE THAT SURVEY QUESTIONS CAUSE THEM PROBLEMS?

The discussion above assumes that our lab subjects truly *are* aware of the fact that questions cause them cognitive problems. But what if they are not? Rho and Sangster (2003) concluded that their cognitive interview subjects "were not always reliable informants about their cognitive processes and their ability to comprehend and answer the survey questions" (p. 2), and this mirrors a range of findings concerning subjects' relative inability to realize when they are having difficulties (e.g., Cosenza, 2001). I do not see this as a fundamental flaw, however. It is, of course, useful if our subjects are aware of difficulties and can make them known to us; our use of Reactive probing is, to some extent, dependent on these realizations. However, there are also many cases in which our reliance on verbal reports is not dependent on the assumption that subjects have subjective insight or recognize that problems exists. Once again, the phenomenon of silent misunderstanding, as described in Chapter 6, has been found to be rampant—and we conduct Proactive forms of probing, in particular, because subjects cannot of their own accord provide insight into their comprehension abilities. Rather, subjects reveal how they are comprehending the item, and the *researcher* decides whether a problem exists. This is why we do not normally ask our subjects to critique the questions or their own performance; it is up to us to assess these factors, based on their performance during the interview.

Referring again to the math word problem that opened Chapter 1, when a first grader answers a targeted word problem, and the interviewer probes with "How did you get that answer?" the child may, in turn, provide a verbal report indicating a rational chain of mental operations that suggests a different encoding of the original question than the one intended. We do not, however, expect the child to have awareness of the nature of the cognitive problem, let alone its existence. Rather, the interviewer diagnoses the problem, relying on the verbal report as a record of the byproducts of the child's cognitive effort.

Of course, a critic might object that even a logically clear and convincing description by the child may be pure fabrication, rather than a literal byproduct of cognition, and that we are led to misdiagnose the problem (admittedly, even very young subjects may try to give us what we ask for, including a potentially useless verbal report). However, such a conclusion requires that we regard the six-year-old as capable of answering our probe by imaginatively creating, on the spot, a fanciful alternative description of her thinking that is not only relevant to the evaluated math word problem but also convincing. The simpler explanation would be that the child has produced a report that is closely enough associated with just-terminated cognitive processes that it can be regarded as veridical.

DO WE EVEN NEED OUR SUBJECTS
TO REVEAL THEIR THOUGHT PROCESSES?

The preceding discussion implies a subtle distinction between (a) subjects' conscious awareness of *question flaws* and (b) their awareness of *what they are thinking as they answer the questions*. I have argued that at times the former of these conditions applies (subjects are aware that the questions produce problems), and at other times the latter is a better description (they tell us what they think, and *we* decide if a problem exists). More extremely, however, there are still other times when we do not even require condition (b) to hold. That is, to reject a major premise of our underlying cognitive theory, *we find problems even when subjects cannot effectively articulate or reflect upon their own thought processes.* In other words, we do not directly concern ourselves with verbal reports that indicate what they are thinking.

By adopting an Expansive probing perspective, as detailed in Chapter 7, we do rely on verbal reports, but these are of a very different nature than the ones described by Ericsson and Simon. Rather than asking what they are thinking, we simply ask subjects to answer the survey questions (e.g., on their job history) and then to provide an Expansive description—say, of all the jobs they have ever had. The subject may report three jobs but during the elaborated discussion make evident that she, all told, had six. After observing such a trend across a series of interviews, the investigators may decide that the target question is flawed and likely to produce an undercount.

At no point, however, did the interviewing process require subjects to provide reports on their cognitive processes in the usual sense. Rather, subjects gave the answer and then talked more about the issue. This version of verbal report can be conceptualized as the overt *product* of cognition, rather than a record of the thought *processes* giving rise to that product. In such cases, subjects may even be unaware that there is a conflict between the product they provide in answer to the target question and the one that they produce under an elaborated description (although in practice they do tend to notice this after a point, and make comments like "Boy, that answer I first gave you was way off, wasn't it?"). Overall, from the point of view of the Expansive interview approach, we don't worry about whether we are in fact mind readers because this is not a necessary requirement of problem discovery. In any event, we certainly are not burdened by a requirement that we use verbal report methods to drill into the subjects' heads and pull out their thoughts.

SUMMARY: THEORY IS STILL USEFUL

In one sense, I have addressed the issue of theory by challenging the usual assertion that the cognitive interview is dependent on cognitive theory, especially as it involves a reliance on verbal report methods as espoused by Ericsson and Simon. Rather, to the degree that Expansive interviewing procedures in particular are not inherently cognitive in perspective, and may not rely strongly on verbal reports in the usual sense, our techniques may call for a different variety of as-yet-undeveloped theoretical support. Or, we may decide that attempts to impose theory overburden the system, and that cognitive interviewing in essence should be guided by a combination of common sense and the overt demonstration that it is useful. Certainly it is possible to conduct cognitive interviewing without becoming a theoretician.

On the other hand, theory is useful in guiding practice, especially where a methodology gives rise to complex decisions concerning best—or flawed—practice. Also, given that answering survey questions by definition does require cognitive processing, a cognitive theoretical perspective is still very attractive. In particular, as pointed out previously by Forsyth and Lessler (1991), it is imperative to further consider the conditions under which verbal report procedures of various types are veridical when applied to the cognitive interview. We also need to further clarify our views of exactly what we demand of ourselves, and of our subjects, as we apply these methods. For one, I have argued that even from the current cognitive viewpoint, we do not require that our subjects articulate, themselves, the problems they have in answering survey questions. Rather, their verbal reports indicate to the researcher that problems exist. We still have not determined, however, the best means for eliciting such indications of trouble (see Willis, in press, for a more extensive discussion). I conclude this discussion by emphasizing that in evaluating the cognitive interview by making reference to theory, we need to be careful to first determine what theory best pertains. This remains an unfinished task.

Empirical Evaluation of Cognitive Interviewing

Aside from considering the interesting—but somewhat conjectural—notions of subjective awareness, windows to the mind, and other theoretic constructs, we can also take a more objective, empirical approach to evaluation. As Tucker (1997) forcefully argued, methods that claim to be scientific should be required to demonstrate their effectiveness. However, the issue of whether "the cognitive approach works" is itself vague (in the same sense that our survey questions often are), and requires further clarification, especially concerning what is meant by "the cognitive approach," and whether it "works." Our approaches are multifaceted; some of these could work, and others not. Second, in deciding what works, we also need to establish valid measures of effectiveness.

Because these challenges are complex and varied, it is vital to first formulate an evaluation model that establishes criteria for assessing method utility—that is, our ground rules. In order to make sense of the tangled web of evaluation efforts done to date, and to spur future work in this area in an organized fashion, I will organize the discussion around the framework described in Table 13.1.

This chapter focuses on within-method studies; between-method evaluation will be deferred to Chapter 14, following a wider description of pretesting methods. The existence of a diverse set of models does complicate the evaluation task. However, it also allows researchers to adopt varied perspectives and to conduct a range of limited studies that may be inconclusive in themselves but that point to consistent overall themes.

EVALUATION MODEL 1: DOES
COGNITIVE INTERVIEWING FIX PROBLEMS?

The most superficially compelling evaluation criterion is simple: Is there any evidence that cognitive interviewing improves survey questions? I have often endeavored to demonstrate to clients that a result of our testing has been to improve their questions, as this is usually their

Table 13.1   Models for the Evaluation of Cognitive Interviewing

(A) Within-Method Evaluation	
Model 1	Question improvement: Are evaluated questions "fixed" through cognitive testing?
Model 2	Criterion validation: Are known problems found through cognitive testing?
Model 3	External validation: Are cognitive interviewing results replicated in the field environment?
Model 4	Reliability/Consistency analysis: Do independent cognitive tests, laboratories, or approaches identify the same problems in evaluated questions?
Model 5	Process evaluation: Are cognitive interviewing results useful in the broad scheme of survey development?
(B) Between-Method Evaluation	
Are the problems found in cognitive interviewing in agreement with those found by other pretesting methods?	

fundamental concern. For example, for a final report of cognitive testing of a set of questions on drug use (Willis, 2000), I submitted both the initial draft and the final version to a set of linguistic analyses, and obtained the results shown in Table 13.2.

These results do seem to represent an improvement on multiple linguistic fronts and could be seen as evidence that cognitive testing was effective. To muddy the waters considerably, however, more systematic studies of question improvement by Forsyth, Rothgeb, and Willis (in press) and by DeMaio and Landreth (in press) have produced results that were less positive; using either additional cognitive testing results or measures of overt problems observed in field administration, neither was able to demonstrate clear superiority of questions that were revised based on cognitive testing results. (I will have more to say about these studies in Chapter 14.)

In any event, results concerning question improvement may be beside the point. Based on the contention that "cognitive testing doesn't improve survey questions, questionnaire designers improve survey questions," a critic might reject attempts to either credit or blame the cognitive testing process itself for question improvement or lack thereof. This objection

Table 13.2   Linguistic Analysis of Initial and Recommended Drug
Dependence Questions

	Number of long sentences	"Big words"	Average number of words/ sentences	Sentence complexity index (0-100)	Flesch-Kincaid reading level
Initial Draft	10	53	28.5	83	13.1
Recommended Draft	2	43	23.3	65	10.9

does force us to clarify our expectations: do we believe that cognitive interviewing directly improves survey questions, or preliminary to that, that it only identifies problems that can then be remedied? Willis et al. (1999) termed this distinction as *finding* versus *fixing*. In discussing the skills and training necessary for cognitive interviewing in Chapter 9, I suggested that finding problems is generally easier than fixing them, as the latter poses requirements (such as expertise at the level of the individual practitioner) that extend beyond the strict domain of the cognitive interview itself. Consequently, cognitive interviewing might result in clear evidence of a specific problem (e.g., of 10 subjects, none have any idea of what we mean by "natural gas distribution charges"), but these testing results may not directly tell us what to do to improve the question. Optimally, cognitive testing results point us toward a specific hypothesis concerning the root of the problem. Finding a solution that improves the question, however, remains the job of the questionnaire designer, who must make intelligent use of the cognitive interviewing results (Tourangeau, Rips, et al., 2000).

Paradoxically, then, evaluations of cognitive interviewing that simply ask, "Was the questionnaire improved?" can be misleading. If the answer turns out to be "No," this could be only because of a limitation in ability or imagination of the questionnaire designer(s). Conversely, as Conrad and Blair (1996) and Willis et al. (1999) point out, demonstrations of absolute improvements to questions following cognitive testing and subsequent revision are also inconclusive, as this could reflect only the skill of designers, apart from any particular contribution of cognitive testing. So simply observing that our questions have either improved or failed to improve following cognitive interviewing is not, in itself, particularly informative for evaluating cognitive interviewing in a general sense.[2] As a result, Evaluation Model 1, though seemingly the crux of the entire matter, is unsatisfactory.

EVALUATION MODEL 2: DOES COGNITIVE INTERVIEWING FIND PROBLEMS?

Because of ambiguities related to fixing problems, the most straight-forward and easily interpreted assessments of cognitive interviewing outcomes detach the finding and fixing stages of question development and address the former through a simplified evaluation question: Is cognitive interviewing effective in identifying known problems contained in survey questions? Here a useful evaluation model does exist: We can adopt principles from epidemiology and psychological testing as used to evaluate diagnostic tests (e.g., for depression, breast cancer, etc.). We determine whether the test exhibits both (a) *sensitivity* in successfully identifying positive occurrences (finding problems in survey items that really exist) and (b) *specificity* in rejecting negative occurrences (labeling questions *without* problems as acceptable). This model also requires that we have a criterion measure, or gold standard, by which to determine sensitivity and specificity. For example, to evaluate a psychological screening test for major depression, we must have some independent means (such as a full clinical evaluation) to determine whether our subjects are, in fact, depressed. Or, in order to evaluate a protocol for mammogram review, we might mix a set of X-rays for cases that resulted in breast cancer diagnoses with others that did not, to determine whether the protocol can effectively distinguish them.

As applied to questionnaire pretesting, a similar logic dictates that we stock the pond, by mixing "good" and "bad" questions, and determine whether cognitive interviewing is effective in discriminating between them. Although this is an attractive model, we unfortunately lack clear independent measures of survey question quality that allow us to conduct such a sensitivity analysis. In fact, a general challenge to the survey methods field is to know whether our questions in fact produce error. As discussed in Chapter 2, one approach has been to conduct record check studies, which compare objective records with self-reports and determine which types of questions produce accurate results. However, such objective records are normally elusive. First, the concept of a "record" may make little sense: for attitudinal measures, such as favorability toward a political candidate, or self-assessment of life happiness, there normally exists no gold standard record that one could possibly make use of. Such measures are by definition latent constructs—they are presumed to exist but unobservable—and we have, in practice, no measure that can be used to determine directly whether the report of an attitudinal question is "correct" or not. Even for factual and autobiographical questions, gold standard measures may only exist in theory, given that the spectrum of behaviors we are interested in assessing, such as number of sexual partners, generally fails to produce objective records.

Lacking records, are there other ways that we can assign levels of "goodness" to survey questions in order to evaluate cognitive interviews? Interestingly, one older study by Hunt et al. (1982) made such an attempt. Hunt et al. selected three techniques: (a) think-aloud via phone, (b) in-person think-aloud, and (c) a debriefing procedure that seemed to have included retrospective probing. They assessed the performance of each for its ability to detect questions the researchers believed (apparently based on expert judgment) to exhibit defects. Even though subjects were instructed to be critical, the procedures all produced unimpressive levels of detection of the problematic embedded survey questions: only 12.5% were detected on average, although surprisingly, telephone-based think-alouds were found to be more productive than those conducted in person.

Although the Hunt et al. results were fairly negative, it is difficult to know how much confidence to place in them in evaluating cognitive techniques that are used today, especially given that (a) the authors did not provide many details of their pretest procedures, (b) the most frequent cognitive interviewing approach currently employed (again, a heavily probed interview) was not evaluated, and (c) although not totally clear, their procedure appears to have relied heavily on the ability of subjects to critique questions and ferret out problems, which does not reflect modern practice. Surely, though, an appropriate replication of the Hunt et al. approach would be a welcome development in the field.

Beyond this, it would be instructive to use more recent developments in question quality measurement that are more rigorous than experimenter opinion but that do not rely on a full-blown record-check study. For example, researchers can make use of (a) questions that are found through reinterview studies to differ in their reliability, (b) questions that have been found by record-check studies to differ in degree of response error produced (e.g., those assessing accurate self-reports of medical conditions versus inaccurate reports), or (c) questions that have been determined in field studies to produce overt problems or problematic data distributions (such as very high numbers of "don't know" responses).

Such studies likely represent a very promising approach to the evaluation of cognitive interviewing, or of any pretesting technique. I leave this as a recommendation for future work.

EVALUATION MODEL 3: ARE COGNITIVE TESTING RESULTS RELEVANT TO THE FIELD ENVIRONMENT?

A few studies have incorporated an evaluation model that assesses the use of cognitive interviewing in finding problems but that does not rely on absolute measures of question quality. Rather, *lab-to-field carryover studies* are based on the assertion that if problems found through cognitive interviewing are real, they should at least have external validity—some measurable impact in the field environment to which they are intended to apply. In perhaps the earliest evaluation studies of cognitive interviewing, Lessler et al. (1989) demonstrated that problems found in a series of dental questions as a result of think-aloud interviewing appeared to be similar to those uncovered in a field pretest of the same instrument. However, foreshadowing a difficulty of such studies, the results were ambiguous because it was not possible to maintain strict independence between laboratory and field outcomes; the demands of field survey development often simply do not allow for controlled experimentation.

More recently, Willis and Schechter (1997) carried out a controlled experiment designed to directly assess the degree of carryover from the cognitive laboratory to the field environment. The investigators developed alternate wording for each of five target survey questions, based on cognitive testing results. The testing results had indicated that the alternate versions could be expected to produce predictably divergent data distributions when fielded. Rather than simply selecting the version that appeared superior, they instead chose to test both in a field environment. That is, as a fairly stringent test, the researchers examined the extent to which cognitive interviewing outcomes could be used to predict the directionality of data distributions obtained from Version A (original) relative to Version B (revised).

For example, cognitive interviews of the question on physical activity contained in Table 13.3 resulted in an explicit prediction: Relative to the original version of a single question that simply asked *how much* activity the person engaged in (Version A), a revision that included a filter question first asking whether the respondent engaged in *any* physical activity (Version B) would result in lower overall levels of reporting. That is, the former appeared to induce lab subjects to report some non-zero amount, in order to avoid saying "none" and appearing to be completely inactive,

Table 13.3   Alternate Version of Physical Activity Question

VERSION A (No screener):

On a typical day, how much time do you spend doing strenuous physical activities such as lifting, pushing, or pulling? __ None __ Less than 1 hour __ 1–4 hours __ 5 + hours

VERSION B (Screener):

On a typical day, do you spend *any* time doing strenuous physical activities such as lifting, pushing, or pulling?
　　　　　IF YES: Read Version A

	Mean number of hours of physical activity reported										
	0	<1	1–4	5+	0	<1	1–4	5+	0	<1	1–4	5+
	FIELD PRETEST				CLINIC SURVEY				TELEPHONE SURVEY			
	(*n* = 78)				(*n* = 191)				(*n* = 989)			
No screener (A)	32%	32%	35%	0%	4%	42%	50%	4%	–	45%	34%	22%
Screener (B)	72%	18%	10%	0%	49%	16%	27%	8%	–	62%	29%	9%

SOURCE: Adapted from Willis and Schechter, 1997.

whereas presenting the same question as an initial "yes/no" choice allowed subjects to select "no" and to make comments like "I just have a desk job," therefore avoiding the forced choice concerning how much activity one engages in.[3]

In three subsequent field studies of various sizes (ranging from 78 to almost 1,000 respondents) and involving a range of survey types (face-to-face household, telephone, and clinical environment), these predictions were borne out in striking fashion (see Table 13.3). The authors concluded that qualitative cognitive testing results could be used to make predictions concerning the functioning of targeted questions across a range of field environments.

Finally, Davis and DeMaio (1993) conducted a study that compared cognitive interviewing results with field outcomes, and that can be viewed as a lab-to-field carryover study. In departure from the Willis and Schechter (1997) approach, however, they focused not on the *problems with survey questions* found through cognitive interviewing, but rather on the *answers* given to those questions in the cognitive interview. In essence, they focused on the classic question of whether verbal reports induce reactivity by determining whether the answers to a tested series in a think-aloud cognitive interview were similar to one completed under field conditions (absent cognitive interviewing). Although theirs was a small study consisting of 10 subjects who completed each version of a dietary recall questionnaire, they found no evidence that think-aloud altered the overall number of food items reported. As does the Willis and Schechter study, the Davis and DeMaio results buttress the contention that cognitive interviews are similar enough to field interviews that similar mental processes are involved, and that the qualitative results from cognitive interviews can reasonably be expected to carry over to the environments to which they are intended to generalize. Future evaluation studies that incorporate split-sample approaches, such as that by Willis and Schechter, will be facilitated to the extent that researchers have access to vehicles for methodological survey research (Fowler, 2003). To this end, Rothgeb (2003) has described the Questionnaire Design Experimental Research Study (QDERS) that has been implemented at the U.S. Census Bureau.

EVALUATION MODEL 4: ANALYSIS OF RELIABILITY AND CONSISTENCY

As Tucker (1997) has pointed out, in order to be valid, results should at least be reliable within the laboratory (i.e., reproducible under identical testing conditions) and consistent between labs (i.e., at least similar—testing conditions may be somewhat different but outcomes theoretically should converge). Measures of within-lab reliability are infrequent, especially because any one laboratory does not typically collect independent measures of testing outcomes for the same targeted questions. However, once a cognitive laboratory has been in operation for a sufficient time, it should be possible to keep track of testing results for identical, or at least similar, items that have been targeted in different investigations. We can then determine whether the same problems tend to emerge each time.

To my knowledge, at least two organizations have begun to catalogue tested questions in computerized database systems (Collins & Becher, 2001; Miller, Canfield, Beatty, Whitaker, & Wilson, 2003), and this promises to further promote reliability analysis. Short of this, most assessments of this type are admittedly sporadic and anecdotal. It is at least reassuring to come across, in one's own work, case studies that suggest that we are unearthing persistent problems; for example, the illustration in Figure 13.1 of a key issue (the presence of an ambiguous reference period) that arose when testing very similar questions in different studies.

STUDY 1 TARGET QUESTION: Have you ever seriously thought about quitting smoking?

INTERVIEWER COMMENT: My 17-year-old subject said "Yes, but not now." He's thought about quitting at a future time, when he goes to college. This may be OK if we have a generally wide intent for the question, but not if we really mean whether they've thought about quitting in the sense of "current intent."

STUDY 2 TARGET QUESTION: Do you want to completely stop smoking cigarettes?

INTERVIEWER COMMENT: One reaction was "Sure, by the time I'm 40." The question doesn't indicate a time frame. Do we mean "Would you completely stop smoking cigarettes <u>right now</u>, if you could?"

Figure 13.1   Cognitive Interviewing Studies of Teenage Smokers

SOURCE: Studies conducted at the Research Triangle Institute Cognitive Research Laboratory (previously unpublished, by the author).

BETWEEN-LAB STUDIES

Methodological studies of consistency of results *across* rather than within cognitive laboratories have been more frequent. Willis, Schechter, and Whitaker (1999) compared the results of interviews of the same set of target questions from two cognitive laboratories that used different approaches to cognitive interviewing (the former involving experienced interviewers and Spontaneous probes, the latter less experienced using mainly Anticipated probes) to determine whether the same questions were identified as problematic. Using a quantitative measure of problem severity, they found fairly good correspondence across labs (a correlation of .68), suggesting good intra-method reliability. On the other hand, Rothgeb et al. (2001) applied a similar design to a comparison of three cognitive laboratories and found substantially lower agreement across them concerning intensity of problem severity (in general, r = .3). However, Rothgeb et al. did note that their questionnaire contained survey questions that were extremely problem-ridden, possibly resulting in ceiling effects, and therefore a restriction in range that minimized the magnitude of statistical relationships.

In a more recent well-controlled study, DeMaio and Landreth (in press) determined whether cognitive laboratories produced similar outcomes when testing a common questionnaire (a 48-item telephone survey of household recycling practices). Across three organizational teams representing different "packages" of cognitive pretesting techniques, they obtained a mixed bag of outcomes: (a) The teams tended to agree on the particular questions that were problematic (overall 81% agreement) but (b) failed to concur concerning the qualitative types of problems, for both interviewers and respondents, that were found in those questions (overall 34% agreement). This finding brings to life the distinction between the objectives of (a) identifying problematic questions and (b) identifying the exact *source* of the problem so that the problems can be directly addressed, and suggests that the former is likely a more straightforward pursuit.

The Rothgeb et al. and DeMaio and Landreth studies are somewhat disturbing, in that they indicate that cognitive interviewing may produce somewhat unstable results; different interviewing teams may come to different conclusions concerning the nature of problems contained in survey questions. However, it is not clear what conclusions should be drawn on the basis of low level of agreement concerning problem identification. In particular, this begs the question of what it means to "agree." The fact that teams identified different problems for the same question does not necessarily imply that they literally disagreed concerning the existence of problems—they may simply have noted different problems where multiple ones existed, especially given that the tested questionnaires appear to have been riddled with defects. One simple conclusion might be that the conduct of additional interviews brings out more (actual) problems. As an analogy, if we view cognitive interviewing teams as teams of inspectors—say, of a vessel that is very minimally seaworthy—it is possible that the different teams may locate a range of areas of the ship that exhibit problems (to pursue the analogy, rust, holes, missing parts, and so on). The fact that these inspectors focus on different sets of defects does not mean that they disagree—only that once they identify deficiencies, they come to different conclusions concerning which ones require immediate attention. It is quite possible that they are all correct and, in combination, are effective in covering the true range.

Parenthetically, as a final illustration that is relevant to the assessment of between-lab testing outcomes, I cite one more example from my testing archives (documenting testing at NCHS of a mid-1990s National Health Interview Survey, administered to adults), and simply urge the reader to compare this with the results of testing of the teen smoking questions later conducted at RTI, presented previously in Figure 13.1:[4]

Would you like to completely quit smoking cigarettes?

The question doesn't indicate "right now." One subject said "yes," but means he wants to stop someday. If this is the intention of the question, this is OK.

EVALUATION MODEL 5: DO FINDINGS
GET IMPLEMENTED INTO ONGOING PROCESSES?

Yet another evaluation question can be expressed very directly: Even if cognitive testing results otherwise satisfy all of the demands of our evaluation models, can they be made use of in a practical sense? That is, once we work out the complex issues concerning finding problems versus fixing them, whether they can be proved to be real problems, and so on, we are still left with the vital issue of whether we can really impact survey practice (Rothgeb et al., 2000). In particular, we could establish that cognitive techniques exhibit impressive sensitivity and specificity, but for reasons related to logistical or organizational resistance, the results might be practically unusable. Rothgeb et al. identified the following as impediments to implementation:

- The need to avoid question changes in order to maintain *time series* (i.e., asking the question the same way over time, so estimates can be compared)

- Resistance of decision makers to the results of qualitative methods

- A tendency to treat testing results as a "stamp of approval" for the survey, even where none of the recommendations are implemented

- Lack of resources to implement recommended changes

Issues of timing are paramount: If sufficient testing takes so long that critical results are available only after the instrument is finalized and put into the field, our demonstrations of effectiveness represent, at best, a Pyrrhic victory. Further, as a very real concern, if computer-based administration imposes programming-related requirements that make cognitive testing untenable, then it will likely fall by the wayside, no matter how useful it may have been in the past.

To date, evidence for the value of cognitive interviewing has largely consisted of documentation showing how it is embedded into the routine process of developing survey questionnaires, and in some cases is part of an official pretesting policy. A recent statement on survey development policy from the U.S. Census Bureau (2003) has reiterated the value of cognitive (and other) pretesting techniques, and despite the changes occurring in the survey world, cognitive interviewing results continue to be used across a wide variety of questionnaire development projects.

Rothgeb et al. (2000) state that several strategies have been used successfully to gain acceptance of cognitive testing at the Census Bureau:

- Communicating expectations with sponsors or clients from the very earliest development stages

- Identifying early the "unchangeables" in the existing instrument

- Inviting clients to observe cognitive interviews

- Writing convincing outcome reports that rely on case study quotes to bring life to abstract comments and prioritizing recommendations

In summary, if we define the validity of cognitive interviewing in terms of its implementation, it appears to have made the appropriate impact. This, however, has not been an automatic outcome but rather the result of considerable proactivity by its practitioners.

Are We Evaluating the Right Outcome?

Most of the above discussion assumes a particular criterion: cognitive interviewing is effective to the degree that it serves as a type of "metal detector," sweeping the questionnaire in search of defects. This objective is of course vital, but it is incomplete. I have stressed a range of potential positive outcomes, including (a) forcing us to respecify and define our measurement objectives, and therefore choose the right questions to ask in the first place;[5] (b) determining what types of information can and can't be measured effectively in a self-report survey, due to cognitive or other limitations; (c) detecting problems at the questionnaire (rather than question) level that involve higher-order issues of section ordering and organization; and (d) helping us to understand more about the relative trade-offs associated with different approaches to asking questions and then choose the form that best fits our current objectives (Beatty, 2003, 2004).

This last point is particularly significant, and can be restated as a statistical Bayesian viewpoint that emphasizes the evolution of subjective probability assessments over time. That is, our development process consists of the following:

(a) We begin with *a priori* expectations concerning question functioning, based on expert review activities or other sources of background information.

(b) Through the conduct of empirical cognitive testing, we gain additional information about how items function when administered to live subjects.

(c) Based on this accrual of knowledge, we adjust our initial expectations, possibly make further changes, and test further.

(d) At the end of the process, based on what we have observed, we select the question form that we now believe most likely to provide the best measure in the context of the current investigation.

The outcomes resulting from this sequence cannot be evaluated within a simple, metal-detector-based evaluation design that considers only the issue of problem identification in an absolute sense. Although we sometimes may be separating wheat from chaff, there are also many cases when the pertinent question may instead be "Which of several question variants (if any) will be useful for my particular application?" We do not obtain an answer to this based on the very limited measures that we normally claim represent markers of question quality or validity. Some years ago Oppenheim (1966) made this fundamental point in suggesting that *to the extent a question may have a number of potential objectives, it may also have different validities.* Cognitive interviewing may itself be valid to the extent that it forces the testers and designers to think about this very issue.

Limitations of Cognitive Interviewing

I have talked a great deal *about* evaluation—how it has been done and how it might be done better—without coming to a solid answer to the opening question: How do we know for sure that cognitive interviewing is valid? At this point, this is a difficult case to prove, even though, as an advocate, I have taken a liberal approach throughout and suggested a range of purposes to which cognitive interviewing can profitably be applied. Given this orientation, it is appropriate to conclude a chapter on evaluation on a more conservative note and to list some caveats to cognitive interviewing practice, with a balanced discussion that acknowledges potential drawbacks.

1. *Cognitive laboratory subjects are not survey respondents.* Volunteers for cognitive interviews are, by definition, self-selected and are therefore not likely to be representative of the survey population as a whole (although the case can also be made that for a household survey with a 50% response rate, respondents are somewhat self-selected). Most importantly, unless explicit steps are taken to counter the effect, laboratory volunteers may tend to be higher in level of education than the

average survey respondent. We can counter this somewhat by avoiding recruitment of subjects who all have very high levels of education (e.g., advertising for people "with at most a high school education" has been effective).

2. *The cognitive laboratory environment is different from that of the field.* Especially if one makes use of a cognitive lab, the physical and social environment will not replicate the field interview, and this may influence the obtained results. The extent to which the differences in question-answering contexts matter likely depends on the type of question administered and the cognitive processes involved. In particular, the cognitive lab cannot easily be used to study issues of respondent motivation to think hard to answer a question—they are much more likely to *satisfice* (Krosnick, 1991) in the field than under the conditions of cognitive testing. Lab subjects are generally patient and forgiving, especially when paid, and I have never had a break-off during a cognitive interview (that is, except for one medical emergency involving allergic reaction to herbal tea). Cognitive testing results may, for this reason, underestimate problems in the field. On the other hand, it is sometimes surprising to find that even in the laboratory, subjects may pay only cursory attention to tested materials, such as study brochures (Landreth, 2003); to our benefit, even paid subjects are not enticed to pay close attention to materials they find boring or confusing.

3. *Cognitive interviewers are (normally) not field interviewers.* Cognitive and field interviewing require different skills and priorities, and in general, cognitive interviewing is not useful for detecting measurement errors attributable to the field interviewer (Von Thurn & Moore, 1994). Further, because cognitive interviewers focus mainly on the respondent side of the interaction, they have a tendency to neglect question features that cause problems for interviewers. This is not, however, an inherent limitation of the process, as we can choose to attend to such problems if we are mindful of them.

4. *Our sample sizes are generally tiny.* Our samples do tend to be small, and it is sometimes argued that the cognitive approach is generally deficient because the samples used do not support reasonable inferences. I do agree that, to an extent, the more interviews we can do, the better. In defense of cognitive interviews, however, there at least three defects in the argument that small samples are a fatal drawback:

(a) *The purpose of cognitive interviewing is not statistical estimation.* The point is not to obtain sample sizes large enough to supply precision in statistical estimates. Rather, we strive to interview a *variety of individuals* who will be useful in informing our decisions. Statisticians strive to minimize (error) variance, whereas cognitive interviewers maximize (subject) variance.

(b) *The nature of laboratory interviews is qualitative, not quantitative.* As discussed previously, we trade off quantity of observation for intensity and depth of focus. Further, we do not evaluate survey questions simply by counting the number of interviews in which a problem occurs. Of course, if every interviewer reports a problem with a particular question in every interview, that is significant. However, a finding can be based on one interview; an interviewer may say that "I had a person with a particular disease for which this question does not work," and we need not verify this by testing a large number of other individuals with the same disease. *Logical and structural problems in particular are sample-size independent,* in the sense that sources of question illogic persist whether we test one subject or a thousand.

(c) *The apparent quantitative superiority of the field pretest may be illusory.* Again, questionnaires often contain initial screening or filter questions and then long follow-up sections that apply only if one "passes" the gatekeeper. However, in cases where respondents infrequently receive the follow-up questions, field pretests of the general population tend to provide only a few cases in which these follow-ups are actually administered. For example, for one evaluation exercise (Willis, 1989), I found that a field pretest of almost 300 households routed less than 12 individuals to an important section on use of assistive devices (canes, wheelchairs, etc.). Not surprisingly, that section received little comment at a field interviewer debriefing following the pretest. Prior cognitive laboratory testing of the same questionnaire, on the other hand, had specifically incorporated recruitment of subjects who would naturally screen in to the follow-up questions. As a result, the effective sample size of the lab sample turned out to be substantially larger than that in the field pretest. Hence there are times when the effective sample size of the lab sample is not all that poor, relative to those obtained through other mechanisms.

Chapter Summary

THEORETICAL ASPECTS OF VALIDITY

- In defense of our use of cognitive interviewing, we can refer to theoretical and logical grounds; in particular, our reliance on a model of the survey response process at least suggests that *verbal reports are related to the mental processing of survey questions.*
- The finding that subjects don't always have insight into the failures of their own cognitive processes has been cited as a challenge to our use of verbal reports, but it is somewhat of a red herring, as we do not require that subjects have perfect self-awareness.
- Rather, we expect that subjects *provide us information* that is useful to us in evaluating questions—some of this relates to cognitive processes, and some is informative in a more general sense, as it provides elaborated context.
- Overall, theories of cognitive interviewing remain in skeletal form, and are ripe for further development.

EMPIRICAL ASPECTS OF VALIDITY

- *Empirical evaluation* of cognitive interviews is not straightforward, as it is not clear what we mean when we ask whether this "works" to "fix bad survey questions."
- In particular, cognitive interviewing is normally only required to *find* problems; whether these can then be *fixed* is another matter.
- There are means for conducting evaluation studies under a number of models (criterion validation, external validation, reliability/consistency analysis, and process evaluation). In review of these, cognitive interviewing earns mixed grades; we appear to find problems that are real, but it is not as clear whether we do so reliably, as the fundamental principle of repeatability across practitioners remains undemonstrated.
- An alternative way to view the effectiveness of cognitive interviewing is in terms of its value in assessing trade-offs between alternative versions; this view presupposes that questions themselves are not simply "good" or "bad," *but may have multiple validities,* each relative to a different potential measurement objective.

LIMITATIONS TO COGNITIVE INTERVIEWING

- Four limitations to cognitive interviewing were described in terms of the ways it departs from the survey field environment: (a) the individuals interviewed are different, (b) the testing context is different, (c) the interviewers are different, and (d) the samples are smaller. We must adjust to these limitations in order to create a testing environment that has sufficient applicability.

Notes

1. It is possible that this situation does not literally reflect retrieval failure but the subject's unwillingness to attempt to recall. This, however, still provides information that is useful in evaluating the tested question.

2. Another potentially unfortunate, but not unusual, outcome is that cognitive interviewing results were accurate but were not used by clients or design staff, for whatever reason, resulting in no improvement to the questions. In other words, even if cognitive interviewing is necessary for question improvement, it is in no way sufficient to produce that outcome.

3. Note that this finding is consistent with guidance contained in rule-based questionnaire appraisal systems, such as the QAS, which suggest that questions of the form "How often do you do X?" induce bias, relative to questions simply asking "Do you do X?"

4. I acknowledge the anecdotal nature of this example and the fact that a single case in no way proves that cognitive lab results are generally consistent. However, I have chosen to include this as a model of an evaluation approach that could be more systematically pursued through careful documentation of results. I was also struck by the degree to which this particular problem has persisted through time.

5. Beyond *what* to ask, cognitive interviewing may also direct us as far as *whom* to ask the questions of. Hess (1999) describes a case in which the cognitive tester made recommendations concerning the appropriate universe of respondents, based on the anticipated analysis.

14

Beyond Cognitive Testing

Affiliated Pretesting Methods

Methods are the tools of the trade for any discipline.

Couper (1999, p. 281)

Chapter Overview

Couper's observation may seem unremarkable, but note his use of the plural. Because this book is about cognitive interviewing, to this point I have treated it as *the one* tool of choice for evaluating survey questions and other materials. Other tools do exist, however, and even the most enthusiastic advocate must recognize that cognitive testing is not the sole means at our disposal. Because the well-informed practitioner should not just attain proficiency in cognitive techniques, but also become knowledgeable about these other methods, the current chapter reviews the use of (a) expert review, (b) focus groups, (c) behavior coding, and (d) reinterview surveys. Consistent with arguments made by Snijkers (2002), I purposely refer to these not as *alternative* methods, but as *affiliated* methods, because we normally do not select any of these because it is a "better" method in an absolute sense. Rather, methodologists focus on methods integration: *when each method should be used and how they can be combined into an overall pretesting strategy.* I will introduce each method separately, and then consider the challenge of combining them.

(Formal) Expert Review

In Chapter 2, I suggested that one form of expert review—expert appraisal—should always be carried out before cognitive testing. Beyond that, expert *review*, as I describe it here, is a more formal and proactive procedure which is considered to be an empirical pretesting method because it involves the systematic collection and processing of reviews from sources outside the immediate design team (Ramirez, 2002). To date, expert review procedures have not been well documented. Several issues affect the nature and effectiveness of such reviews, but the one I will focus on concerns selecting the experts who will assist us.

WHO IS AN EXPERT?

There are four categories of experts we may rely upon:

(a) Questionnaire design experts

(b) Subject matter experts

(c) Questionnaire administration experts (i.e., experienced interviewers)

(d) Computer-based expert systems

General questionnaire design experts have considerable experience writing and evaluating questionnaires and are well schooled in the design principles explicated in Chapter 2. It is useful to consult this type of expert, or expert team, when the designer needs assistance in developing a draft or feels that an independent questionnaire review would be beneficial. Beyond this type of review, especially for topics that are somewhat unusual, specific, or unfamiliar to the researchers themselves, we can obtain review by a subject matter expert—someone who knows about the topic under investigation through either scholarly study or personal experience. A few examples might be surveys involving

(a) use of assistive devices (wheelchairs, walkers, etc.)

(b) salmon farming

(c) cocaine or heroin use and methods used for quitting drug abuse

Such topics present a host of issues that are simply not familiar to most questionnaire designers. At an early point, it may be useful to at least run the questions by someone who has more than a passing familiarity with the topic. In this way we become informed about factors such as the relevant set of questions to ask, the terminology that may apply, and the ranges of response categories that make sense (e.g., a survey on salmon farming might require a comprehensive list of health problems that afflict farmed salmon).

The distinction between expert review and other development methods may become blurred, especially when the expert feedback is oral rather than written. In particular, a cultural anthropologist might choose to relabel the expert an *informant* and the investigator an *ethnographic investigator*. Tying this concept back to issues discussed in Chapter 7, this application of expert review has many features in common with the ethnographic interview. It may, in some cases, be difficult to say where expert review stops and pretesting-by-interview begins.

A heavy reliance on subject matter experts does potentially create drawbacks. In particular, though they will often attempt to revise survey questions, such experts may not be very good questionnaire designers. Academically or professionally oriented experts (e.g., medical doctors) often know the subject so well that they propose vocabulary or make subtle distinctions that are simply out of the reach of the average survey respondent. As always, the opinions of experts must be accepted with discretion and considered to be modifiable based on cognitive and other testing results.

A sometimes neglected but valuable type of expert is the experienced field interviewer, who can evaluate questions in a way that is enhanced through experience in the field or on the telephone. For example, early in the process of a mid-1990s redesign of the questionnaires for the National Health Interview Survey, NCHS staff conducted a focus group of Census Bureau interviewers in order to determine the problems that respondents typically had with the questions. An extension of the interviewer-based expert review that combines elements of expert opinion and empirical observation is the *interviewer debriefing,* where interviewer guidance is obtained after a field pretest, so that opinions can be based on recent experience. If the interviewers are to systematically rate each item according to a classification scheme (e.g., whether a question presents serious problems, moderate problems, or few problems), then the activity is referred to as an *interviewer rating.*

One caveat to interviewer-based review is that due to the unique set of pressures they face, field interviewers tend to focus mainly on operational aspects of the interview or questionnaire features that interfere with the smooth and quick completion of the interview. As a result, they may be less attuned to covert problems that do not really "hang up the interview" but that may adversely affect data quality.

A final category of expert review is computer-based, such as QUEST (Graesser, Kennedy, Wiemer-Hastings, & Ottati, 1999). Such a system attempts to identify explicit sources of difficulty in question clarity based on a linguistic model of text comprehension. Entering the question "Have you ever had chronic pain in the abdomen?" into such a system typically causes the computer to object that we have selected terms (chronic, abdomen) that may not be familiar to some respondents. Computer-based expert review can be used to screen large numbers of survey questions quickly to search for such problems. However, although this approach evaluates comprehension issues, it provides no way of assessing potential difficulties related to other cognitive processes such as retrieval, because existing computer models cannot duplicate the knowledge base of the human survey respondent.

Concerning the actual conduct of the expert review, there are many variations involving (a) the timing of communication with experts; (b) the use of single versus multiple experts (i.e., the "panel review" described by Presser and Blair, 1994, and by Snijkers, 2002); and (c) the use of multiple experts and group meetings, as opposed to multiple independent reviews. These issues are beyond the scope of this book. However, as a general observation, it is generally best to obtain such guidance early in the questionnaire design process, before we have expended much energy in word-crafting our questions, let alone cognitive testing (especially given that one result of expert review may be that we need to "go back to the drawing board" and ask somewhat different questions).

Focus Groups

Focus groups have been used very extensively, especially by market researchers and public opinion pollsters, to investigate the ways in which people think about various topics (e.g., new products, policy, relevant issues, etc.). Survey researchers appear to differ markedly in the degree to which they rely on focus groups to inform questionnaire design. Based on discussions with colleagues at NCHS, the U.S. Census Bureau, and the Bureau of Labor Statistics, it appears that the U.S. federal agencies most involved in questionnaire design and pretesting use focus groups rather sporadically. Interestingly, despite the generally wide use of both cognitive interviews and focus groups to evaluate draft materials, the cultures of researchers who conduct focus groups and those who conduct cognitive interviews do not greatly overlap, and it seems relatively few individuals do both.

Concerning when to use a focus group rather than a cognitive interview, there appears to be consensus that there are qualitative differences between these techniques—the focus group is not simply a group cognitive interview. Rather, the objectives and targeted materials differ; both are used to gain further understanding, but the focus group is typically used at a more general level, to investigate *topics*, whereas the cognitive interview is intended more to evaluate *specific survey questions* that ask about those topics (Snijkers, 2002). Krueger (1994) suggests that "the focus group is beneficial for the identification of major themes but not so much for the micro-analysis of subtle difference" (p. X). Similarly, Eisenhower (1994) states that the focus group approach "is more suited to exploration of potential questionnaire topics than to detailed assessment of existing questions" (p. 1377), and Cosenza and Fowler (2000) agree that "focus groups are not the best places to test specific question wording" (p. 997). Fowler (1995) suggests that focus groups are useful in questionnaire- based studies for examining our assumptions about (a) the reality about which people will be asked (what I would term logical problems), and (b) participants' thinking about key concepts.

SIMILARITIES AND DIFFERENCES BETWEEN FOCUS GROUPS AND COGNITIVE INTERVIEWS

An excellent description of the intricacies of focus group practices is Krueger's (1994) *Focus Groups: A Practical Guide for Applied Research.* Krueger makes several points that serve to differentiate focus groups from cognitive interviews. First, as far as similarities between the methods:

(1) Sample sizes that are effective are similarly small—for study of complex topics, it is best to have only 5–7 people in the focus group.

(2) The focus group allows the interviewer to probe, as does the cognitive interview. Krueger also distinguishes between "structured" and "free" inquiries (probes) by the moderator—these are very reminiscent of the various forms of Proactive and Reactive probes that I have described.

(3) Consistent with my view that cognitive interviewers should be cordial and exhibit some degree of personality while also

refraining from behavior that creates bias with respect to the material to be tested, Krueger states that "small talk" surrounding the focus group should be used to put people at ease but should avoid the issues that define the purpose of the focus group.

Apart from issues related to "topic versus question" emphasis, cognitive interviews and focus groups also differ in key ways:

(1) *Group dynamic versus individualism.* The group focus imposes very different dynamics—in particular, social interaction, bouncing ideas back and forth, and so on. In fact, the group emphasis is vital: Krueger argues that because we are products of our environment and are influenced by people around us, a deficiency of face-to-face interviews is that they assume people form opinions in isolation. This may be true, but is probably not a drawback of the cognitive interview, given that our usual objective is, in fact, to study the individual in isolation. (Surveys may involve social interaction with the interviewer but generally should not include interaction with other respondents!)

(2) *Scope of questioning.* The number of questions in a focus group protocol is fewer than in a cognitive interview. Krueger suggests that a typical focus group will ask about a dozen questions in order to obtain a full, in-depth discussion of a topic—far fewer than the number of combined target questions and probes that will be typically asked in a cognitive interview.

(3) *Nature of data and analysis.* Chapter 11 describes the particularities of analyzing and documenting data from cognitive interviews. As subjective and impressionistic as these data may seem, the use of focus groups tends to exacerbate these problems. Krueger admits that a limitation to focus groups is that group-based data are notoriously difficult to analyze, although Fowler (1995) suggests that the key is to conduct focus groups that have very limited, focused objectives. Recently, researchers have applied computer-based scaling and analysis procedures (such as NUD*IST: Analysis of Non-numerical Unstructured Data by processes of Indexing, Searching, and Theory-building, from QSR International) for organizing themes that emerge from focus groups.

TIMING OF THE FOCUS GROUP

It generally makes sense to conduct the focus group before the target questions are evaluated via cognitive interviewing (Fowler, 1995). However, in keeping with the theme that flexibility is a virtue, Schechter, Trunzo, and Parsons (1993), Eisenhower (1994), and Gower, Belanger, and Williams (1998) have advocated the use of focus groups subsequent to cognitive interviewing. Eisenhower views the cognitive interview as a useful warmup for the focus group, and states that a one-day delay between them orients each participant and results in a wide range of contributions in the focus group. Schechter et al. present a case study that represents a different approach, in which cognitive interviewing prompted a "back to the drawing board" reaction and the researchers decided to reexamine the topic using a group approach. Again, we select pretesting methods from our toolbox based on their utility in dealing with the problem at hand; such an approach favors imagination over adherence to dogma.

Miller (2002a) conducted a direct comparison between focus groups and cognitive interviews for a Canada-U.S. health survey. She found the focus group to be unsuited to the evaluation of specific questions, as this environment put the participants into the role of question evaluator and resulted in questionnaire design recommendations that were clearly unwise. Further, the focus group situation tended to lead members to speculate about what other individuals might do when answering survey questions, as opposed to reporting how they would react. In agreement with a number of other researchers, Miller suggested that the focus group is useful for the study of social and cultural dynamics, but that question testing should be reserved for the cognitive laboratory.

Behavior Coding

Behavior coding is also referred to as interaction analysis, and as these titles imply, focuses on the overt behaviors of the interviewer and the respondent as they interact during the survey interview (Cannell, Fowler, Kalton, Oksenberg, & Bischoping, 1989; Cannell, Fowler, & Marquis, 1968; Fowler, 1995; Fowler & Cannell, 1996; Morton-Williams, 1979; Morton-Williams & Sykes, 1984; Oksenberg, Cannell, & Kalton, 1991; Sykes & Morton-Williams, 1987). Behavior coding was developed by Cannell and colleagues at the University of Michigan. The initiators of the method were initially most concerned with monitoring interviewer performance in a field environment to determine whether interviewers administered questions, controlled pacing, and otherwise followed procedures as trained (Cannell et al., 1968; Cannell et al., 1977). However, the system has also been found to be very useful for assessing the respondent side of the interaction, and recent applications of this method have tended to focus largely on sources of response error.

Behavior coding encompasses the following features:

(1) It is a passive endeavor, in which the evaluator "eavesdrops" on the interview to assess the interviewer-respondent interaction and introduces no probing or other forms of interference.

(2) Behavior coding can be done live, similar to basic interview monitoring done by telephone survey call centers, but is more often accomplished by subsequent analysis of recordings (once tape-recorded, and now increasingly in digitized form).

(3) The interaction is systematically coded with respect to several behaviors that are manifested by the interviewer and the respondent.

A range of coding systems have emerged, and more recent applications, such as by Dijkstra (2002), tend to be extensive, as they are oriented toward a detailed description of the interaction as a type of code-able conversation. However, Table 14.1 lists a core set of codes that are currently applied for purposes of question pretesting and evaluation.

Each time the (trained) coder hears evidence of one of these problems, she or he applies that code for the relevant question, for each of a number of interviews. Because it is a quantitative endeavor, behavior coding provides aggregate coding summaries over a number of interviews. One complication is that the effective sample size obtained may vary markedly, depending on skip patterns and other sequencing instructions (e.g., men won't get asked a pregnancy history series). Therefore the number of times the question is actually administered needs to be taken into account, and the critical measure becomes the percentage of time that a question produced (a) each type of code or (b) any code (i.e., collapsing over coding category).

A representative table of behavior coding results would look like Table 14.2. In brief, Question 1 seems difficult to read correctly, whereas Question 2 suffers from respondent interruptions, Question 3 appears to present a host of problems for respondents, and Question 4 induces responses that often fail to match the intended categories. At first glance,

Table 14.1 Common Behavior Codes

Interviewer-Oriented Codes

(1) Reads question correctly
(2) *Skip* error (which may not be necessary with computer-based presentation unless programming errors have crept in)
(3) Reading errors (misreads), sometimes divided into *Minor and Major* changes to question wording
(4) Other interviewer probing behaviors (e.g., inducing a respondent to select a codeable response, such as when given a response of "5 or 10," asking "Which would you say is closer, 5 or 10?")

Respondent-Oriented Codes

These involve some type of verbal behavior by the respondent (R):
(1) R request for *Repeat* of question ("Run that by me again"; "Uh, what?")
(2) R requests *Clarification* ("When you say TV reception, do you mean cable or through the airwaves?")
(3) R provides an *Uncodeable* response ("Oh, I smoke between 10 or 20 cigarettes a day")
(4) R *Interrupts* with an answer to the question before the interviewer is done reading it
(5) R expresses *Uncertainty* (although he or she does answer, so this is different from a "Don't Know" response; e.g., "I'm not exactly sure . . . maybe three times in the past year")

SOURCE: Based on Fowler (1995).

Question 5 appears to be perfect except for a huge level of Uncodeable responses. However, note that this question was asked only twice (and one of these times the response was Uncodeable), so the results are not meaningful. Normally a question should be asked at least a dozen or more times before we even consider taking a serious look at the code distribution.[1]

Besides the obvious systematic and quantitative nature of the data produced, there are a few clear differences between behavior coding and cognitive interviewing:

1. *Focus on overt versus covert problems*. Again, a key purpose of cognitive interviewing is to provide a means for detecting covert problems

Table 14.2   Sample Behavior Coding Results Table (Percentage of Question Administrations Exhibiting Problems)

	INTERVIEWER			RESPONDENT			
	Misread (major)	Probe	Interrupt	Repeat	Clarification	Uncertain	Uncodeable
Question 1: (n = 20)	20%	4%	3%	6%	2%	7%	3%
Question 2: (n = 50)	5%	5%	28%	2%	3%	5%	9%
Question 3: (n = 32)	0%	2%	3%	15%	18%	12%	3%
Question 4: (n = 50)	2%	5%	5%	5%	5%	3%	25%
Question 5: (n = 2)	0%	0%	0%	0%	0%	0%	50%

NOTES:

a.   n = sample size for question.

such as silent misinterpretation, as verbal report methods are our means for externalizing processes that are otherwise hidden from view. Behavior coding focuses instead on observable—or overt—problems (and therefore shares that feature with Reactive forms of verbal probing) (Sykes & Morton-Williams, 1987).

2. *Timing.* Behavior coding is done when the questionnaire is in a form appropriate for field administration and is not normally conducted with early drafts. For this reason, behavior coding is typically conducted in the context of a field pretest or a "dress rehearsal," after rounds of cognitive interviewing are completed. There is no theoretical reason why a separate set of interviews could not be conducted strictly for purposes of behavior coding, but for most surveys it is more efficient to make use of existing field interviews.

3. *Focus on interviewer versus respondent.* Because behavior coding often involves interviews by field interviewers and focuses explicitly on

interviewer behavior much more than does cognitive interviewing, it is particularly useful for identifying questions that are difficult to administer (e.g., those that have awkward wording or formats that induce reading errors).

4. *Item level of measurement.* Behavior coding focuses strictly on the question level, rather than across questions. Because coding is done at this level, it is similar in focus to checklist-oriented expert review systems, such as the Question Appraisal System described in Chapter 2, and suffers the same limitation of imposing a very narrow view—in effect, analyzing each tree rather than the overall forest.

5. *Sample size.* Behavior coding depends on aggregation over a number of interviews, which is another reason that behavior coding is typically done as part of the field pretest, for which one normally conducts a relatively large number of interviews (30–300; Zukerberg, Von Thurn, and Moore (1995) recommend that behavior coding studies contain at least 50 respondents). This feature may appear to favor behavior coding over cognitive interviewing, which generally involves much smaller samples. However, as pointed out in Chapter 13, this advantage is sometimes illusory. Because behavior coding can only reflect the number of times that any question is actually asked, questions that are buried under layers of skip patterns can demonstrate vanishingly small effective samples.

6. *Conditions of participant selection and questionnaire administration.* Under the usual behavior-coded interview, the exchange takes place under realistic (rather than "laboratory") survey conditions. Respondents are not paid volunteers, so their degree of motivation to answer questions carefully is likely to be more similar to that of field survey respondents. Respondents in behavior coding studies are also typically less self-selected than cognitive interviewing subjects because their participation is somewhat more passive in nature (as this involves simple agreement to participate in an interview when approached, as opposed to actively seeking participation through response to a recruitment advertisement). As such, behavior coding participants are perhaps more representative of the target population for the survey.

7. *Nature of data obtained.* Behavior coding is more oriented toward counting problems than identifying reasons for those problems. As is clear from Table 14.2, behavior coding does provides a measure of problem severity—if one or more codes appear in 80% of interviews for one question, and only 10% for another, then it seems advisable to devote more additional attention to the former than the latter. On the

other hand, even the most detailed level of coding may not be very illuminating. Knowing that a question produces a large number of requests for clarification in itself does not reveal exactly what feature of the question creates the problem. Such diagnostic functions are more clearly the purview of our qualitative testing techniques, such as cognitive interviewing, which (at least in intent) sacrifice quantity of observation for quality of information.

Interestingly, Fowler (1995) has attempted to address this particular limitation of behavior coding by instituting a qualitative feature consisting of a *coder debriefing*. It does make sense that coders, having heard the same problem emerge a dozen or more times, would have something useful to say about the nature of the problem and how to fix it. Further, recent technological innovations may be helpful in this regard: The advent of digitized recording potentially provides a means for the researcher to have quick access to audio records of the exchanges that are associated with each code. That is, if requests for clarification are found to be pronounced for a particular question, it may be possible to easily select and listen to recordings of the interactions that gave rise to those codes, in order to better understand the specific question defects that led respondents to require clarification.

Reinterview Surveys

One weakness of cognitive interviewing is that it does not explicitly provide standard measures developed in the field of psychometrics, such as measurement reliability. We can label an item unreliable to the extent that we judge it unlikely to produce stable answers, but cognitive interviews are not normally conducted in order to firmly assess this. However, an affiliated procedure that can sometimes be useful in this regard is the reinterview survey, introduced in Chapter 2, which makes the assumption that a question asked twice of the same respondent should produce the same answer. This procedure is dependent on two field administrations of the targeted questions. Reinterview is not normally practical as a pretesting method, but can be used as a question evaluation procedure, after the questionnaire is in the field, and potentially as a pretest for later rounds of a repeated or cyclical survey (Biemer & Forsman, 1992; Marquis, Marquis, & Polich, 1986). The U.S. Census Bureau has long carried out a Response Variance Reinterview Program in which a subset of respondents in field surveys (or pretests) are recontacted, and a small number of questions are readministered (Forsman & Schreiner, 1991).

Although done largely to check for interviewer falsification ("curbstoning"), this procedure can also be used to evaluate question quality, with several important caveats:

1. Responses may change in the reinterview because the true answer has changed. Clearly, reinterview of the question "Did you work at all yesterday?" may produce discord over time because the underlying behavior may vary.

2. Answers may differ because the same respondent is not selected at both original and reinterview. If proxy responses are accepted for the second interview, this will create a source of variance that cannot easily be attributed to the question itself, unless we are demanding that the question function the same under proxy response as for self-report.

3. Reinterview assumes two independent responses that can be compared, but if the interval between interview and reinterview is short, there is the chance that the respondent will remember the act of answering in the initial interview, rather than answer independently. So a respondent may be thinking "Last time I said I went to the doctor three times last year, and although I later remembered two more times, I'll still say three to be consistent." In such cases, item reliability will be overestimated.

As an example of the results of reinterviewing, Albright et al. (2000) used an Index of Inconsistency for measurement of categorical variable agreement (response variance/total variance, or the complement of the more familiar kappa statistic) and found that targeted questions varied widely in terms of reliability. Demographic items and health insurance status had lower response variance than nonwage assets (bank accounts, stocks), income from government programs (welfare, AFDC), and disability.

Finally, although the above review covers the majority of questionnaire pretesting techniques in common use, it is not comprehensive. For example, Bassili and Scott (1996) have described the use of response latency (literally, how long it takes a respondent to answer) as an indicator of problematic questions. Note that this procedure could be incorporated into existing designs, such as a behavior coding study that assesses the time between interviewer administration and the respondent's answer.

How Do Pretesting Methods Compare?

As alluded to in the previous chapter, it is interesting to know whether different survey pretesting methods are working to the same end, or at least do not produce conflicting results. Several studies have examined the results of cognitive interviewing in comparison with other pretesting methods, such as expert review and behavior coding. Studies that directly compare cognitive interviewing to other methods focus on one or more outcomes: (a) *productivity*, or the number of problems identified; (b) qualitative *categorization* of the types of problems found by each method; and (c) degree of *overlap* in identifying the same items as problematic, especially when the methods are applied to a constant set of survey materials (e.g., Campanelli, 1997; DeMaio, Mathiowetz, et al., 1993; Oksenberg et al., 1991; Presser & Blair, 1994; Willis et al., 1999; Forsyth, Rothgeb, & Willis, in press).

Several researchers have assessed pretesting methods in the context of development of a large-scale federal survey (Esposito & Rothgeb, 1997; Fowler & Roman, 1992; Lessler et al., 1989). However, these are mainly useful as descriptive case studies, as it has proved difficult to provide adequate experimental control in such situations and to produce quantitative data that permit direct comparisons across methods. Therefore methodological studies that attempt to simulate critical conditions of questionnaire development, but that incorporate controls appropriate for purposes of technique comparison, are necessary.

In the first systematic attempt to compare pretesting techniques under controlled conditions, Presser and Blair (1994) applied three rounds of cognitive interviewing involving 10 to 12 subjects each, two expert group panels, two conventional field pretests involving interviewer debriefing, and behavior coding of 29 and 30 interviews, respectively, from these pretests. As their basic dependent measure, they recorded the total number of problems—across all survey questions—detected by each technique (productivity). Overall, the expert panel labeled the most questions as problematic, whereas behavior coding and cognitive interviewing assigned problematic status relatively less frequently, although they also noted very wide within-method variation (especially across the two conventional pretests). Presser and Blair also developed a qualitative coding scheme to describe the problems found in survey questions. Based on this analysis, they found that respondent-based semantic problems dominated the cognitive interviewing results (60–70% of problems found by the cognitive interviews fell into this category), whereas behavior coding and conventional pretests were more adept at revealing problems for interviewers than were cognitive interviews (for the former, 10–20% of problems found involved the interviewer, whereas for the latter, two of three rounds revealed *no* interviewer problems).

Finally, Presser and Blair also assessed the degree of overlap between pretesting methods, finding generally positive but partial agreement. Concerning the comparison of cognitive interviewing with other methods, the most significant results were that (a) cognitive interviews and behavior coding tended to overlap moderately (generally, a Yule's Q agreement statistic of about .4), and that (b) cognitive interviews overlapped more strongly with expert review (for which agreement values were more variable, but reached the .9 level). One interpretation might be that for whatever reasons, cognitive interviewing as carried out in this study (which was not described in detail, other than as a combination of follow-up probes and concurrent and retrospective think-alouds) had more in common with an appraisal-based method than with one based purely on observation.

To extend the Presser and Blair approach, Willis et al. (1999) similarly conducted a study that not only compared variants of cognitive interviewing (reviewed in Chapter 13) but that also compared the results of cognitive interviewing, expert review, and behavior coding. Table 14.3 contains the (previously unpublished) details of that study.

Overall, Willis et al. found that expert review produced the highest productivity (27% of questions had a "problem"), in accordance with Presser and Blair's (1994) findings. The two behavior coding studies also produced fairly high—and fairly similar—levels of identified problems (21% versus 26%, respectively). On average, the cognitive interviews reported the lowest levels of problems (about 12%). However, the authors argued that measures of productivity are inconclusive; in the absence of independent information concerning question quality, the finding of more problems cannot be viewed as evidence that a particular pretesting technique is superior. In particular, "more is better" reasoning focuses solely on the issue of sensitivity; it ignores the possibility that a highly sensitive procedure may as well exhibit poor specificity and produce a large number of false positive results. Instead, the authors focused more on the issue of overlap between methods, through correlation analysis (see Table 14.4).

Note first that all correlations are positive and significantly greater than zero, indicating a general positive direction of agreement. The highest correlations were among different expressions of the same pretesting methods, in particular for behavior coding ($r = .79$) and, as mentioned in the previous chapter, cognitive interviewing ($r = .68$). This lends some

Table 14.3   Design Used for Willis et al. (1999) Cross-Method Evaluation
Study

A. Questionnaire

93 questions relating to a range of general health behavior topics, including:

1. During the past 12 months, that is, since [*12-month date*] a year ago, ABOUT how many days did illness or injury keep you in bed more than half of the day? (Include days while an overnight patient in a hospital.)

2. During the past 12 *months*, were you seen *at home* by a health care professional such as a medical doctor, nurse, nurse's aide, social worker, or therapist?

3. Altogether, during the past 12 *months, how many times* have you seen a medical doctor or other health care professional about your own health at *a doctor's office, a clinic, or some other place*? DO NOT INCLUDE TIMES YOU WERE HOSPITALIZED OVERNIGHT, VISITS TO HOSPITAL EMERGENCY ROOMS, HOME VISITS, OR TELEPHONE CALLS.

4. In the past 2 weeks, that is, since [*date*], how many TIMES did you do VIGOROUS exercise (such as fast walking or bicycling, jogging, strenuous swimming or sports play, vigorous aerobic dance, and so on) that caused HEAVY sweating or LARGE increases in breathing or heart rate?

B. Cognitive Interviews

1. 43 interviews by 5 experienced interviewers at U.S. National Center for Health Statistics.

2. 40 interviews by 4 inexperienced interviewers at National Opinion Research Center at the University of Chicago (NORC).

C. Expert Review

21 expert reviewers from 5 U.S. federal agencies: NCHS, the Bureau of Labor Statistics (BLS), the Census Bureau, the General Accounting Office (GAO), and the National Agricultural Statistical Service (NASS).

D. Behavior Coding

1. *Household Behavior Coding:* 29 interviews conducted by the U.S. Census Bureau in the field.

2. *Telephone Behavior Coding:* 89 telephone interviews.

E. Outcome Measure

For cognitive interviews and expert reviews, the mean percentage of interviews or reviews in which a problem was reported for a given item.

For behavior coding, the percentage of times a question was read that *any* behavior code was assigned.

Table 14.4   Problem Percentage Score Correlations Between Pretesting Method Types and Between Technique Variants

	NCHS Cognitive Interviews	NORC Cognitive Interviews	Behavior Coding (household)	Behavior Coding (telephone)	Expert Review
NCHS Cognitive Interviews:	–	.68	.49	.59	.48
NORC Cognitive Interviews:	.68	–	.53	.73	.33
Behavior Coding (household):	.49	.53	–	.79	.54
Behavior Coding (telephone):	.59	.73	.79	–	.54
Expert Review:	.48	.33	.54	.54	–

SOURCE: Willis et al. (1999).

NOTES:

Correlation coefficients are based on 93 questionnaire items.

All $p < .001$

credence to the notion that these methods are consistent in terms of identifying the same questions as defective.

At first glance, the between-method values appear to present a sea of moderate correlations; cognitive interviewing generally tended to agree moderately with both expert review and behavior coding. At a closer level, however, it is interesting that the NORC-based cognitive interviews agreed more with the behavior coding results, whereas the NCHS cognitive interviewing results were more similar to the expert reviews. This may reflect, in part, an emphasis on the ways in which the cognitive interviews were conducted across laboratories; NORC interviewers were relatively less experienced, focused more on overt subject behavior, and largely "stuck to a script" that included structured (Anticipated) probes. NCHS interviewers were, on the other hand, freer to make use of both unscripted Spontaneous forms of probing and Reactive (Emergent) probing. The use of a less constrained probing style may have, in this case, imposed more of an expert-review-like approach.

Finally, Rothgeb et al. (2001) conducted a study that omitted behavior coding but instead focused on the overlap between the outcomes of (a) cognitive interviewing, (b) informal expert review, and (c) a checklist-based question appraisal system (the QAS). In terms of overall productivity in the sense defined by Presser and Blair (1994), they found that informal expert review and cognitive interviews were similar, with the QAS almost twice as productive. However, like Willis et al. (1999), they cautioned against "more is better" reasoning, as the QAS is best seen as a screening device that forces the user to actively consider the presence of a wide range of potential problems, some of which presumably do not demand any type of question revision. Overall, we should be very hesitant to consider the pretesting method that proves to "dig up the most dirt" on our target questions to be superior. Despite having a personal connection to the QAS, I would resist the conclusion that these data demonstrate that it is twice as good as cognitive interviewing, simply because Rothgeb et al. found that it identifies a prodigious number of defects. Rather, we need to consider the extent to which identified problems are both real and serious in magnitude, and whether our methods generally agree concerning the presence of a core of such problems.

In any event, note that the finding that cognitive interviews tend to produce fewer problem identifications than other methods is somewhat informative, as it relates to a discussion in Chapter 7 of Conrad and Blair's (1996) fear that our common techniques involve over-probing, and therefore the production of phantom problems. If anything, the cumulative empirical evidence seems to show that cognitive interviewing that is heavily based on aggressive (Proactive) forms of probing produces *fewer* problems than do other methods. On this basis, cognitive interviews could be viewed as relatively conservative, and therefore not likely to be especially prone to false positive outcomes.

With respect to agreement across methods on exactly *which* questions are causing problems, Rothgeb et al. (2001) found that QAS results could not be meaningfully evaluated due to ceiling effects (again, the system tended to find problems with virtually everything), but that standard expert review and cognitive interviewing produced a level of agreement somewhat lower than that of the other two studies cited above ($r = .3$). Returning to a point from the last chapter, in accounting for this discrepancy, Rothgeb et al. suggested that this outcome may have been in part due to the very poor condition of the target questions they evaluated.

Again, given a multitude of inherent problems, the different techniques may have successfully identified varied subsets of a very large set of inherent question deficiencies.

From a methodological point of view, this analysis suggests that perhaps a better approach would be to identify and evaluate questions that exhibit a limited number of subtle problems (rather than evaluating the proverbial kitchen sink) and to ascertain the sensitivity of various pretesting techniques in detecting those problems. This again leads me to advocate evaluation based on the embedding of known but subtle problems, as presented in the previous chapter. More basically, however, I would still argue that there are inherent limitations to studies that compare the results of cognitive interviewing to other methods. In particular, it is difficult to see how such a study can cleanly account for the fact that cognitive interviewing normally relies on multiple iterative testing rounds, especially as our somewhat contrived methodological comparisons are based on the results of a single round. Parenthetically, this argument also extends logically to the previous chapter concerning the evaluation of cognitive interviewing methods, which also is typically based on the erroneous assumption that only one cognitive round is conducted. To be fair, we must find ways to evaluate the method at full strength, as it is actually practiced.

SHOULD PRETESTING METHODS BE COMPARED HEAD-TO-HEAD?

Several authors (Eisenhower, 1994; Esposito & Rothgeb, 1997; O'Brien et al., 2001; Sykes & Morton-Williams, 1987; Willis et al., 1999) have challenged the notion that our methodological "holy grail" consists of identifying the pretesting method that is superior in an absolute sense. Rather, different methods seem to fit naturally at particular points in the survey development process, largely as a function of the nature of their core features (DeMaio et al., 1998). As a result, we are not usually interested in determining "Which single pretesting method should I choose over the others?" but rather "How can I efficiently combine these into a system of pretesting that is likely to be effective, given real-world constraints?" Researchers across several countries have addressed this issue independently, and seem to have reached a similar conclusion. For example, Table 14.5 is a model of questionnaire development presented by Akkerboom and Luiten (1996).

Note that this sequence is well-satisfied by the ordering—(a) expert review, (b) focus group, (c) cognitive interview, (d) field pretesting—that

Table 14.5   Model of Questionnaire Development

1. Determine how respondents view the topic and procedures of the survey
2. Determine how respondents fare when answering the questions
3. Conduct qualitative test to find efficient ways to operationalize data collection
4. Conduct quantitative pilot study (monitoring, etc.)
5. Conduct ongoing quality assessment

SOURCE: Akkerboom and Luiten (1996).

is generally applied in the United States. Further, Akkerboom and Luiten note that "the weight of various options for pretesting programs cannot be determined solely from the cognitive perspective" (p. 916). In other words, there are many considerations within the total system of quality assurance, with the study of cognition just one facet. Finally, the authors emphasize system flexibility—the steps are not invariant, but procedures can be used at different points. This again reflects, for example, Schechter et al.'s (1993) view concerning the conduct of "late" focus groups.

Revisiting the overall patterns identified across the Presser and Blair (1994), Willis et al. (1999), and Rothgeb et al. (2001) studies, it is not surprising that there is some correspondence between the problems found by different pretesting methods, although the overlap is not complete. This view is consistent with the *Relative Confidence Model* espoused by Esposito and Rothgeb (1997), in which the various methods tap separate but overlapping subsets of the population of questionnaire problems. They suggest that a common but limited set of serious problems will likely be identified by a range of pretest methods, but that there will also exist further problems for which one method is best suited (e.g., problems for interviewers or problems that surface when respondent motivational level is relatively low tend to reveal themselves best under behavior coding).

As a guide to the selection of pretesting techniques, Campanelli (1997) produced a tabular summary that takes into account not only overall usefulness, but also the range of problems covered, reliability, and cost. I reproduce some elements of her table in Table 14.6 (in which a larger number of "+" values represents a more desirable rating). I have chosen to omit the critical element of "usefulness" contained in the original because (a) based on the available evaluation data, it is premature to

Table 14.6   Features of Survey Pretesting Methods

	Range of problems covered	Reliability	Cost
(1) Expert review	++	++	+++
(2) Cognitive interviewing	++	++	++
(3) Traditional field pretest with interviewer debriefing	++	+	+
(4) Behavior coding	+	+++	+

SOURCE: Based on Campanelli (1997).

make such conclusions, and (b) again, my key conclusion is that the usefulness of any method depends on how and where it is applied. Overall, the table suggests some themes that I have already covered: Behavior coding is reliable, but limited in its scope; expert review and behavior coding are cheaper, and relatively broad in emphasis, but perhaps at the price of reliability. Based on Campanelli's analysis, the only pretesting method that appears to be a poor choice is the conventional field pretest followed by interviewer debriefing. Ironically, this approach was the standard for some years and is still sometimes used as the lone method of pretesting!

A CASE STUDY IN THE COORDINATION OF PRETESTING METHODS

Based on the notion that pretesting techniques are best when combined rather than competed, I make reference to a case study that combined methods and also made use of variations on the theme of cognitive interviewing. Schechter and Beatty (1994) developed and tested a questionnaire on seatbelt use via a three-phase plan:

Phase 1: Expert review and development involving subject matter (traffic) experts as collaborators

Phase 2: Face-to-face cognitive interviews using concurrent verbal probing

Phase 3: Simulated (laboratory-based) telephone interviews involving retrospective cognitive probing

Schechter and Beatty (1994) anticipated adverse cognitive effects in their initial expert review phase and made changes even prior to cognitive interviewing. For the question "Regardless of the type of medical emergency, are you confident that the EMS personnel would know what to do?" they believed that "EMS personnel," even if defined previously, is too technical—so they instead tried "ambulance or other emergency workers." Further, given the question "If a vehicle has an air bag, does the law require a driver to also wear a seat belt?" the experts pointed out that the survey measurement objectives didn't actually concern laws but rather knowledge of what protective behavior consists of. As such, it seemed that the wrong question was being asked (as opposed to "the right question being asked wrong"), and the key issue was better expressed by the question "True or false: if a car has a driver-side air bag, I don't need to wear my seat belt when driving."

It may appear to the reader (as it does to me) that the seat belt question is still problematic—it is not entirely clear what we mean by "I don't need to." (Does that mean "by law" or "in order to be safe in an accident"?) But the development of the question at least seems to be moving in the right direction, and the purpose of cognitive interviews is to examine this further. Based on our suspicions about the question, we could probe Proactively (e.g., by asking "Why do you say you don't need to wear your seat belt?") and then listen to whether the person expounds upon the law or mentions issues of occupant safety.

During Phase 2 cognitive testing, the researchers used targeted recruitment—for three iterative rounds, they made sure that at least half of tested subjects had children under the age of six, so child safety belt questions would be meaningful. Some unanticipated problems were detected, such as difficulty with terminology used to describe "seat belt," given that people don't normally split hairs further in order to distinguish "lap belt," "shoulder belt," and so on. Also, people who reported wearing a seat belt "All of the time" were sometimes found to be able to report the last time they failed to wear one, when probed about this. However, they failed to regard this as contradictory because, as a rule, they wear it all of the time (as an aside, note how this finding buttresses my continual assertion that lab subjects often are completely oblivious to inconsistencies in their own reporting behaviors). In response to this finding, the sponsor decided to convert the relevant probe into the question "When was the last time you did not wear your seat belt?" in order to achieve a more sensitive measure of usage. I note that this decision further demonstrates the point that cognitive probes sometimes serve as Expansive follow-up questions pertinent to the queried topic, as opposed to a means for delving into specific cognitive processes.

Finally, in Phase 3, although a true field pretest was not carried out (and this may have occurred apart from the study as described), Schechter and Beatty conducted two rounds of testing involving telephone interviews (the intended administration mode), representing an abbreviated form of field pretesting. In addition, face-to-face retrospective probing techniques—equivalent to respondent debriefing in the field—were used in each round to provide a further opportunity for intensive study of problems anticipated to persist during field administration. For example, for a question on the type of seat belt law the person favored (e.g., police stopping people for not wearing one versus only ticketing for failure when they violated another law), subjects on the phone tended to respond with "the first one" or "the second one you said," indicating potential problems with remembering the complex wording. In the retrospective debriefing session it was found that subjects couldn't paraphrase these items well and tended to talk about their knowledge of the laws, as opposed to what they favored. So some evidence was obtained that subjects misunderstood the intent and reported knowledge rather than opinion.

The Schechter and Beatty (1994) study reflects a key recommendation made by DeMaio, Mathiowetz, et al. (1993) and Esposito and Rothgeb (1997) concerning the selection of a method from an arsenal of pretesting methods: choose the method that best fits the current developmental state of the questionnaire. One does not normally conduct a behavior-coding field pretest on an embryonic questionnaire. On the other hand, the final dress rehearsal of a forms-designed questionnaire does not incorporate cognitive interviews. The overall challenge in pretesting is to utilize a cohesive developmental plan that takes advantage of the strengths of each method.

Certainly there may be times when methods integration is not feasible, and the researcher must make a hard choice between pretesting methods. We may have enough time, money, or staff, to do either cognitive interviewing or behavior coding, but not both. In this case, what should we do? I suggest considering the nature and state of the survey questions that we're evaluating. Does the survey involve the scripting of a number of new questions on novel topics? If so, I would be inclined to make sure that some cognitive testing gets done—it may be very risky to wait for a field pretest and then find out that the questions are clearly on the wrong track. On the other hand, if the design team has already carefully reviewed and revised a number of questions that have been used in previous surveys (that is, they have a history), and the developmental schedule dictates an upcoming field pretest, then perhaps the more reasonable approach is to carry out a behavior coding study—along with respondent debriefing and/or coder debriefing—to verify that the new versions at least appear to function properly. Even in this case, however, it may still be worth conducting a few "pseudo cognitive interviews" on appropriate colleagues or friends, as this can be most illuminating.

Chapter Summary

Besides the cognitive interview, several other survey pretesting methods are at our disposal. Each of these has optimal uses—especially with respect to when it is applied—and also has strengths and limitations. In brief,

- *Expert review* can be done by questionnaire design experts, subject matter experts, survey interviewers, or by special-purpose computer programs. Expert opinion helps to clarify objectives, to ensure that our questions are not logically flawed, and to iron out basic questionnaire design deficiencies. Generally, expert review is most valuable early in the questionnaire development process.

- *Focus groups* of individuals have been incorporated throughout the questionnaire development, testing, and fielding cycle, but are most often used in the formative stages, to research concepts and the manner in which our target population tends to think about them. Focus groups are not usually the best way in which to evaluate the specifics of question wording, however.

- *Behavior coding,* or interaction coding, is a systematic means for recording and quantifying overt indicators of error or difficulties in the interaction between interviewer and respondent. Behavior coding is normally conducted using field interviews, such as during a field pretest, and relies on the review of interview recordings by specially trained coders, who apply codes targeted toward both interviewer behavior (misreading of questions, probing behavior) and respondent behavior (interruptions, requests for repeat of question, requests for clarification, uncodeable responses, and indications of uncertainty in answers). Behavior coding is less effective than cognitive interviewing in detecting hidden problems, or the sources of difficulty, but is especially useful for establishing the severity of questionnaire defects.

- The *Reinterview,* sometimes referred to as response variance analysis, is a means for establishing degree of reliability of responses to survey questions asked at multiple time points. This method is not often used, but does provide quantitative measures of consistency at the level of the individual item. One must be careful, when implementing this method, to consider the degree to which reliability may be affected by issues such as true changes in the respondent's status and potential lack of independence between data collection points.

- In comparison, the reviewed pretesting procedures tend to produce results that are overlapping but not identical. This is not surprising, given their respective strengths and limitations, and according to a Relative Confidence Model, suggests that they should be combined whenever possible.

Note

1. Such decisions are judgment calls. If a question was only asked six times but produced the same code in all six cases, I might be inclined to at least take a look at the question for an obvious explanation.

15

Recommendations
and Future Directions

Within a relatively short period, the cognitive approach to survey errors has helped to change the face of an old art form. It is still too soon to say how profound those changes will turn out to be.

Tourangeau, Rips, et al. (2000, p. 340)

Chapter Overview

Tourangeau, Rips, et al.'s conclusion pertains not only to the cognitive approach in general (CASM), but also to cognitive interviewing as a means to develop and evaluate survey questions and other materials. Will new challenges increasingly call on cognitive interviewing as a fundamental tool? If so, to what extent must the core methods that I have described evolve? This final chapter will first reiterate some overall themes, in the context of recommendations for practitioners, and then turn to the area of potential new directions.

Twelve Recommendations
for Cognitive Interviewing Practice

Although I have made many recommendations concerning the conduct of cognitive interviewing, I select the following major themes as vital, and worthy of restating.

RECOMMENDATION 1: INTEGRATE COGNITIVE
INTERVIEWING INTO THE OVERALL DESIGN PROCESS

Due to its breadth of application, cognitive interviewing can be conducted at a variety of points. Even subsequent to survey fielding, it can provide quality assurance or determine the particular uses to which our data can be put. For example, on the basis of cognitive interviews with parents of young children, we may decide that detailed information on children's immunizations that had been collected in the absence of records might not be accurate—yet we might decide to rely on global reports of whether the child is up-to-date.

More often, however, cognitive interviewing is not intended for after-the-fact quality assurance but for questionnaire pretesting, so that results can be incorporated into later instrument drafts. To this end, issues of timing and integration are fundamental, as cognitive testing is not a stand-alone activity, but sits most comfortably at an intermediate level, subsequent to initial question development and appraisal but prior to field pretesting (see Chapters 10 and 14). In this sense, although it may be a stretch to assert that "timing is everything," the issue of *when* to conduct testing can be nearly as important as *how* to do this testing. Further, we must allow enough time to recruit subjects; develop the cognitive protocol; conduct and write up interviews; consider the implications of any proposed changes, perhaps in conjunction with collaborators or clients; and then implement these changes. In the best of worlds, we repeat this procedure for at least two iterative cycles.

RECOMMENDATION 2: WHEN PREPARING
QUESTIONS FOR COGNITIVE TESTING, ATTEND
TO FIRST PRINCIPLES OF QUESTION DESIGN

Even if the time is right for testing, the content must also be right. It normally makes little sense to conduct cognitive testing on questions that are obviously defective (that is, unless these defects are not obvious to the client or sponsor, and cognitive interviewing will be used to settle the issue). When first presented a questionnaire for cognitive testing, the evaluator can normally expect to conduct an initial cycle of question appraisal, discussion, and modification. This practice not only results in questions that are purged of major pitfalls, so that cognitive testing can focus on more subtle issues, but is instrumental for developing cognitive probe questions (see Chapter 5).

RECOMMENDATION 3: REVISIT
QUESTION OBJECTIVES—OFTEN

If a question presents difficulty for subjects—or even if it does not—we may wonder about its utility as a measure, independent of whether it may be possible to address its cognitive limitations. Subjects may be able to answer the question "When you go out at night, how often do you take something with you that could be used for protection such as a dog, mace, gun, or knife?" But are analysts likely to be able to make meaningful use of a question that pools people who walk their dog nightly with those who carry a concealed weapon? As a rule, pay attention not only to subjects' difficulties, but as well to potential difficulties in using the questions for projected purposes of analysis. Although not normally viewed as key to the cognitive method, the issue of "Why exactly are we asking this question?" is well within scope.

RECOMMENDATION 4: APPLY COGNITIVE
INTERVIEWING TECHNIQUES THAT ARE
APPROPRIATE TO THE SURVEY ADMINISTRATION MODE

This recommendation must be tempered, because we do not always strictly select telephone-based cognitive interviewing for telephone surveys, or self-administered techniques for mail and Web surveys (see Chapter 12). Rather, there may some benefit to an initial round of face-to-face cognitive interviewing for a range of surveys, simply because of the advantages of interacting with subjects and carrying out free discussion. However, there is a point at which we must take into account the fact that the fielded survey may not rely on face-to-face interaction, and adjust our cognitive interviewing approach to test the questionnaire as it will be administered. So in a final round of cognitive testing, cognitive researchers may use the telephone or a laptop computer in the cognitive laboratory. Further, we may decide to limit concurrent forms of probing and to rely more on retrospective debriefing. Our overall objective is to apply cognitive interviewing in such a way that we depart from field interviewing procedures (e.g., we probe to obtain supplemental information useful for questionnaire evaluation), while at the same time retaining significant features of questionnaire administration (e.g., mode). The tension between these opposing requirements causes us to make compromises. Ideally, we implement a plan that allows us, over subsequent rounds of cognitive testing, to evolve toward field conditions.

RECOMMENDATION 5: KEEP IN MIND
POTENTIAL PROBLEMS FOR FIELD INTERVIEWERS

For interviewer-administered questionnaires, a potential drawback of cognitive testing is that interviewers pay so much attention to subjects' problems that they ignore those confronting the interviewer. It is not necessarily our destiny to suffer this outcome, however, if we remain mindful of it. This argument suggests yet another reason to make explicit use of a question appraisal system which forces us to consider the interviewer's role from the start. Further, during the conduct of the cognitive interview, we can be primed to attend to difficulties of administration. It makes little sense to wait until a field pretest produces an onslaught of protests from field interviewers that our questions cause them to stumble.

RECOMMENDATION 6: UTILIZE AN APPROACH THAT
COMBINES A RANGE OF VERBAL REPORT TECHNIQUES

There should be little debate concerning whether to select think-aloud versus interviewer-based probing techniques, as these can effectively be integrated in the same interview (see Chapter 4). With respect to choosing between the varieties of probing techniques, such as Proactive versus Reactive, or Concurrent versus Retrospective (see Chapters 6 and 7), this can be guided by a number of factors, including proficiency of the interviewers, mode of survey administration, nature of the questions being asked, degree to which problems are anticipated ahead of time, and amount of previous development and pretesting that questions have received. The selection of appropriate verbal report techniques is itself a decision-making process, rather than the blind application of an established algorithm.

RECOMMENDATION 7:
EMPHASIZE QUALITY OVER QUANTITY

Cognitive interviewing is an intensive activity that by nature involves small samples of interviews. Because we sacrifice quantity of interviews for depth of information, the more attention that can be given each interview, the better. As DeMaio and Landreth (in press) discovered, it may be very worthwhile to review audio- or videotapes of cognitive interviews whenever possible, to attend to subtle issues that may have been missed during the live interview. It is generally better to conduct a dozen careful interviews than simply to go through the motions in order to achieve a result that may appear impressive (e.g., 50 completions) but that is lacking in information value.

RECOMMENDATION 8: DO NOT SIMPLY
APPLY TESTING RESULTS—INTERPRET THEM FIRST

Without doubt, the objective results from cognitive interviews—what we actually observe—constitute our key data and must, therefore, serve as the basis for our conclusions and recommendations. That said, recognize as well that these data do not directly speak for themselves, in terms of indicating what problems will exist in the fielded survey and how serious these problems will be. Rather, we must apply an intermediate, interpretive phase, in which we judge the degree to which, and exactly how, each finding should be addressed. For purposes of meeting some measurement objectives, even very clear problems may be judged to be effectively irrelevant. For example, our subjects may think a question about whether "they can get around easily" is ridiculous, as it is obvious that they traveled to the cognitive laboratory. The same question might be received very differently in a field survey where at least some respondents are house-bound.

RECOMMENDATION 9: DOCUMENT RESULTS FOR POSTERITY

Practitioners in the cognitive interviewing field have been somewhat guilty of reinventing the wheel when we may have simply forgotten about previous results or failed to make those results available to others. Consistent themes that do not require continual rediscovery may emerge if these results can be documented and communicated generally, rather than be tied to a single project report that is read once and then shelved. I will have more to say about this as I anticipate future directions, below.

RECOMMENDATION 10: KEEP IN MIND
THE VITAL IMPORTANCE OF SUBJECT RECRUITMENT

Cognitive interviewing is an empirical method that relies on the presence of real people as subjects. We must, therefore, make use of imaginative and varied forms of recruitment. A variety of advertising approaches have been found effective, as have practices such as providing remuneration at a level that is sufficient to induce participation, and interviewing in a variety of environments in which subjects can be found. Especially where our surveys involve particular groups (e.g., farmers, heavy industrial users of electrical energy, single mothers), we must rely on targeted recruitment strategies. Remember that for some groups (e.g., deans of medical schools), financial remuneration may not be the most important factor. In general, the research team must be prepared to devote significant staff resources to dealing with gatekeepers and intermediaries, and working through intermediate levels of access (e.g., churches, community leaders) where key individuals can be influential proponents of our research.

RECOMMENDATION 11: LEARN BY DOING

Just as it is impossible to learn to fly only from the manual, without once taking to the sky, it is also not possible to learn cognitive interviewing simply by reading this book (or any other written work). To facilitate the learning process, I have included a training curriculum in Chapter 9, but this, to some extent, assumes the incorporation of interviewers in an ongoing cognitive laboratory operation. For lone operators, the necessary alternative is simply to prepare as much as possible and then dive in. It should be relatively easy to do so by attending to the basics: Ask subjects to think aloud, craft and administer Anticipated probe questions, and record the verbal reports that seem relevant. Beyond this, the interviewer who is close to the questionnaire, and has considered its potential defects, will be in a good position to follow up with Reactive probes when a subject gives responses that suggest potential question pitfalls. The major attribute required is the willingness to listen and to carefully relate what subjects are telling us to what we are attempting to ask of them.

RECOMMENDATION 12: KEEP IN MIND THE VARIED POTENTIAL OUTCOMES OF COGNITIVE INTERVIEWING

Cognitive interviewers do not simply "patch leaky roofs" through finding and then fixing problems in survey questions. Royston and Bercini (1987) recognized the need for a wider perspective very early, and suggested that we simultaneously (a) find what can't be asked in a survey (avoid error); (b) establish limits on data uses (measure error); and (c) find better ways to ask questions (reduce error). To the extent that we focus on the last of these, and our ambitions lead us naturally to want to improve questions, we must still keep in mind a few important limitations. No question will function perfectly for all respondents, and there may be no question form that exactly fulfills our objective. Rather, we must consider the relative merits of the different potential expressions of our concept and choose the one that appears best.

Future Directions for Cognitive Interviewing

The final discussion in a book that describes an evolving field should be forward looking: Where is the field headed, and what can we do to help it to get there? In the absence of a truly effective crystal ball, I base my projections on rumblings from several existing sources, as these have either anticipated future directions or made incipient attempts at novel applications (in particular, see Snijkers, 2004). I divide these roughly into (a) varieties of *methodological development,* or advancements in the conduct of cognitive interviewing itself; and (b) developments in *application,* or new areas to which cognitive interviewing can be devoted.

DEVELOPING BEST PRACTICES OF INTERVIEWING

I have resisted the notion that there is an optimal way to conduct cognitive interviewing, because a one-size-fits-all notion is overly simplistic. This does not mean that we should engage in procedural free-for-all, as presumably there are variants of the cognitive interview that apply best to particular situations, such as for self-administered paper-based administration. Development in this area largely falls under the guise of evaluation research, as reviewed in Chapter 13 where I have already made some recommendations concerning general issues of method utility. Beyond that, I suggest, in conclusion, that future endeavors focus on assessing the effectiveness of various tools (e.g., probing approaches, specialized techniques such as vignettes, etc.) on particular survey subtypes (e.g., when classed according to administration mode, individual versus establishment focus, degree of question sensitivity, or some other critical dimension).

In keeping with earlier discussion, it may be particularly useful to focus on the detection of embedded problems—where we seed test instruments with questions of known (or likely) sources of error and determine which techniques are most efficient in finding them, but without also flagging questions that we independently believe to be less problematic. We might even rely on an embedded defect approach as a means to improve the efficiency of the cognitive interviewing process, by developing question appraisal methods that are effective in prescreening a wide range of defects. In particular, it may be that with advances in artificially intelligent systems, computer-based appraisal tools will be found to be of substantial use. In this way, cognitive interviews can focus on particularly complex problems, rather than serving as back-up to an incomplete prior review process.

DETERMINING WHETHER CERTAIN
QUESTION FEATURES SPELL COGNITIVE TROUBLE

A second potential methodological development involves the further pursuit of our "holy grail": the general establishment of the cause-and-effect relationship between questionnaire features and components of response error (Collins, 2003; Snijkers, 2004). Borrowing terms introduced in Chapter 3, an ultimate goal of Applied CASM research is to provide feedback information to the Basic CASM level in facilitating the general development of questionnaire design principles, as opposed to always restricting our view to the current set of targeted questions in trial and error fashion (O'Muircheartaigh, 1999; Schwarz, 1999; Sirken & Schechter, 1999). This two-way flow of information is described in the medical literature as Translational Research, in which information flows from the laboratory to the clinic and also in the reverse direction (Pober, Neuhauser, & Pober, 2001).

To this end, Table 15.1 includes a few sample "rules" governing the relationships between question features and observed outcomes that I have gleaned from an array of cognitive testing reports. Although these examples are perhaps not profound (although it is my hope that they are also not completely banal), these move us toward a translational approach that informs the CASM field generally and in turn sets the stage for the refinement of our cognitive models of self-reporting. At the least, such rules represent a marked improvement over the current state of the art, which largely involves scattered reports containing individual exemplars of these relationships.

Systematic developments that are based on particular markers of response errors in survey questions will require that we not only attend to the documentation of the types of cognitive (and other) errors that we identify (e.g., the various coded subclasses of comprehension errors described by Presser and Blair, 1994), but simultaneously code question features that are presumably linkable to such errors. I have already made reference to one effort in this direction, a U.S. interagency effort labeled Q-BANK, dedicated to developing a computerized database that will record and allow for subsequent analysis of cognitive interview results,

Table 15.1   Sample Rules Relating Cognitive Features to Resultant
Response Error Tendencies

Rule 1: Questions requiring judgments of *behavioral frequency* that include lifetime reference periods tend to produce massive errors of information retrieval (e.g., number of times one has changed residences).

Rule 2: Questions that involve *multiple conceptual elements* such as frequency, duration, and intensity within them (e.g., those concerning exercise and physical activity) tend to overburden cognitive processes and lead respondents to ignore one or more of these elements; it is usually more efficient to decompose such questions into multiple items, even at the cost of increasing the number of questions in the instrument.

Rule 2a: Rule 2 applies most clearly to *orally administered instruments*, and especially to the telephone. For visually based self-administered paper questionnaires, relatively more complexity can sometimes be embedded in the question in cases where the benefits of decomposing questions are offset by the increased burden of skip patterns the respondent must follow.

Rule 3: *Hypothetical questions* related to future decisions tend to lead to failures to answer, or answers that are not representative of respondent thought, because such questions fail to specify enough relevant information of the type that respondents use in order to make decisions (e.g., "Would you support an increase in taxes for the purpose of fighting terrorism?").

---

and that explicitly codes both question features and testing outcomes (Miller et al., 2003).

As the system is in draft form, this remains a future direction, but I list the current set of coded question features in Table 15.2. Current plans call for the database to be populated by outcomes across a number of organizations that conduct cognitive testing, across a range of areas (health, labor force, demographics, etc.), and across surveys of establishments as well as of household populations.

COMPUTERIZATION

As I have already covered in Chapter 12, questionnaire development and pretesting must increasingly adapt to advances in Computer Assisted Interviewing, or CAI (Couper, 1999; Marquis & Kasprzyk, 1999), in which questionnaires are presented via computer, such as through CAPI and CATI systems. To this point, however, this development has not

264 OTHER ISSUES AND TOPICS

Table 15.2   Q-BANK Project: Question Characteristics Potentially Related to Categories of Response Error

Question Type	Demographics
	Events, actions, and behaviors
	Objective characteristics
	Subjective characteristics
	Speculations
	Attitudes
	Knowledge tests
	Explanation
	Individual ID
	Other
Response Category Type	Yes/No
	Quantity—open
	Quantity—from list
	Point in time—open
	Point in time—from list
	Scale/rating
	Select one
	Mark all that apply
	Allocation
	Textual response
	Other

SOURCE: Based on Miller et al. (2003).

had a significant influence on the cognitive interviewing field, as our procedures have not departed greatly from those used under paper-based interviewer administration. However, recent developments in the survey field threaten to challenge this status quo, and to force cognitive interviewers not only to modify their techniques but to also consider the prospects of an increased convergence of cognitive testing and usability testing. As stated by Tourangeau, Couper, Tortora, and Miller-Steiger (2000), "the development of new methods for collecting survey data—particularly Web surveys and administration of recorded questions by telephone—may be ushering in a golden age for self-administered surveys" (p. 476). As this trend continues and the machine is substituted for the survey interviewer, designers and evaluators must ensure that respondents not only process survey questions appropriately but also find usable the vehicle that is presenting those questions. When evaluating such systems, cognitive interviewers will therefore face directly the challenges of usability testing, in addition to those posed by the need to conduct question testing.

Increasingly, large-scale survey development organizations (such as the U.S. Census Bureau and Bureau of Labor Statistics) have recognized that the surveys of the future will likely require a coordination of cognitive and usability testing; what is not clear is whether staffing and equipment devoted to each type of laboratory will be integrated. In some ways, it makes sense to fully combine approaches, as both are at their core dependent on respondents' cognitive processes. Computer-based self-administration does present novel issues to cognitive interviewers who are used to orally administered questions, as we must now consider visual features such as screen layout, clarity of navigation (i.e., getting around the screen and between screens), and use of color and font.

Such features, however, are in another sense not novel at all. In fact, each of these is reflected in paper self-administered questionnaires, to which cognitive testing has frequently been applied with success. Therefore cognitive interviewers who are already adept at testing self-administered paper instruments may be able to adapt their existing methods to Web surveys and other computer-based applications. Further, from a theoretical point of view, issues of computer survey navigation (i.e., Where should I go next?) bear close resemblance to the problem-solving tasks initially envisioned by Ericsson and Simon (1980, 1984) as amenable to verbal report methods, and in some ways much more so than does the task of answering interviewer-administered survey questions. From this perspective, our usual cognitive interviewing techniques should be at least as applicable to computer usability testing as they are to questionnaire pretesting. Ironically, we may even come full circle and find that traditional think-aloud techniques are eminently suited to the testing of Web surveys and other computer-based applications that include strong elements of problem solving.

SURVEY AND RESEARCH PARTICIPATION

Increasingly, researchers face new challenges to their research as changes in society lead to members of the public being less likely to participate in surveys. In the survey research field, declining response rates have been cited as a problem for at least a decade (Groves, Cialdini, & Couper, 1992). Similarly, medical research that involves case-control studies requires the participation of members of the public (controls), yet usual methods for control selection, such as random-digit-dialed telephone calling, may no longer be effective. More generally, in the area of human subject protections that are considered by Institutional Review Boards located in all research institutions, there is an increasing concern that consent forms are effectively unreadable and uninterpretable by many study subjects, calling into question the notion that fully informed consent is obtained.

Each of these areas may be addressed, to one extent or another, by applications of cognitive interviewing. In general, it may be advisable to consider, as an important research area, "The Cognitive Aspects of Research Participation." Potentially effective methods are wide in scope. Some of these already exist—for example, focus groups to determine not only why respondents do *not* refuse to participate in surveys, but why they *do* choose to complete an interview. Further, cognitive interviews can be used to evaluate the comprehensibility of materials developed to convince subjects to participate. Potential applications to the development of research consent forms are especially clear. Because cognitive probing seems especially useful in assessing comprehension processes, it should be easy to adopt these techniques in order to ascertain level of understanding of various versions of consent documents, and to compare alternative approaches (e.g., a fully explanatory form as opposed to a shorter, schematic version accompanied by a descriptive brochure).

CROSS-CULTURAL INVESTIGATION

I anticipate that one direction in particular will increasingly frame the focus of cognitive interviewing. As an extension of the discussion of the ethnographic approach in Chapter 7, a current challenge to survey methods is the development of questionnaires that are explicitly intended for diverse populations, especially where a major survey objective is to make statistical comparisons across these groups (Carrasco, 2003; Kagawa-Singer & Blackhall, 2001; Snijkers, 2004; Stewart & Napoles-Springer, 2000). To this end, a key challenge is to establish *cross-cultural equivalence*; we endeavor to produce questions that are mentally processed in a similar manner across groups that may be defined according to ethnicity, race, nationality, or some other distinction (Johnson, 1998). Further, our goal is not only to establish such equivalence for subgroups that extend beyond the demographically normative population, but as well for questionnaires that are translated into different languages (Harkness, Van de Vijver, & Mohler, 2003; McKay et al., 1996).

Large population-based surveys, such as the NCHS National Health Interview Survey, have for years been translated into Spanish, but the trend toward multiple-language translation is increasing (de la Puente & Pan, 2003). For example, the 2001 California Health Interview Survey was administered in seven languages (California Health Interview Survey, 2002). Across language versions, researchers have begun to seriously question whether these demonstrate cross-cultural equivalence in the sense that responses obtained from different groups can be meaningfully compared. For instance, Harkness et al. (2003) suggest that although questions on empathy presented to Koreans and to Norwegians may produce different means, the interpretation of this cross-cultural (or cross-national) discrepancy is not clear. Rather than variations in underlying levels of empathy, this result may reflect differences in the social desirability of demonstrating or conveying empathy when queried about this topic.

Although Harkness et al. (2003) discuss at length cognitive and cultural issues of cross-cultural equivalence, they make little mention of the potential use of empirical question development methods to this end. However, Harkness and colleagues do suggest that "pretesting strategies, such as focus groups, cognitive interviews, split pretests with bilinguals and monolinguals, as well as respondent and field staff debriefing, are important sources of feedback that can help improve different aspects of the translated questionnaire versions" (p. 41). In particular, I believe that because of its intensive investigative role, cognitive interviewing may be particularly well-suited to the pursuit of both within- and between-language varieties of cross-cultural equivalence. There are, however, several features vital to the development of cross-cultural cognitive interview methods, especially across language, that require further development:

(a) Interviewer selection and training, and especially the challenges of identifying individuals who meet all the criteria for selection of cognitive interviewers identified in Chapter 9 but who are also bilingual

(b) Monitoring of interviewer performance by lead researchers who may be unable to evaluate cognitive interviews that are conducted in a language they do not speak

(c) Similarly, investigators' interpretation of the documentation of interview outcomes when these involve unfamiliar languages

(d) From a logistical point of view, the coordination of interviews across groups or languages, as the scope and complexity of development may exponentially increase with the number of groups or languages involved

A Final Case Study

Chapter 1 opened by posing the question "What is cognitive interviewing?" I have spent 15 chapters attempting to answer that question from a range of viewpoints, relying on logical and conceptual arguments, on appropriate data where they exist, and on a range of examples. To conclude, I revisit the issue of what cognitive interviewing is one more time, relying on an example that conveys many broad themes that I have discussed. McKay and de la Puente (1995) conducted an intensive, multistep cognitive interviewing project in order to answer a specific set of questions: What is the effect of the addition of a multi-racial category to a question on racial self-identification, and how exactly should this be worded? Further, should Hispanicity be included on a race question or separated? Would it be best to use "African American" or "Black"?

For recruitment, the investigators relied on community centers to obtain particular varieties of subjects (e.g., American Indian/Alaskan Native, Hispanics, and Asians). The researchers conducted three phases of research and obtained a number of findings that are not only interesting but important for purposes of establishing methods for the collection of racial and ethnicity data across federal surveys. Most significantly, they found that traditional methods of assessing self-reports of race and ethnicity routinely used by U.S. federal surveys seemed lacking; in particular, many members of the surveyed population simply do not think of these concepts in the same manner as do government demographers. For example, when asked "You selected [race] from the list I read to you. Do you also have a more specific group that you belong to?" subjects did not mention categories established by federal agencies, but instead gave responses such as "Christian," "Masons," "Black Muslim," and "rebellious teenager."

Further, many people, including those who think of themselves as Hispanic (e.g., Mexican, Mexican American, Puerto Rican, Cuban, etc.), considered this to constitute their racial composition, rather than a separate measure of ethnicity. Hence it seemed best to first ask whether respondents believed themselves to be Hispanic and then to ask a separate question on racial identification. The researchers also concluded that a multi-racial category can be useful for respondents with multiple-race backgrounds. To some extent, the results of this and similar studies have been incorporated into federal surveys, which points to the very important requirement—that we not only detect important problems through testing but implement them into survey practice.

Apart from the general findings from the McKay and de la Puente study, I summarize a few of their more detailed findings in Table 15.3 because they reiterate themes that persist throughout this book. The details of the table are illustrative. In Phase 1, it seemed that the attempted probe questions presented too much information at once and would need to be decomposed into several parts to be understood. So, as others have found, probes obey the same laws as the survey questions they aim to test and can themselves be confusing. To their credit, the authors both (a) indicated what probes they used, and (b) admitted when these failed to work, an unusual practice that, if performed generally, would greatly benefit the cognitive interviewing field.

Concerning Phase 2, the outcome of cognitive interviewing was not specifically to improve questions. Rather, a result of the investigation was to eliminate questions that represented unrewarding directions because they exhibited unacceptable forms of sensitivity. Finally, in Phase 3, the investigators doggedly pursued a systematic program of iterative testing in order to develop a question version that resulted in the intended outcome (an accurate answer that is literally provided as a "Yes" or "No"), even though a successful outcome required considerable effort and imagination.

Overall, McKay and de la Puente applied cognitive testing for varied purposes. For some components of the investigation, the investigators fully paid attention to the cognitive issues related to racial and ethnic identification through standard probing approaches, noting the underlying basis for the answers given by subjects (that is, why they classify themselves in particular ways). For the third phase, however, an important objective was to focus not on how respondents interpreted the question, but on how they literally answered it. From the point of view of a cognitive model, they initially isolated and investigated comprehension processes and later tacked on the response matching process as efforts were made to lead subjects to provide responses that matched the investigators' conception (simply, "Yes" or "No" to a question on Hispanic origin). In pursuing the latter aim, the investigators established a focus on overt problems of the type one might typically target through behavior coding (in particular, the "uncodeable response" code, as described in Chapter 14), as opposed to a reliance on heavy doses of cognitive probing to detect covert flaws. In this case, several small iterative rounds appeared to have been

Table 15.3   Cognitive Investigation of Hispanicity Questions

---

Phase 1 (20 interviews):

Finding: There were problems with comprehension of cognitive probe questions, especially when they targeted abstract concepts.

    (a) In response to the probe "You selected [race] from the list I read to you. Do you also have a more specific group that you belong to?" answers included "Christian" "Masons," "Black Muslims," "rebellious teenager." (The probe question was itself vague, and failed to invoke thinking about racial or ethnic identification.)

    (b) The probe "Do you think there is any difference between race, ethnicity, and ancestry?" was found to be abstract and difficult, and failed to produce useful information.

Phase 2 (54 interviews conducted across 9 regions of the U.S.):

Finding: Several questions elicited strong negative emotionality and were eliminated.

Phase 3 (9 respondents)

Simple observation of subject responses (absent probing) were used to modify a question in iterative fashion in order to induce the desired response (YES or NO).

Version 1: "First, let me begin by asking whether or not you consider yourself to be Hispanic, Latino, or of Spanish origin."

Finding: No one answered YES or NO, but instead gave their race or ethnicity.

Version 2: "Are you Hispanic, Latino, or of Spanish origin?"

Finding: Some subjects still responded to the question with "I'm white" rather than YES or NO.

Version 3: "Are you Hispanic, Latino, of Spanish origin, or none of these?"

Finding: Subjects still tended to answer with race/ethnicity rather than YES or NO.

Version 4: "First, are you one of the following: Hispanic, Latino, of Spanish origin?"

Finding: This was tested again on 48 non-Hispanics and 6 Hispanics; all answered with YES or NO.

SOURCE: McKay & de la Puente (1995).

effective and efficient (one can only imagine the number of behavior coding exercises that might have been necessary to achieve the same result).

Finally, the investigators also tested a Spanish version of the questionnaire, illustrating appropriate attention to cultural issues and to those of cross-cultural equivalence. In sum, the McKay and de la Puente example well reflects the flexible and varied nature of the cognitive interviewing approach as it can be systematically applied to a particular questionnaire development challenge. I stress that their study implicitly addresses the question "What is cognitive interviewing?" by demonstrating that it is many things, some cognitive, some not, some that are specific core elements of that method and others that overlap with the many development and pretesting procedures that, in combination, serve to produce effective survey questions.

In Conclusion

Cognitive interviewing is a flexible activity that encompasses a wide range of elements but nevertheless follows a logical and systematic approach to the evaluation of materials that the human mind must be able to comprehend and respond to in a rational manner. I both assert and acknowledge that the involved activities are not set in stone, static, or stagnant—cognitive testing is best viewed as dynamic, changing with the times, and evolving as necessary. Consequently, the procedures I have described will surely continue to change as the field matures, and the practices that I have described will perhaps eventually become outdated. However, I do hope that some of the key elements I advocate will persist. Most generally, for those who plan to conduct cognitive interviewing based on the principles and procedures that I espouse, I very much hope that this proves to be a useful endeavor and is not only productive but enjoyable. It has been for me.

Appendix 1

Example of Cognitive Testing Protocol

A. INSTRUCTIONS FOR COGNITIVE INTERVIEWER

1. Review the questionnaire to make sure you can "get through it" and to determine probes to ask.

2. To start the interview, read the INSTRUCTIONS TO SUBJECT either verbatim or paraphrased.

3. When you start, make sure to enter the START TIME.

4. Make sure the subject isn't reading the questionnaire as you administer it (i.e., make sure he or she is only listening to you).

5. Go for up to one hour. If you don't get done, just mark where you ended. If something is difficult to administer or you can't figure out exactly how to read a question, make a comment to the effect that this is a problem, and ask it the best you can.

6. Use the suggested probes that are written in and other probes you can think of. Don't feel that you need to probe every question extensively.

7. Enter comments, under each question, about problems or issues that come up. Try to make them readable because we're going to use them (these are data for the project).

8. When you're done, enter the END TIME.

9. Look back over the questionnaire and add other comments as appropriate.

10. Save each commented protocol so that later you can pool these into one version that covers all the interviews you conduct.

B. INSTRUCTIONS TO BE READ TO SUBJECT[1]

Notes to Interviewer

(a) *Either read these instructions in their entirety or paraphrase them (but make sure to include elements 1–7)*

(b) *Note that this form is set up to be administered after subject has signed the Confidentiality Form[2]*

Thanks for coming in. Let me tell you a little more about what we'll be doing today.

1. We're testing a new questionnaire with the help of people such as yourself.

2. I'll ask you questions and you answer them, just like a regular survey.

3. However, our goal here is to get a better idea of how the questions are working. So I'd like you to *think aloud* as you answer the questions—just tell me *everything* you are thinking about as you go about answering them.

4. At times I'll also stop and ask you more questions about the terms or phrases in the questions and what you think a question is asking about. I'll also take notes.

5. Please keep in mind that I really want to hear all of your opinions and reactions. Don't hesitate to speak up whenever something seems unclear, is hard to answer, or doesn't seem to apply to you.

6. Finally, we'll do this for an hour, unless I run out of things to ask you before then.[3]

7. Do you have any questions before we start?

[Next Page]

Optional Think-Aloud Practice[4]

Let's begin with a couple of practice questions. Remember to try to think aloud as you answer.

Practice question 1: How many windows are there in the house or apartment where you live?

[Probe as necessary]: How did you come up with that answer?

Practice question 2: How difficult was it for you to get here to do the interview today: very difficult, somewhat difficult, a little difficult, or not at all difficult?

[Probe as necessary]: Tell me more about that. Why do you say [ANSWER]?

OK, now let's turn to the questions that we're testing.

C. SAMPLE COGNITIVE INTERVIEWING PROTOCOL[5]

Date _____ Interview # _____ Interviewer initials _____

ENTER START TIME OF INTERVIEW: _____

Consumer Expenditure Module

NOTE FOR INTERVIEWER *(not to be read to subjects): The objectives of this module are to obtain data on household telephone expenses and information about the characteristics of the newest automobile owned by anyone in the household. (It is one component of a larger survey that collects data on consumer expenditures.)*[6]

Telephone Expenses for Owned and Rented Properties

1. Since the first of last month, that is, DECEMBER, have you received any bills for telephone services? Do not include bills for telephones used entirely for business purposes.

Yes - Ask 2   No - Go to 11

Probes:

In your own words, what is this question asking?

What does the term "telephone services" mean to you in this question?

What type of services do you think should be included in this question?

What type of services do you think should be excluded in this question?

[ENTER INTERVIEW NOTES] _____

_____

_____

_____

2. What property(ies) was (were) the telephone bill for?

Mobile (car) phone
Rented sample unit
Other rented unit
Property not owned or rented by HH

Probes:

How did you arrive at your answer?
In your own words, what is this question asking?
What does the term "properties" mean to you, in this question?
What about cell phones or car phones? Do you think they should be included in this question?

[ENTER INTERVIEW NOTES] _____

_____

_____

_____

3. What is the name of the company that provides telephone services for [PROPERTY DESCRIPTION]?

_____

Probes:

In your own words, what is this question asking?
How did you arrive at your answer?
Did you report your local telephone service carrier, your long distance telephone service carrier, a cellular phone service carrier, or
some other company?

[ENTER INTERVIEW NOTES] _____

_____

_____

_____

4. How many telephone bills were received for [PROPERTY DESCRIPTION] from [COMPANY NAME]?

_____

Probes:

How did you arrive at your answer?
What time period are you thinking of?

[ENTER INTERVIEW NOTES] _____

_____

_____

_____

5. What was the total amount of bills [BILL NUMBERS]? Exclude any unpaid bills from a previous billing period.

$ _____

Probes:

How did you arrive at your answer?
How sure are you of your answer?

[ENTER INTERVIEW NOTES] _____

_____

_____

_____

6. In what month was the bill received?

_____

Probes:

How did you arrive at your answer?
Do you receive more than one telephone bill per month?
[IF YES, ASK:] How did you decide which to report here?

[ENTER INTERVIEW NOTES] _____

_____

_____

_____

7. Does the total amount of the bill include

    (a) a basic service charge?   Yes   No

    (b) long distance call charges?   Yes   No

    (c) equipment purchases such as
       the purchase of a telephone? Yes   No

Probe:

How sure are you about the different specific services your bill covers?

[ENTER INTERVIEW NOTES] _____

_____

_____

_____

8. Is any of the total charge to be deducted as a business expense?

    Yes   Ask 9   No Go to 10

Probe:

In your own words, what is this question asking?

[ENTER INTERVIEW NOTES] _____

_____

_____

_____

9. What percentage will be deducted?

_____ percent

Probes:

How did you arrive at your answer?
How sure are you of your answer?
Would it be easier for you to report a percentage of the expenses or a dollar amount?

[ENTER INTERVIEW NOTES] _____

_____

_____

_____

10. What is the year, make, and model of your newest car or truck?

Year _____ Make _____ Model _____

Probes:

How did you arrive at your answer?
What does the term "newest" mean to you in this question?
How sure are you of the exact year, make, and model?
Is there any specific part of this question that is more difficult to answer than another?

[ENTER INTERVIEW NOTES] _____

_____

_____

_____

11. How many cylinders does it have?

_____

Probes:

What, to you, is a cylinder?
How sure are you of your answer?

[ENTER INTERVIEW NOTES]_____

_____

_____

_____

12. How many doors does it have? _____

Probes:

How did you arrive at your answer?
If a car is a hatchback, would you count the hatchback as one of the doors?
What about an SUV or a station wagon? Would you count the back opening as one of the doors?

[ENTER INTERVIEW NOTES] _____

_____

_____

_____

13. How many miles are currently on the vehicle?

_____

Probes:

How sure are you that it's about [X] miles?
How much attention do you pay to the mileage?

[ENTER INTERVIEW NOTES] _____

_____

_____

_____

Environmental Module

NOTE: *The objective of this module is somewhat unclear, but appears to focus on assessing the respondent's perceptions concerning a range of environmental issues.*[7]

1. First, I am going to read you a list of different issues that may or may not occur in your area. Some issues are about the urban environment and others are about topics such as schools and roads. I am going to read the list of issues and I want you to tell me how high or low a priority each is in your area. Use a scale of one to ten, with one meaning "very low priority" and ten meaning "very high priority."

Probe:

Can you repeat what I just read to you in your own words?

General Probe:

(For all 1–10 ratings below): "Why do you say [#]?"
Issue: Rating

(a) Air pollution from cars   1 2 3 4 5 6 7 8 9 10

PROBES: Are you thinking here of just cars, or all vehicles?

What does it mean to you, for this to be "a high priority"—a high priority to whom?

(b) Air pollution from businesses or
    industrial sites   1 2 3 4 5 6 7 8 9 10

PROBE: How much air pollution from business or industry do you think there is in your area?

(c) Air pollution from burning leaves 1 2 3 4 5 6 7 8 9 10

PROBE: How much of this happens in your area?

(d) Ozone alerts in the community   1 2 3 4 5 6 7 8 9 10

PROBE: Who do you think considers this to be a priority?

(e) Depletion of the water table   1 2 3 4 5 6 7 8 9 10 DK

PROBE: What does "depletion of the water table" mean to you?

(f) Streams, rivers, lakes, and oceans in the urban area are polluted
    1 2 3 4 5 6 7 8 9 10 DK

PROBES: Do you think that these are polluted?
How do you get your information about this?

2. Now I would like you to rate the following groups and organizations on how well they provide you with information about environmental conditions in your area. Please rate these groups using a scale from 1 to 10, with 10 being excellent and 1 being very poor.

Let's start with . . . [READ EACH. CIRCLE APPROPRIATE RATING]

Issue: Rating

(a) Television 1 2 3 4 5 6 7 8 9 10

PROBE: What type of information on "environmental conditions" do you get from TV?

(b) Radio   1 2 3 4 5 6 7 8 9 10

PROBE: What type of information on "environmental conditions" do you get from radio?

(c) Newspaper   1 2 3 4 5 6 7 8 9 10

PROBE: What type of information on "environmental conditions" do you get from newspapers?

3. The next few questions are about your household and the environment. When we use the word "environment" we mean the air you breathe; the water you drink; the place where you live, work, and play; and the food you eat. It also means the climate, wild animals, recycling, and more. When you think about the environment this way, have you or anyone else in your household aged 18 and older:

    (a) Requested environmental information in person, in writing, or by phone?

Yes ☐

No ☐

DK ☐

PROBES: Can you remember what we defined as the "environment" in this question?
What type of environmental information have you requested? From whom?

    (b) Subscribed to an environmental publication such as a magazine?

Yes ☐

No ☐

DK ☐

Refuse ☐

PROBE: [IF YES] What type of publication?

    (c) Read a book or brochure or done a library search about an environmental issue?

Yes ☐

No ☐

DK ☐

Refuse ☐

PROBE: Tell me more about that.

Transportation Module

NOTE: *The objective of this module is to collect data on availability and usage of public transportation services.*

1. Is local bus service available in your town or city?

Yes
No [SKIP NEXT QUESTION]

Probes:

What does the phrase "local bus service" mean to you?
What geographic area did you think of when you heard "town or city"?

[ENTER INTERVIEW NOTES] _____

_____

_____

_____

2. How far is it from your home to the nearest bus stop?

_____ blocks OR miles

Probes:

How did you arrive at your answer?
Is it easier for you to answer this question in terms of "number of blocks" or "number of miles" or does it not matter?

[ENTER INTERVIEW NOTES] _____

_____

_____

_____

3. Is subway, commuter train, or streetcar service available in your town or city?

Yes
No Go to 5

Probes:

In your own words, what is this question asking?
What does the term "commuter train" mean to you?
What does the term "streetcar service" mean to you?

[ENTER INTERVIEW NOTES] _____

_____

_____

_____

4. Which of these are available?

[CODE ALL THAT APPLY]
Subway
Commuter train
Streetcar

Probe:

Tell me more about this service.

[ENTER INTERVIEW NOTES] _____

_____

_____

_____

5. How many minutes does it usually take you to get from home to
   work?

_____ Minutes

Probes:

How did you arrive at your answer?
Do you usually go straight from home to work, or do you make other
stops along the way?

[ENTER INTERVIEW NOTES] _____

_____

_____

_____

ENTER END TIME OF INTERVIEW: _____

Notes

1. Instructions are appropriate for interviewer-administered questionnaires.

2. This form is set up to be administered after an appropriate consent form has been signed. Typically such a form contains elements that describe the voluntary nature of the activity, steps taken to assure privacy and confidentiality, and so on (these forms may be institution specific). Although the consent form also describes the purpose of the research and tends to be duplicative of the information above, it is still helpful for the cognitive interviewer to explain, out loud, these steps and features.

3. This instruction assumes a one-hour interview. It is sometimes useful to repeat the agreed-upon duration of participation to head off any subject tendency to "speed up" the interview based on the expectation that we need to accomplish a certain amount. We want them to be thoughtful and certainly don't want them to hurry their answers.

4. Organizations differ in the extent to which they teach think-aloud prior to beginning the interview. Some evidence indicates that, by nature, the cognitive interview induces think-aloud activity and that such instruction may not be vital (DeMaio & Landreth, in press). However, it is certainly not harmful to begin with a warm-up exercise such as this.

5. Based on a testing protocol used by Rothgeb, Forsyth, and Willis (2001) to evaluate cognitive interviewing results, as described in Chapters 13 and 14. This protocol contains more Anticipated probe questions than would generally be administered in a cognitive interview; these are made available to be selected by the interviewer as necessary.

6. Question objectives may be provided to give the interviewer a summary of the intent of the questions. These are notes, and are not to be read to subjects.

7. Although the designer of the cognitive protocol may intend to provide information to cognitive interviewers about question or section objectives, these may not be altogether clear!

Appendix 2

Examples of Findings From Cognitive Testing Reports

The question-specific comments listed below are from interviews done at three cognitive labs, either in original or minimally revised form. For each example, I have appended *general comments* that are relevant to the cognitive testing process.

Four sets of comments are presented. For the first two (Set A and Set B), little information is given about *how* the conclusions were arrived at (e.g., what probes were asked, etc.). In many cases, clients or sponsors are less interested in how we arrived at our results than in what the results are. This approach represents a common, but not universal, practice. Sets C and D illustrate an alternative practice of showing both the Anticipated probes that were embedded in the questionnaire and comments that effectively "answer" the probe questions.

SET A: Teenage Smoking
Self-Administered Questionnaire

1. Do you think young people who smoke cigarettes have more friends?

   a. Definitely yes

   b. Probably yes

   c. Probably not

   d. Definitely not

COMMENT: The response categories produced consistent, major problems. Respondents tended to believe that "smoking makes no differ-ence" in terms of the number of friends one has, and that none of the given categories adequately captured this opinion (they appeared to believe that a "not" response implied that smokers had fewer friends). The question might be rephrased, "Do you believe that young people who smoke cigarettes have more friends, fewer friends, or the same number of friends as those who don't smoke?"

To make this revision work, one would also have to change the response categories:

a. People who smoke cigarettes have more friends

b. People who do NOT smoke cigarettes have more friends

c. People who smoke and those who don't have the same number of friends

GENERAL COMMENT: *The adequacy of response categories is in the eye of the beholder—in this case, the teen subject. It may not occur to the expert reviewer that a problem exists, but this can become clear when dealing with "real people."*

2. During this school year, did you practice in any of your classes ways to say "no" to tobacco (for example, in role plays)?

a. Yes

b. No

c. Not sure

COMMENT: The question was very unrealistic for my subjects and doesn't appear to apply well for their age group; they did not engage in the type of "role playing" that the question implies (these activities may occur in lower grades). Further, some respondents mentioned programs directed toward illicit drugs, rather than tobacco, and the question may be misinterpreted on this basis as well. If the question is to be retained, it may help to make the wording a little less awkward: "During this school year, did you practice ways to say "no" to tobacco in any of your classes (for example, by role playing)?"

GENERAL COMMENT: *This could be seen as representing a prob-lem with our assumptions concerning respondents and the world in which they live. This case also demonstrates the value of conducting interviews of an appropriate range of subjects (in this case, older and younger subjects, and both smokers and nonsmokers).*

3. During the past 30 days, about how often have you seen anti-smoking commercials on TV, or heard them on the radio, or seen antismoking ads on the Internet?

   a. None

   b. 1–3 times in the past 30 days

   c. 1–3 times per week

   d. Daily or almost daily

   e. More than once a day

COMMENTS: We anticipated that the triple-barreled nature of the question would present problems, but that wasn't evident. The more serious problem was that the term "antismoking" was not well understood, or perhaps just misheard, so some respondents interpreted the question completely backwards and answered with respect to tobacco advertisements. The wording of the question might be changed to "During the past 30 days, have you seen TV commercials about the dangers of cigarette smoking, or heard them on the radio, or seen them on the Internet?"

OR, if we don't want to emphasize "dangers" specifically, "Have you seen TV commercials that try to get people not to smoke?"

It still may be a better idea to ask this in checklist form—(a) TV, (b) radio, (c) Internet—especially if the objective is to count these separately.

Also, the first response category ("none") does not match the "how often" phrasing of the question, and would be better as "never in the past 30 days."

GENERAL COMMENT: For this example, the researchers expected one type of problem but observed others. The interviewer suggests several different candidate solutions but also brings up the critical issue of defining the question objectives (Does this involve dangers of smoking versus something more general about not smoking?; Do the analysts have an interest in combining sources or counting them separately?).

4. Besides yourself, does anyone who lives in your home smoke cigarettes now?

   a. Yes

   b. No

COMMENT: Our smoker-subjects found this clear. However, the phrasing "besides yourself" may be confusing for nonsmokers. It therefore might be best to change the wording to "Does anyone who lives with you now smoke cigarettes?"

GENERAL COMMENT: The recommendation is not based on any observable problem that was noted during the interviews. It simply occurred to the interviewer that the question could produce problems for another class of individual (nonsmokers). One of the functions of cognitive interviewing is to make allowances for the acknowledged fact that testing may be restricted, and that we must always keep in mind the broader population of respondents to be administered the questions.

SET B: Teenage Smoking Telephone Survey

1. Think about the last 30 days. On about how many days, if any, did you smoke? (Give your best guess.) [READ CATEGORIES]

   a. 0 days

   b. 1 or 2 days

   c. 3 to 5 days

   d. 6 to 9 days

   e. 10 to 19 days

   f. 20 to 29 days

   g. All 30 days

COMMENT: This would be OK for a self-administered form, but over the phone, reading all these categories doesn't work very well. I would just ask this as open-ended and have the interviewer code in the exact number. The ranges could be used as a follow-up if the person says that he or she doesn't know.

GENERAL COMMENT: Very often the act of administering questions out loud in the cognitive interview makes clear where we have failed to appropriately reformat questions originally intended for self-administration. This should have been evident based on prior expert review; however, this is the very type of problem that tends to get overlooked by reviewers, who tend not to actually read the questions out loud as they review them. (Perhaps this suggests the need for the novel science of "The Cognitive Aspects of Questionnaire Review.")

2. Have you ever seriously thought about quitting smoking?

   a. Yes

   b. No

   c. Already (just) quit

COMMENTS: Interviewer #1 - My 17-year-old subject said "yes, but not now." He's thought about quitting at a future time, when he goes to college. This may be OK if we have a generally wide intent for the question but not if we really mean whether they've thought about quitting in the sense of "current intent."

Interviewer #2: - My 15-year-old subject had difficulty with this question because she says she really doesn't smoke, although she has the rare cigarette. She has not smoked more than 100 cigarettes in her entire life, although she did have one cigarette in the past month. Given that she's not (yet!) a regular smoker, the question did not seem appropriate for her.

Interviewer #1 - The comment above reminds me that sometimes smoking surveys ask how old the respondent was when he or she started smoking fairly regularly, with "never smoked regularly" as one option. If we included this, those who said "never smoked regularly" could be skipped out of the quit questions.

GENERAL COMMENT: Two interviewers noted two very different problems. In one sense, they didn't "agree," but they could still both be making useful points. Note also the interplay between interviewers, where the compiler of the notes (who was also Interviewer #1) is led to make a recommendation based on reading another interviewer's comment.

3. Have you ever used chewing tobacco, snuff, or dip, such as Redman, Levi Garrett, Beechnut, Skoal, Skoal Bandits, or Copenhagen?

   a. Yes

   b. No

COMMENTS: Interviewer #1 - I didn't observe a problem, but I have never liked the question in this form because the term "used" is really vague. Does this mean "used regularly" or "used once"? If we mean TRIED, use that instead of USED. If we mean USED REGULARLY, say that (still vague, but less so).

Interviewer #2 - My subjects were unclear about whether we mean just once or something else—there needs to be clarification of what we mean by "used" (how many times).

GENERAL COMMENT: Both interviewers made the same comment, the first based on opinion/expert review, the second via testing outcomes.

4. During the past 7 days, on how many days did you ride in a car with someone who was smoking cigarettes?

   a. 0 days

   b. 1 or 2 days

   c. 3 or 4 days

   d. 5 or 6 days

   e. 7 days

COMMENT: Interviewer #1 - One of my subjects wanted to say NO because he was driving, rather than riding. Should this just say "On how many days were you in a car with someone who was smoking cigarettes"?

GENERAL COMMENT: A result based on a single interview prompts the interviewer/analyst to suggest a rewording. This is a very typical outcome.

5. What are the rules (if any) about smoking in your home? Would you say: [OR]

   a. People can't smoke in the house

   b. People can smoke only in certain rooms of the house

   c. You can't smoke around your parents

   d. There are no rules about smoking at home

COMMENTS: Interviewer #1 - This misses some possibilities that one subject mentioned: there may be rules, but not the ones we mention (can't smoke in the morning, or need to open a window). We need to include a "something else" category to capture this.

Interviewer #2: To make this easier and straightforward, it would be easier to ask if a person has any rules about smoking at home first and then, if so, follow up with a second question about the specific rule.

GENERAL COMMENT: *The interviewers note the same problem and then pose two different potential solutions. Note that for a telephone survey it is feasible to decompose the question into two parts; this would not be as good a solution under paper-based self-administration where skip patterns would be needed.*

> 6. Most people your age think it is okay to work for tobacco companies.
>
> a. Definitely yes
>
> b. Probably yes
>
> c. Probably not
>
> d. Definitely not

COMMENTS: Interviewer #1 - This clearly didn't apply for my 12-year-old subject. She said that kids her age didn't think about this type of thing (I believe that). Then, to try to answer it anyway, she suggested that it might be bad because if they worked for a cigarette company they'd be around it all day and probably start using it (she was probably thinking of being on an assembly line, making cigarettes, or selling them). My 17-year-old also said that he never thought about this and wondered whether we meant working in a factory. I think we're attempting to ask about something that most respondents in this survey will not have an existing opinion on.

Interviewer #2 - My respondent wanted a neutral response for this question.

Interviewer #3 - My 12-year-old respondent understood this question to mean people working in a factory making cigarettes, and had no opinion because kids her age are not thinking about this.

GENERAL COMMENT: *Interviewers #1 and #3 both noted the degree to which children think in concrete rather than abstract terms (working in a cigarette factory) and that this is perhaps not a meaningful task for these respondents.*

> 7. Do you think it is safe to smoke for only a year or two, as long as you quit after that?

    a. Definitely yes

    b. Probably yes

    c. Probably not

    d. Definitely not

COMMENT: Interviewer #1 - I have found repeatedly in testing this question that some subjects tend to say NO, because once you start, you won't be able to quit. That is, they reject the conditional premise of the question. To really get at this, it would be nice to first ask how likely they think it would be that a person COULD quit after smoking for a year or two, and for those who say that it's possible, then ask them this as a follow-up question.

GENERAL COMMENT: The interviewer might have done better by indicating whether this was only his opinion, or whether he observed these problems for the current set of interviews. In any case, the question seems to make the erroneous assumption that respondents will agree to accept the hypothetical precondition on which answering the question is based.

    8. Do you believe there is any harm in having an occasional cigarette?

    a. Definitely yes

    b. Probably yes

    c. Probably not

    d. Definitely not

COMMENT: Interviewer #1 - My 22-year-old male subject wanted to know what is meant by "occasional."

Interviewer #2 - This is vague. What does "occasional" mean? Two subjects said that it depended and had a hard time answering.

Interviewer #3 - My subjects tended to say "yes, because then you'll start smoking more," so they're thinking about future addiction, rather than direct health effects of the occasional cigarette. This may be OK if our intent is to include extended effects.

GENERAL COMMENT: The first pair of interviewers identified the same problem, and the third a further issue. They may all be correct in their assessments.

9. Do you think smoking cigarettes makes young people look cool or fit in?

   a. Definitely yes

   b. Probably yes

   c. Probably not

   d. Definitely not

COMMENT: Interviewer #1 - This question appeared to be very sensitive to the issue of what we meant by "young people." I heard that a 13-year-old smoking a cigarette doesn't look very cool, but that an 18-year-old might. Here's a case where I'd go with "people your age."

GENERAL COMMENT: Another very common issue arose— vagueness concerning the meaning of a key term ("young people"). The suggested solution is to tie this to the individual respondent. This modification could be tested in another iterative round.

SET C: Testing a National Health Interview Survey (Household) Questionnaire

1. During the past 12 months, was there any time when someone in the family needed eyeglasses but could not get them?

PROBE: Find out whether subjects know that we mean NEW eyeglasses as well as ANY eyeglasses.
COMMENT: As anticipated by the probe, one subject said "no," but actually needed *new* eyeglasses.

2. How often do you or the person who shops for your food buy items that are labeled "low salt"?

PROBES: Who shops for your food?
Tell me in your own words how (you/they) decide how to choose foods that contain salt.
COMMENT: Several problems here:

(a) One subject was thinking of low fat, not low salt.

(b) Several subjects said "yes," but meant that they get foods that they *know* are low in salt—they don't necessarily say so on the label.

(c) One subject just read the #mg of sodium in the food—does that count as a label of "low salt"? (I don't think so.)

(d) This asks about two different people (you, another person)—they may both shop and have different behaviors ("My wife always checks; I never do").

(e) It's also not clear how to interpret a given answer such as "seldom." This could be because they rarely buy the types of foods that contain sodium, or that they buy lots of such foods but not the low-sodium varieties.

To get around all these problems, I would try breaking it up and asking something like the following:
THE NEXT QUESTIONS ARE ABOUT SALT OR SODIUM IN FOODS.
(A) Who shops for most of the food you eat—you or someone else?

(B) When (you/that person) shops for your food, how often do (you/they) buy *low-salt or low-sodium* varieties of foods, when (you/they) have a choice?

(C) How (do you/does that person) usually select a food that is low in salt? Does it say "low salt" on the label, or do (you/they) just know it is low in salt?

One issue that this solution raises is that we may just want to restrict the line of questions to the person who does the shopping—it's not clear whether the respondent knows how his or her spouse figures out what is low- sodium.

GENERAL COMMENT: The person who wrote up these results chronicled a range of problems and went to some length in attempting an alternative approach.

3. How often do you add salt to your food at the table? Would you say . . .

COMMENT: At least one subject missed the part about "at the table"—this may be buried, as it is. How about "When you sit down at the table to eat, how often do you add salt to your food?"

GENERAL COMMENT: *We can't always anticipate what parts of the question just don't get heard—the cognitive interview can help make this clear.*

4a. When you buy a food item for the first time, how often would you say you read the INGREDIENT list on the package?

4b. When you buy a food item for the first time, how often would you say you read the information about calories, fat and/or cholesterol content?

COMMENT: When answering 4a, every one of my subjects meant the types of information asked about in 4b (probing shows that they are thinking about fat, etc.). How about reversing the order of the questions?

GENERAL COMMENT: *Comments may involve interactions between questions, as opposed to being purely question-specific.*

5. During the past TEN years, have you had a tetanus shot?

COMMENT: This is very difficult for people to say—they simply do not remember. I would ask a confidence question to this, if they say "yes": "How sure are you that you had a tetanus shot in the last ten years: very sure, somewhat sure, or not at all sure?"

GENERAL COMMENT: *Note that the suggested additional question is itself very much like a cognitive probe.*

SET D: Telephone Lines—For Telephone Administration

1. How many residential telephone numbers do you have? Exclude dedicated fax, computer lines, and wireless phones.

Total telephone numbers: _____

PROBE: *What, to you, is a residential telephone number?*
COMMENT: This was difficult to understand for at least two of my elderly persons—they didn't understand the technical language we're using. At the other extreme, one very technically sophisticated subject was unsure about whether to include his cell phone.

PROBE: What is included or not included? Would you count a computer or a fax line? What about a cell phone or wireless phone?

COMMENT: Use of the term "wireless" produced considerable error here, as this was often mistaken for a cordless phone. As an alternative, the term "cell phone" or "cellular phone" tended to be understood even by very elderly subjects when I probed about that.

Overall, I prefer the approach asking for the number of telephone numbers that can be used to reach a person at the household. But we'd then need to decide whether a business line should be counted (because presumably a respondent could be reached that way) or not.

It seems that we want two things: (a) number of telephones that can be used to reach the household, and (b) whether there are any cell phones (and I'm not even sure whether this means phones that are owned by HH members, or that are even kept in the household, or something else). But there are two separate issues: one is statistical (how we want to define and count the various possibilities—cell phone kept in car in driveway, carried around by 16-year-old son, etc.), and the second is questionnaire-design based. Once the decision is made about what's to be included and excluded, then we can determine the wording to be used.

GENERAL COMMENT: A seemingly simple question produces a slew of results and discussion. There is no way this can be resolved until the researchers retrench and determine what it is they are attempting to measure. As often as not, cognitive interviewing serves the purpose of making clear the defects in the proposed measures, as opposed to simply improving questions on an assembly-line basis.

References

Aday, L. A. (1996). *Designing and conducting health surveys* (2nd ed.). San Francisco: Jossey-Bass.

Ahola, A. (2004). Cognitive model of the question-answering process and development of pretesting. *Proceedings of the 4th Conference on Questionnaire Evaluation Standards, Zentrum fur Umfragen, Methoden und Analysen (ZUMA)*, 26-33.

Ainsworth, B. E. (2000). Issues in the assessment of physical activity in women. *Research Quarterly for Exercise and Sport, 71,* s37–42.

Akkerboom, H., & Dehue, F. (1997). The Dutch model of data collection development for official surveys. *International Journal of Public Opinion Research, 9,* 126–145.

Akkerboom, H., & Luiten, A. (1996). Selecting pretesting tools according to a model of questionnaire development, with illustrations concerning patient satisfaction with medical care. *Proceedings of the Section on Survey Research Methods, American Statistical Association,* 911–916.

Albright, K. A., Reichart, J. W., Flores, L. R., Moore, J. C., Hess, J. C., & Pascale, J. (2000). Using response reliability to guide questionnaire design. *Proceedings of the Section on Survey Research Methods, American Statistical Association,* 157–162.

Austin, J., & Delaney, P. F. (1998). Protocol analysis as a tool for behavior analysis. *Analysis of Verbal Behavior, 15,* 41–56.

Bartlett, F. C. (1932). *Remembering.* Cambridge: Cambridge University Press.

Bassili, J. N., & Scott, B. S. (1996). Response latency as a signal to question problems in survey research. *Public Opinion Quarterly, 60,* 390–399.

Bates, N., & DeMaio, T. (1989). Using cognitive research methods to improve the design of the decennial census form. *Proceedings of the U.S. Bureau of the Census Annual Research Conference,* 267–277.

Beatty, P. (1995). Understanding the standardized/non-standardized interviewing controversy. *Journal of Official Statistics, 11,* 147–160.

Beatty, P. (2003). Answerable questions: Advances in the methods for identifying and resolving questionnaire problems in survey research (Doctoral Dissertation, University of Michigan, 2003). *Dissertation Abstracts International, 64* (09), 3504A.

Beatty, P. (2004). Paradigms of cognitive interviewing practice, and their implications for developing standards of best practice. *Proceedings of the*

4th Conference on Questionnaire Evaluation Standards, Zentrum fur Umfragen, Methoden und Analysen (ZUMA), 8-25.

Beatty, P. (in press). The dynamics of cognitive interviewing. In S. Presser, J. Rothgeb, M. Couper, J. Lessler, E. Martin, J. Martin, et al. (Eds.), *Methods for testing and evaluating survey questionnaires*. New York: John Wiley & Sons.

Beatty, P., Schechter, S., & Whitaker, K. (1996). Evaluating subjective health questions: Cognitive and methodological investigations. *Proceedings of the Section on Survey Research Methods, American Statistical Association*, 956–961.

Beatty, P., Schechter, S., & Whitaker, K. (1997). Variation in cognitive interviewer behavior: Extent and consequences. *Proceedings of the Section on Survey Research Methods, American Statistical Association*, 1064–1068.

Beatty, P., Willis, G. B., & Schechter, S. (1997). Evaluating the generalizability of cognitive interview findings. In *Seminar on statistical methodology in the public service: Statistical policy working paper 26* (pp. 353–362). Washington, DC: Federal Committee on Statistical Methodology, Office of Management and Budget.

Belson, W. A. (1981). *The design and understanding of survey questions*. Aldershot, UK: Gower.

Bercini, D. H. (1992). Pretesting questionnaires in the laboratory: An alternative approach. *Journal of Exposure Analysis and Environmental Epidemiology*, 2, 241–248.

Bethlehem, J., & Hundepool, A. (2002). *On the documentation and analysis of electronic questionnaires*. Division of Technology and Facilities, Methods and Informatics Department, Statistics Netherlands.

Bickart, B., & Felcher, E. M. (1996). Expanding and enhancing the use of verbal protocols in survey research. In N. Schwarz & S. Sudman (Eds.), *Answering questions: Methodology for determining cognitive and communicative processes in survey research* (pp. 115–142). San Francisco: Jossey-Bass.

Biemer, P. P., & Forsman, G. (1992). On the quality of reinterview data with application to the current population survey. *Journal of the American Statistical Association*, 87(420), 915–923.

Blair, E., & Burton, S. (1986). Processes used in the formulation of behavioral frequency reports in surveys. *Proceedings of the Section on Survey Research Methods, American Statistical Association*, 481–487.

Blair, E. A., & Burton, S. (1987). Cognitive processes used by survey respondents in answering behavioral frequency questions. *Journal of Consumer Research*, 14, 280–288.

Blair, J., & Presser, S. (1993). Survey procedures for conducting cognitive interviews to pretest questionnaires: A review of theory and practice. *Proceedings of the Section on Survey Research Methods, American Statistical Association*, 370–375.

Blixt, S., & Dykema, J. (1993). Before the pretest: Question development strategies. *Proceedings of the Section on Survey Research Methods, American Statistical Association*, 1142–1147.

Bolton, R. N. (1993). Pretesting questionnaires: Content analysis of respondents' concurrent verbal protocols. *Marketing Science*, 12, 280–303.

Bolton, R. N., & Bronkhorst, T. M. (1996). Questionnaire pretesting: Computer-assisted coding of concurrent protocols. In N. Schwarz & S. Sudman

(Eds.), *Answering questions: Methodology for determining cognitive and communicative processes in survey research* (pp. 37–64). San Francisco: Jossey-Bass.

Bowker, D., & Dillman, D. A. (2000, May). *An experimental evaluation of left and right oriented screens for web questionnaires.* Paper presented at the Annual Meeting of the American Association for Public Opinion Research, Portland, Oregon.

Bradburn, N. M., & Sudman, S. (1991). The current status of questionnaire research. In P. Biemer, R. M. Groves, L. E. Lyberg, N. A. Mathiowetz, & S. Sudman (Eds.), *Measurement errors in surveys* (pp. 29–40). New York: John Wiley & Sons.

Bradburn, N. M., Sudman, S., & Associates. (1979). *Improving interview method and questionnaire design.* San Francisco: Jossey-Bass.

Brannen, J. (1988). The study of sensitive subjects. *Sociological Review, 36,* 552–563.

Brewer, M. B., Dull, V. T., & Jobe, J. B. (1989). *Social cognition approach to reporting chronic conditions in health surveys* (DHHS Publication No. PHS 89–1078). Washington, DC: U.S. Government Printing Office.

Brewer, M. B., & Lui, L. N. (1996). Use of sorting tasks to assess cognitive structures. In N. Schwarz & S. Sudman (Eds.), *Answering questions: Methodology for determining cognitive and communicative processes in survey research* (pp. 373–385). San Francisco: Jossey-Bass.

Burton, S., & Blair, E. (1991). Task conditions, response formulation processes, and response accuracy for behavioral frequency questions in surveys. *Public Opinion Quarterly, 55,* 50–79.

California Health Interview Survey. (2002). *Sample Design* (CHIS 2001 Methodology Series, Report 1). Los Angeles: UCLA Center for Health Policy Research.

Campanelli, P. (1997). Testing survey questions: New directions in cognitive interviewing. *Bulletin de Methodologie Sociologique, 55,* 5–17.

Campanelli, P., Martin, E., & Rothgeb, J. M. (1991). The use of respondent and interviewer debriefing studies as a way to study response error in survey data. *The Statistician, 40,* 253–264.

Cannell, C. F., Fowler, F., Kalton, G., Oksenberg, L., & Bischoping, K. (1989). New quantitative techniques for pretesting survey questions. *Proceedings of the International Association of Survey Statisticians, Paris,* Vol. 2.

Cannell, C. F., Fowler, F. J., & Marquis, K. (1968). *The influence of interviewer and respondent psychological and behavioral variables on the reporting in household interviews.* Vital and Health Statistics, Series 2, No. 26 (PHS No. 1000, PB80-128275). Washington, DC: U.S. Government Printing Office.

Cannell, C. F., Marquis, K. H., & Laurent, A. (1977). A summary of studies of interviewing methodology. *Vital and Health Statistics,* Series 2, No. 69 (DHEW Publication No. HRA 77-1343) Washington, DC: U.S. Government Printing Office.

Cannell, C. F., Miller, P. V., & Oksenberg, L. (1981). Research on interviewing techniques. In S. Leinhardt (Ed.), *Sociological methodology* (pp. 389–437). San Francisco: Jossey-Bass.

Cantor, D., & Phipps, P. (1999). Adapting cognitive techniques to establishment surveys. In M. Sirken, T. Jabine, G. Willis, E. Martin, & C. Tucker (Eds.), *A new agenda for interdisciplinary survey research methods: Proceedings of the CASM II seminar* (pp. 74–78). Hyattsville, MD: National Center for Health Statistics.

Cantril, H. (1944). *Gauging public opinion.* Princeton, NJ: Princeton University Press.

Cantril, H., & Fried, E. (1944). The meaning of questions. In H. Cantril (Ed.), *Gauging public opinion.* Princeton, NJ: Princeton University Press.

Carrasco, L. (2003). *The American Community Survey (ACS) en Español: Using cognitive interviews to test the functional equivalency of questionnaire translations.* Paper presented at the 2003 Federal Committee on Statistical Methodology Research Conference, Arlington, VA.

Caspar, R. A., & Biemer, P. P. (1999). The use of cognitive laboratory interviews for estimating production survey costs and respondent burden. *Proceedings of the Section on Survey Research Methods, American Statistical Association,* 192–197.

Clark, H. H., & Brennan, S. E. (1991). Grounding in communication. In L. B. Resnick, J. M. Levine, & S. D. Teasley (Eds.), *Perspectives on socially shared cognition* (pp. 127–149). Washington, DC: American Psychological Association.

Clark, H. H., & Schaeffer, E. F. (1987). Collaborating on contributions to conversations. *Language and Cognitive Processes, 2,* 19–41.

Clark, H. H., & Schaeffer, E. F. (1989). Contributing to discourse. *Cognitive Science, 13,* 259–294.

Collins, D. (2003). Pretesting survey instruments: An overview of cognitive methods. *Quality of Life Research, 12,* 229–238.

Collins, D., & Becher, H. (2001). Question testing and archiving of results to make best use of limited resources. *Proceedings of the QUEST 2001 Conference, U.S. Census Bureau,* 36–44.

Conrad, F. (1999). Customizing survey procedures to reduce measurement error. In M. Sirken, D. Herrmann, S. Schechter, N. Schwarz, J. Tanur, & R. Tourangeau (Eds.), *Cognition and survey research* (pp. 301–317). New York: John Wiley & Sons.

Conrad, F., & Blair, J. (1996). From impressions to data: Increasing the objectivity of cognitive interviews. *Proceedings of the Section on Survey Research Methods, American Statistical Association,* 1–9.

Conrad, F., & Blair, J. (2001). Interpreting verbal reports in cognitive interviews: Probes matter. *Proceedings of the Section on Survey Research Methods, American Statistical Association* [CD-ROM].

Conrad, F., Blair, J., & Tracy, E. (2000). Verbal reports are data! A theoretical approach to cognitive interviews. *Office of Management and Budget: Proceedings of the 1999 Federal Committee on Statistical Methodology Research Conference,* 317–326.

Converse, J. M. (1987). *Survey research in the United States: Root and emergence 1890–1960.* Berkeley: University of California Press.

Converse, J. M., & Presser, S. (1986). *Survey questions: Handcrafting the standardized questionnaire.* Newbury Park, CA: Sage.

Cosenza, C. (2001). Standardized cognitive testing: Will quantitative results provide qualitative answers? *Proceedings of the Section on Survey Research Methods, American Statistical Association* [CD-ROM].

Cosenza, C. (2002). *Not your grandparent's cognitive testing: Exploring innovative methods in cognitive evaluations of questions.* Paper presented at the International Conference on Questionnaire Development, Evaluation, and Testing (QDET), Charleston, SC.

Cosenza, C., & Fowler, F. J. (2000). Prospective questions and other issues in cognitive testing. *Proceedings of the Section on Survey Research Methods, American Statistical Association*, 994–997.

Couper, M. P. (1999). The application of cognitive science to computer assisted interviewing. In M. Sirken, D. Herrmann, S. Schechter, N. Schwarz, J. Tanur, & R. Tourangeau (Eds.), *Cognition and survey research* (pp. 277–300). New York: John Wiley & Sons.

Couper, M. P. (2001). Web survey research: Challenges and opportunities. *Proceedings of the Section on Survey Research Methods, American Statistical Association* [CD-ROM].

Couper, M. P., Baker, R. P., Bethlehem, J., Clark, C. Z. F., Martin, J., Nicholls, W. L., et al. (1998). *Computer assisted survey information collection.* New York: John Wiley & Sons.

Crutcher, R. J. (1994). Telling what we know: The use of verbal report methodologies in psychological research. *Psychological Science, 5*, 241–244.

Daugherty, S., Harris-Kojetin, L., Squire, C., & Jaël, E. (2001). Maximizing the quality of cognitive interviewing data: An exploration of three approaches and their informational contributions. *Proceedings of the Section on Survey Research Methods, American Statistical Association* [CD-ROM].

Davis, W. L., & DeMaio, T. J. (1993). Comparing the think-aloud interviewing technique with standard interviewing in the redesign of a dietary recall questionnaire. *Proceedings of the Section on Survey Research Methods, American Statistical Association*, 565–570.

Davis, W., DeMaio, T., & Zukerberg, A. (1995). *Can cognitive information be collected through the mail? Comparing cognitive data collected in written versus verbal format* (Working Papers in Survey Methodology No. 95/02). Washington, DC: U.S. Census Bureau. Retrieved February 11, 2004, from www.census.gov/srd/papers/pdf/sm9502.pdf

de la Puente, M., & Pan, Y. (2003). *An overview of proposed Census Bureau guidelines for the translation of data collection instruments and supporting materials: Census Advisory Committee of Professional Associations.* Paper presented at the 2003 Federal Committee on Statistical Methodology Research Conference, Arlington, VA.

de Leeuw, E., Borgers, N., & Strijbos-Smits, A. (in press). Pretesting questionnaires for children and adolescents. In S. Presser, J. Rothgeb, M. Couper, J. Lessler, E. Martin, J. Martin, et al. (Eds.), *Methods for testing and evaluating survey questionnaires.* New York: John Wiley & Sons.

de Leeuw, E., & Collins, M. (1997). Data collection methods and survey quality: An overview. In L. Lyberg, P. Biemer, M. Collins, E. de Leeuw, C. Dippo, N. Schwarz, & D. Trewin (Eds.), *Survey measurement and process quality* (pp. 199–220). New York: John Wiley & Sons.

DeMaio, T. J., et al. (1983). *Statistical policy working paper 10: Approaches to developing questionnaires*. Washington, DC: U.S. Office of Management and Budget, Statistical Policy Office.

DeMaio, T., & Hughes, K. (2003). *Report on cognitive testing of question to address the respondent identification policy* (Survey Methodology #2002–06). Washington, DC: U.S. Census Bureau, Statistical Research Division.

DeMaio., T., & Landreth, A. (in press). Do different cognitive interivew techniques produce different results? In S. Presser, J. Rothgeb, M. Couper, J. Lessler, E. Martin, J. Martin, et al. (Eds.), *Methods for testing and evaluating survey questionnaires*. New York: John Wiley & Sons.

DeMaio, T., Landreth, A., & Hughes, K. (2003). *Report of cognitive research on the School Crime Supplement for the 2001 National Crime Victimization Survey* (Study Series, Survey Methodology #2003–01). Washington, DC: U.S. Census Bureau, Statistical Research Division.

DeMaio, T., Mathiowetz, N., Rothgeb, J., Beach, M. E., & Durant, S. (1993). *Protocol for pretesting demographic surveys at the Census Bureau* (Working Papers in Survey Methodology No. 93/04). Washington, DC: U.S. Census Bureau. Retrieved February 10, 2004, from www.census.gov/srd/papers/pdf/sm93–04.pdf

DeMaio, T. J., & Rothgeb, J. M. (1996). Cognitive interviewing techniques: In the lab and in the field. In N. Schwarz & S. Sudman (Eds.), *Answering questions: Methodology for determining cognitive and communicative processes in survey research* (pp. 177–195). San Francisco: Jossey-Bass.

DeMaio, T. J., Rothgeb, B., & Hess, J. (1998). *Improving survey quality through pretesting* (Working Papers in Survey Methodology No. 98/03). Washington, DC: U.S. Census Bureau. Retrieved February 11, 2004, from www.census.gov/srd/papers/pdf/sm98–03.pdf

DeMaio, T., & Wellens, T. (1997). *Cognitive evaluation of proposed disability questions for the 1998 dress rehearsal* (Working Papers in Survey Methodology No. 97/07). Washington, DC: U.S. Census Bureau. Retrieved February 11, 2004, from www.census.gov/srd/papers/pdf/sm97–07.pdf

Dijkstra, W. (2002). Transcribing, coding, and analyzing verbal interactions in survey interviews. In D. W. Maynard, H. Houtkoop-Steenstra, N. C. Schaeffer, & J. van der Zouwen (Eds.), *Standardization and tacit knowledge: Interaction and practice in the survey interview* (pp. 401–425). New York: John Wiley & Sons.

Dijkstra, W., & van der Zouwen, J. (1988). Types of inadequate interviewer behavior in survey interviews. In W. E. Saris & I. N. Gallhafer (Eds.), *Data collection and scaling* (pp. 24–35). New York: St. Martin's.

Dillman, D. A., & Bowker, D. K. (2001). *The web questionnaire challenge to survey methodologists*. Retrieved May 27, 2002, from www.survey.sesrc.wsu.edu/dillman/zuma_paper_dillman_bowker.pdf

Dillman, D. A., & Redline, C. D. (in press). Testing paper self-administered questionnaires: Cognitive interview and field test comparisons. In S. Presser, J. Rothgeb, M. Couper, J. Lessler, E. Martin, J. Martin, et al. (Eds.), *Methods for testing and evaluating survey questionnaries*. New York: John Wiley & Sons.

Dillman, D. A., Tortora, R. D., Conradt, J., & Bowker, D. (1998). *Influence of plain vs. fancy design on response rates for web surveys*. Paper presented at Joint Statistical Meetings, Dallas, Texas.

Dippo, C. (1989). The use of cognitive laboratory techniques for investigating memory retrieval errors in retrospective surveys. *Proceedings of the International Association of Survey Statisticians, International Statistical Institute,* 323–342.

Edwards, W. S., & Cantor, D. (1991). Toward a response model in establishment surveys. In P. Biemer, R. M. Groves, L. Lyberg, N. A. Mathiowetz, & S. Sudman (Eds.), *Measurement errors in surveys* (pp. 211–233). New York: John Wiley & Sons.

Eisenhower, D. (1994). Design-oriented focus groups and cognitive laboratories: A comparison. *Proceedings of the Section on Survey Research Methods, American Statistical Association,* 1374–1379.

Eisenhower, D., Mathiowetz, N. A., & Morganstein, D. (1991). Recall error: Sources and bias reduction techniques. In P. Biemer, R. M. Groves, L. Lyberg, N. A. Mathiowetz, & S. Sudman (Eds.), *Measurement errors in surveys* (pp. 127–144). New York: John Wiley & Sons.

Embretson, S. E., & Reise, S. P. (2000). *Item response theory for psychologists.* Mahwah, NJ: Lawrence Erlbaum.

Ericsson, K. A., & Simon, H. A. (1980). Verbal reports as data. *Psychological Review, 87,* 215–251.

Ericsson, K. A., & Simon, H. A. (1984). *Protocol analysis: Verbal reports as data.* Cambridge: MIT Press.

Esposito, J., & Hess, J. (1992). *The use of interviewer debriefings to identify problematic questions on alternative questionnaires.* Paper presented at the annual meeting of the American Association for Public Opinion Research, St. Petersburg, FL.

Esposito, J. L., & Rothgeb, J. M. (1997). Evaluating survey data: Making the transition from pretesting to quality assessment. In L. Lyberg, P. Biemer, M. Collins, E. de Leeuw, C. Dippo, N. Schwarz, et al. (Eds.), *Survey measurement and process quality* (pp. 541–571). New York: John Wiley & Sons.

Fisher, R. P., & Geiselman, R. E. (1992). *Memory-enhancing techniques for investigative interviewing: The cognitive interview.* Springfield, IL: Thomas.

Foddy, W. (1998). An empirical evaluation of in-depth probes used to pretest survey questions. *Sociological Methods and Research, 27,* 103–133.

Forsman, G., & Schreiner, I. (1991). The design and analysis of reinterview: An overview. In P. Biemer, R. Groves, L. Lyberg, N. Mathiowetz, & S. Sudman (Eds.), *Measurement errors in surveys* (pp. 279–301). New York: John Wiley & Sons.

Forsyth, B. (1990). *A summary of agency interviews.* Unpublished manuscript, Research Triangle Institute, Research Triangle Park, NC.

Forsyth, B. H., & Lessler, J. T. (1991). Cognitive laboratory methods: A taxonomy. In P. P. Biemer, R. M. Groves, L. E. Lyberg, N. A. Mathiowetz, & S. Sudman (Eds.), *Measurement errors in surveys* (pp. 393–418). New York: John Wiley & Sons.

Forsyth, B. H., Lessler, J. T., & Hubbard, M. L. (1992). Cognitive evaluation of the questionnaire. In C. F. Turner, J. T. Lessler, & J. C. Gfroerer (Eds.), *Survey measurement of drug use* (pp. 13–52). Rockville, MD: U.S. Department of Health and Human Services.

Forsyth, B., Rothgeb, J., & Willis, G. B. (in press). Does Questionnaire Pretesting Make a Difference? An Empirical Test. In S. Presser, J. Rothgeb, M. Couper, J. Lessler, E. Martin, J. Martin, et al. (Eds.), *Methods for testing and evaluating survey questionnaires.* New York: John Wiley & Sons.

Forsyth, B. H., Weiss, E. S., & Miller Anderson, R. (2002). *A comparison of appraisal and cognitive interview methods for testing organizational survey questionnaires.* Paper presented at the International Conference on Questionnaire Development, Evaluation, and Testing (QDET), Charleston, SC.

Fowler, F. J. (1992). How unclear terms affect survey data. *Public Opinion Quarterly, 56,* 18–231.

Fowler, F. J. (1995). *Improving survey questions.* Thousand Oaks, CA: Sage.

Fowler, F. J. (2004). More on the value of split ballots. *Proceedings of the 4th Conference on Questionnaire Evaluation Standards, Zentrum fur Umfragen, Methoden und Analysen (ZUMA),* 43–51.

Fowler, F. J., & Cannell, C. F. (1996). Using behavioral coding to identify problems with survey questions. In N. Schwarz & S. Sudman (Eds.), *Answering questions: Methodology for determining cognitive and communicative processes in survey research* (pp. 15–36). San Francisco: Jossey-Bass.

Fowler, F. J., & Cosenza, C. (2002). *The value of systematic question appraisal prior to cognitive interviewing.* Paper presented at the International Conference on Questionnaire Development, Evaluation, and Testing (QDET), Charleston, SC.

Fowler, F. J., & Mangione, T. (1990). *Standardized survey interviewing: Minimizing interviewer-related error.* Newbury Park, CA: Sage.

Fowler, F. J., & Roman, A. M. (1992). *A study of approaches to survey question evaluation.* Unpublished manuscript, University of Massachusetts.

Friedenreich, C. M., Courneya, K. S., & Bryant, H. E. (1997). *The lifetime total physical activity questionnaire: Development and reliability.* Unpublished manuscript, Division of Epidemiology, Alberta Cancer Board, Canada.

Fuson, K. C., & Willis, G. B. (1988). Subtracting by counting up: More evidence. *Journal for Research in Mathematics Education, 19*(5), 402–420.

Garas, N., Blair, J., & Conrad, F. (2003, November). *Inside the black box: Analysis of interviewer-respondent interaction in the cognitive interview.* Paper presented at the 2003 Federal Committee on Statistical Methodology Research Conference, Arlington, VA.

Gerber, E. R. (1994). *Hidden assumptions: The use of vignettes in cognitive interviewing* (Working Papers in Survey Methodology No. 94/05). Washington, DC: U.S. Census Bureau. Retrieved February 12, 2004, from www.census.gov/srd/papers/pdf/sm9405.pdf

Gerber, E. R. (1999). The view from anthropology: Ethnography and the cognitive interview. In M. Sirken, D. Herrmann, S. Schechter, N. Schwarz, J. Tanur, & R. Tourangeau (Eds.), *Cognition and survey research* (pp. 217–234). New York: John Wiley & Sons.

Gerber, E. R., & Wellens, T. R. (1997). Perspectives on pretesting: "Cognition" in the cognitive interview? *Bulletin de Methodologie Sociologique, 55,* 18–39.

Gerber, E. R., Wellens, T. R., & Keeley, C. (1996). "Who lives here?": The use of vignettes in household roster research. *Proceedings of the Section on Survey Methods Research, American Statistical Association,* 962–967.

Giesen, D. (2004). Evaluation plan for the Dutch Structural Business Statistics questionnaires: Using output to guide input improvements. *Proceedings of the 4th Conference on Questionnaire Evaluation Standards, Zentrum fur Umfragen, Methoden und Analysen (ZUMA)*, 73–80.

Goldenberg, K. L. (1996). Using cognitive testing in the design of a business survey questionnaire. *Proceedings of the Section on Survey Research Methods, American Statistical Association*, 944–949.

Goldenberg, K. L., Anderson, A. E., Willimack, D. K., Freedman, S. R., Rutchik, R. H., & Moy, L. M. (2002). *Experiences implementing establishment survey questionnaire development and testing at selected U.S. government agencies.* Paper presented at the International Conference on Questionnaire Development, Evaluation, and Testing, Charleston, SC.

Goldenberg, K. L., & Phillips, M. A. (2000, June). *Now that the study is over, what did you really tell us? Identifying and correcting measurement error in the job openings and labor turnover survey pilot test.* Paper presented at the International Conference on Establishment Surveys II, Buffalo, New York.

Gower, A. R., Belanger, B., & Williams, M. J. (1998). Using focus groups with respondents and interviewers to evaluate the questionnaire and interviewing procedures after the survey has taken place. *Proceedings of the Section on Survey Research Methods, American Statistical Association*, 404–409.

Gower, A. R., & Dibbs, R. (1989). Cognitive research: Designing a 'respondent friendly' questionnaire for the 1991 Census. *Proceedings of the U.S. Bureau of the Census Annual Research Conference (V)*, 257–266.

Graesser, A. C., Kennedy, T., Wiemer-Hastings, P., & Ottati, V. (1999). The use of computational cognitive models to improve questions on surveys and questionnaires. In M. Sirken, D. Herrmann, S. Schechter, N. Schwarz, J. Tanur, & R. Tourangeau (Eds.), *Cognition and survey research* (pp. 199–216). New York: John Wiley & Sons.

Grice, H. P. (1975). Logic and conversation. In P. Cole & J. L. Morgan (Eds.), *Syntax and semantics: Vol. 3. Speech acts* (pp. 41–58). New York: Academic Press.

Groenvold, M., Klee, M. C., Sprangers, M. A. G., & Aaronson, N. K. (1997). Validation of the EORTC QLQ-C30 Quality of Life Questionnaire through combined qualitative and quantitative assessment of patient-observer agreement. *Journal of Clinical Epidemiology, 50*(4), 441–50.

Groves, R. M. (1989). *Survey errors and survey costs.* New York: John Wiley & Sons.

Groves, R. M. (1991). Measurement errors across the disciplines. In P. Biemer, R. M. Groves, L. E. Lyberg, N. A. Mathiowetz, & S. Sudman (Eds.), *Measurement errors in surveys* (pp. 1–25). New York: John Wiley & Sons.

Groves, R. M. (1996). How do we know what we think they think is really what they think? In N. Schwarz & S. Sudman (Eds.), *Answering questions: Methodology for determining cognitive and communicative processes in survey research* (pp. 389–402). San Francisco: Jossey-Bass.

Groves, R. M., Cialdini, R. B., & Couper, M. P. (1992). Understanding the decision to participate in a survey. *Public Opinion Quarterly, 56*, 475–495.

Hak, T., van der Veer, K., & Jansen, H. (2004). *The Three-Step Test-Interview (TSTI): An observational instrument for pretesting self-completion questionnaires* (ERIM Report ERS-2004-029-ORG). Rotterdam: Erasmus Research

Institute of Management. Retrieved May 21, 2004, from hdl.handle.net/ 1765/1265

Hansen, S. E., Couper, M. P., & Fuchs, M. (1998). Usability evaluation of the NHIS CAPI instrument. *Proceedings of the Section on Survey Research Methods, American Statistical Association,* 928–933.

Harkness, J. A., Van de Vijver, F. J. R., & Mohler, P. (Eds.). (2003). *Cross-cultural survey methods.* Hoboken, NJ: John Wiley & Sons.

Harlow, S. D., & Linet, M. S. (1989). Agreement between questionnaire data and medical records: The evidence for accuracy of recall. *American Journal of Epidemiology, 129,* 233–248.

Hasher, L., & Griffin, M. (1978). Reconstructive and reproductive processes in forgetting. *Journal of Experimental Psychology: Human Learning and Memory, 4,* 318–330.

Heath, A., & Martin, J. (1997). Why are there so few formal measuring instruments in social and political research? In L. Lyberg, P. Biemer, M. Collins, E. de Leeuw, C. Dippo, N. Schwarz, et al. (Eds.), *Survey measurement and process quality* (pp. 71–86). New York: John Wiley & Sons.

Herrmann, D. J. (1999). Potential contributions of the CASM movement beyond questionnaire design: Cognitive technology and survey methodology. In M. Sirken, D. Herrmann, S. Schechter, N. Schwarz, J. Tanur, & R. Tourangeau (Eds.), *Cognition and survey research* (pp. 267–275). New York: John Wiley & Sons.

Hess, J. (1995). *The role of respondent debriefing questions in questionnaire development* (Working Papers in Survey Methodology No. 95/18). Washington, DC: U.S. Census Bureau. Retrieved May 25, 2004, from www .census.gov/srd/papers/pdf/sm9518.pdf

Hess, J. (1999). *Report on cognitive interviewing results for the Survey of Program Dynamics Children's Residential History Module.* Washington, DC: U.S. Census Bureau, Center for Survey Research Methods.

Hess, J. C., Rothgeb, J. M., & Nichols, E. M. (1998). *Report on cognitive interview results for the 1999 Survey of Program Dynamics.* Washington, DC: U.S. Census Bureau, Statistical Research Division.

Hippler, H., Schwarz, N., & Sudman, S. (Eds.). (1987). *Social information processing and survey methodology.* New York: Springer-Verlag.

Holland, L., & Willis, G. B. (1991). *Innovative pretesting methods for surveys of adolescent populations.* Paper presented at the National Field Directors Conference, San Diego, CA.

Houtkoop-Steenstra, H. (2000). *Interaction and the standardized survey interview: The living questionnaire.* Cambridge: Cambridge University Press.

Hughes, K., & DeMaio, T. (2003). *Final report of cognitive research on the new computer crime questions for the 2001 National Crime Victimization Survey* (Study Series, Survey Methodology #2003–02). Washington, DC: U.S. Census Bureau, Statistical Research Division.

Hunt, S. D., Sparkman, R. D., & Wilcox, J. B. (1982). The pretest in survey research: Issues and preliminary findings. *Journal of Marketing Research, 14,* 269–273.

Hunter, J., & Hughes, K. (2003). *Results and recommendations from the cognitive pretesting of the SIPP cash balance pension question* (Study Series,

Survey Methodology #2003–12). Washington, DC: U.S. Census Bureau, Statistical Research Division.

Jabine, T. B., Straf, M. L., Tanur, J. M., & Tourangeau, R. (Eds.). (1984). *Cognitive aspects of survey methodology: Building a bridge between disciplines.* Washington, DC: National Academy Press.

Jenkins, C. R., & Von Thurn, D. (1996). *Cognitive research on the Teacher Listing Form for the Schools and Staffing Survey* (Working Paper Series No. 96–05). Washington, DC: U.S. Department of Education, National Center for Education Statistics.

Jobe, J. B., & Hermann, D. J. (1996). Implications of models of survey cognition for memory theory. In D. Herrmann, C. McEvoy, C. Herzog, P. Hertel & M. Johnson (Eds.), *Basic and Applied Memory Research: Vol. 2. Practical application* (pp. 193–205). Hillsdale, NJ: Erlbaum.

Jobe, J. B., Keller, D. M., & Smith, A. F. (1996). Cognitive techniques in interviewing older people. In N. Schwarz & S. Sudman (Eds.), *Answering questions: Methodology for determining cognitive and communicative processes in survey research* (pp. 197–219). San Francisco: Jossey-Bass.

Jobe, J. B., & Mingay, D. J. (1990). Cognitive laboratory approach to designing questionnaires for surveys of the elderly. *Public Health Reports, 105,* 518–524.

Jobe, J. B., & Mingay, D. J. (1991). Cognition and survey measurement: History and overview. *Applied Cognitive Psychology, 5,* 175–192.

Jobe, J. B., Tourangeau, R., & Smith, A. F. (1993). Contributions of survey research to the understanding of memory. *Applied Cognitive Psychology, 7,* 567–584.

Johnson, T. P. (1998). Approaches to equivalence in cross-cultural and cross-national survey research. *ZUMA–Nachrichten Spezial, 3,* 1–40.

Jourard, S. M. (1964). *The transparent self.* New York: Van Nostrand Reinhold.

Kagawa-Singer, M., & Blackhall, L. J. (2001). Negotiating cross-cultural issues at the end of life. *Journal of the American Medical Association, 286,* 2993–3001.

Kennet, K., Wilson, B. F., Calvillo, A., Whitaker, K. R., Garber, M., & Pinder, G. (2000). *Development of a brochure to counter mistrust-based survey refusals: Putting Tuskagee in perspective* (Cognitive Methods Staff Working Paper No. 29). Hyattsville, MD: Centers for Disease Control and Prevention/National Center for Health Statistics.

Kirk, J., & Miller, M. L. (1986). *Reliability and validity in qualitative research.* Newbury Park, CA: Sage.

Krosnick, J. A. (1991). Response strategies for coping with the cognitive demands of attitude measures in surveys. *Applied Cognitive Psychology, 5,* 213–236.

Krueger, R. A. (1994). *Focus groups: A practical guide for applied research* (2nd ed.). Thousand Oaks, CA: Sage.

Labaw, P. J. (1980). *Advanced questionnaire design.* Cambridge, MA: Abt Books.

Laffey, F. (2002). *Business survey questionnaire review and testing at Statistics Canada.* Paper presented at the International Conference on Questionnaire Development, Evaluation, and Testing (QDET), Charleston, SC.

Landreth, A. (2001). *SIPP advance letter research: Cognitive interview results, implications and letter recommendations* (Working Papers in Survey

Methodology No. 01/01). Washington, DC: U.S. Census Bureau. Retrieved February 15, 2004, from www.census.gov/srd/papers/pdf/sm2001-01.pdf

Landreth, A. (2003). *Results and recommendations from cognitive interviews with selected materials accompanying the American Community Survey* (Study Series, Survey Methodology #2003-10). Washington, DC: U.S. Census Bureau, Statistical Research Division.

Lansing, J. B., Ginsburg, G. P., & Braaten, K. (1961). *An investigation of response error.* Urbana: University of Illinois, Bureau of Economic and Business Research.

Lashley, K. S. (1923). The behavioristic interpretation of consciousness II. *Psychological Review, 30,* 329–353.

Lee, L., Brittingham, A., Tourangeau, R., Ching, P., Willis, G., et al. (1999). Are reporting errors due to encoding limitations or retrieval failure? Surveys of child vaccination as a case study. *Applied Cognitive Psychology, 13,* 43–63.

Lee, R. M. (1993). *Doing research on sensitive topics.* London: Sage.

Lessler, J. T., & Forsyth, B. H. (1996). A coding system for appraising questionnaires. In N. Schwarz & S. Sudman (Eds.), *Answering questions: Methodology for determining cognitive and communicative processes in survey research* (pp. 259–291). San Francisco: Jossey-Bass.

Lessler, J. T., & Sirken, M. G. (1985). Laboratory-based research on the cognitive aspects of survey methodology: The goals and methods of the National Center for Health Statistics study. *Milbank Memorial Fund Quarterly, 63*(3), 565–581.

Lessler, J. T., Tourangeau, R., & Salter, W. (1989). *Questionnaire design research in the cognitive research laboratory* (DHHS Publication No. PHS-89-1076). Washington, DC: U.S. Government Printing Office.

Loftus, E. (1984). Protocol analysis of responses to survey recall questions. In T. B. Jabine, M. L. Straf, J. M. Tanur, & R. Tourangeau (Eds.), *Cognitive aspects of survey methodology: Building a bridge between disciplines* (pp. 61–64). Washington, DC: National Academy Press.

Loomis, L. (2000). *Report on cognitive interview research results for questions on welfare reform benefits and government health insurance for the March 2001 Income Supplement to the CPS.* Washington, DC: U.S. Census Bureau, Center for Survey Research Methods.

Magliano, J. P., & Graesser, A. C. (1991). A three-pronged method for studying inference generation in literary text. *Poetics, 20,* 193–232.

Marquis, K., & Kasprzyk, D. (1999). CASM in a changing survey environment. In M. Sirken, T. Jabine, G. Willis, E. Martin, & C. Tucker (Eds.), *A new agenda for interdisciplinary survey research methods: Proceedings of the CASM II seminar* (pp. 45–50). Hyattsville, MD: National Center for Health Statistics.

Marquis, K. H., Marquis, M. S., & Polich, J. M. (1986). Response bias and reliability in sensitive topic surveys. *Journal of the American Statistical Association, 81*(394), 381–389.

Martin, E. (1983). Surveys as social indicators: Problems in monitoring trends. In P. H. Rossi, J. D. Wright, & A. B. Anderson (Eds.), *Handbook of survey research* (pp. 677–743). New York: Academic Press.

Martin, E. (in press). Vignettes and respondent debriefing for questionnaire design and evaluation. In S. Presser, J. Rothgeb, M. Couper, J. Lessler,

E. Martin, J. Martin, et al. (Eds.), *Methods for testing and evaluating survey questionnaires*. New York: John Wiley & Sons.

Martin, E., & Polivka, A. E. (1995). Diagnostics for redesigning survey questionnaires: Measuring work in the Current Population Survey. *Public Opinion Quarterly, 59*, 547–567.

Martin, E., & Tucker, C. (1999). Toward a research agenda: Future development and applications of cognitive sciences to surveys. In M. Sirken, D. Herrmann, S. Schechter, N. Schwarz, J. Tanur, & R. Tourangeau (Eds.), *Cognition and survey research* (pp. 363–381). New York: John Wiley & Sons.

Martin, J. (1964). Acquiescence—measurement and theory. *British Journal of Social and Clinical Psychology, 3*, 216–225.

McCurdy, D. W. (1997). Using anthropology. In J. Spradly & D. W. McCurdy (Eds.), *Conformity and conflict: Readings in cultural anthropology*. New York: Longman.

McKay, R. B., Breslow, M. J., Sangster, R. L., Gabbard, S. M., Reynolds, R. W., Nakamoto, J. M, et al. (1996). Translating survey questionnaires: Lessons learned. In M. T. Braverman & J. K. Slater (Eds.), *Advances in survey research* (pp. 93–104). San Francisco: Jossey-Bass.

McKay, R. B., & de la Puente, M. (1995). Cognitive research in designing the CPS Supplement on Race and Ethnicity. *Proceedings of the U.S. Bureau of the Census Annual Research Conference, 435–445.*

Means, B., Nigam, A., Zarrow, M., Loftus, E., & Donaldson, M. (1989). Autobiographical memory for health-related events (DHHS Publication No. PHS 89–1077). Washington, DC: U.S. Government Printing Office.

Miller, K. (2002a). *A comparison of focus groups and one-on-one cognitive interviewing for question evaluation*. Paper presented at the International Conference on Questionnaire Development, Evaluation, and Testing (QDET), Charleston, SC.

Miller, K. (2002b). *Cognitive analysis of sexual identity, attraction and behavior questions* (Cognitive Methods Staff Working Paper No. 32). Hyattsville, MD: Centers for Disease Control and Prevention/National Center for Health Statistics.

Miller, K. (2002c). *The role of social location in question response: Rural poor experience answering general health questions*. Paper presented at the Annual Meeting of the American Association for Public Opinion Research, St Pete Beach, FL.

Miller, K., Canfield, B., Beatty, P., Whitaker, K., & Wilson, B. (2003). *Q-BANK: Development and implementation of an evaluated-question database*. Paper presented at the 2003 Federal Committee on Statistical Methodology Research Conference, Arlington, VA.

Morrison, R. L, Stettler, K., & Anderson, A. E. (2002). *Using vignettes in cognitive research on establishment surveys*. Paper presented at the International Conference on Questionnaire Development, Evaluation, and Testing, Charleston, SC.

Morton-Williams, J. (1979). The use of 'verbal interaction coding' for evaluating a questionnaire. *Quality and Quantity, 13*, 59–75.

Morton-Williams, J., & Sykes, W. (1984). The use of interaction coding and follow-up interviews to investigate the comprehension of survey questions. *Journal of the Market Research Society, 26*, 109–127.

Neisser, U., & Winograd, E. (1988). *Remembering reconsidered: Ecological and traditional approaches to the study of memory.* New York: Cambridge University Press.

Neter, J., & Waksberg, J. (1964). A study of response errors in expenditures data from household interviews. *Journal of the American Statistical Association, 59,* 18–55.

Newell, A., & Simon, H. A. (1972). *Human problem solving.* Englewood Cliffs, NJ: Prentice-Hall.

Nisbett, R. E., & Wilson, T. D. (1977). Telling more than we know: Verbal reports on mental processes. *Psychological Review, 84,* 231–259.

Nunnally, J. C. (1978). *Psychometric theory.* New York: McGraw-Hill.

O'Brien, E., Fisher, S., Goldenberg, K., & Rosen, R. (2001). Application of cognitive methods to an establishment survey: A demonstration using the Current Employment Statistics Survey. *Proceedings of the Section on Survey Research Methods, American Statistical Association* [CD-ROM].

Oksenberg, L., Cannell, C., & Kalton, G. (1991). New strategies for pretesting survey questions. *Journal of Official Statistics, 7*(3), 349–365.

O'Muircheartaigh, C. (1999). CASM: Successes, failures, and potential. In M. Sirken, D. Herrmann, S. Schechter, N. Schwarz, J. Tanur, & R. Tourangeau (Eds.), *Cognition and survey research* (pp. 39–62). New York: John Wiley & Sons.

Oppenheim, A. N. (1966). *Questionnaire design and attitude measurement.* New York: Basic Books.

Oppenheim, A. N. (1992). *Questionnaire design, interviewing and attitude measurement* (2nd ed.). London: Pinter Publishers.

Pascale, J. (2003). *Questionnaire Design Experimental Research Survey (QDERS) 2004: Cognitive testing results on health insurance questions.* Washington, DC: U.S. Census Bureau, Center for Survey Research Methods.

Pascale, J., & Mayer, T. S. (2002). *Alternate methods for exploring confidentiality issues related to dependent interviewing.* Paper presented at the International Conference on Questionnaire Development, Evaluation, and Testing (QDET), Charleston, SC.

Payne, S. L. (1951). *The art of asking questions.* Princeton, NJ: Princeton University Press.

Pickle L. W., Herrmann, D. J., Kerwin J., Croner, C. M., & White, A. A. (1994). The impact of statistical graphic design on interpretation of disease rate maps. *Proceedings of the Statistical Graphics Section, American Statistical Association,* 111–116.

Pober, J. S., Neuhauser, C. S., & Pober, J. M. (2001). Obstacles facing translational research in academic medical centers. *The FASEB Journal, 15*(13), 2303–2313.

Presser, S., & Blair, J. (1994). Survey pretesting: Do different methods produce different results? In P. V. Marsden (Ed.), *Sociological methodology* (Vol. 24, pp. 73–104). Washington, DC: American Sociological Association.

Prufer, P., & Rexroth, M. (2004). Paraphrasing can be dangerous: A little experiment. *Proceedings of the 4th Conference on Questionnaire Evaluation Standards, Zentrum fur Umfragen, Methoden und Analysen (ZUMA),* 52–59.

Ramirez, C. (2002). *Strategies for subject matter expert review in questionnaire design.* Paper presented at the International Conference on Questionnaire Development, Evaluation, and Testing (QDET), Charleston, SC.

Redline, C., Smiley, R., Lee, M., DeMaio, T., & Dillman, D. (1998). *Beyond concurrent interviews: An evaluation of cognitive interviewing techniques for self-administered questionnaires* (Working Papers in Survey Methodology No. 98/06). Washington, DC: U.S. Census Bureau. Retrieved February 12, 2004, from www.census.gov/srd/papers/pdf/sm98–06.pdf

Reeve, B. B., & Masse, L.C. (in press). Item response theory modeling for questionnaire evaluation. In S. Presser, J. Rothgeb, M. Couper, J. Lessler, E. Martin, J. Martin, et al. (Eds.), *Methods for testing and evaluating survey questionnaires*. New York: John Wiley & Sons.

Rho, C., & Sangster, R. L. (2003). *How much can you trust the answers you get using cognitive interviews?* Paper presented at the meeting of the American Association for Public Opinion Research, Nashville, TN.

Rothgeb, J. (2001). *Summary of cognitive testing of the American Community Survey New York City Special Study on the Effects of September 11.* Washington, DC: U.S. Census Bureau, Statistical Research Division.

Rothgeb, J. (2004). A valuable vehicle for question testing in a field environment: The Census Bureau's Questionnaire Design Experimental Research Survey (QDERS). *Proceedings of the 4th Conference on Questionnaire Evaluation Standards, Zentrum fur Umfragen, Methoden und Analysen (ZUMA)*, 92–98.

Rothgeb, J., Loomis, L., & Hess, J. (2000). Challenges and strategies in gaining acceptance of research results from cognitive questionnaire testing. In J. Blasius, J. Hox, E. de Leeuw, & P. Schmidt (Eds.), *Proceedings of the Fifth International Conference on Logic and Methodology, Cologne, Germany* [CD-ROM].

Rothgeb, J., Willis, G., & Forsyth, B. (2001). Questionnaire pretesting methods: Do different techniques and different organizations produce similar results? *Proceedings of the Section on Survey Research Methods, American Statistical Association* [CD-ROM].

Royston, P. N. (1989). Using intensive interviews to evaluate questions. In F. J. Fowler, Jr. (Ed.), *Health survey research methods* (DHHS Publication No. PHS 89–3447, pp. 3–7). Washington, DC: U.S. Government Printing Office.

Royston, P., & Bercini, D. (1987). Questionnaire design research in a laboratory setting: Results of testing cancer risk factor questions. *Proceedings of the Section on Survey Research Methods, American Statistical Association*, 829–833.

Royston, P. N., Bercini, D., Sirken, M., & Mingay, D. (1986). Questionnaire design research laboratory. *Proceedings of the Section on Survey Research Methods, American Statistical Association*, 703–707.

Rutchik, R. H., & Freedman, S. R. (2002). *Establishments as respondents: Is conventional cognitive interviewing enough?* Paper presented at the International Conference on Questionnaire Development, Evaluation, and Testing (QDET), Charleston, SC.

Sangster, R., & Fox, J. E. (2000). *Housing Rent Stability Bias Study.* Washington, DC: U.S. Bureau of Labor Statistics, Statistical Methods Division.

Schaeffer, N. C. (1991). Conversation with a purpose—or conversation? Interaction in the standardized interview. In P. Biemer, R. M. Groves, L. Lyberg, N. A. Mathiowetz, & S. Sudman (Eds.), *Measurement errors in surveys* (pp. 367–391). New York: John Wiley & Sons.

Schaeffer, N. C. (1999). Asking questions about threatening topics: A selective overview. In A. A. Stone, J. S. Turkkan, C. A. Bachrach, J. B. Jobe, H. S. Kurtzman, & V. S. Cain (Eds.), *The science of self-report: Implications for research and practice* (pp. 105–122). Mahwah, NJ: Lawrence Erlbaum.

Schaeffer, N. C., & Dykema, J. L. (in press). Improving the clarity of closely related concepts. In S. Presser, J. Rothgeb, M. Couper, J. Lessler, E. Martin, J. Martin, et al. (Eds.), *Methods for testing and evaluating survey questionnaires*. New York: John Wiley & Sons.

Schechter, S. (1993). *Investigation into the cognitive processes of answering self-assessed health status questions* (Cognitive Methods Staff Working Paper No. 2). Hyattsville, MD: Centers for Disease Control and Prevention/National Center for Health Statistics.

Schechter, S. (Ed.). (1994). *Proceedings of the 1993 NCHS conference on the cognitive aspects of self-reported health status* (Cognitive Methods Staff Working Paper No. 10). Hyattsville, MD: Centers for Disease Control and Prevention/National Center for Health Statistics.

Schechter, S., & Beatty, P. (1994). *Conducting cognitive laboratory tests by telephone* (Cognitive Methods Staff Working Paper No. 8). Hyattsville, MD: Centers for Disease Control and Prevention/National Center for Health Statistics.

Schechter, S., Blair, J., & Vande Hey, J. (1996). Conducting cognitive interviews to test self-administered and telephone surveys: Which methods should we use? *Proceedings of the Section on Survey Research Methods, American Statistical Association,* 10–17.

Schechter, S., Trunzo, D., & Parsons, P. E. (1993). Using focus groups in the final stages of questionnaire design. *Proceedings of the Section on Survey Research Methods, American Statistical Association,* 1148–1153.

Schober, M. F. (1999). Making sense of questions: An interactional approach. In M. Sirken, D. Herrmann, S. Schechter, N. Schwarz, J. Tanur, & R. Tourangeau (Eds.), *Cognition and survey research* (pp. 77–93). New York: John Wiley & Sons.

Schober, M. F., & Conrad, F. G. (1997). Does conversational interviewing reduce survey measurement error? *Public Opinion Quarterly, 61,* 576–602.

Schober, M. F., & Conrad, F. G. (2002). A collaborative view of standardized survey interviews. In D. W. Maynard, H. Houtkoop-Steenstra, N. C. Schaeffer, & J. van der Zouwen (Eds.), *Standardization and tacit knowledge: Interaction and practice in the survey interview* (pp. 67–94). New York: John Wiley & Sons.

Schober, M., & Conrad, F. (2003, August). *Variability in question interpretation.* Paper presented at the Annual Meeting of the American Statistical Association, San Francisco.

Schuman, H. (1966). The random probe: A technique for evaluating the validity of closed questions. *American Sociological Review, 21,* 218–222

Schuman, H. (1982). Artifacts are in the mind of the beholder. *The American Sociologist, 17,* 21–28.

Schuman, H., & Presser, S. (1981). *Questions and answers in attitude surveys: Experiments on question form, wording, and context.* New York: Academic Press.

Schwarz, N. (1997). Questionnaire design: The rocky road from concepts to answers. In L. Lyberg, P. Biemer, M. Collins, E. de Leeuw, C. Dippo, N. Schwarz, et al. (Eds.), *Survey measurement and process quality* (pp. 29–45). New York: John Wiley & Sons.

Schwarz, N. (1999). Cognitive research into survey measurement: Its influence on survey methodology and cognitive theory. In M. Sirken, D. Herrmann, S. Schechter, N. Schwarz, J. Tanur, & R. Tourangeau (Eds.), *Cognition and survey research* (pp. 65–75). New York: John Wiley & Sons.

Schwarz, N., & Bienias, J. (1990). What mediates the impact of response alternatives on frequency reports of mundane behaviors? *Applied Cognitive Psychology, 4,* 61–72.

Schwarz, N., Hippler, H., Deutsch, B., & Strack, F. (1985). Response scales: Effects of category range on reported behavior and comparative judgments. *Public Opinion Quarterly, 49,* 388–395.

Schwarz, N., Strack, F., & Mai, H. (1991). Assimilation and contrast effects in part-whole question sequences: A conversational logic analysis. *Public Opinion Quarterly, 55,* 3–23.

Schwarz, N., & Sudman, S. (Eds.). (1996). *Answering questions: Methodology for determining cognitive and communicative processes in survey research.* San Francisco: Jossey-Bass.

Selltiz, C., Jahoda, M., Deutsch, M., & Cook, S. W. (1959). Research methods in social relations. New York: Holt, Rinehart & Winston.

Sirken, M. G., Herrmann, D. J., Schechter, S., Schwarz, N., Tanur, J. M., & Tourangeau, R. (1999). *Cognition and survey research.* New York: John Wiley & Sons.

Sirken, M., & Schechter, S. (1999). Interdisciplinary survey methods research. In M. Sirken, D. Herrmann, S. Schechter, N. Schwarz, J. Tanur, & R. Tourangeau (Eds.), *Cognition and survey research* (pp. 1–10). New York: John Wiley & Sons.

Skinner, B. F. (1950). Are theories of learning necessary? *Psychological Review, 57,* 193–216.

Smith, A. F., Mingay, D. J., Jobe, J. B., & Weed, J. A. (1992). A cognitive approach to mortality statistics. *Proceedings of the Section on Survey Research Methods, American Statistical Association,* 812–817.

Smith, E. R., & Miller, F. D. (1978). Limits on perception of cognitive processes: A reply to Nisbett and Wilson. *Psychological Review, 85,* 355–362.

Smith, T. W. (2003). Developing comparable questions in cross-national surveys. In J. A. Harkness, F. J. R. Van de Vijver, & P. Mohler (Eds.), *Cross-cultural survey methods* (pp. 69–91). Hoboken, NJ: John Wiley & Sons.

Snijkers, G. (2002). *Cognitive laboratory experiences: On pretesting computerised questionnaires and data quality.* Unpublished doctoral dissertation, Utrecht University, Netherlands.

Snijkers, G. (2004). Cognitive laboratory experiences and beyond: Some ideas for future research. *Proceedings of the 4th Conference on Questionnaire Evaluation Standards, Zentrum fur Umfragen, Methoden und Analysen (ZUMA),* 190–203.

Stettler, K., Willimack, D. K., & Anderson, A. E. (2001). Adapting cognitive interviewing methodologies to compensate for unique characteristics of establishments. *Proceedings of the Section on Survey Research Methods, American Statistical Association* [CD-ROM].

Stewart, A. L., & Napoles-Springer, A. (2000). Health-related quality-of-life assessments in diverse population groups in the United States. *Medical Care, 38*(9), II-102–II-124.

Stone A. A., Turkkan, J. S., & Bachrach, C. E. (Eds.). (1999). *The science of self-report: Implications for research and practice.* Mahwah, NJ: Lawrence Erlbaum.

Stussman, B. J., Willis, G. B., & Allen, K. F. (1993). Collecting information from teenagers: Experiences from the cognitive lab. *Proceedings of the Section on Survey Research Methods, American Statistical Association,* 382–385.

Suchman, L., & Jordan, B. (1990). Interactional troubles in face-to-face survey interviews. *Journal of the American Statistical Association, 85,* 232–241.

Sudman, S., & Bradburn, N. (1982). *Asking questions: A practical guide to questionnaire design.* San Francisco: Jossey-Bass.

Sudman S., Bradburn, N. M., & Schwarz, N. (1996). *Thinking about answers. The application of cognitive processes to survey methodology.* San Francisco: Jossey-Bass.

Sykes, W., & Morton-Williams, J. (1987). Evaluating survey questions. *Journal of Official Statistics, 3,* 191–207.

Tanur, J. (Ed.). (1992). *Questions about questions. Inquiries into the cognitive bases of surveys.* New York: Russell Sage Foundation.

Tanur, J. M. (1999). Looking backwards and forwards at the CASM movement. In M. Sirken, D. Herrmann, S. Schechter, N. Schwarz, J. Tanur, & R. Tourangeau (Eds.), *Cognition and survey research* (pp. 13–19). New York: John Wiley & Sons.

Tomaskovic-Devey, D., Leiter, J., & Thompson, S. (1994). Organizational survey nonresponse. *Administrative Science Quarterly, 39,* 439–457.

Tourangeau, R. (1984). Cognitive science and survey methods: A cognitive perspective. In T. Jabine, M. Straf, J. Tanur, & R. Tourangeau (Eds.), *Cognitive aspects of survey design: Building a bridge between disciplines* (pp. 73–100). Washington, DC: National Academy Press.

Tourangeau, R. (1987). Attitude measurement: A cognitive perspective. In H. Hippler, N. Schwarz, & S. Sudman (Eds.), *Social information processing and survey methodology* (pp. 149–162). New York: Springer-Verlag.

Tourangeau, R. (1992). Attitudes as memory structures: Belief sampling and context effects. In N. Schwarz & S. Sudman (Eds.), *Context effects in social and psychological research* (pp. 35–47). New York: Springer-Verlag.

Tourangeau, R., Couper, M. P., Tortora, R., & Miller-Steiger, D. (2000). Cognitive issues in the design of web surveys. *Proceedings of the Section on Survey Methods Research, American Statistical Association,* 476–480.

Tourangeau, R., & Rasinski, K. (1988). Cognitive processes underlying context effects in attitude measurement. *Psychological Bulletin, 103,* 299–314.

Tourangeau, R., Rips, L. J., & Rasinski, K. (2000). *The psychology of survey response.* Cambridge: Cambridge University Press.

Trabasso, T., & Suh, S. (1993). Understanding text: Achieving explanatory coherence through on-line inferences and mental operations in working memory. *Discourse Processing, 16,* 3–34.

Tucker, C. (1997). Measurement issues surrounding the application of cognitive psychology in survey research. *Bulletin de Methodologie Sociologique, 55,* 67–92.

Turner, C. F., & Martin, E. (1984). *Surveying subjective phenomena.* New York: Russell Sage.

U.S. Census Bureau. (1998). *Pretesting policy and options: Demographic surveys at the Census Bureau.* Washington, DC: Author.

U.S. Census Bureau. (2003). *Census Bureau standard: Pretesting questionnaires and related methods for surveys and censuses.* Washington, DC: Author.

U.S. Office of Management and Budget. (2001). *Measuring and reporting sources of error in surveys* (Statistical Policy Working Paper 31). Washington, DC: Author. Retrieved February 5, 2004, from www.fcsm .gov/01papers/SPWP31_final.pdf

van der Zouwen, J. (2002). Why study interaction in the survey interview? Response from a survey researcher. In D. W. Maynard, H. Houtkoop-Steenstra, N. C. Schaeffer, & J. van der Zouwen (Eds.), *Standardization and tacit knowledge: Interaction and practice in the survey interview* (pp. 47–65). New York: John Wiley & Sons.

van Someren, M. W., Barnard, Y. F., & Sandberg, J. A. C. (1994). *The think-aloud method: A practical guide to modelling cognitive processes.* San Diego, CA: Academic Press.

Viterna, J. S., & Maynard, D. W. (2002). How uniform is standardization? Variation within and across survey research centers regarding protocols for interviewing. In D. W. Maynard, H. Houtkoop-Steenstra, N. C. Schaeffer, & J. van der Zouwen (Eds.), *Standardization and tacit knowledge: Interaction and practice in the survey interview* (pp. 365–397). New York: John Wiley & Sons.

Von Thurn, D., & Moore, J. (1993). The use of anthropological interviewing methods in survey research pretesting. *Proceedings of the Section on Survey Research Methods, American Statistical Association,* 571–576.

Von Thurn, D., & Moore, J. (1994). Results from a cognitive exploration of the 1993 American Housing Survey. *Proceedings of the Section on Survey Research Methods, American Statistical Association,* 1210–1214.

Warnecke, R. B., Johnson, T. P., Chavez, N., Sudman, S., O'Rourke, D. P., Lacey, L., et al. (1997). Improving question wording in surveys of culturally diverse populations. *Annals of Epidemiology, 7*(5), 334–342.

Wellens, T. (1994). The cognitive evaluation of the nativity questions for the Current Population Survey. *Proceedings of the Section on Survey Research Methods, American Statistical Association,* 1204–1209.

Whitney, P., & Budd, D. (1996). Think-aloud protocols and the study of comprehension. *Discourse Processing, 21,* 341–351.

Willimac, D. K., Martin, J., Whitridge, P., Japec, L., & Lyberg, L. (in press). Current practices in questionnaire development, evaluation and testing for establishment surveys: An international overview. In S. Presser, J. Rothgeb, M. Couper, J. Lessler, E. Martin, J. Martin, et al. (Eds.), *Methods for testing and evaluating survey questionnaires.* New York: John Wiley & Sons.

Willis, G. B. (1989). *Evaluation of 1990 NHIS pretest findings.* Unpublished manuscript, National Center for Health Statistics, Hyattsville, MD.

Willis, G. B. (1994). *Cognitive interviewing and questionnaire design: A training manual* (Cognitive Methods Staff Working Paper No. 7). Hyattsville, MD: Centers for Disease Control and Prevention/National Center for Health Statistics.

Willis, G. B. (1996). *The use of the psychological laboratory to study sensitive survey topics: Can cognitive techniques supplement field study?* (Cognitive Methods Staff Working Paper No. 20). Hyattsville, MD: Centers for Disease Control and Prevention/National Center for Health Statistics.

Willis, G. B. (1999). *Cognitive interviewing: A 'how to' guide*. Rockville, MD: Research Triangle Institute. Retrieved May 12, 2003, from www.appliedresearch .cancer.gov/areas/cognitive/interview.pdf

Willis, G. B. (2000). *Cognitive testing of the 2000–2001 National Household Survey on Drug Abuse* (Report submitted to the Substance Abuse and Mental Health Services Administration). Rockville, MD: Research Triangle Institute.

Willis, G. B. (in press). Cognitive interviewing revisited: A useful technique, in theory? In S. Presser, J. Rothgeb, M. Couper, J. Lessler, E. Martin, J. Martin, et al. (Eds.), *Methods for testing and evaluating survey questionnaires*. New York: John Wiley & Sons.

Willis, G. B., Al-Tayyib, A., & Rogers, S. (2001). The use of touch-screen ACASI in a high-risk population: Implications for surveys involving sensitive questions. *Proceedings of the Section on Survey Research Methods, American Statistical Association* [CD-ROM].

Willis, G. B., Bornstein, G., Sand, K., & Alakoye, A. (2000). *Telephone-based cognitive interviewing of the Behavioral Risk Factor Surveillance System*. Rockville, MD: Research Triangle Institute.

Willis, G. B., DeMaio, T. J., & Harris-Kojetin, B. (1999). *Is the bandwagon headed to the methodological promised land? Evaluating the validity of cognitive interviewing techniques*. In M. Sirken, D. Herrmann, S. Schechter, N. Schwarz, J. Tanur, & R. Tourangeau (Eds.), *Cognition and survey research* (pp. 133–153). New York: John Wiley & Sons.

Willis, G. B., & Lessler, J. (1999). *The BRFSS-QAS: A guide for systematically evaluating survey question wording*. Rockville, MD: Research Triangle Institute.

Willis, G. B., Reeve, B. B., & Barofsky, I. (in press). The use of cognitive interviewing techniques in quality of life and patient-reported outcomes measurement. In J. Lipscomb, C. C. Gotay, & C. Snyder (Eds.), *Outcomes assessment in cancer: Findings and recommendations of the cancer outcomes measurement working group*. Cambridge: Cambridge University Press.

Willis, G. B., Royston, P., & Bercini, D. (1991). The use of verbal report methods in the development and testing of survey questionnaires. *Applied Cognitive Psychology, 5*, 251–267.

Willis, G., & Schechter, S. (1997). Evaluation of cognitive interviewing techniques: Do the results generalize to the field? *Bulletin de Methodologie Sociologique, 55*, 40–66.

Willis, G. B., Schechter, S., & Whitaker, K. (1999). A comparison of cognitive interviewing, expert review, and behavior coding: What do they tell us? *Proceedings of the Section on Survey Research Methods, American Statistical Association*, 28–37.

Wilson, B. F., & Peterson, L. S. (1999). Using the NCHS cognitive lab to help design cycle VI of the National Survey of Family Growth. *Proceedings of the Section on Survey Research Methods, American Statistical Association,* 997–1002.

Wilson, B. F., Whitehead, N., & Whitaker, K. (2000). Cognitive testing proposed questions for PRAMS in the NCHS Questionnaire Design Research Laboratory. *Proceedings of the Section on Survey Research Methods, American Statistical Association,* 989–993.

Wilson, T., LaFleur, S., & Anderson, D. (1996). The validity and consequences of verbal reports about attitudes. In N. Schwarz & S. Sudman (Eds.), *Answering questions: Methodology for determining cognitive processes in survey research* (pp. 91–114). San Francisco: Jossey-Bass.

Wolfgang, G. S., Lewis, P. J., & Vacca, E. A. (1994). Cognitive research for the 1997 Census of Agriculture Report form. *Proceedings of the Section on Survey Research Methods, American Statistical Association,* 503–508.

York, R. O. (1998). *Conducting social work research: An experimental approach.* Needham Heights, MA: Allyn & Bacon.

Zukerberg, A. L., & Hess, J. (1996). Uncovering adolescent perceptions: Experiences conducting cognitive interviews with adolescents. *Proceedings of the Section on Survey Research Methods, American Statistical Association,* 950–955.

Zukerberg, A. L., Von Thurn, D. R., & Moore, J. C. (1995). *Practical considerations in sample size selection for behavior coding pretests. Proceedings of the Section on Survey Research Methods, American Statistical Association,* 1116–1121.

Index

Aaronson, N. K., 107
ACASI. *See* Audio-Computer-
   Assisted Self-Interview
Aday, L. A., 23, 136
Adolescents, interviewing, 203
Advanced Research Seminar on
   Cognitive Aspects of Survey
   Methodology (CASM I), 3
Affiliated pretesting methods,
   230-254
  behavior coding, 236-241
  case study in coordination of,
    250-253
  comparing, 243-253
  expert review, 231-233
  focus groups, 233-236
  reinterview surveys, 241-242
Age of respondent, 202-204
Ahola, A., 37
Ainsworth, B. E., 109
Akkerboom, H., 78, 155, 248, 249
Alakoye, A., 93
Albright, K. A., 16, 242
Allen, K. F., 203
Al-Tayyib, A., 92
Analysis:
  once-through vs. revisitation,
    168-169
  probed interview, 159-168
  think-aloud interview, 156-159
Anderson, A. E., 58, 196, 197
Anderson, D., 200, 201
Anderson, R., 24
Anticipated probing, 88, 92, 163
Applied CASM research, 40, 262

Appraisal-based probing, 79-80
Apt Associates, 10
Attitudes, testing questions
  on, 199-202
Attitude surveys, logical problems
  in, 78
Audio-Computer-Assisted Self-
  Interview (ACASI), 178, 195
Austin, J., 209
Autobiographical questions,
  cognitive processes and, 36

Bachrach, C. E., 13
Back channeling, 47, 67
Backup ethnography, 110
Barnard, Y. F., 42
Barofsky, I., 3
Bartlett, F. C., 38
Bassili, J. N., 242
Bates, N., 58, 183
Beach, M. E., 58
Beatty, P., 20, 28, 57, 93, 101n2,
  103, 104, 105, 106, 116, 117,
  121, 135, 160, 169, 180, 209,
  220, 224, 250-252
Becher, H., 37, 220
Behavioral frequency, questions
  about, 263
Behavioral Risk Factor Surveillance
  Survey (BRFSS), 24
Behavior coding, 236-241
  cognitive interviewing vs., 238-241
  features of, 237
  interviewer-oriented codes, 238
  respondent-oriented codes, 238

Belanger, B., 236
Belson, W. A., 17, 24, 29, 40, 48, 52, 118
Bercini, D., 37, 40, 49, 77, 260
Bercini, D. H., 40
Best practices, 261-262
Bethlehem, J., 188
Between-lab studies, cognitive interviewing evaluation and, 221-222
Bias, 14
  avoiding, 116-117
  think-aloud technique and, 53, 55
  verbal probing techniques and, 56
Bickart, B., 54, 55, 157-158
Biemer, P. P., 140, 154, 155, 204, 241
Bienias, J., 39
Bischoping, K., 236
Blackhall, L. J., 141, 266
Blair, E., 38
Blair, E. A., 16
Blair, J., 40, 48, 78, 90, 91, 94, 103, 115, 120, 124, 134, 160, 165, 166, 179, 215, 233, 243, 244, 247, 249, 262
Blixt, S., 80
Bolton, R. N., 46, 47, 54, 156, 158, 159
Borgers, N., 117
Bornstein, G., 93, 119, 140
Bowker, D., 188
Bowker, D. R., 188
Braaten, K., 16, 35
Bradburn, N., 23
Bradburn, N. M., 17, 27, 37
Brannen, J., 195
Brennan, S. E., 18
Brewer, M. B., 60
BRFSS. See Behavioral Risk Factor Surveillance Survey
Bronkhorst, T. M., 46, 47, 158, 159
Bryant, H. E., 107
Budd, D., 46
Burden issues, 154-155

Bureau of Labor Statistics, interviewing outcome reports from, 124
Burton, S., 16, 38

CAI. See Computer Assisted Interviewing
Calvillo, A., 205
Campanelli, P., 40, 243, 249, 250
Canfield, B., 220
Cannell, C. F., 35, 16, 236, 237
Cantor, D., 196, 197
Cantril, H., 48
CAPI, 263
CAPI. See Computer-Assisted Personal Interview
Card sorting, 60-61
Carrasco, L., 266
CASI. See Computer-Assisted Self Interview
CASIC. See Computer-assisted survey information collection
CASM. See Cognitive Aspects of Survey Methodology (CASM) research
Caspar, R. A., 140, 154, 155, 204
CATI, 263
CATI. See Computer-Assisted Telephone Interview
Centers for Disease Control and Prevention, Behavioral Risk Factor Surveillance
Children, interviewing, 203-204
Cialdini, R. B., 265
Clark, H. H., 17, 18
Coding schemes:
  probed interview, 164-168
  think-aloud interview, 157-159
Cognitive Aspects of Survey Methodology (CASM) research, 34
  applications of, 37-41
  applied, 40, 262
  basic, 262
  in formal statistical sense, 114n1
  origins of, as orienting framework, 34-37

Cognitive interview:
  computer-based instruments,
    186-188
  focus groups vs., 236-236
  length of, 143-144
  number of rounds, 145-146
  small-scale informal, 148
  timing of, 6
  verbal reports and, 209-210
  See also Cognitive interviewing
Cognitive interviewing:
  behavior coding vs., 238-241
  best practices of, 261-262
  broad view of, 102-109
  defined, 3
  empirical evaluation of,
    213-224
  future directions for, 261-268
  generality of, 3-4
  integrating into design
    process, 256
  limitations of, 225-228
  merging expansive interviewing
    and, 113
  outcome report, 162-164
  quality vs. quantity with,
    258-259
  recommendations for practice,
    255-261
  See also Cognitive interview
Cognitive laboratory, 6
  environment, field vs., 226
  physical requirements of,
    148-149
Cognitive probing:
  examples of, 68-77
  logical and structural problems
    with, 77-78
  question pitfalls model, 79-84
  traditional, 106
  See also Probe(s); Probing;
    Verbal probing
Cognitive testing:
  defined, 5
  question inspection, 7
  sensitive questions, 189-196
  staffing for, 147
  steps for, 7-8

Cognitive testing process, 5-11
  characterizing outcomes,
    152-156
  cognitive interviewing
    as part of, 10
  general features of, 6-7
  interviewing process, 142-143
  logistical issues and considerations,
    143-149
  overall design sequence
    and, 136
  selecting and training
    interviewers, 129-131
  subject recruitment, 137-141
Cognitive testing protocol,
    8, 273-286
Cognitive testing reports, examples
    of findings from, 287-298
Collins, D., 37, 220, 262
Collins, M., 178
Computer Assisted Interviewing
    (CAI), 263
Computer-Assisted Personal
    Interview (CAPI),
    178, 186-189
Computer-Assisted Self Interview
    (CASI), 178
Computer-assisted survey
    information collection
    (CASIC), 186
Computer-Assisted Telephone
    Interview (CATI), 178, 186-189
Computer-based coding, for think-
    aloud interview, 158
Computer-based instruments,
    cognitive interviewing and,
    186-188
Concurrent probe group, 183
Concurrent probing,
    51-52, 90-92
Confidentiality issue, 149
Confirmatory probes, 106
Conrad, F., 78, 90, 91, 94,
    115, 120, 124, 134, 151,
    160, 165, 189, 215, 247
Conrad, F. G., 19, 20, 21, 93
Conradt, J., 188
Conversation, as negotiated, 18

Converse, J. M., 13, 23, 27, 61, 107, 121
Cook, S. W., 48
Cosenza, C., 24, 78, 88, 106, 107, 134, 160, 210, 234
Couper, M. P., 186, 187, 188, 230, 263, 264, 265
Courneya, K. S., 107
Coverage error, 13-14
CPS. See U.S. Current Population Survey
Croner, C. M., 204
Cross-cultural equivalence, 266
Cross-cultural investigation, 266-268
Cross-method evaluation study, design for, 245
Crutcher, R. J., 209
Cultural variation, 109-110
subject recruitment and, 140-141
See also Ethnographic interview
Curbstoning, 242
Current Population Survey, 139, 188

Data collection, 159-160
Daugherty, S., 167, 181, 183
Davis, W., 197
Davis, W. L., 219, 220
Debriefing:
interviewer, 232
probes, 61
script, 182
subject, 52
Dehue, F., 78
Delaney, P. F., 209
De la Puente, M., 267, 268, 269, 270, 271
Delayed retrospective probing, 52
De Leeuw, E., 117, 178, 203
DeMaio, T., 52, 57, 58, 120, 125, 133, 143, 144, 163, 166, 167, 168, 170, 171, 181, 183, 205, 214, 243, 252, 258, 286n4
DeMaio, T. J., 40, 46, 57, 61, 92, 197, 219, 220, 221, 222, 248
Demand characteristics, biases as, 40
Deutsch, B., 39
Deutsch, M., 48
Dibbs, R., 182

Dijkstra, W., 94, 237
Dillman, D., 181
Dillman, D. A., 181, 188
Dippo, C., 40
Donaldson, M., 16
Double-barreled questions, 23
Dull, V. T., 60
Durant, S., 58
Dykema, J., 80
Dykema, J. L., 140

Edwards, W. S., 196
Eisenhower, D., 36, 234, 236, 248
Elaborative probing, 103-108.
See also Expansive probing
Elderly people, interviewing, 204
Embedded defect approach, 261
Embedded probing, 61
Embretson, S. E., 22
Emergent probing, 90, 96, 98-101, 103
Ericsson, K. A., 42, 44, 45, 46, 47, 52, 55, 57, 95, 130, 208, 211, 212, 265
Error:
coverage, 13-14
extended reactivity effects, 115
gross, 15
interviewer, 13-14
local reactivity effects, 115
net, 14
nonobservation, 14
nonresponse, 13-14
observation, 14
post-observation, 14
response, 13-17, 263
sampling, 13-15
self-report surveys and, 13-17
sources of, probes for, 81-83
specification, 29
See also Survey-related error
Esposito, J., 40
Esposito, J. L., 243, 248, 249, 252
Establishment surveys, 196-199
Ethnographic interview, 109-112
application of, 112
cognitive interview as, 110-111
considerations for using, 110

need for explicit, 111-112
use of term, 103
Ethnographic investigator, 232
Ethnography of Business, 197
Evaluation of cognitive interviewing:
  between-lab studies and, 221-222
  empirical, 213-224
  finding problems, 216-218
  fixing problems, 213-216
  implementing findings, 223-224
  lab-to-field carry-over studies,
    218-220
  models for, 214
  potential outcomes and, 224-225
  reliability and consistency, 220
Expansive interviewing, 102-114
  merging cognitive interviewing
    and, 113
  nonstandardized pretest interview,
    108-109
  use of term, 103
Expansive probing, 105-106
  application of, 112
  dual checking function of, 106
  thought process and, 211-212
  See also Elaborative probing
Expert review, 231-233
Extended reactivity effects, 115, 121

Face-to-face surveys:
  interviewer-administered, 178-179
  verbal probing techniques for,
    47-51
Feedback probes, 106
Felcher, E. M., 54, 55, 157-158
Field-based probes, 61-62
Field interviewers, potential
  problems for, 258
Filter questions, 139
Fisher, R. P., 5
Fisher, S., 197
Flexible Processing Model, 37
Flores, L. R., 16
Focus groups, 233-236
  cognitive interviews vs., 234-236
  timing of, 236
Focus Groups: A Practical Guide for
  Applied Research (Krueger), 234

Foddy, W., 80
Follow-up questions, 150n1
Formal review. See Expert review
Forsman, G., 16, 241, 242
Forsyth, B., 10, 80, 214, 243, 286n5
Forsyth, B. H., 24, 58, 79, 212
Fowler, F., 236, 238
Fowler, F. J., x, 20, 23, 24, 29,
    62, 77, 78, 106, 107, 164,
    220, 234, 235, 236, 241, 243
Fox, J. B., 121
Freedman, S. R., 196, 197, 199
Free-form probing, standardized
  probing vs., 94-97
Fried, E., 48
Friedenreich, C. M., 107
Fuchs, M., 187
Functional remarks, 106
Fuson, K. C., 3

Garas, N., 124
Garber, M., 205
Gateway questions, 139
Geiselman, R. E., 5
Gerber, E. R., 58, 109, 110, 111,
    112, 167
Giesen, D., 196
Ginsburg, G. P., 16, 35
Goldenberg, K., 197
Goldenberg, K. L., 125,
    196, 197, 198
Gower, A. R., 182, 236
Graesser, A. C., 46, 233
Grand Tour approach, 103
Grice, H. P., 17-18
Griffin, M., 38
Groenvold, M., 107, 108
Gross error, 15
Gross redundancy, 154
Grounding, 18, 29, 93, 210
Groves, R. M., 13-15, 103,
    114n1, 208, 265

Hak, T., 181, 184, 185
Hansen, S. E., 187
Harkness, J. A., 266, 267
Harlow, S. D., 16
Harris-Kojetin, B., 40

Harris-Kojetin, L., 167
Hasher, L., 38
HCI. *See* Human-Computer
  Interaction, 187
Heath, A., 22
Hermann, D., 37
Herrmann, D. J., 35, 40, 204
Hess, J., 40, 57, 61, 117, 118, 125,
  147, 163, 203, 229n5
Hess, J. C., 16, 143, 145
Hippler, H., 35, 39
Hispanicity questions, cognitive
  investigation of, 270
Holland, L., 56, 203
Houtkoop-Steenstra, H., 21
Hubbard, M. L., 24
Hughes, K., 125, 143, 155,
  170, 171, 205
Human-Computer Interaction
  (HCI), 187-188
Human subject protections, 266
Hundepool, A., 188
Hunt, S. D., 121, 123, 217
Hunter, J., 143, 155
Hypothetical questions, 263

Immediate retrospective
  probing, 51-52
Index of Inconsistency, 242
Indirect probing, 192
Informant, expert as, 232
Information processing chain, 51
Information retrieval processes,
  studies of, 37-38
Institutional Review Boards (IRBs),
  140, 266
Intensive interview, 48, 102
Interaction analysis, 236.
  See also Behavior coding
Interviewer:
  cognitive vs. field, 226
  continuing education for, 134-135
  instructions for, 273-274
  multiple, 147-148
  neutral approach, sensitive
    questions and, 193
  novice, Anticipated probing
    and, 92

opinionating about problems,
  171-172
personality traits, 129-131
social contact between subject
  and, 46-47
technical background of, 131
training for, 53, 131-134
Interviewer, field:
  potential problems for, 258
  training for cognitive interviewing,
    133-134
Interviewer-administered face-to-face
  surveys, 178-179
Interviewer-administered telephone
  surveys, 179-180
Interviewer debriefing, 232
Interviewer error, 13-14
Interviewer falsification, 242
Interviewer-oriented codes, 238
Interviewer rating, 232
Interviewer style, professional vs.
  personal approach, 94
Intrusive threat, 190
IRT. *See* Item Response Theory
Item Response Theory (IRT), 22
Item-specific recommendations, 152
Iterative testing, 7

Jabine, T. B., 34, 35
Ja?l, E., 167
Jahoda, M., 48
Jansen, H., 181, 185
Japec, L., 197
Jay, A., 12
Jenkins, C. R., 117
Jobe, J. B., 35, 37, 40, 58, 60, 204
Johnson, T. P., 141, 266
Jordan, B., 20
Jourard, S. M., 194

Kagawa-Singer, M., 141, 266
Kalton, G., 236
Kasprzyk, D., 263
Keeley, C., 58
Keller, D. M., 204
Kennedy, T., 233
Kennet, K., 205
Kerwin, J., 204

Kirk, J., 22
Klee, M. C., 107
Krosnick, J. A., 226
Krueger, R. A., 20, 29, 195, 234, 235

Labaw, P. J., 23
Laboratory:
   cognitive, physical requirements
      of, 148-149
   testing, 6
Lab-to-field carry-over studies,
   218-220
Laffey, F., 196
LaFleur, S., 200, 201
Landreth, A., 52, 57, 120, 133, 143,
   144, 166, 167, 168, 170, 171,
   205, 214, 221, 222, 226, 258,
   286n4
Lansing, J. B., 16, 35
Laurent, A., 16
Law enforcement, cognitive
   interviews in, 5
Lazarsfeld, P, 29
Lee, L., 16, 37
Lee, M., 181
Lee, R. M., 58, 190
Leiter, J., 197
Lessler, J., 24, 26, 78
Lessler, J. T., 24, 40, 46, 49, 58, 79,
   93, 212, 218, 243
Lewis, P. J., 181
Linet, M. S., 16
Local reactivity effects, 115
Loftus, E., 16, 42, 43, 45, 62
Logical problem:
   cognitive probing and, 77-78
   expansive interview and, 103-104
Loomis, L., 113, 124, 139, 163
Lui, L. N., 60
Luiten, A., 155, 248, 249
Lyberg, L., 197

McCurdy, D. W., 197
McKay, R., 266
McKay, R. B., 268, 269, 270, 271
Magliano, J. P., 46
Mai, H., 153
Mangione, T., 20

Mapping processes, 71
Mapping techniques, 204
Marquis, K., 236, 263
Marquis, K. H., 16, 241
Marquis, M. S., 241
Martin, E., 22, 35, 40, 58, 59, 109
Martin, J., 22, 117, 197
Mathiowetz, N., 58, 243, 252
Mathiowetz, N. A., 36
Mayer, T. S., 58, 117
Maynard, D. W., 21, 116
Means, B., 16, 38
Measurement theory, 22
Method, xi
Methodological development, 261
Miller, F. D., 209
Miller, K., 119, 125, 141, 170, 194,
   195, 220, 236, 263, 264
Miller, M. L., 22
Miller, P. V., 35
Miller-Steiger, D., 264
Mingay, D., 40, 44
Mingay, D. J., 58, 204, 35
Mohler, P., 266
Moore, J., 16, 54, 56, 80, 109, 226
Moore, J. C., 16, 240
Morganstein, D., 36
Morrison, R. L., 58
Morton-Williams, J., 236, 239, 248
Moy, L. M., 196
Multiple conceptual elements, 263

Napoles-Springer, A., 266
National Center for Health Statistics
      (NCHS):
   cognitive lab, 10, 116
   focus group use, 233
   interviewing outcome reports, 124
   National Health Interview
      Survey, 267
   Questionnaire Design Research
      Laboratory, 49
National Centre for Social Research
   in the United Kingdom, 10
National Health Interview Survey
   (NHIS), 68, 187-188, 267
   Podiatry Supplement (1990), 139
   testing questionnaire, 295-297

National Opinion Research
    Center, 10
Neisser, U., 41
Neter, J., 38
Net error, 14
Neuhauser, C. S., 262
Newell, A., 45
NHIS. See National Health
    Interview Survey
Nichols, E. M., 143
Nigam, A., 16
Nisbett, R. E., 208, 210
Nonobservation, errors of, 14
Non-questionnaire materials,
    testing, 204-205
Nonresponse error, 13-14
Non-standardized cognitive
    interview, 103
Nonstandardized interview, 20
Nonstandardized pretest interview,
    expansive interview as, 108-109
NUD*IST, 235
Nunnally, J. C., 22

O'Brien, E., 197, 248
Observation, errors of, 14
Office of Management
    and Budget, 145
Off-site interviewing, 130
Oksenberg, L., 35, 236, 243
O'Muircheartaigh, C., 207, 262
Once-through procedure,
    revisitation vs., 168-169
Opinions, testing questions on,
    199-202
Oppenheim, A. N., 13, 14, 16,
    21, 23, 29, 35, 89, 225
Ordering:
    interview methods, 248-249
    outcomes and, 153-154
    present-to-past, 42
Organized testing report, 162
Ottati, J., 233
Outcome:
    categories, 152-156
    evaluation of right, 224-225
    field, cognitive interviewing
        results and, 219-220

    report, 162-165
    typical, of probed interview, 125
    varied potential, 260-261

Pan, Y., 267
Paradigmatic sequence, 94
Paraphrasing, 117-118
Parsons, P. E., 236
Pascale, J., 16, 58, 113,
    117, 125, 162
Payne, S. L., 23
Peterson, L. S., 107
Phillips, M. A., 125, 198
Phipps, P., 197
Pickle, L. W., 204
Pinder, G., 205
Pober, J. M., 262
Pober, J. S., 262
Polich, J. M., 241
Polivka, A. E., 59
Post-observation error, 14
Present-to-past recall ordering, 42
Presser, S., 13, 17, 23, 27, 40, 48,
    61, 103, 107, 121, 165, 166,
    233, 243, 244, 247, 249, 262
Pretesting methods, affiliated.
    See Affiliated pretesting methods
Privacy issue, 149
Proactive probing, 88, 91-94, 182
Probe(s):
    common cognitive, 48
    confirmatory, 106
    feedback, 106
    paraphrase, 117-118
    reorienting, 116
    See also Cognitive probing;
        Probing; Verbal probing
Probe administration, 88
Probe construction, 87
Probed interview, analysis of:
    coding schemes, 164-168
    data collection, 159-160
    informal analysis of, 160-164
Probe questions, 8
Probing:
    Anticipated, 88, 92, 163
    appraisal-based, 79-80
    balanced questions, 117

concurrent, 51-52
conditional, 90-92
conservative use of, 120-121
elaborative, 103
embedded, 61
emergent, 90, 96, 98-101, 103
establishment surveys and, 198
expansive, 105-106, 211-212
field-based, 61
immediate retrospective, 51-52
indirect, for sensitive
    questions, 192
misinterpretation of, 118-119
proactive, 88-94, 124, 182
proactive vs. reactive, 91-94
prospective, 107
reactive, 89-94, 182
retrospective, 52
sources of error and, 81-83
speculative, limiting, 119-120
spontaneous, 88, 95
standardized vs. free-form, 94-97
standard model of, 87
See also Cognitive probing; Probe;
    Verbal probing; Verbal
    probing techniques
Problems:
avoiding artificial, 116-125
cognitive probes vs. cognitive
    problems, 113
embedded, detection of, 261
finding vs. fixing, 215
finding nonexistent, 115-116
frequency of, 169-170
interviewers opinionating about,
    171-172
overt vs. covert, 6, 238-239
potential, for field
    interviewers, 258
Procedure, xi
Prospective probing, 107
Protocol, use of term, 86n2
Protocol analysis, 45
Prufer, P., 117
Psychometrics, 22

QAS. *See* Question Appraisal System
Q-BANK Project, 262, 264

Quality-of-life research, 107
QUEST, 233
Question:
attitudes and opinions, 199-202
autobiographical, 36
comprehension process, 46
different validities of, 225
double-barreled, 23
follow-up, 150n1
frequency of problems with,
    169-170
hypothetical, 263improvement
    of, 213
need for testing, 27-29
pragmatic meaning of, 17
probe, 8
problems in. *See* Problems
redesigning, 173-174
revising, 9
sensitive, 36
sources of misunderstanding,
    30-31
standardized, 20-21
target, 4
vagueness of, 17-18
Question Appraisal System
    (QAS), 24-25
codes, 25-26
developing probe questions
    using, 81-86
error sources in telephone
    surveys, 25-26
probe development
    framework, 80
Question design:
first principles of, 256
rules for, 27-28, 31-33
Questionnaire:
limitations of, 155
pretesting, good vs. bad
    questions, 216
self-administered paper, 180-181
steps for cognitive testing of, 7-8
See also Survey
Questionnaire design:
avoiding problems in, 21-27
checklist approaches to, 23-27
first principles of, 12-33

psychometrics and, 22
texts on, 23
Questionnaire development process:
cognitive testing in context of, 138
model, 249
sequence of, 137
Question objectives, revisiting,
152, 257
Question pitfalls model, 79-80

Ramirez, C., 231
Rasinski, K., x, 199
Reactive probing, 89-94, 182
Reactivity effects, 115, 121,
181-182
Recall task, 71
Record check study, 16, 38
Recruitment, subject. *See* Subject
recruitment
Redline, C., 181, 182, 206n1
Redline, C. D., 181
Redundancy:
gross, 154
subtle forms of, 78
Reeve, B. B., 3
Reference period, 9
Reichart, J. W., 16
Reinterview surveys, 16, 241-242
Reise, S. P., 22
Relative Confidence Model, 249
Reliability, 22, 220
Reorienting probes, 104-105, 116
Repair mechanisms, 18
Research Triangle Institute
International, 10, 24
Re-specification of objectives,
152-153
Respondent:
age of, 202-204
cognitive processes of, 6
debriefing, 61
survey, cognitive laboratory
subject vs., 225-226
Respondent-oriented codes, 238
Response error, 13-14
cognitive features and
resulting, 263
evidence of, 16-17

self-report questionnaire, 15-16
sociolinguistic perspective on,
17-21
Response processes, 71
Response rates, declining, 265
Results, interpreting, 259
Retrospective probing, 52, 181-182
Revisitation, once-through vs.,
168-169
Rexroth, M., 117
Rho, C., 107, 117, 210
Rips, L. J., x, 37, 38, 112, 132, 160,
164, 178, 199, 202, 215, 255
Rogers, S., 92
Roman, A. M., 62, 243
Rosen, R., 197
Rothgeb, B., 57
Rothgeb, J., 58, 80, 117, 125, 153,
163, 164, 166, 168, 214, 220,
221, 222, 223, 247, 286n5
Rothgeb, J. M., 40, 61, 92, 143,
243, 248, 249, 252
Royston, P., 37, 46, 49, 77, 260
Royston, P. N., 40, 54, 56, 77
Royston, T., 102
Rutchik, R. H., 196, 197, 199

Salter, W., 46
Sample size:
behavior coding, 240
cognitive interviews, 7, 226-288
focus group, 234
Sampling error, 13-15
Sand, K., 93
Sandberg, J. A. C., 42
Sangster, R., 107, 121
Sangster, R. L., 117, 210
Schaeffer, E. F., 17, 18
Schaeffer, N. C., 17, 19, 20, 94,
116, 140, 189
Schechter, S., 35, 37, 40, 57, 74,
103, 104, 117, 135, 165,
166, 179, 180, 183, 201,
218, 219, 220, 221, 236,
249, 250-252, 262
Schober, M. F., 18, 19, 20, 21, 93
Schreiner, I., 16, 242
Schuman, H., 17, 48-49, 61

Schwarz, N., x, 28, 35, 37, 39, 40, 41, 153, 262
Scott, B. S., 242
Screener questions, 139
Self-administered questionnaire:
    concurrent and mixed approaches, 182-185
    paper, 180-181
    teenage smoking, 287-290
    think-aloud vs. retrospective probing for, 181
Self-fulfilling prophecy, proactive probing and, 124
Self-report surveys, sources of error in, 13-17
Selltiz, C., 48
Semi-structured interview, 20
Sensitive question:
    cognitive processes and, 36
    cognitive testing of, 189-196
    defined, 190
    intensive cognitive testing of, 190-191
    procedures for testing, 191-195
Sex, questions about, 170, 191-194
Show cards, 179
Silent Misinterpretation (DeMaio and Rothgeb), 92-93
Simon, H. A., 42, 44, 45, 46, 47, 52, 55, 57, 95, 130, 208, 211, 212, 265
Sirken, M., 35, 37, 40, 46, 262
Sirken, M. G., 40
Skinner, B. F., 209
Skip errors, concurrent probe group and, 183
Skip-outs, 78
Skip patterns, 19, 182, 203
Smiley, R., 181
Smith, A. F., 40, 58, 204
Smith, E. R., 209
Smith, T. W., 46
Snijkers, G., 37, 52, 54, 78, 177, 230, 233, 234, 261, 262, 266
Social desirability effects, 72
Sociolinguistic analysis, of response error, 17-21
Sparkman, R. D., 121

Specification error, 29
Spontaneous probing, 88, 95
Sprangers, M. A. B., 107
Squire, C., 167
Standardized probing, 94-97
Standardized questions, 20-21
Statistics Canada, 10, 196
Statistics Finland, 10
Statistics Netherlands, 10
Statistics New Zealand, 10
Statistics Norway, 10
Statistics Sweden, 10
Stettler, K., 58, 197
Stewart, A. L., 266
Stone, A. A., 13
Strack, F., 39, 153
Straf, M. L., 34
Strijbos-Smits, A., 117
Structural problem:
    cognitive probing and, 77-78
    expansive interview and, 103-104
Stussman, B. J., 203
Subject:
    awareness of questionnaire problems, 123
    cognitive laboratory, survey respondent vs., 225-226
    instructions for, 274-275
    protections for human, 366
    remuneration for, 144-145
    social contact between interviewer and, 46-47
    written instructions and, for establishment surveys, 198
Subject debriefing, 52
Subject recruitment, 137-141
    cross-cultural perspective, 140-141
    establishment surveys, 198
    importance of, 259-260
    quota sampling for, 140
    sample newspaper advertisement for, 141
    sources of subject names, 140
    specialized, 6
    the "right" people, 139-140
Suchman, L., 20
Sudman, S., x, 17, 23, 27, 35, 37, 132

Suh, S., 46, 205
Survey:
  establishment, 196-199
  filtering function, 139
  interviewer-administered,
    178-179
  reinterview, 16
  self-report, sources of error
    in, 13-17
  See also Questionnaire
Survey administration mode:
  adjusting to, 177-189
  techniques appropriate to, 257
Survey-related error, general
  categories of, 13-15
Survey response process,
  four-stage model, 36
Sykes, W., 236, 239, 248

Tanur, J. M., 34, 35, 40
Target questions, 4
Technique, xi
Teenage smoking:
  self-administered questionnaire
    on, 287-290
  telephone survey on, 290-295
Telephone survey:
  interviewer-administered,
    179-180
  teenage smoking, 290-295
  telephone lines for, 297-298
Telescoping, 38
Textbook, questionnaire design, 23
Theoretical perspectives, 50-51,
  208-213
Think-aloud interview, 42-47
  advantages of, 53
  analysis of, 156-159
  conducting, 44
  disadvantages of, 53-55
  inducing "pure," 57
  interpreting, 172-173
  introducing subjects to, 143
  non-reactive, 45
  procedures, 6
  retrospective probing vs.,
    181-182
  survey questions and, 46-47

theory of verbal reports, 44-46
verbal probing techniques
  and, 52-58
verbal record of, 43
Thompson, S., 197
Threat of sanction, 190
Three-Step Test Interview
  (TSTI), 184
Time series, 223
Tomaskovic-Devey, D., 197
Tortora, R., 264
Tortora, R. D., 188
Tourangeau, R., x, 34, 35, 36,
  37, 38, 40, 46, 62, 112,
  132, 160, 164, 178, 199,
  202, 215, 255, 264
Trabasso, T., 46, 205
Tracy, E., 78, 120
Traditional cognitive probes, 106
Training cognitive interviewers,
  131-134
Translational Research, 262
Trunzo, D., 236TSTI. See Three-Step
  Test Interview
Tucker, C., 109, 134, 207,
  213, 220
Turkkan, J. S., 13
Turner, C. F., 22

U.S. Bureau of Labor Statistics,
  131, 265
  cognitive lab at, 10
  establishment surveys by, 196
  unemployment index, 28
  use of focus groups, 233
U.S. Census Bureau, 35, 131, 265
  cognitive lab at, 10
  establishment surveys by, 196
  focus groups use, 233
  interviewing outcome reports
    from, 124
  Response Variance Reinterview
    Program, 241
  survey development, 223-224
  Survey of Income and Program
    Participation, 19
U.S. Current Population Survey
  (CPS), 59

U.S. General Accounting Office, 10, 196
U.S. Office of Management and Budget, 15
Unit nonresponse, 13
Usability testing, 186

Vacca, E. A., 181
Validity, 22, 56
Vande Hey, J., 179
Van der Veer, K., 181, 185
Van der Zouwen, J., 20, 78, 94, 178
Van de Vijver, F. J. R., 266
Verbal probing:
    avoiding pitfalls, 115-126
    classification of, 87-91
    ethnographic interview, 109-112
    proactive probes, 88-89
    procedures, 6
    reactive probes, 89-90
    standard cognitive probes, 67-86
    standardized vs. free-form probes, 94-97
    See also Cognitive probing
Verbal probing techniques, 47-51
    advantages of, 55-56
    choosing between think-aloud and, 52-58
    concurrent vs. retrospective, 51-52
    disadvantages of, 56-57
    historical basis of, 48-50
    information processing chain, 51
    theoretical basis for, 50-51
    think-aloud with, 57
    training interviewers in, 132
Verbal report:
    cognitive interviewing and, 209-210
    data, 151
    procedures, 6
    techniques, combining range of, 258
    theory of, 44-46
Vignettes, 58-60
Viterna, J. S., 21, 116
Von Someren, M. W., 42

Von Thurn, D., 16, 54, 56, 80, 109, 117, 226
Von Thurn, D. R., 240

Waksberg, J., 38
Warnecke, R. B., 109
Weed, J. A., 58
Weiss, E. S., 24
Wellens, T., 27, 54, 56, 110, 118, 163
Wellens, T. R., 58, 167
Westat, 10
Whitaker, K., 57, 80, 103, 165, 220, 221
Whitaker, K. R., 205
White, A. A., 204
Whitehead, N., 80
Whitney, P., 46
Whitridge, P., 197
Wiemer-Hastings, P., 233
Wilcox, J. B., 121
Williams, M. J., 236
Willimac, D. K., 196, 197
Willis, G. B., 3, 10, 24, 26, 35, 37, 40, 45, 47, 51, 56, 57, 68, 74, 77, 78, 80, 87, 92, 93, 104, 105, 116, 119, 131, 140, 164, 165, 166, 191, 203, 207, 209, 213, 214, 215, 218, 219, 220, 221, 227, 243, 244, 245, 246, 247, 248, 249, 286n5
Wilson, B., 220
Wilson, B. F., 80, 107, 154, 205
Wilson, T., 200, 201, 202, 206n2
Wilson, T. D., 208, 210
Winograd, E., 41n1
Within-methods studies, 213
Wolfgang, G. S., 181, 198
Wording effects studies, 17
Wrong Question Effect, 153

York, R. O., 20

Zarrow, M., 16
Zukerberg, A., 197
Zukerberg, A. L., 203, 240
ZUMA, 10

About the Author

Gordon Willis, Ph.D., is Cognitive Psychologist in the Applied Research Program, National Cancer Institute, National Institutes of Health. Previously, he was Research Methodologist at Research Triangle Institute's Rockville, Maryland, office, where he established a cognitive laboratory. He also worked for over a decade in the Questionnaire Design Research Laboratory at the National Center for Health Statistics, Center for Disease Control, developing and applying cognitive interviewing techniques. Dr. Willis attended Oberlin College and received a Ph.D. in cognitive psychology from Northwestern University. He now works mainly in the development and evaluation of questionnaires that collect information on cancer risk factors. His main research interest is the evaluation of survey pretesting techniques, especially the cognitive interview. Dr. Willis is an authority on the use of cognitive interviewing, based on the development and practice of these methods at three organizations. He has personally conducted hundreds of such interviews and overseen the work of teams of interviewers. He has taught cognitive interviewing in short courses at survey conferences and in university lectures, and has written extensively on the practice and the theoretical and empirical evaluation of cognitive interviewing techniques.

errors
1
2
3

Question

C Interviewer

↑↓ survey interview

Answer

errors   Right Person
1 coverage
2 sampling
3

p14

respondent

errors
1
2

data

Pure, Ideal, Perfect
Knowledge

Research
Finding

if not
exact is
error